Handbook of Research in Enterprise Systems

Thank you for choosing a SAGE product!
If you have any comment, observation or feedback,
I would like to personally hear from you.

Please write to me at **contactceo@sagepub.in**

Vivek Mehra, Managing Director and CEO, SAGE India.

Handbook of Research in Enterprise Systems

Edited by

SANJAY KUMAR, JOSE ESTEVES,
and ELLIOT BENDOLY

Los Angeles | London | New Delhi
Singapore | Washington DC | Melbourne

First published in 2011 by

SAGE Publications India Pvt Ltd
B1/I-1 Mohan Cooperative Industrial Area
Mathura Road, New Delhi 110 044, India

SAGE Publications Inc
2455 Teller Road
Thousand Oaks, California 91320, USA

SAGE Publications Ltd
1 Oliver's Yard, 55 City Road
London EC1Y 1SP, United Kingdom

SAGE Publications Asia-Pacific Pte Ltd
3 Church Street
#10-04 Samsung Hub
Singapore 049483

Published by Vivek Mehra for SAGE Publications India Pvt Ltd, typeset in 11/13 pt Times New Roman by Star Compugraphics Private Limited, Delhi.

Library of Congress Cataloging-in-Publication Data

Handbook of research in enterprise systems / edited by Sanjay Kumar, Jose Esteves, Elliot Bendoly.
   p. cm.
  Includes bibliographical references.
  1. Management information systems. 2. Business planning. I. Kumar, Sanjay. II. Esteves, Jose, 1970– III. Bendoly, Elliot.

HD30.213.H3535	658.4′038011—dc22	2011	2011000948

ISBN: 978-93-528-0993-6 (PB)

The SAGE Team: Rekha Natarajan, Swati Sengupta and Vijay Sah

Contents

Section 2: Enterprise Systems—Implementation and Management

Section 3: Enterprise Systems—Case Studies and Field Applications

Detailed Contents

1

THE ENTERPRISE SYSTEMS INDUSTRY LANDSCAPE
Sachin B. Modi and *Vincent A. Mabert*

The objective of this chapter is to provide a description of the enterprise systems industry landscape for the interested reader. Towards that end, first, a brief description of the main components of enterprise systems and the primary organizations involved in the implementation of enterprise systems is provided. Second, a discussion of the enterprise system ecosystem with a focus on application product providers in the industry is presented. Third, a review of the various architectural components of the enterprise system and major organizations which provide these components. The final section speculates the future direction of the industry.

2

ENTERPRISE INTEROPERABILITY AND ENTERPRISE SYSTEMS
Peter Loos, Dirk Werth, Silke Balzert, Thomas Burkhart, and *Sebastian Kämper*

The objective of this chapter is to investigate on the nature of enterprise interoperability and to assess the way it directs the implementation of enterprise systems. The chapter deals with the origin of the term interoperability, namely the technical disciplines. It expands this property of a technical object to the business-orientated domain, resulting in the concept of enterprise interoperability. The chapter then describes the special characteristics of enterprise interoperability. It decomposes the concept into partial relationships, namely the interoperability between businesses, processes, and information systems. At the end of this chapter, the authors consolidate these partial concepts into the Enterprise Interoperability Framework.

3

SERVICE-ORIENTED COMPOSITE APPLICATIONS: ENABLING ENTERPRISE AGILITY AND REUSE
Sudeep Mallick

Composite applications development built on the foundation of sound principles of service orientation and agile methodologies enables rapid marketing of new IT systems, by reusing pieces of logic from the pre-existing IT system portfolio within an enterprise. This has implications for speed and degree of flexibility of an enterprise to respond to new business context and trends and remain competitive. Being able to roll out new automation systems by rapidly assembling together pre-built, pre-tested, and re-configurable IT assets can prove to a game changer for a business, by enabling it in the quick capitalization of new business opportunities in a reliable manner. In addition to this, composite applications present a business case for the reuse of IT assets resulting into enhanced ROI and TCO of the existing IT architecture of an enterprise.

4

ES AS INFRASTRUCTURE FOR ANALYTICS AND KNOWLEDGE MANAGEMENT
Gita A. Kumta

This chapter discusses the evolution of Enterprise Systems to the role infrastructure for Knowledge Management (KM) and analytics. The use of IT in organizations has therefore moved from mere problem-solving to enterprise-wide IT strategies. IT is redefining the business model, and creating major opportunities for companies positioned to take advantage. No longer is it adequate to simply get the system to run. Now, we must see the enterprise holistically as the implementation itself so it can be dynamically reshaped and redefined as the environmental change and complexity escalate.

5

TOWARDS SERVICE-ORIENTED ENTERPRISE SYSTEMS: A BUSINESS INTELLIGENCE PERSPECTIVE
Jayanthi Ranjan and *B.S. Sahay*

Service orientation in enterprises is a business-centric IT enabled architectural plan that supports integrating all the businesses as linked, repeatable business tasks, or services. A Service Oriented Architecture (SOA) is essentially a collection of services. The communication can involve either simple data passing or it could involve two or more services coordinating some activity. Service orientation starts as a powerful technical idea to operationalize the goal of rapid enterprise change by allowing business processes to negotiate diverse systems. This is a technical advantage as it becomes easier to integrate systems in enterprises and to reposition existing capabilities for new purposes. In this chapter service-oriented enterprise systems are explained with respect to business intelligence perspective. SOA for business intelligence in enterprises has been explained to make it possible the integration of technologies into a coherent business intelligence environment, which automatically enables simplified data delivery and low-latency analytics.

6

ENTERPRISE TOMOGRAPHY: AN EFFICIENT APPLICATION LIFECYCLE MANAGEMENT APPROACH SUPPORTING SEMI-AUTOMATIC LOCALIZATION, DELTA-TRACKING, AND VISUALIZATION OF INTEGRATION ONTOLOGIES IN VLBAs
Jorge Marx Gómez and *Jan Aalmink*

Enterprise Tomography, a new methodology in software diagnostics, enables efficient application lifecycle management of enterprise platforms and Very Large Business Applications (VLBA). Enterprise Tomography semi-automatically identifies and localizes semantic integration concepts and visualizes integration ontologies categorized in semantic genres. Especially delta determination of integration concepts is performed in dimensions of space and time. Enterprise Tomography supports root cause analysis as well as software and data comprehension. Visualization of integration ontologies from Enterprise Systems streamlines the communication flow between the parties—enterprise, consulting industry, and Enterprise Software supplier. Large-scale development and maintenance and implementation organizations can benefit from this new approach.

7

THE PARADOXICAL IMPACT OF ENTERPRISE-WIDE INTEGRATION ON FLEXIBILITY
Judy E. Scott

Enterprise-wide Integration (EWI) is a recent phenomenon made feasible by technologies such as Enterprise Resource Planning (ERP) systems, Enterprise Application Integration, and web services. While EWI facilitates flexibility, which is critical in hypercompetitive markets, it also introduces constraints under certain conditions. Conflicting reports suggests an EWI flexibility paradox. The objective of this research is to investigate the paradox with an in-depth analysis of the EWI and flexibility constructs and relationship between them. We study integration dimensions: reach, range and modularity, and dimensions of flexibility—versatility, responsiveness, and adaptability at the strategic and operational level. This study sheds light on contradictory findings in prior research by synthesizing information processing, coordination, dynamic capabilities, organizational learning, and institutional theories to support a research model and eight propositions which future research can convert into testable hypotheses.

8

BUILDING KNOWLEDGE-INTENSIVE CUSTOMER-CENTRIC SUPPLY CHAIN ORGANIZATIONS
Minwir Al-Shammari

This chapter proposes the development of customer knowledge management (CKM) as a strategic change model for supply chain (SC) organizations in changing business environments. The basic premise of the chapter is that business organizations need to strive to adapt to opportunities as well as challenges brought by constant, complex, rapid, and discontinuous environmental changes. In their quest for sustainable competitive advantage, organizations need to leverage their distinctive core competencies and craft knowledge-intensive customer-centric SC organizations.

The chapter proposes a knowledge-intensive customer-centric SCM model based on four components: customer relationship management (CRM), enterprise resource planning (ERP), supplier relationship management (SRM), and business process re-engineering (BPR).

9

THE 'SIX IMPERATIVES' FRAMEWORK FOR THE EVALUATION OF AN ERP PROJECT
Maria Argyropoulou, George Ioannou, Dimitrios N. Koufopoulos, and *Jaideep Motwani*

This chapter analyzes and tests a novel framework for the evaluation of an ERP project. The framework incorporates specific performance measures, which are linked to a previously developed model (the 'six-imperatives' framework), and are relevant to ERP implementation. A case study illustrates the use of the framework in a Greek company. The main results indicate that the 'six-imperatives' framework provides a comprehensive methodology based on the profound exploration and understanding of specific business processes and objectives that should be met in order to assess an ERP project.

10

ENTERPRISE RESOURCE PLANNING SYSTEMS IMPLEMENTATION: A PRACTICAL APPROACH
Manoj Jha

This chapter attempts to view Enterprise Solution from different perspectives right from the Enterprise Solution Vendors to Management Consultant and ES Implementation Consultants. A new Enterprise Systems Adoption Model is proposed. The Model has been analyzed with simple examples and has been presented in an easy-to-comprehend format. In the last segment of this chapter, the 'Seven Stage Enterprise Systems Adoption Model' has been applied on a real-life case of a successful adoption. The chapter provides an overview of implementation of Oracle HRMS solution for a reputed airlines organization. The examples used in this chapter are from large and reputed organizations. They represent live examples for the sole purpose of learning.

11

A MODEL FOR ERP SYSTEMS MANAGEMENT: AN EXPLORATORY STUDY IN COMPANIES USING SAP R/3

Cesar Alexandre de Souza and *Ronaldo Zwicker*

Enterprise Resource Planning (ERP) systems are now an important component of IT architecture. Activities undertaken to align this component to business requirements conduct its evolution and ensure its performance and availability to become increasingly important to companies' IT areas. Success of these activities relies upon knowledge and participation of various actors inside and outside the IT area, imposing challenges not observed in internally developed systems. Many authors have researched the implementation processes of ERP systems with diverse approaches and stressing the benefits achieved by its application. However, few have analyzed the management of already implemented ERP systems. This work proposes a model for the analysis of ERP systems management, including the activities and actors engaged in this effort. An exploratory survey has been conducted with 85 Brazilian companies whose results also comprise this text.

12

CRITICAL SUCCESS FACTORS FOR THE ACQUISITION OF ENTERPRISE RESOURCE PLANNING (ERP): EMPIRICAL VALIDATION

Tariq Bhatti and *Veerappan Jayaraman*

Enterprise Systems are high cost propositions as they place tremendous demands on the organization's time and resources. Successful investments in ERP require a sound understanding of the acquisition and implementation processes of these enterprise-wide systems. The ERP implementation literature contains many examples of organizations that have implemented it successfully. However, there have been cases where organizations did not achieve success due to wrong acquisition of ERP systems. Few studies have scientifically developed and tested constructs that represent critical success factors of ERP acquisition projects. Based on a survey of 53 organizations in Australia, the results suggest 60-item instrument measures 10 dimensions of CSFs of ERP acquisition is well-validated. It is argued that the model proposed in the chapter is valuable to researchers and practitioners interested in acquiring Enterprise Resource Planning systems.

13

INTEGRATING ENTERPRISE RESOURCE PLANNING SYSTEMS AND THE BALANCED SCORECARD IN PERFORMANCE MANAGEMENT
Noorhayati Mansor and *Asniati Bahari*

This chapter reviews the existing literature of Enterprise Resource Planning (ERP) and Balanced Scorecard (BSC) systems. Two major objectives of this study are: *(a)* to examine the current practice of performance management, and *(b)* to determine managers' perception of the combined effect of ERP and BSC. A framework to examine the effects of integrating the two systems on organizational performance is proposed.

14

UPGRADE YOUR 'RENOVATION CYCLES' TO 'INNOVATION WAVES' USING KNOWLEDGE MANAGEMENT AND ENTERPRISE SYSTEM CAPABILITIES
Rakesh Kumar Mishra

Innovation and knowledge management are going to be key differentiators in tomorrow's enterprise. And hence enterprises must understand the complete anatomy of innovation such as what is return that enterprise can expect from innovation, how does innovation process work, what nurtures the innovation, what hinders the innovation, what are the human factors involved, etc. This chapter will discuss some of these issues in detail and also share a case study of real-life experiment that author has successfully delivered combining knowledge management and innovation.

15

BALANCED SCORECARD AND ITS ROLE IN STRATEGIC MANAGEMENT OF INFORMATION: A REVIEW OF PRACTICE
D.P. Sinha

The chapter discusses the evolution of the use of balanced scorecard (BSC) in managing organizations. The authors have traced the use of the BSC by a number of industries and present the zones of effectiveness in this usage. The use of enterprise systems in this process for strategic management of the enterprise is then discussed.

16

A CASE OF MRO PROCESS TRANSFORMATION THROUGH ERP: ENABLING GROWTH THROUGH IMPROVED INTRA- AND INTER-COMPANY COLLABORATION
Alexandra Bizerova

The transformation is often viewed as one complete process rather than giving different weight of the contribution of each of the activities. The task for evaluating the effectiveness of the Enterprise Resource Planning (ERP) component as part of the entire company transformation is limited and not representative. The usefulness of the systems solution and its effect towards achieving the company goals can be assessed by comparing user satisfaction and actual usage data. In the evaluation of the success of the Inventory Component Exchange program in Delta Air Lines, the criteria have been user satisfaction, time savings achieved, and improvement of service (increase in the number of transactions, fewer days for service, and decrease in overdue exchanges).

17

THE ROLE OF MOBILE COMPUTING AND COMMUNICATION TECHNOLOGIES IN MOBILE GOVERNANCE
Shashank Garg and *Krishna Sundar Diatha*

In this chapter, the authors describe how two large governance initiatives, the Public Distribution System and the Public Health System, could be improved significantly through the application of mobile communication and computing technologies. Technology is merely an enabler but if government services could be provided at the doorstep of the citizen, it would help in providing an efficient and transparent model for governance services. It contends that it is not enough to convert governance into e-governance, but to take the next logical step into mobile governance, or m-governance, by leveraging on the success of the cellular telephony infrastructure. Clearly, any improvements in the Public Distribution System and Public Health System will create a positive social impact through systemic efficiencies and transparency. The socio-economic divide will be reduced and will also help bridge the 'digital divide' as people start using mobile communication and computing technologies for applications that become a part of their daily lives.

Introduction

The *Handbook of Research in Enterprise Systems* was conceived to collate and present to the reader the fast changing landscape of enterprise systems in one convenient volume.

Briefly, the evolution of enterprise systems can be broken into three distinct phases:

1. The evolution of the client server based Enterprise Resource Planning (ERP) systems which emerged during the 1990s. These monolithic systems were developed largely inside a single vendor firm and many functional applications were developed with an integrated logic, and engineered to work in an integrated fashion across the different functional areas of an organization. Thus, intra-organizational integration of application functionality was achieved by these applications.

2. In Phase 2, demand for additional functionality by customers led to the development of various software modules. However, the highly engineered ERP systems were not very amenable to changes or development of software to provide additional functionality, as the dependencies of the processes embedded in the software were not clear to developers and users. This led to the breakup of ERP systems into more self-sufficient and smaller software modules—each covering only a small part of the functionality, and not a whole process (e.g., procurement) as developed earlier. Thus, the integrated and monolithic nature of enterprise systems has changed to a more modular nature.

3. The shift to a Service Oriented Architecture (SOA) for ERP systems led to the development of software as services. Underlying the evolution of 'services orientation' was the widespread adoption of the object-oriented methods for developing software and the emphasis on software reuse. Thus, SOA led to the development of compatible 'composite' software which was developed by third party vendors, but could be tested and certified by ERP vendors as compatible to their software.

   The evolution of SOA for enterprise systems (along with the adoption of international standards for ensuring inter-operability of software using a services orientation) has resulted in increasing integration and inter-operability between disparate Information Technology (IT) systems—whether installed inside an organization or in multiple organizations. Thus, the integration first achieved by enterprise systems is now deepening and extending across the boundaries of the organization. However, integration alone is not enough. Advances in the 'Internet technology' and 'Internet-based applications' have evolved into WEB 2.0 and WEB 3.0 generation of applications. Major developments are taking place in software related to Business Analytics. Most enterprise system applications have now become Internet-enabled and so the integral use of 'Internet applications' as a part of enterprise systems is evolving faster than imagined. The evolution of the mobile phone as a platform for delivery of information, music, and entertainment has led to its development as an interface for accessing enterprise systems. New languages are being developed to allow managers to express their requirements amongst themselves and to business analysts, viz. Business Process Modeling Notation (BPMN). In such exciting times the *Handbook of Research in Enterprise Systems* attempts to provide the readers with a collection of research which will provide them with a better understanding of the evolving trends in the field of enterprise systems.

The *Handbook* is structured as follows: Section 1 comprises research-based chapters which describe the current and evolving landscape of enterprise systems; Section 2 comprises research-based chapters which deal with the implementation and management of enterprise systems; and Section 3 comprises chapters which describe the implementation of enterprise systems and its various functional application in the form of case studies. The chapters are discussed section-wise in brief ahead.

SECTION 1: ENTERPRISE SYSTEMS—EVOLVING LANDSCAPE AND TECHNOLOGICAL TRENDS

Most appropriately, the section opens with Chapter 1 by Sachin B. Modi and Vincent A. Mabert who discuss the enterprise systems industry landscape. Their chapter includes a brief description of the main components for enterprise systems and the primary organizations involved in the implementation of enterprise systems. A discussion of the enterprise system ecosystem, with a focus on application product providers in the industry, is also presented by the authors. This is followed by a review of the various architectural components of the enterprise systems and major organizations which provide these components.

In Chapter 2, Peter Loos, Dirk Werth, Silke Balzert, Thomas Burkhart, and Sebastian Kämper discuss the various issues related to the development of an 'Enterprise Interoperability Framework'. The authors investigate the nature of Enterprise Interoperability and assess the way it directs the implementation of enterprise systems. The chapter deals with the origin of the term 'interoperability', viz. the technical disciplines. It expands this property of a technical object to the business-orientated domain, resulting in the concept of Enterprise Interoperability. The chapter then describes its special characteristics. It decomposes the concept into partial relationships, viz. the interoperability between businesses, processes, and information systems. Finally, the authors consolidate these partial concepts into an 'Enterprise Interoperability Framework'.

In Chapter 3, Sudeep Mallick explains how composite applications development built on the foundation of sound principles of service orientation (SO) and agile methodologies enables rapid time to market new IT systems by reusing pieces of logic from the pre-existing IT system portfolio within an enterprise. The author discusses how this has implications for speed and degree of flexibility of an enterprise to respond to new business context and trends and remain competitive. Being able to roll out new automation systems by rapidly assembling pre-built, pre-tested, and re-configurable IT assets can prove to be a game changer for a business by enabling it in the quick capitalization of new business opportunities in a reliable manner. In addition to this, composite applications present a business case for the reuse of IT assets resulting in enhanced return on investment (ROI) and (total cost of ownership) TCO of the existing IT architecture of an enterprise.

In Chapter 4, Gita A. Kumta discusses the evolution of enterprise systems for the role of infrastructure for knowledge management and analytics. The use of IT in organizations has moved from mere problem-solving to enterprise-wide IT strategies. IT is redefining the business model and creating major opportunities for companies positioned to take advantage. The enterprise system today is an essential infrastructure for developing business analytics for better and more informed decision-making. The author proposes a knowledge management framework so that the enterprise system can be dynamically reshaped and redefined to meet escalating environmental change and complexity.

In Chapter 5, Jayanthi Ranjan and B.S. Sahay define SO in enterprises as a business-centric IT enabled architectural plan that supports integrating all the businesses as linked, repeatable business tasks, or services. They present service-oriented enterprise systems with respect to a business intelligence perspective. The authors argue that an SOA for business intelligence in enterprises makes it possible for the integration of technologies into a coherent business intelligence environment, which automatically enables simplified data delivery and low-latency analytics.

In Chapter 6, Jorge Marx Gómez, Jan Aalmink, and Carl von Ossietzky explain how Enterprise Tomography, a new methodology in software diagnostics, enables efficient Application Lifecycle Management of Enterprise Platforms and Very Large Business Applications (VLBA). Enterprise Tomography semi-automatically identifies and localizes semantic integration concepts and visualizes integration ontologies categorized in semantic genres. Especially delta determination of integration concepts is performed in dimension space and time. Enterprise Tomography supports root cause analysis as well as software and data comprehension. Visualization of integration ontologies from enterprise systems streamlines the communication flow between the parties—enterprise; consulting industry, and enterprise software supplier. Large-scaled development, maintenance, and implementation organizations can benefit from this new approach.

In Chapter 7, Judy E. Scott discusses the paradoxical impact of enterprise-wide integration (EWI) on organizational flexibility. The author investigates this with an in-depth analysis of the EWI and flexibility constructs and the relationship between them. The author further studies integration dimensions: reach, range and modularity, and dimensions of flexibility–versatility, responsiveness, and adaptability at the strategic and operational level. This chapter sheds light on contradictory findings in prior research by synthesizing information processing, coordination, dynamic capabilities, organizational learning, and institutional theories to support a research model and eight propositions regarding this issue.

In Chapter 8, Minwir Al-Shammari proposes the development of customer knowledge management (CKM) perspective as an organizational strategic change model that consolidates programmes such as Enterprise Systems (ES) implementation, Business Process Reengineering (BPR), strategic information systems (SIS), total quality management (TQM), just-in-time (JIT), knowledge management (KM), organizational learning (OL), customer relationship management (CRM), and electronic business (e-biz).

SECTION 2: ENTERPRISE SYSTEMS—IMPLEMENTATION AND MANAGEMENT

This section of the *Handbook* discusses issues related to the implementation and management of enterprise systems. Various models for successful ERP implementation, critical success factors for ERP implementation, and issues in managing ERP systems on a day-to-day basis are discussed in this section.

Maria Argyropoulou, George Ioannou, Dimitrios N. Koufopoulos, and Jaideep Motwani present a 'six imperatives framework' for the evaluation of an ERP project in Chapter 9. It analyzes and tests a novel framework for the evaluation of an ERP project. The framework incorporates specific performance measures, which are linked to a previously developed model, the 'six-imperatives' framework, and are relevant to ERP implementation. A case study illustrates the use of the framework in a Greek company. The main results indicate that the 'six imperatives' framework provides a comprehensive methodology based on the profound exploration and understanding of specific business processes and objectives that should be met in order to assess an ERP project.

In Chapter 10, Manoj Jha proposes a new Enterprise Systems Adoption Model. This model attempts to view Enterprise Solution from different perspectives right from the Enterprise Solution Vendors to Management Consultant and ES Implementation Consultants. The author analyzes the model with simple examples, and it has been presented in an easy-to-comprehend format. Last, the model is illustrated through a real-life case study, where the author used his seven-stage model for a successful ERP implementation.

Chapter 11 discusses the most important issue of day-to-day management of an ERP system, and the issues which arise. Cesar Alexandre de Souza and Ronaldo Zwicker discuss the activities undertaken to align enterprise systems to business requirements and other elements of the IT architecture. Success of these activities relies upon knowledge and participation of various actors inside and outside the IT area, imposing challenges not observed in internally developed systems. Many authors have researched the implementation processes of ERP systems with diverse approaches and have stressed the benefits achieved by its application. However, few have analyzed the management of already-implemented ERP systems. This chapter proposes a model for the analysis of ERP systems management, including the activities and actors engaged in this effort. It includes the results of an exploratory survey conducted with 85 Brazilian companies on the issue of ERP systems management.

Chapter 12, by Tariq Bhatti and Veerappan Jayaraman, discusses critical success factors (CSFs) in acquisition and implementation of ERP systems. Successful investments in ERP requires a sound understanding of the acquisition and implementation processes of these enterprise-wide systems. However, there have been cases where organizations did not achieve success due to wrong acquisition of ERP systems. The authors have scientifically developed and tested constructs that represent critical success factors of ERP acquisition projects. Based on a survey of 53 organizations in Australia, the results suggest that a 60-item instrument measures 10 dimensions of CSFs of ERP systems acquisition and implementation.

Chapter 13, by Noorhayati Mansor and Asniati Bahari discusses the integration of ERP systems and the Balanced Scorecard (BSC) for performance management. The authors explore existing literature to develop a framework for integrating the two tools. The chapter examines the current practice of performance management and attempts to determine the managers' perception of the combined effect of ERP and BSC. In the chapter, a framework to examine the effects of integrating the two systems on organizational performance is proposed.

The last chapter in this section, Chapter 14, is by Rakesh Kumar Mishra, who proposes using knowledge management capability to upgrade 'renovation cycles' to 'innovation waves'. He argues that innovation and knowledge management are going to be key differentiators in tomorrow's enterprise. Hence, enterprises must understand the anatomy of innovation such as what is the return that enterprise can expect from innovation, how does innovation process work, what nurtures the innovation, what hinders the innovation, what are the human factors involved, etc. There is a very strong link between innovation and knowledge management, and according to the author, a strong knowledge management platform can enable the innovation to a great extent if organizations are able to figure out how to leverage the knowledge management platform to integrate and resonate with the innovation lifecycle.

SECTION 3: ENTERPRISE SYSTEMS—CASE STUDIES AND FIELD APPLICATIONS

This section is more application-oriented as the focus is on case studies of actual applications in the field. The case studies cover implementation of various technical and functional capabilities of enterprise systems.

Chapter 15, by D.P. Sinha discusses the implementation of BSC systems in various organizations, and the role of enterprise systems in evolving a strategic information system to meet the needs of the top management. The author uses various case studies of BSC implementation along with enterprise systems to bring out and discuss various issues and implementation of best practices in the integration and implementation of these two systems.

Chapter 16, by Alexandra Bizerova discusses the transformation of the maintenance, repair, and overhaul (MRO) processes through implementation of an ERP system. The author argues that the transformation is often viewed as one complete process rather than giving different weight of the contribution of each of the activities. The task for evaluating the effectiveness of the ERP component as part of the entire company transformation is thus limited and not representative. The usefulness of the systems solution and its effect towards achieving the company goals can be assessed by comparing user satisfaction and actual usage data. The author cites the case of Delta Air Lines, and the evaluation of the success of their Inventory Component Exchange program as an illustration.

Finally, in Chapter 17, Shashank Garg and Krishna Sundar Diatha describe the case of two large governance initiatives, the Public Distribution System (PDS) and the Public Health System (PHS), and how they could be improved significantly through the application of mobile communication and computing technologies. The authors contend that it is not enough to convert governance into e-governance, but to take the next logical step into mobile governance, or m-governance, by leveraging on the success of the cellular telephony infrastructure. Clearly, any improvements in the PDS and PHS will create a positive social impact through systemic efficiencies and transparency.

Section 1

Enterprise Systems—Evolving Landscape and Technological Trends

The Enterprise Systems Industry Landscape

SACHIN B. MODI
Department of Information Operations and Technology Management
College of Business Administration, University of Toledo, Ohio
E-mail: sachin.modi@utoledo.edu

VINCENT A. MABERT
Department of Operations and Decision Technologies
Kelley School of Business, Indiana University, Bloomington, Indiana
E-mail: mabert@indiana.edu

INTRODUCTION

The world economy today is more global than ever. Every organization is a potential global player with operations and/or trading partners spanning continents and time zones. As the physical boundaries of organizations expand, achieving synchronization within and across organizational boundaries becomes more critical. This synchronization is typically achieved through a technology platform—enterprise system, which enables the organization to deal with large volumes of data and coordinate their business processes across functional and organizational boundaries. Organizations are commonly split into multiple functions and operate with intricate management hierarchies. Traditionally, every function is driven by its own data and information requirements. This leads to the adoption of multiple fragmented information systems. While this may be essential to the functioning of an organization, it leads to data and information fragmentation through the use of multiple systems. The result is large volumes of data which is redundant and almost impossible to translate into the information required for decision-making across the enterprise's managerial hierarchy. An enterprise system is a valuable tool to eliminate the information fragmentation caused by the use of multiple legacy information systems employed across an organization. Enterprise systems are designed to seamlessly integrate and support multiple business processes across functional and organizational boundaries. Implementing enterprise systems is a major undertaking for any organization. Any implementation involves multiple components and subsystems which are provided by various vendor organizations in the enterprise systems industry.

The objective of this chapter is to provide a description of the enterprise systems industry landscape for the interested reader. Towards that end, a brief description of the main components for enterprise systems and the primary organizations involved in the implementation of enterprise systems is provided initially. Second, a discussion of the enterprise system ecosystem, with a focus on application product providers in the industry, is presented. This is followed by a review of the various architectural components of the enterprise system and major organizations which provide these components. The final section speculates on the future direction of the industry. It is important to note that this chapter provides a description of the enterprise system industry landscape with respect to the manufacturing industry sector. While some sections would also be relevant to the retail and services industry sectors, the enterprise systems for these industry sectors are not explicitly considered in this chapter.

As a starting point, Figure 1.1 shows the typical elements of an enterprise system, with major components briefly reviewed here.

ENTERPRISE PORTAL

The term portal initially emerged in the information technology (IT) industry to refer to websites (or web portals) such as MSN, AOL, and Yahoo, which provided users the access point for information content for a set of features (news, e-mail, weather, games, finance, stock quote, etc.). Enterprise portals are essentially an organization's internal website, serving as an interface for a set of organizational users. Enterprise portals offer an organization the ability to provide the target audience with a single entry point to access organizational information assets (e.g., content, applications, functionality, business processes, knowledge base) housed within the enterprise system, in a highly personalized manner. While an organization can create multiple portals, the three most commonly created portals are: Business-to-Employee (B2E), Business-to-Customer (B2C), and Business-to-Business (B2B): they allow the organization to provide an interface to its employees, customers and supply chain partners, respectively. Multiple options are available to an organization for choosing a portal vendor. IBM, Microsoft, Oracle (and BEA), Sun Microsystems, SAP, Hummingbird (Open Text Corp), Vignette, Tibco, and BroadVision are some examples of organizations offering portal solutions. While specific features may vary, the underlying objective of providing composite and customizable interface with Single Sign-On (SSO) and role-based access to organizational users is served by all.

APPLICATION SOFTWARE/APPLICATION SUITES

Application software contains the logic and functionality to perform business processes, such as procurement, scheduling, production management, forecasting and demand planning, customer relationship management, supply management, human resource management, team

FIGURE 1.1
Enterprise System of a Large Enterprise

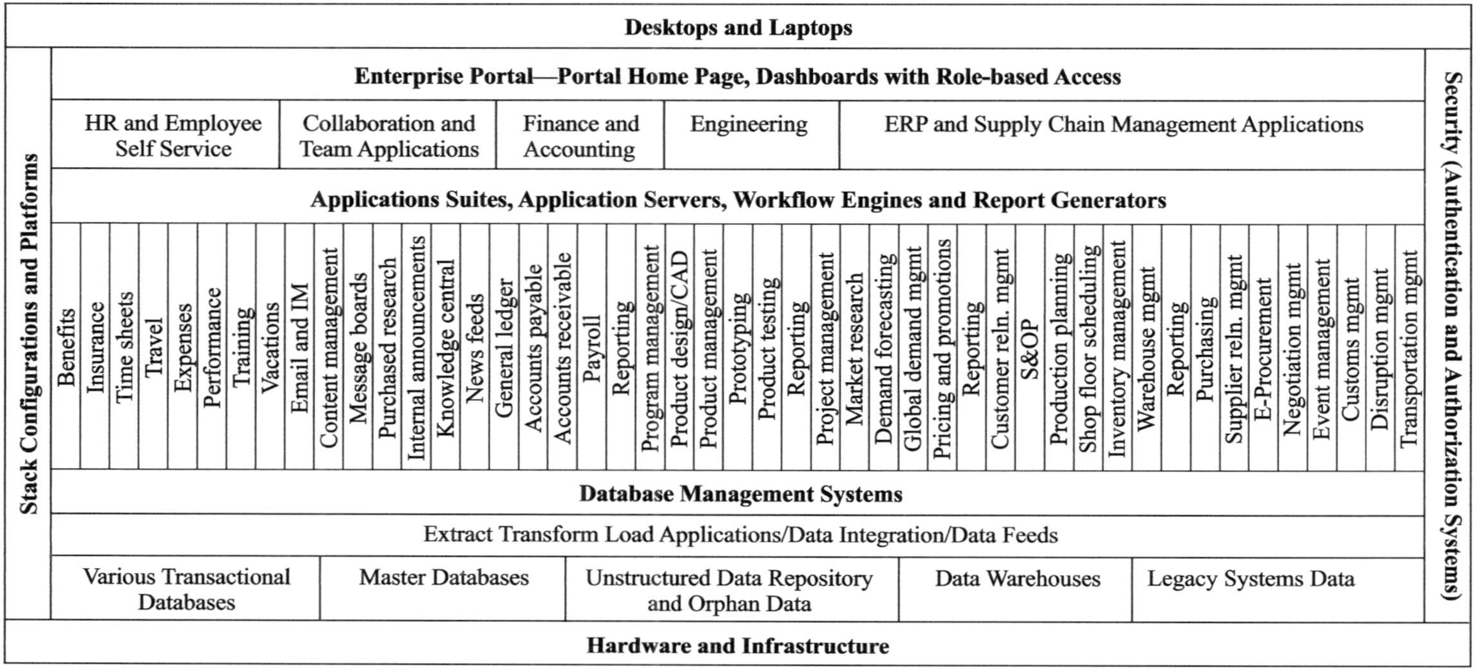

Security (Authentication and Authorization Systems)

Desktops and Laptops

Enterprise Portal—Portal Home Page, Dashboards with Role-based Access

HR and Employee Self Service	Collaboration and Team Applications	Finance and Accounting	Engineering	ERP and Supply Chain Management Applications
Benefits	Email and IM	General ledger	Program management	Market research
Insurance	Content management	Accounts payable	Product design/CAD	Demand forecasting
Time sheets	Message boards	Accounts receivable	Product management	Global demand mgmt
Travel	Purchased research	Payroll	Prototyping	Pricing and promotions
Expenses	Internal announcements	Reporting	Product testing	Reporting
Performance	Knowledge central		Reporting	Customer reln. mgmt
Training	News feeds		Project management	S&OP
Vacations				Production planning
				Shop floor scheduling
				Inventory management
				Warehouse mgmt
				Reporting
				Purchasing
				Supplier reln. mgmt
				E-Procurement
				Negotiation mgmt
				Event management
				Customs mgmt
				Disruption mgmt
				Transportation mgmt

Applications Suites, Application Servers, Workflow Engines and Report Generators

Database Management Systems

Extract Transform Load Applications/Data Integration/Data Feeds

Various Transactional Databases	Master Databases	Unstructured Data Repository and Orphan Data	Data Warehouses	Legacy Systems Data

Hardware and Infrastructure

Stack Configurations and Platforms

Source: Authors.

collaboration, content management, knowledge management, etc. Application software is often bundled together as a package—commonly referred to as Application Suite, which caters to the needs of specific organizational function such as Manufacturing, Engineering, Human Resources, Supply Management, Marketing, Accounting, etc. Application software/suites allow an organization to integrate its processes across various levels and functions into a system, which is represented as a collection of workflows. Ideally the various application suites of an enterprise system integrate several data sources and minimize data redundancy. Application suites catering to the needs of specific functions are often integrated, allowing cross functional coordination between business processes. The extent of integration across applications varies by organization and is influenced by individual organizational needs. A number of vendors provide application software/suites, including, SAP, Oracle, Infor, i2 Technologies, JDA, Manhattan Associates, Logility, and Epicor to name a few.[1] Application providers are often categorized as broad-based enterprise resource planning (ERP) providers (e.g., SAP, Oracle, Infor) and best of breed application providers (e.g., i2 Technologies, JDA, Logility).

SECURITY (AUTHENTICATION AND AUTHORIZATION SYSTEMS)

Enterprise portals provide the interface for various applications to the organization's employees, customers, and partners. As such, a key component of an enterprise system is the security system for user authentication and authorization. Authentication and authorization can be carried at multiple points in the system. Initial authentication verifies the user's access right to the enterprise portal and authorization allows the user access the authorized applications on their personalized web interface commonly referred to as dashboard. A directory service is commonly used for authentication and authorization. Lightweight Directory Access Protocol (LDAP) directories and authentication have become quite common in an enterprise systems infrastructure. SSO systems frequently use LDAP authentication. Other options include Central Authentication Service (CAS) and Java Authentication and Authorization Service (JAAS). SSO authentication and authorization systems allow users to have a single entry point to the enterprise system for accessing multiple applications/application suites which are authorized for the user. An organization can choose from a number of vendors (e.g., CA Inc, IBM, Microsoft, Novell, and Sun Microsystems) who provide the products and services for enterprise system security.

DATA MANAGEMENT SYSTEMS

Enterprise systems are very data intensive and all organizations, large and small, have to deal with a significant amount of data. Often, the availability of data is not as much of an issue

---

[1] JDA Software Inc. completed its acquisition of i2 Technologies Inc. in the first quarter of 2010.

as it being in the desired format at a required level of granularity. Data often are available in fragmented systems and may be more aggregate or granular then required. Organizations employ a multitude of systems ranging from excel files to data warehouses to store and manage data. A typical enterprise system commonly involves data that are stored in a transactional database, master data, data stored in legacy systems, and home grown applications with orphan data. All application/application suites have their own database schema. Integration between different data elements across systems can be enabled by using extract, transform, and load (ETL) adaptors between systems which are available with applications or may be developed. The various databases that may be part of an enterprise system reside on relational database management systems (RDBMS). A number of organizations such as Oracle, IBM (DB2, INFORMIX), and Microsoft (SQL server, Microsoft Access) provide data management tasks commonly used by organizations.

STACK CONFIGURATIONS

Stack configurations refer to a combination of sub-systems needed to deliver an enterprise system. These commonly include an operating system, web server, and database management system. Common stacks used for enterprise systems are Unix, IBM WebSphere, IBM-DB2 and Microsoft-Windows, BEA-Weblogic, and Oracle.

HARDWARE AND INFRASTRUCTURE

This is the physical part of the enterprise systems which includes physical servers, computers, and network circuitry. Organizations such as IBM, Dell, HP, and Apple are major providers of computer hardware.

IMPLEMENTATION

Enterprise systems are complex products which an organization most often acquires. A number of partner organizations are normally involved in bringing these systems to reality. Viewing the enterprise system as the end product and the organization implementing an enterprise system as the customer, this allows one to define the enterprise system's supply chain. Figure 1.2 shows a simplified representation of such a supply chain with respect to the major components which are involved in the development and implementation of enterprise systems.

Generally, an organization has to partner with multiple vendors to procure the products and services required to implement an enterprise system. These include:

FIGURE 1.2
Primary Organizations Involved in Providing Enterprise System Components

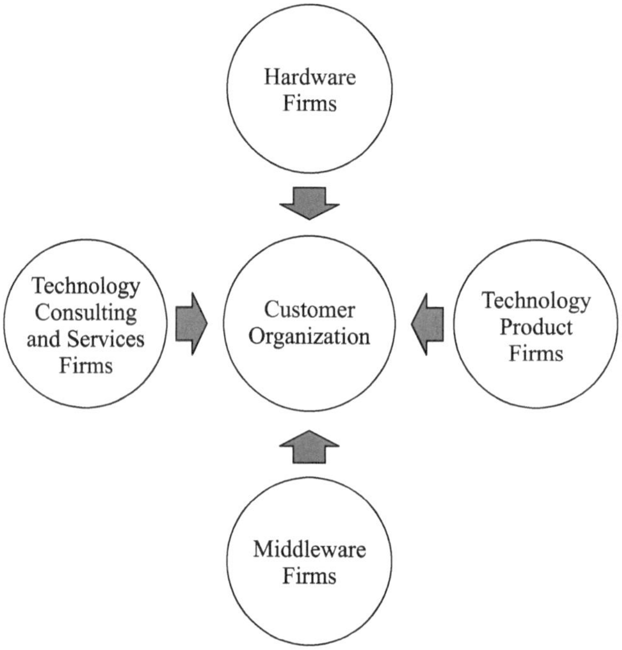

Source: Authors.

Technology consulting and services firms: These firms provide services for implementing and maintaining enterprise systems across the organization. Examples of technology consulting and services firms commonly referred to as system integrators (SI) include Accenture, Gapgemini, Tata Consultancy Services, Wipro, Infosys, etc. Table 1.1 provides a sample of the organizations providing services for enterprise system implementation. Consulting services are also provided by product firms. And what is the primary difference? Product firms provide implementation and maintenance services just for their own products while technology consulting and services firms provide implementation and maintenance services for products by multiple product vendors. In some cases technology consulting and service firms also act as a selling channel for product firms.

Product firms: Product firms (like SAP, i2 Technologies, JDA, and Manhattan Associates) for the enterprise systems market are organizations which develop applications and application suites. Application providers traditionally were divided into two broad categories—broad-based ERP providers and best of breed application providers. Table 1.1 provides a sample list of the organizations which provide applications/application suites. This distinction was more obvious in the past versus today. A number of broad-based ERP providers now sell standalone best of breed applications and application providers with a historical niche focus have broadened

TABLE 1.1
Sample of Firms Providing Enterprise System Applications and Services

	Application providers		*Service providers*
1	Oracle		Accenture
2	SAP**	Board based ERP	Bearing Point
3	Infor	Application Providers	Capgemini
4	Epicor		Cognizant
5	IFS*		Deloitte
6	IBS*		EDS
7	AspenTech		HP Technology Solutions Group
8	Manhattan Associates	Best of Breed Application	Infosys
9	i2 Technologies	Providers	Satyam
10	ILOG		Tata Consultancy Services
11	JDA		Unisys
12	Logility		Wipro

Source: Authors.

their application footprints. All product organizations also provide services for consulting, implementation, and maintenance of their products and product licensing makes up for only a part of their total revenue. Table 1.2 provides the total and new licence revenue breakdowns for a sample of enterprise system product firms. Licence revenues typically make up between one-quarter to one-third of the total revenue for most organizations, with the rest of the revenue coming from ongoing licence renewals, consulting services, and maintenance contracts.

TABLE 1.2
Total and Licence Revenues for a Sample of Product Firms

		Revenue ($M)		*License revenue ($M)*		*License revenue as % of revenue*	
	Application providers	*2007*	*2006*	*2007*	*2006*	*2007*	*2006*
1	Oracle	17996	14380	5882	4905	32.69%	34.11%
2	SAP**	15823.89	14512.185	5263.815	4639.635	33.26%	31.97%
3	Infor***	2100	790	Not Available	Not Available	Not Available	Not Available
4	Epicor	429.832	384.096	109.443	99.53	25.46%	25.91%
5	IFS*	388.74	364.485	78.87	71.445	20.29%	19.60%
6	IBS*	372.9	375.87	80.85	84.48	21.68%	22.48%
7	AspenTech	341.029	294.416	199.761	153.73	58.58%	52.22%
8	Manhattan Associates	337.401	288.868	73.031	66.543	21.65%	23.04%
9	i2 Technologies	260.31	279.677	47.721	76.243	18.33%	27.26%
10	ILOG	161.459	133.559	74.97	66.376	46.43%	49.70%
11	JDA	98.463	88.649	22.44	17.734	22.79%	20.00%
12	Logility	43.763	37.303	16.242	13.889	37.11%	37.23%

Source: Authors (based on financial reports available on individual company websites).
Note: Conversion Exchange rates used *1 SEK = 0.165 USD; **1 Euro = 1.545 USD; ***Obtained from company website.

Middleware firms: These organizations supply software systems that enable web hosting and integration of multiple applications and application suites, which comprise an enterprise system. Some middleware firms include web servers such as IBM, BEA systems, etc.; databases such as IBM, Oracle, Microsoft, etc.; and data integration adaptors/data management such as Informatica and Teradata. Often the middleware components for applications will be provided as packaged with the products or through the technology consulting firms.

Hardware firms: These organizations provide the hardware to host the enterprise systems and provide the infrastructure to enable users to access it. Apple, Dell, HP, Toshiba, Seagate, Hitachi, IBM, NEC, and Sun are major players in this market.

ENTERPRISE SYSTEM APPLICATIONS ECOSYSTEM

The enterprise systems market continues to grow every year with expected growth between 4 per cent and 6 per cent in 2008 (Bartels, 2008). As organizations become more global and pressures for reducing inefficiency increase organizations need to have more visibility and connectivity across different functions in the firm and with their supply chain. An enterprise system can enable the organization to achieve such visibility and connectivity to make informed business decisions. An enterprise system will consist of multiple modules or applications or application suites which cater to the specific planning and execution needs of particular functions or business units. Business units and functions commonly choose applications catering to their specific strategic and tactical needs. Ideally, organizations would like to have the enterprise system from one vendor. However, the needs of various business units and functions may not be completely fulfilled by products provided by a single vendor, and even in situations where multiple modules are obtained from the same vendor, they are implemented at different times. Therefore, applications or application suites from multiple vendors are integrated to provide the broader enterprise system functionality for an organization with a common look and feel across all applications or application suites. Users across multiple business units and the extended supply chain can access the required application or application suites through the enterprise portal. For an enterprise system which has multiple business unit specific applications or application suites, the ERP system commonly forms the backbone with other applications being integrated to form the complete enterprise system. Figure 1.3 provides a simplified representation of major application suites which come together to form an organization's enterprise system.

Enterprise systems, historically, were broadly grouped into two categories: (*a*) broad-based ERP providers; and (*b*) best of breed providers. As the industry continues to evolve the lines between these two categories of providers are more blurred. The broad-based ERP provider today offers standalone applications for planning, optimization, and collaboration for an organization and its supply chain, at the same time niche players who provided best of breed application in specific areas have broadened their product offerings with applications which allow for planning,

FIGURE 1.3
A Simple Representation of an Enterprise System

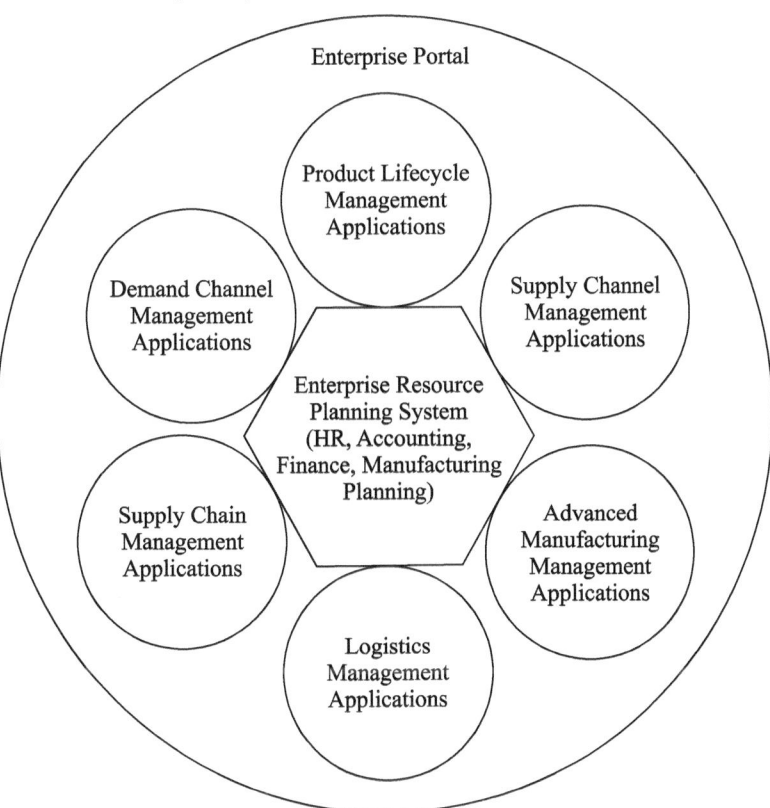

Source: Authors.

optimization, and collaboration across multiple areas of an organization and its supply chain. Another distinction between the two categories is that early ERP providers offered integrated solutions which tapped into the same database and explicit integration was not needed across different solution modules. However, the industry has evolved to modular solutions and the modules provided through the traditional ERP providers today require explicit integration to be a complete system. Table 1.3 provides a snapshot of application offerings by some of the major organizations in the enterprise systems industry categorized by functional areas.

The two major ERP providers today are SAP and Oracle. Over the last decade both have expanded their product footprint to provide application suites for extended enterprise integration as modules outside the traditional ERP domain. SAP has largely followed an organic growth strategy expanding its application footprint primarily with alliances, though it has recently completed some acquisitions (e.g., BI firm Business Objects). Oracle has largely followed an

TABLE 1.3
Sample of Firms Providing Applications or Application Suites by Application Areas

		Oracle	SAP	Infor	JDA	i2 Technologies	Manhattan associates	Logility	Ariba	IBM
Enterprise Portals	Enterprise Portals	X	X							X
Product Lifecycle Management	Product Data Management	X	X	X		X				X
	Project Portfolio/Program Management	X	X	X		X				X
Demand Channel Management	Customer Relationship Management	X	X	X	X					
	Marketing Resource Management	X	X	X						
	Sales Promotion Management	X	X	X	X	X				
	Pricing Optimization	X	X	X	X	X				
	Demand Planning	X	X	X	X	X	X	X		
	Order Fulfillment	X	X	X	X	X	X	X		
Enterprise and Manufacturing Management	Enterprise Resource Management	X	X	X						
	Enterprise Financial and Asset Management	X	X	X						
	Enterprise Human Capital Management	X	X	X						
	Manufacturing Planning and Execution	X	X	X	X	X				
	Advanced Planning and Scheduling	X	X	X	X	X		X		
Supply Chain Management	Sales and Operations Planning	X	X			X		X		
	Network Design	X	X	X		X				
	Inventory Optimization	X	X	X	X	X	X	X		
	Event Management	X	X	X	X	X	X	X		
	Performance Management/ Business Intelligence	X	X	X	X	X	X	X		X
Supply Channel Management	Supplier Relationship Management	X	X			X			X	
	Contract Management	X	X			X			X	
	Supplier Collaboration and Visibility	X	X		X	X			X	
	Spend Optimization	X	X			X		X	X	
	Reverse Auctions	X	X						X	
Logistics Management	Transportation Management	X	X	X	X	X	X	X		

Source: Authors.

acquisition strategy and its growth in the ERP segment was largely due to its acquisition of other ERP vendors such as JD Edwards and PeopleSoft. In addition to SAP and Oracle, Infor presents itself as another major ERP vendor and the largest privately owned enterprise systems organization. Infor offers the traditional ERP package offerings and has an expanded footprint of applications for the extended organization. However, it does have a gap in the application offerings for supply management.

Examples of the major organizations offering applications and application suite products other than ERP packages but with multiple areas include JDA, i2 Technologies, Manhattan Associates, and Logility. Over the last half decade these organizations have greatly expanded their application footprint. While having a broad application footprint, they still primarily provide applications which are optimization-based planning and execution tools. Very few niche application vendors providing best of breed applications in one application area remain today as most have been acquired by larger organizations. For example, Demantra, an application provider for demand management applications, is now part of Oracle. As indicated in Table 1.3, Ariba remains as one of the very few application providers with focused offerings for just supply management. Some application providers who offer products by different solution areas are now looked at.

ENTERPRISE AND MANUFACTURING MANAGEMENT

Central to enterprise systems is the ERP system. An ERP system commonly forms the backbone of an enterprise system which is integrated with multiple function or business unit specific application suites. ERP systems can be quite broad in their scope and may be implemented to provide support for accounting, finance and asset management, human resources, production and manufacturing, marketing, logistics, and purchasing functions. With such a broad scope there is often confusion regarding how ERP systems differ from enterprise systems. The two terms are often used interchangeably. Two main distinctions can be drawn between ERP systems and enterprise systems. First, ERP systems traditionally include systems which help the coordination and integration of business units or with functions which lie within the organizational boundaries. Enterprise systems assist the coordination and integration of business units or functions which lie within the organizational boundaries and also help the firm to coordinate and integrate across organizational boundaries with its supply chain trading partners.

Second, while an ERP system may be provided by a vendor who offers applications with the breath of functionality required across the entire organization and across the supply chain the applications are often not integrated as a single system upfront. A key component of an ERP system is a common integrated database across the multiple functions which are supported by the ERP system. Only a portion of the functionality required across the organization is integrated and available standard out of the box. This commonly includes the functionality required for planning and execution in the areas of finance, accounting, human resources, manufacturing, and, to a smaller extent, marketing, logistics, purchasing, etc., often with gaps in functionality. These gaps in functionality and additional functionality needed by the organization to manage and coordinate activities within the firm and across the supply chain are available as modules, which are integrated with the ERP system. This integrated set of solutions, which provide the organization with an ability to manage and coordinate internally and externally form the enterprise system for that organization.

Over the last few years the ERP industry has consolidated to a large extent and fewer organizations provide broad-based ERP packages. As such, a user organization's choice is more restricted today than in the past, with major vendors for ERP packages including SAP, Oracle, and Infor. In addition to ERP systems, all these vendors provide application suites across the board for a broad range of enterprise activities. In addition to broad-based ERP providers like SAP, other vendors also provide applications for manufacturing planning, scheduling, and execution systems as standalone applications. These standalone applications can be integrated with the ERP system for production and manufacturing management. Examples of vendors providing advanced planning and scheduling systems include SAP, Oracle, i2 Technologies, and JDA.

PRODUCT LIFECYCLE MANAGEMENT APPLICATIONS

One of the most challenging tasks for an organization is the management and maintenance of information related to its products. Product information needs careful management right from the conception of a product idea to the disposal of the product. Computer-aided design (CAD) and computer-aided manufacturing (CAM) systems are commonly used for the actual design of products and manufacturing processes the information systems required to manage the new product development programs and information regarding the organization's product portfolio.

Project or program management applications allow an organization to manage multiple new product development projects concurrently, sharing material, and resources. These applications allow the organization to have visibility and coordinate program management from strategic planning to actual execution of new product development efforts. SAP, Oracle, Infor, i2 Technologies, and IBM are some vendors providing leading edge applications for project or program management for new product development. In addition to managing information for new product development an organization is faced with challenges to manage information on its product. Organizations can effectively address this challenge through the use of Product Information Management (PIM) applications, which are focused on capturing and maintain information on the organizations product in a central repository. The application market for PIM has grown approximately 40–50 per cent in the last two years with the growth rate expected to grow in the near future (White, 2007). IBM, SAP, Oracle, Tibco Software, Fulltilt Solutions, i2 Technologies, and GXS are some vendors an organization can choose for PIM systems.

DEMAND CHANNEL MANAGEMENT APPLICATIONS

Managing the downstream supply chain efficiently and effectively is critical to an organization's success. Demand channel management applications fall under the broad umbrella of Customer Relationship Management (CRM) systems and Demand Management systems. CRM is a multi-faceted approach that organizations use to manage it customer relationships. In practice, CRM systems are often seen as application suites for sales force automation, account management, territory management, and customer service and support applications. Demand Management systems refer to systems used for forecasting and demand planning, order fulfillment, pricing optimization, promotions planning and management, and distributed order management which allows organizations to use point of sale or similar data to forecast their future product sales, manage product pricing, promotions, and manage customer orders.

While no single comprehensive solution is available for all the facets for demand channel management, a number of standalone applications allow an organization to implement and integrate multiple packages that can be aligned with the organizations requirements. Commonly used vendors for CRM by organizations include, Oracle (Siebel Systems, PeopleSoft and Oracle E-Business Suit, and CRM on Demand), SAP (SAP—CRM), Infor (CRM-Epiphany), and Salesforce.com. Similarly, sample of vendors with demand management application offerings include SAP, Oracle (Oracle E-Business Suit, CRM on Demand, and Demantra), Infor (Demand Planning Suite), i2 Technologies (Total Channel Management, Demand Manager, Demand Planner, Markdown Price Optimizer, and Order Fulfillment), JDA (Price and Promotion Management, Demand Management, and Allocation and Replenishment), Manhattan Associates (Planning and Forecasting Suite), and Logility (Voyager Demand Planning). Demand channel management applications such as demand planning and forecasting, order management, and order promising are expected to have growth rates of approximately 5–6 per cent in 2009–2010 (Hillman et al., 2005).

SUPPLY CHANNEL MANAGEMENT APPLICATIONS

As organizations seek to improve bottom line performance they are increasing efforts to manage the supply channel and collaborate better with suppliers with the use of information technology. Applications for supply channel management fall under the umbrella of Supplier Relationship Management (SRM) suite of applications. A typical SRM suite includes applications for strategic sourcing, contract management, spend optimization, supplier visibility, reverse auctions, and supplier collaboration. An organization can choose to implement a partial or full functionality offered by the SRM suite. Standalone applications often have overlapping functionality and multiple applications can be integrated to cater to an organization's sourcing needs. Different standalone applications provided by various vendors have similar functionality, which can be customized and configured to individual organizational requirements. Vendors providing applications for supply management include SAP (E-sourcing, Contract Management, Spend Analytics, and Cost and Quotation Management), Oracle (E-Business for Advanced Procurement, PeopleSoft Supplier Relationship Management suite, and JD Edwards Enterprise One Supply Management), Ariba (Supplier Management, Spend Visibility, Contract Management, etc.), and i2 Technologies (Total Supply Management, Collaborative Supply Execution, Negotiate, Product Sourcing, Strategic Sourcing, and Contract Management).

Supply Chain Management (SCM) Applications

For an organization seeking applications to enable efficient supply chain management and collaboration, there are a number of options available in the market. The fact the applications market is riddled with standalone supply chain applications often serves to complicate an organization's choice rather than simplifying it. Applications for SCM are available in the areas of Sales and Operations Planning, Supply Chain Network Design/Supply Chain Planning, Inventory Optimization, Supply Chain Event Management, and Supply Chain Performance Management/Business Intelligence. These are discussed next.

- *Sales and Operations Planning* (S&OP) applications enable organizations to match demand with supply, make decisions regarding the allocation of demand across different supply locations, and evaluate the impact of changes in demand on the firms supply chain network. The detailed demand and supply data required for S&OP are often obtained from standalone supply management applications, demand management applications, legacy systems, and the organizations home grown systems. The S&OP application segment is expected to have a growth rate of 6 per cent over 2009 and 2010 (Hillman et al., 2005). Vendors providing S&OP applications include SAP (xApps Sales and Operations Planning), Oracle (Demantra Real-time Sales, and Operations Planning), i2 Technologies (Sales and Operations Management), and Logility (Voyager Sales and Operations Planning).
- *Supply Chain Network Design* applications enable a firm to design, evaluate, and optimize their supply chain network with respect to decisions regarding the size, location, and numbers of facilities to best meet the demand faced by their organization and organization's service level goals. The Supply Chain Network Design application segment is expected to grow at a rate of 6–8 per cent over 2009–2010 (Hillman et al., 2005). Sample of vendors

providing applications for supply chain network design include, SAP, Oracle (Strategic Network Optimization), Infor (Strategic Network Design), and i2 Technologies (Supply Chain Planning, Supply Chain Strategist).

Tough economic situations faced by the organization in the presence of increased competition, short product life cycles, and increased outsourcing make it critical leading to inventories be managed optimally for maximizing service levels and minimizing costs. Inventory Optimization applications enable an organization to optimize inventory across their organization's facilities by evaluating options such as risk pooling and postponement. The Inventory Optimization application segment is expected to experience a growth rate of 8–10 per cent over 2009–2010 (Hillman et al., 2005). Vendors providing inventory optimization applications include SAP, Oracle, Infor, JDA, i2 Technologies, Manhattan Associates, and Logility.

As organizations have become more decentralized and complexity of supply chain has increased with the increase in global sourcing organizations face a much bigger challenge in maintaining visibility across the organization and its supply chain to manage supply chain risks and disruptions. Improvement visibility and disruption management is often enabled through the use of Supply Chain Visibility and Event Management applications. Supply chain event management applications provide an organization the ability to track supply chain events and set tolerances around an event. The violation of a tolerance is considered a disruption which triggers an alert for the relevant decision makers. As soon as a disruption is detected decision-makers are thus empowered to initiate steps to manage the disruptions or escalation of the issue can be initiated. Vendors providing supply chain event management applications include SAP, Oracle, Infor, JDA, i2 Technologies, Manhattan Associates, and Logility. Applications provided by different vendors offer largely similar functionality and can be customized to individual organizational requirements. The Supply Chain Event Management application segment is expected to have a growth rate of 5–6 per cent over 2009–2010.

- *Business Intelligence or Supply Chain Performance Management* applications integrate, analyze, and present organizational and supply chain performance data at various levels of granularity for the dimensions along which the organization wishes to track key performance indicators and metrics. Business intelligence applications use a data warehouse which houses archival and near-real-time data. Multiple organization specific linked reports for root cause analysis and aggregate reports with drill down capabilities can be developed with such applications to enable the organization to track and manage its supply chain performance. In 2007 the business intelligence applications market experienced a very significant trend of market consolidation and is expected to show a compounded annual revenue growth rate of 8.6 per cent till 2011(Richardson et al., 2008). Leading vendors for business intelligence software include Microsoft (Business Intelligence Suite), IBM (Cognos—acquired in November 2007), Oracle (Hyperion—acquired in July 2007), SAP (Business Objects—acquired in October 2007), and SAS and

MicroStrategy (Richardson et al., 2008). Additionally business intelligence applications are also available through vendors such as i2 Technologies, JDA, Tibco, Logility, etc.

LOGISTICS MANAGEMENT APPLICATIONS

As offshore sourcing expands and organizations increase their efforts to reach global markets, management of logistics to move raw materials through the upstream supply chain to manufacturing locations and finished goods to the customer through its downstream supply chain becomes more important. In light of the increasing oil prices, the pressure faced by an organization to contain transportation costs is immense. Logistics management applications help organizations optimize their transportation costs, maintain logistics visibility, manage freight orders, audit, and manage freight payment. i2 Technologies (Transportation Management Suite) and Oracle (Oracle Transportation Management) continue to lead the Transportation Management Applications Market (Klappich, 2007). Other vendors providing applications for transportation management include SAP, Infor, JDA, Manhattan Associates, Logility, RedPrairie, LeanLogistics, etc. The transportation management applications segment is expected to experience a 5 per cent growth rate in 2009–2010 (Hillman et al., 2005).

ENTERPRISE PORTALS

Enterprise portals enable organizations to provide a single point of access for multiple enterprise applications in essence giving the enterprise system the look and feel of being one system. Organizations continue to invest significant efforts in portal development to provide an interface with its customers, employees, and suppliers. Leading vendors in the portal market include IBM, Microsoft, SAP, Oracle, BEA Systems (acquired by Oracle), Sun, and Vignette (Gootzit et al., 2007). Other vendors include Tibco, Fujitsu, and BroadVision.

ENTERPRISE SYSTEM COMPONENTS ECOSYSTEM

A number of components provided by various organizations come together to bring an enterprise system to reality. Figure 1.4 shows a simplified representation of the enterprise system technical architecture. Organizations may use N-tier architecture for implementing enterprise systems. Commonly a 3-tier or 4-tier architecture is used by most organizations for implementing enterprise systems. The first tier contains the data sources. An enterprise system contains multiple data sources. Each standalone application suite will typically have its own database schema which is independent of other application suites. Often part of the data required for an application

FIGURE 1.4

Simplified Architecture of an Enterprise System

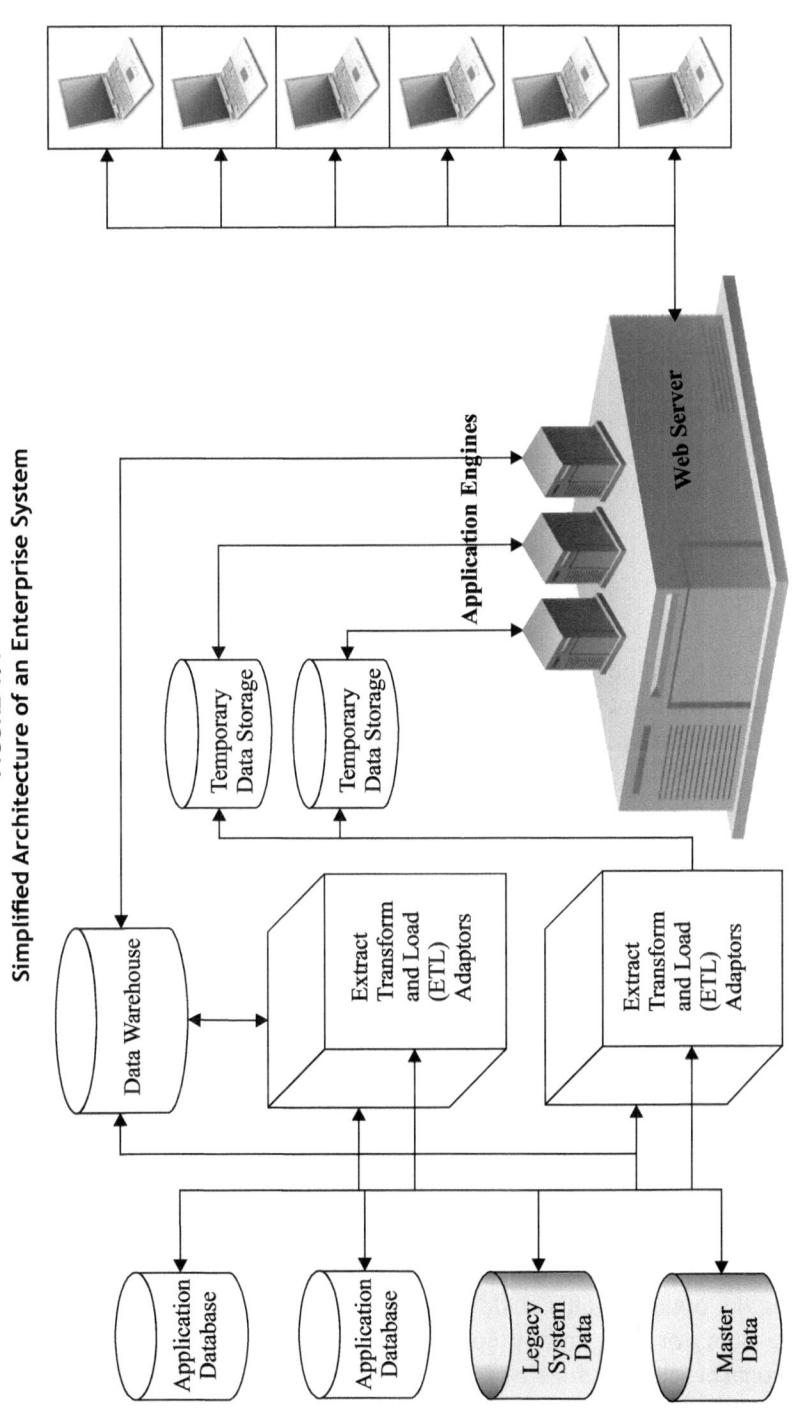

may be available through a legacy system. The enterprise system will have a database which stores the master data and a data warehouse which houses near real-time and archival data.

For any single application the data required are drawn from multiple databases including, other application databases, master data, data warehouse, legacy systems and sometimes orphan data residing in flat files or excel files. The data from multiple data sources are extracted, transformed, and loaded (ETL) into a staging area and/or the applications database for access and manipulation. This is achieved through the help of ETL logic referred to as ETL adaptors. Application engines gather data from the application's database, temporary storage area, and user interface to process it as per the application's logic and business rules. Applications engines are housed in the web server which enable the web interface users to access the application. While web servers and a web interface are commonly used today for most enterprise systems, applications can also be housed in the application servers which use a heavier client and graphic user interface for user access. The different components of an enterprise system are discussed next with examples of organizations supplying these components.

APPLICATION ENGINES

Application engines form the core of the enterprise system and house the processing logic for the business process or business rules for which the application intended. A detailed discussion of application engines was provided in the previous section.

DATABASES

Databases are used to maintain one of the most complex and high volume elements of an enterprise system. Multiple databases come together to provide the complete functionality of an enterprise system. The primary data sources include:

1. *Application databases* house the application specific data. Application databases contain transactional data used and processed by the applications, plus metadata, i.e., data about specific components of the application, e.g., data relating to runtime report structures, etc. Additionally, temporary data stores are also used by applications and form a part of the application database. Schemas for the application databases are application specific and provided by the application vendors.
2. *Master data* are often housed in a separate database. Master data are reference data regarding the organization's customers, products, materials, employees, and suppliers. They are often stored separately, not transactional in nature, but are critical in supporting transactional processing. Ideally, an organization's master data should be stored centrally

with various applications accessing the data from a central source (or backup/image locations). Often different functions and business units in an organization maintain and store separate master data which often leads to inaccurate and duplicate master data in organizations. Therefore, Master Data Management (MDM) is a critical part of enterprise system management and sample vendors which provide products to help a firm manage its master data include, SAP, Oracle, IBM, i2 Technologies, Informatica, and Teradata.

3. *Data warehouses* store organizational near-real time and archival data which are primarily used for analysis and reporting. The primary difference between operational databases (application data and master data) and a data warehouse is that operational databases store data which are normalized and optimized for data integrity. Data warehouses store data in non-normalized form that are optimized for access speed. Data warehouse data may also be redundant and stored at multiple levels of granularity. Primary vendors for data warehouse solutions include Oracle, IBM, and Teradata.

MIDDLEWARE

As the name suggests, this software sits in the 'middle' of the application and database or the application and user interface. Middleware enables the application to communicate with the other components of the enterprise system. The most commonly seen middleware are ETL adaptors and web servers or application servers. ETL adaptors are middleware which enable communication between the application and the databases. Web servers or application servers are the middleware which enable the application to communicate with the client user interface, typically the Internet for most current enterprise systems. ETL adaptors for an application suite are commonly provided by the application vendor; additionally, an organization can write its own ETL adaptors using a middleware platform. ETL adaptors are also available through vendors such as IBM and Informatica. Web servers or application servers enable the web interface between the end user and application. The total web server market was estimated at $2.4 billion and is expected to almost double in five years to $4.1 billion (Natis et al., 2008). Web servers or application servers are often offered by the product firm as part of the product during implementation and can also be obtained as an independent application directly from the organization which developed the servers. Sample of vendors providing web server or application servers include Microsoft, IBM, BEA Systems, Oracle, SAP, Fujitsu, Sun Microsystems, etc.

HARDWARE

This includes all the physical components which enable an enterprise system including servers, computers, network systems, etc., and are available through a number of organizations such as Apple, Dell, HP, Toshiba, Seagate, Hitachi, IBM, NEC, and Sun Microsystems. Hardware for an application system typically forms only a small part of the total cost of the system (generally 1–2 per cent).

CONSULTING SERVICES AND SYSTEM INTEGRATION

Consulting services and system integration services help an organization implement applications, integrate them with the overall enterprise system, and maintain the systems through their lifecycle. The enterprise systems market is continuously evolving and organizations must consider a number of variables such as architecture choice, integration approach, regulatory considerations, governance approach, and enterprise systems risk management approaches, while making the choice of consulting and system integration services. For an application implementation, organizations need to procure services through vendors providing in-depth expertise on the functional and technical aspects of the application. Additionally, the service provider should guide the organization's users through the change while, maintaining stability during implementation in the short term and for system maintenance long term. Figure 1.5 summarizes the role of consulting services relative to the various other elements already discussed here.

With increased information system (IS) outsourcing, most firms have established relationships with some SI who provides advisory and consulting services regarding the organization's enterprise system, in addition to being involved in deployments, integration, and maintenance

FIGURE 1.5
Sample of Vendors Providing Different ES Components

Implementation Consulting and System Integration Services		
SAP consulting, i2 consulting, Oracle consulting, JDA consulting, Capgemini, IBM consulting, Tata Consultancy Services, Accenture, Wipro, EDS, Bearing Point, Deloitte		
Databases	**Middleware**	**Application Engines**
➤ *Oracle* ➤ *IBM – Db2* ➤ *Microsoft –SQL Server*	➤ *ETL Adaptors (e.g., Informatica, TeraData)* ➤ *Web Server (e.g., IBM WebSphere, BEA Weblogic)*	➤ *SAP applications* ➤ *i2 applications* ➤ *Oracle applications* ➤ *Microsoft applications* ➤ *JDA applications*
Hardware and Network Systems		
Apple, Dell, HP, Toshiba, Seagate, Hitachi, IBM, NEC, and Sun Microsystems		

Source: Authors.

of new systems and ongoing support for existing enterprise systems. When choosing an SI to provide a broad range of services, an organization needs to carefully consider the range of core services and the product implementation experience of the SI. What has been their organizational viability and track record? A sample of vendors providing broad-based system integration and consulting services include Accenture, Deloitte, CapGemini, EDS, Infosys, Tata Consultancy Services, Wipro, etc. Additionally, consulting services are also provided by product firms, e.g., SAP, i2 Technologies, Manhattan Associates, JDA, Logility, etc. Product firms provide consulting and system integration services for their own products while SIs provide services for products across products from multiple vendors. Implementation teams today commonly are cross functional and cross organizational, including members from the organization procuring the enterprise application, system integrator, and the application vendor.

ENTERPRISE SYSTEM MARKET TRENDS

Enterprise applications have evolved over the last three decades, with Figure 1.6 showing the changes. During the 1980s systems were developed primarily from a functional perspective.

FIGURE 1.6
Evolution of Enterprise Systems

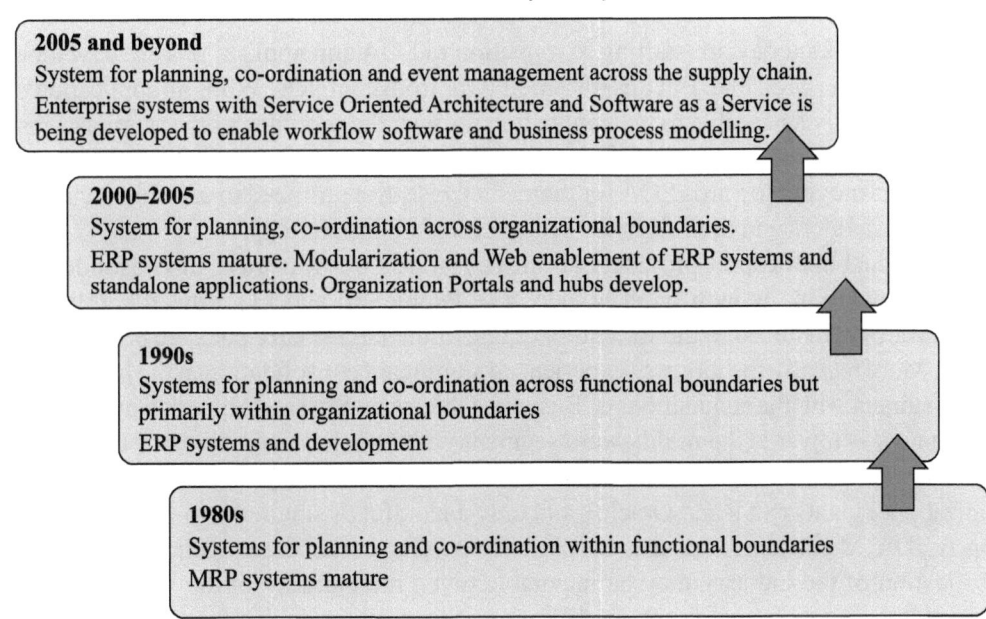

Source: Authors.

Automation within the organization's specific functions was the objective. These systems, like Material Requirement Planning (MRP) and Manufacturing Resources Planning (MRP II), continued to evolve during the early 1990s, and the later part of the decade saw the early development of ERP systems. ERP systems enabled coordination and planning across the functional walls of an organization. While cross functional planning and coordination was enabled with ERP systems; the system laid within the organization's boundary. The early part of 21st century saw the modularization and web enablement of ERP systems, with advanced planning systems and systems for coordination across the supply chain started to be a regular part of enterprise systems. Recent advances in enterprise systems are aimed towards applications which are based on Service Oriented Architecture (SOA) and provide Software as a Service (SaaS) to increase enterprise system flexibility and reduce response time for changes to applications and developing new applications.

SOA is a flexible architecture which enables better integration and sharing of applications, and allows for the linking of data and application resources called services. Applications are built as modules for specific functionality and are referred to as business services. These services are accessible for developing any new application which may be required by the organization. Web services are commonly used to implement a SOA to enable the functionality to be accessed and used easily with standard internet protocols. SOA provides a flexible and agile platform for organizations through the use of a repository of services that can be accessed to quickly develop applications for an organization's need. This enables the IT organization to respond quickly and cost-effectively to the demands of the business organization. Most application vendors today are starting to transition to SOA and applications are developed as services which are accessible. But this transition is far from complete. While an application's services may be easily accessible to the application through the provider's other applications, the access through applications from different vendors may often require additional integration. Organizations moving towards SOA for their enterprise systems need to carefully evaluate the application providers and their fit in the organization's SOA strategy.

As individual application providers all move towards SOA, a wave of consolidation has been in full swing in the industry. The merger of PeopleSoft and J.D. Edwards, followed by the takeover by Oracle led to the formation of one of the largest ERP package providers in the industry. More recently the industry experienced significant consolidation in the business intelligence segment with the acquisitions of Business Objects by SAP and Hyperion by Oracle. The attention now is towards the middleware segment with Oracle's acquisition of BEA Systems in January 2008. Consolidation of the industry has lead to the polarization, leaving large organizational giants (SAP and Oracle), and only a handful of smaller organizations (i2 Technologies, JDA, Manhattan Associates, and Ariba) providing best of breed applications. Continued consolidation of the industry may be inevitable given the maturity of the software industry, which is moving more towards commoditization of its products with a focus on flexibility and easy configurability.

REFERENCES

Bartels, A. 2008. 'Global IT 2008 Market Outlook', *Forrester Research Report* (February). Forrester Research Inc., Cambridge, MA. Available at http://www.forrester.com/rb/research

Gootzit, D., G. Phifer, and R. Valdes. 2007. *Magic Quadrant for Horizontal Portal Products* (August). Gartner Research Inc. Available at http://www.gartner.com/technology/research.jsp

Hillman, M., M. D'Aquila, S. Hochman, and K. Carter. 2005. 'The Supply Chain Management Applications Report', *2005–2010 AMR Research Report*, AMR Research Inc. Available at www. amrresearch.com

Klappich, D.C. 2007. *Magic Quadrant for Transportation Management Systems* (January). Gartner Research Inc. Available at http://www.gartner.com/technology/research.jsp

Natis, Y.V., M. Pezzini, K. Iijima, and R. Favata. 2008. *Magic Quadrant for Enterprise Application Servers.* Gartner Research Inc. Available at http://www.gartner.com/technology/research.jsp

Richardson, J., K. Schlegel, B. Hostmann, and N. McMurchy. 2008. *Magic Quadrant for Business Intelligence Platforms* (February). Gartner Research Inc. Available at http://www.gartner.com/technology/research.jsp

White, A. 2007. *Magic Quadrant for Product Information Management.* Gartner Research Inc. Available at http://www.gartner.com/technology/research.jsp

2

Enterprise Interoperability and Enterprise Systems

PETER LOOS
Institute for Information Systems (IWi)
German Research Center for Artificial Intelligence (DFKI), Saarbrücken, Germany
E-mail: loos@iwi.dfki.de

DIRK WERTH
Institute for Information Systems (IWi)
German Research Center for Artificial Intelligence (DFKI), Saarbrücken, Germany
E-mail: werth@iwi.dfki.de

SILKE BALZERT
Institute for Information Systems (IWi)
German Research Center for Artificial Intelligence (DFKI), Saarbrücken, Germany
E-mail: balzert@iwi.dfki.de

THOMAS BURKHART
Institute for Information Systems (IWi)
German Research Center for Artificial Intelligence (DFKI), Saarbrücken, Germany
E-mail: burkhart@iwi.dfki.de

SEBASTIAN KÄMPER
Institute for Information Systems (IWi)
German Research Center for Artificial Intelligence (DFKI), Saarbrücken, Germany
E-mail: kaemper@iwi.dfki.de

INTRODUCTION

In the past, companies often tried to achieve an increase in efficiency through internal improvements and organic growth. However, companies of all sizes face an ongoing globalization, fast changing technical environments, and increasingly sophisticated customers. Thus, they have to cope with severe competition and high requirements in terms of flexibility (Lucke and Webering, 2003). Consequently, the concentration on the core competencies (Prahalad and Hamel, 1990) and the systematic supplementation of missing abilities and/or products through cooperation becomes more and more important for the success and survival in today's business environment.

Within such an economy of globalization, factor time is becoming more and more business-critical. Enterprises are forced to quickly react on market changes and new business opportunities. In this respect, innovation and flexibility are getting the new critical success factors for businesses (Clark et al., 1988). Apart from 'classical' core competence orientation, a second stream of management is being established—the ability to always be prepared to initiate or to join new businesses (Davidsson et al., 2008). This necessity for preparation to do business with other companies efficiently and efficiently forms the base of the concept of Enterprise Interoperability.

Even as these plug-and-do businesses are becoming more important, this topic has only been modestly evaluated, both in terms of theoretical foundations and in organizational research. Therefore, the objective of this chapter is to investigate the nature of Enterprise Interoperability and to assess the way it directs implementation of enterprise systems. The following section deals with the origin of the term 'interoperability', namely, the technical disciplines. It expands this property of a technical object to the business-orientated domain, resulting in the concept of Enterprise Interoperability. The third section describes the special characteristics of Enterprise Interoperability. It decomposes the concept into partial relationships, namely, the interoperability between businesses, processes, and information systems. At the end of this section, these partial concepts are consolidated into the Enterprise Interoperability Framework. This is followed with a description of the relationship between interoperability and standards. Here, the semantic aspects of interoperability that span another, content-oriented dimension of conceiving Enterprise Interoperability is discussed. Finally, the chapter closes with a discussion that will draw conclusions and provide an outlook on future research directions.

CONCEIVING ENTERPRISE INTEROPERABILITY

The Institute of Electrical and Electronics Engineers formulated in 1990 a widespread definition of interoperability: 'Interoperability is the ability of two or more systems or components to exchange information and to use the information that has been exchanged' (IEEE, 1990).

Following this understanding, interoperability is a property of a (technical) system and appears as a technological phenomenon. Such definition is suitable for the engineering domain, and there are several authors that mainly follow the approach of conceiving Interoperability as a property of technical systems (cf. Lewerenz, 1999). Here, the main prerequisite to enable interoperability is the possibility to exchange data based on a common gateway enabling interactions (Roser, 2008). This implicates that in this technical coherence, interoperability only describes a system feature.

However, the reference object of Enterprise Interoperability is not just a technical system but rather a complex, organizational system, namely the enterprise itself. An enterprise, however, cannot be seen solely from the technical perspective. Strategic, social, and market-related issues have to be considered as well. Thus, it is necessary to transfer the understanding of a mainly technical interoperability into a new business-oriented domain, which takes into account an overall picture of interoperability. Nevertheless, in the context of Enterprise Interoperability this technical understanding provides the foundations on which interoperability occurs. Hence, a shared base in the meaning of common standards and gateways is a crucial requirement to Enterprise Interoperability (Gerst and Bunduchi, 2006).

A business-orientated understanding of interoperability, on the other hand, consists of several aspects that are more complex. Enterprises are not self-contained systems with predefined gateways. The key requirement to enable Enterprise Interoperability is the ability of business partners to collaborate rather than the technical circumstances. Besides the fact that the given technical landscape enables collaboration in general, business partners need to have a common understanding of an aspired partnership. This transforms the understanding of the Enterprise Interoperability terminology from a technical feature of an object to the ability of business partners to be interoperable, based on market-driven as well as personnel circumstances (Bendoly et al., 2004). This in turn leads to a fundamental precondition for Enterprise Interoperability: Business partners are required to have a common goal in terms of an imperative to aim for collaboration. From the economic point of view, this corresponds mainly to the generation of business benefits for both sides. Thus, Enterprise Interoperability has to generate a win-win situation for all collaboration partners in general.

Furthermore, enterprises are changeable, 'organic' systems. Having the ability to change and adapt to whatever requirement there is, they are interoperable per se. However, this does not reflect the understanding of interoperability that is present. Interoperability is more likely the ability to collaborate without any major time delay and without significant effort. Therefore, it can be postulated to achieve interoperability only if the collaboration can be realized without undergoing any fundamental change in the systems and structures involved, neither in the enterprise organization, in its business processes, nor in its enterprise system environment.

Based on these pre-conditions, Enterprise Interoperability can be defined as follows:

> *Enterprise Interoperability* is the ability of multiple firms to perform a generation of added value in division of labour, self-coordinated, within a overlapping business process, based on the exchange of coherent information, with a common goal and without fundamental changes to the initial organizational, procedural, and technical landscapes of the enterprises.

INTEROPERABILITY OF BUSINESSES, PROCESSES, AND INFORMATION SYSTEMS

Emerging from the definition just given, Enterprise Interoperability can be decomposed into three partial concepts that build up the level structure of Enterprise Interoperability (cf. Uption, 1994):

1. *Business Interoperability* is an organizational concept that describes the ability of enterprises to interwork from a strategic point of view. It comprises questions of a cultural compatibility, of the validity of a combined business model as well as of the trust and human relationship between the main actors.
2. *Process Interoperability* is a concept on control and synchronization. It describes the state in which an enterprise is able to be partially steered by another enterprise or vice versa to steer parts of another firm itself.
3. *Information System Interoperability* is the founding base for business operations. It comprises mechanisms and structures that allow the interwork of enterprise systems, i.e., to exchange information and to process this information according to the (common) business purposes.

BUSINESS INTEROPERABILITY

As stated earlier, interoperability is the pure ability to interact and can be achieved within three different concepts. The first concept is the domain of businesses. This means within this perspective the object being addressed is the market itself, which evolves the business drivers for enterprises and which is the place of interaction for enterprises.

The market is divided into different industries. Therein, competitors, suppliers, and customers can be pointed out as the main partners to be considered. Depending on what the mission and the underlying goals are, enterprises choose specific strategies to hold or change their position. In order to do this efficiently, major knowledge from domains like culture, law, geography, etc., is needed (see Figure 2.1).

Every entity acting in the real world is dependent on its environment. The environment shapes enterprises as well (cf. De Groote, 1994). There are different perspectives to decompose the environment in regards of setting up business strategies. On top level, social and physical dimensions can be differentiated.

FIGURE 2.1
Differentiation of Environment

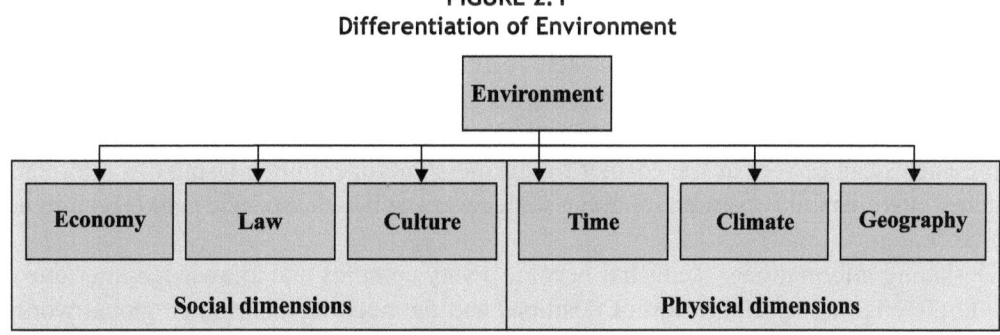

Source: Authors.

The social dimensions are mainly created and affected by humans. Here, the economy can be seen as a set of interrelated enterprises and consumers. The enterprises also comprise information systems. Thus, the economy is a socio-technical system that partly contains enterprise that are socio-technical sub-systems. Depending on where enterprises are located or where they perform their operations, they have to follow different legal regulations. In case of global, multinational enterprises, the legal issues have to be rationalized and included into the strategy. A very complicated aspect is the acquaintance with cultures, especially for those enterprises which sell the same products on diverse markets within different cultures.

While the social dimensions depend on the behaviour of humans, the physical dimensions define the outer frame for interaction of enterprises. The first one, time, is most important when the main goal of information management is considered as the provision of the right information at the right time at the right place to the right person. Because of the distribution of information systems, the geographical aspect can be disregarded in that case, but gets more importance in the case of industrial industries, and additional in handling the aspects of networking and distributed collaboration. Climate is another physical dimension, especially for those enterprises, which are working in, e.g., oil or building industries. The level of interoperability can be augmented by considering different environmental configurations as the context for the process interoperability level. This means that strategies have to consider environmental circumstances on the one hand, but penetrate the process interoperability level in order to transfer the given market requirements into the procedural landscape of a company on the other hand (cf. Werth, 2007).

Process Interoperability

Process interoperability is the ability to immediately change or adapt processes. In this respect, business processes do not only describe the current way of operations. Rather they will specify how an enterprise can adapt. Consequently, the level of description shifts from a present assessment into future potential (Werth, 2006). By this, it is more efficient to meet newly emerged market conditions. Combined with the strategic objectives a company aspires, an enterprise that is process interoperable can align processes and market drivers (cf. Jordan and Graves, 1995). In this way, present market obstacles can be overcome and the targeted goals can be achieved more precisely. Based from the market drivers, the specific market requirements can be tagged using deduction (Fuchs, 1996). Vice versa, the process-based solutions fitting the requirements can be seen as the enabler for business interoperability. Using this information, matched interoperability partners, aligning strategies as well as the specific market requirements can be chosen.

Designing information systems has become a very complex and knowledge-intensive task due to the ongoing specialization of positions and the need for distributed global working.

Displaying these real world requirements for enterprises on to model-level, process architectures can be derived according to the design principles for information system or IS (Becker et al., 2006). Interoperability, however, always implies changes to current process sequences, which results in adjusting the relevance of all processes, involved within the collaboration, to the market requirements. Still more specifically, 'process interoperability' comprises three vertical and two horizontal layers (see Figure 2.2).

The horizontal levels consist of the coordination activities, which are divided into internal and external ones. The internal coordination activities govern the private processes of an enterprise to control the flow of materials, finances, and information within the enterprise. This aspect will not be discussed further in this chapter because it is not within the focus of Enterprise Interoperability. The second coordination activity is the external coordination which controls the public processes [derived from the published parts of private processes (cf. Ziemann et al., 2007)] in order to steer the mentioned flows between enterprises.

FIGURE 2.2
Process Interoperability Framework

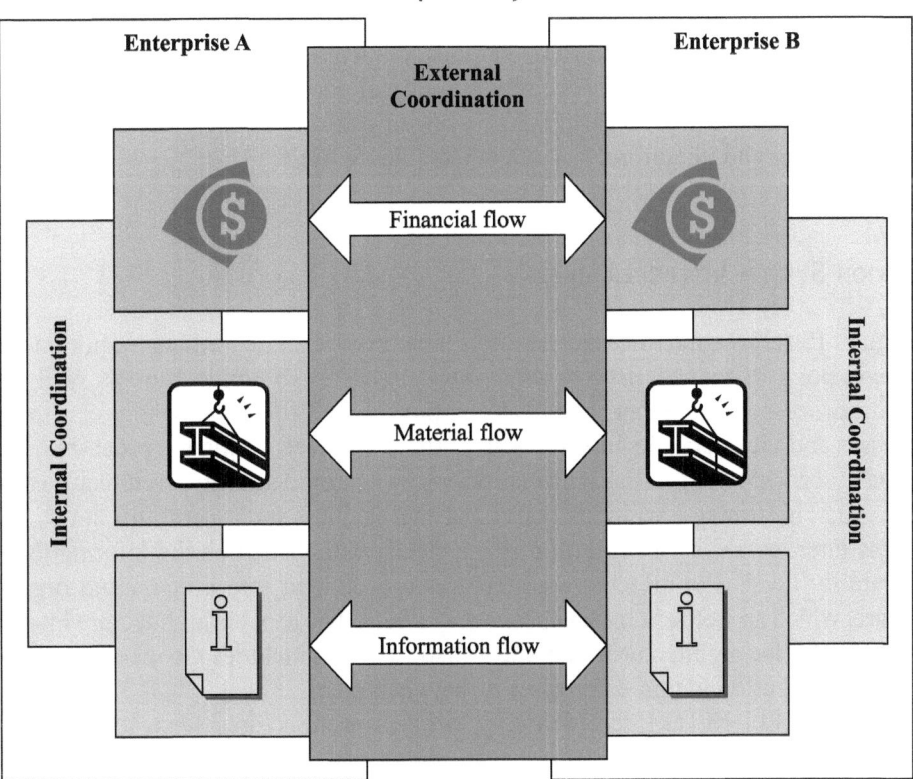

Source: Authors.

The three vertical levels are:

- *Information flows* which handle the transfer of information in between humans as well as applications.
- *Material flows* which are logistically embossed and correspond to the physical transportation of objects in between two locations.
- *Financial flows* which attend to the transfer of financial funds in between partners.

Additionally, these flows may be decomposed into the three sub-dimensions of temporal, spatial, and technical. Through doing so, the quality of achieved interoperability can be measured. Differentiating the service level degree according to the fulfilment in these categories leads to a combined service level evaluation of interoperable processes (Deelmann, 2007).

All these three vertical levels of process interoperability have effect on exchangeable objects. However, the sequence of activities itself constitutes an own flow that describes the synchronization of tasks. This control flow coordinates and supervises all actions and exchanges within the three other levels within the right context and aligned according to the stated business strategy. Partially, the control flow goes in parallel to one of the other flows (in most cases to the information flow); however, in some settings, control has the opposite direction or completely shapes its own structure. Especially in terms of coordination, the control flow acts as an enabler for process interoperability. However, in contrary to the other flows, it does not exchange anything and, therefore, it is not detectable by itself.

INFORMATION SYSTEM INTEROPERABILITY

The design of IS follows the rules and needs of the processes. The business requirements from the strategic point of view constitute the requirements for IS architecture as well as for IS itself. Thus, processes and IS can be seen as components in a life cycle, where IS is the enabler for processes and vice versa. IS integrates all entities involved within the processes. Actually, this can be described based on the Information System Interoperability Architecture described in Figure 2.3. The strategy, which is defined at the business interoperability level, pervades the process interoperability level until it is physically established on the information system interoperability level. The affected architectures are divided into process and organization architecture, which are settled on a business related field. The process architecture integrates all other elements of the architectures into one holistic view. It includes the mentioned flows and shows their distribution within enterprises or between them.

For analyzing Enterprise Interoperability, process architectures seem to be well suited, because they show the relation between the flows and interfaces to connect flows. The organization architecture shows the structure of an enterprise, which cannot explicitly be seen in the process architecture. It comprises the hierarchies and the responsibilities of different roles,

FIGURE 2.3
Information System Interoperability Architecture

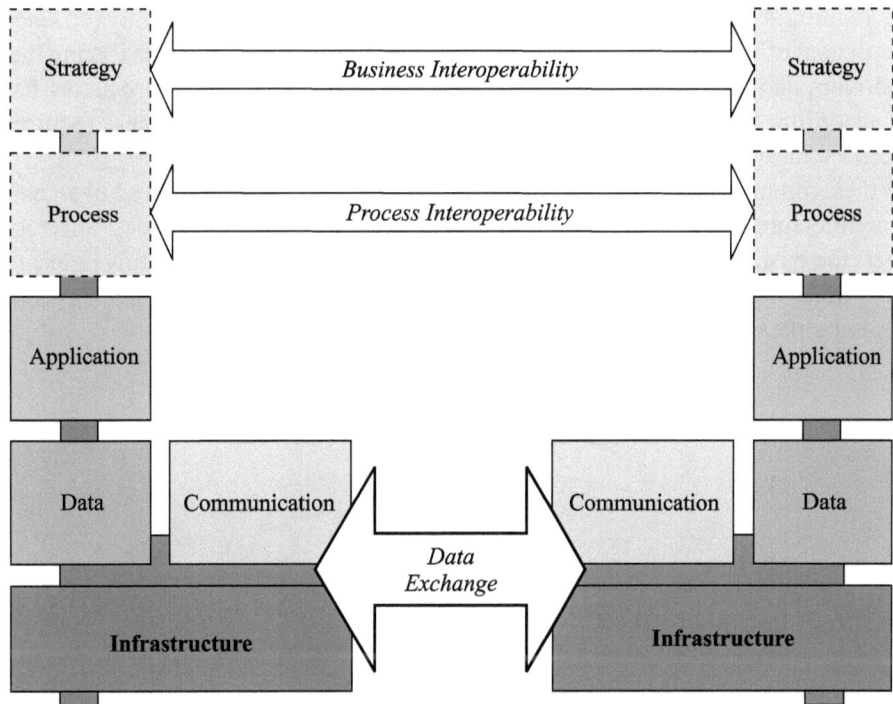

Source: Authors.

departments, and employees (Scheer, 1999). The supporting architectures are the application, data, and communication architectures. The application architecture describes the relations between simple functions, applications, or whole clusters of enterprises. It shows to what degree applications are interoperable in terms of fulfilling functions. The data architecture contains all information about business objects defined on the business interoperability level. This is the source of information that can be used for interoperability purposes. For example, enterprises can intend to share their data in common data warehouses or they can eliminate redundant data to lower the data storage costs. The communication architecture is utilized to enable the possibilities of interconnection between enterprises.

Technically speaking, all these architectures are operated by the infrastructure, which contains all hardware and software systems that are needed to execute business applications. Supported by infrastructure and coordinated by the strategy and the adapted communication architectures, the interoperation between two enterprises should match the requirements set up on the strategic level. However, information system interoperability is the technical implementation of interoperability between enterprises enabled by enterprise architecture management on coordination level and IT infrastructure on execution level.

Enterprise Interoperability Framework

To recap, Figure 2.4 displays an initial framework for Enterprise Interoperability (cf. Chen, 2006). The overall goal of generating benefit for both parties can be achieved by analyzing the specific market drivers and deriving necessary market requirements. Existing processes have to be adapted according to these needs, which lead to the definition of the process requirements to be fulfilled by the system interoperability layer.

Once these premises have been achieved by implementing the required changes into the system architecture, adjusted architecture acts as an enabler for the process interoperability that affects the business interoperability level in the same way. Following this Enterprise Interoperability life cycle, added value can only be generated by constantly meeting the requirements of an upper by the underlying level.

FIGURE 2.4
Enterprise Interoperability Framework

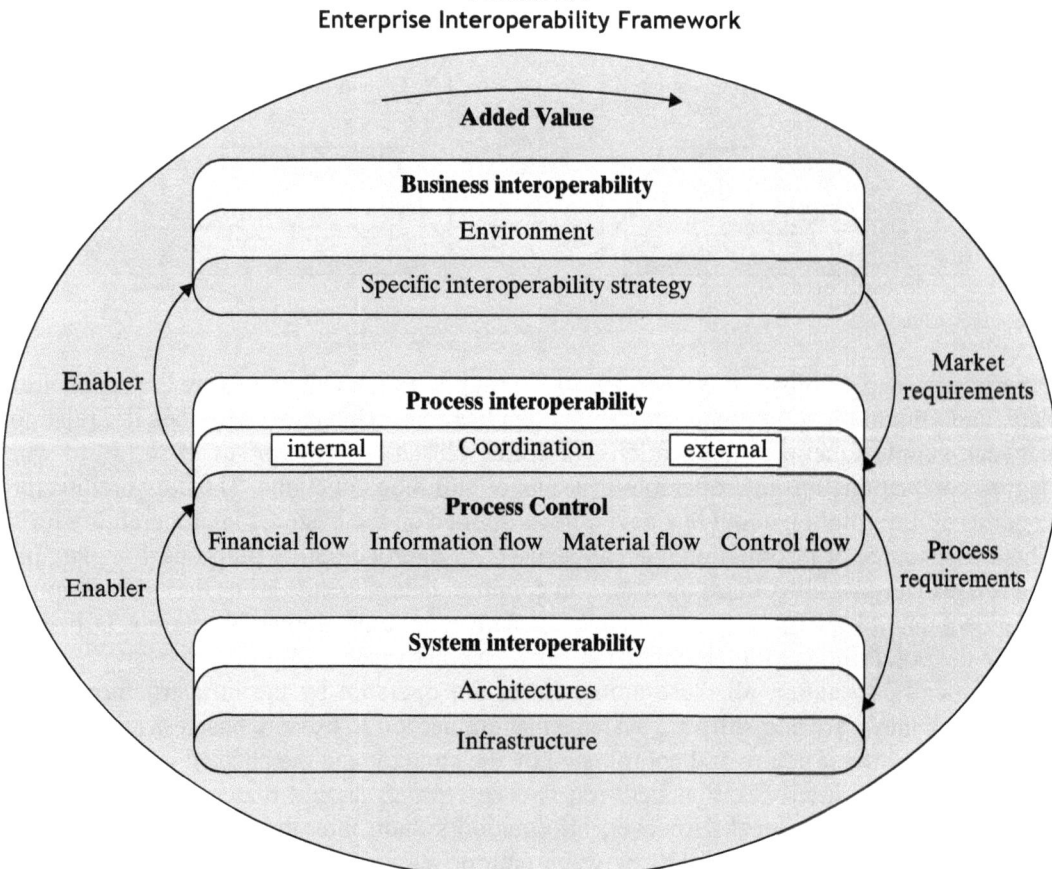

ABOUT THE RELATIONSHIP BETWEEN INTEROPERABILITY AND STANDARDS

In the discussion of interoperability, standards and their treatment is one of the central topics. In this chapter, interoperability is structurally decomposed into the organizational, the process, and the system levels. The organizational level reflects the real business world where enterprises collaborate. From the organizational point of view, interoperability is a phenomenon, which appears when people communicate and exchange information. They have to understand each other's meanings and thoughts to share their mental models for task-oriented activities. The explication of information is error-prone because of different backgrounds of the partners and their different interpretation of information. Barriers in communication can reside in the follow facets of the organization setting (among others):

- *Language* • *Mental models* • *Legal situation* • *Cultures*

On organizational level, the primary goal should be coherency in the use of words. It is important for enterprises to communicate under this premise. Actors in the business need to have the same perception of the 'things' in the real world. Especially, contracts contain ensured, definite information to prevent misunderstandings, and, furthermore, to ensure the correctness in case of deliverables.

To become interoperable connected, the partners have to be coherent in their enterprise descriptions. One way to do this is to use models, which represent the world a bit more formal and simpler. These models describe the business objects and explain the main concepts of enterprise organization, process flow, and rules. The organizational, functional, data, and deliverable perspective are integrated within the process view. Therefore, processes are the most important perspective to describe Enterprise Architectures. These architectures specify the way, how the added value in enterprises and between enterprises is created. The process level is the space where Enterprise Architecture Management is placed to extend the reality on a model-based perspective for planning purposes. Established standards in the field of Enterprise Architecture Management are the different modelling languages itself which are used for different perspectives.

Because of the number of different standards, which occur in running information systems, the heterogeneity between different enterprises may be seen as barrier or as incompatibility in working together. Therefore, it is urgently necessary to treat the differences between the existing standards and handle their differences in the right way to become compatible and interoperable. The main reason for the necessity of interoperability is the diversity of standards in industrial applications. From the technical perspective, the precondition of interoperability is the enabling of communication as basic requirement for the information exchange between partners (Bendoly and Schoenherr, 2005; Bendoly et al., 2007).

On the technical level, interoperability can be measured. As a first-degree measurement, the grade of interoperability corresponds to the number of supported standards and the number of supported interfaces for different purposes. The more the standards exist to fulfill the same function, the higher the grade of interoperability has to be. Possibly, for some domains there are no standards, so that the interoperability has to be initially established. In summary, interoperability can only be established, if there is a minimum of standardization between the objects to be interoperable and, moreover, if these objects have a differentiation between them that makes them not inconsequentially interchangeable. This relationship also (and in actual research mainly) involves the question of semantics (see Figure 2.5).

Newer approaches show that there are some first standards which can be used for describing the organizational and the process level to design information systems on a computation independent model (CIM). This can be done by using ontology to describe and differentiate things occurring in the real world (cf. W3C: OWL Web Ontology). Furthermore, the motivation and business environment can be described by using the Business Motivation Model (BMM) (OMG1: http://www.omg.org/cgi-bin/doc?dtc/2006-08-03). At the end, the way how it should be done is described using the Business Process Model Notation (BPMN) (OMG2: http://www.omg.org/cgi-bin/doc?dtc/2006-11-01). The most accepted definition of an ontology is from Gruber and Studer which was unitized from Probst. In this understanding, an ontology 'is a formal, explicit specification of a common shared conceptualisation' (Gruber, 1993). The important properties of an ontology are its formalism, the explication of implicit knowledge with the aim to share it and to unify it. These ideas underlie the concept of the Semantic Web which was mentioned by Tim-Berner's Lee as a future internet (cf. W3C Semantic Web Activity).

FIGURE 2.5
Semantics of Enterprise Interoperability

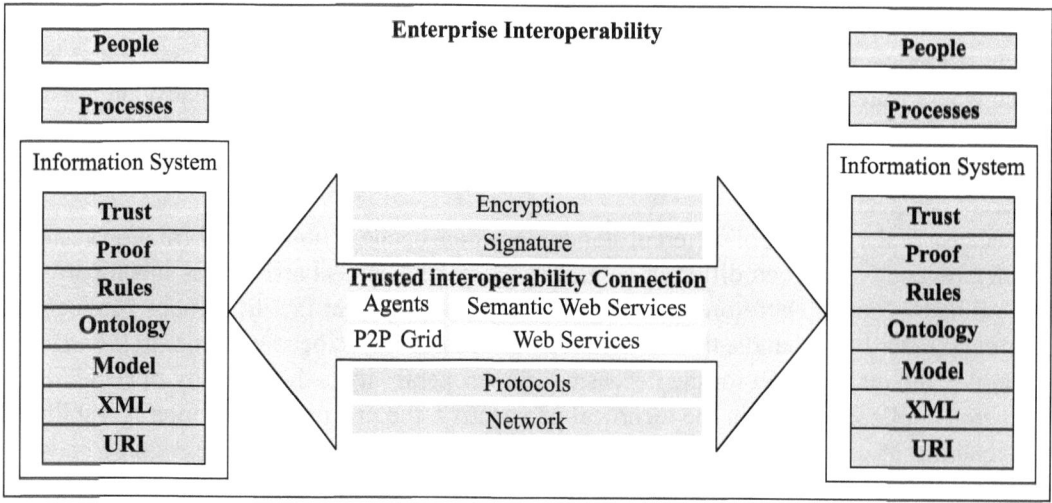

Source: Authors.

The Extensible Mark-up Language (XML) as meta-language is the basis for further languages offering the underlying concepts like Unified Resource Identifier and Unicode. This ensures on the higher levels the unique description of real world-phenomena with the Resource Description Framework (RDF) on the model level (W3C Resource Description Framework Website: http://www.w3.org/RDF/). The Web Ontology Language on the meta-model level is used to subsume those model-entities into generalized concepts and to model differences between classes by using more complex structures like rules, sets and taxonomical aspects (W3C W3C: OWL Web Ontology Language Semantics and Abstract Syntax: http://www.w3.org/TR/owl-feature/). In fact, XML-based ontologies follow the concepts of the Future Internet, namely, Coherency, Openness, Scalability, Dynamicity and Pro-activeness, Partial Predictability (flexibility), and Trust. Interoperation between enterprises is only possible in a trustful economical environment, which addresses the interoperability between processes and people as main objects.

Research on formal structure of information and communication data is quite advanced, whereas the description of the business environment itself is more complicated and treated only in newer approaches. The business environment can be described by using the BMM, an established industrial standard from OMG. BMM standardizes common business terms and business relationships. It provides an open medium for communicating business plans. Furthermore, it bridges the relations between the What and Why to the How by providing specification mechanisms for business processes, business rules, and the organizational structure.

The BMM meta-model is based on four basic concepts and includes ontological aspects showed at the bottom of Figure 2.6 and organizational aspects shown in the left part of it. First, the influencing aspects can be included into the BMM. Influencer can be other competitors, supplier, or customer, but also internal influencer-like employees. On the base of the assessed impact of the influencer the ends and means are described to plan the next steps within the business. Via ends, business goals can be described as a vision, explicate goal, or more detailed objectives. Furthermore, it is possible to express how those goals relate to the mission, the business strategy, and underlying tactics. Additionally, it is possible to enrich the model by rules and policies. These concepts are grouped as means. The last entity is the course of action, which follows as result of the prescribed situation and the goals.

Describing operational sequencing and synchronization is mainly done by using Process Diagram Notations such as Event-driven Process Chain (EPC) or Business Process Modelling Notation (BPMN). Both provide businesses with the capability of defining and understanding their internal and external business procedures through a Business Process Diagram, which will give organizations the ability to communicate these procedures in a standard manner (cf. OMG: http://www.omg.org/cgi-bin/doc?dtc/2006-11-01).

DIRECTIONS/CONCLUSIONS

The discourse of interoperability is based on a technical understanding and has to be extended to achieve a consistent understanding and terminology of the term Enterprise Interoperability.

FIGURE 2.6
The BMM Meta-model

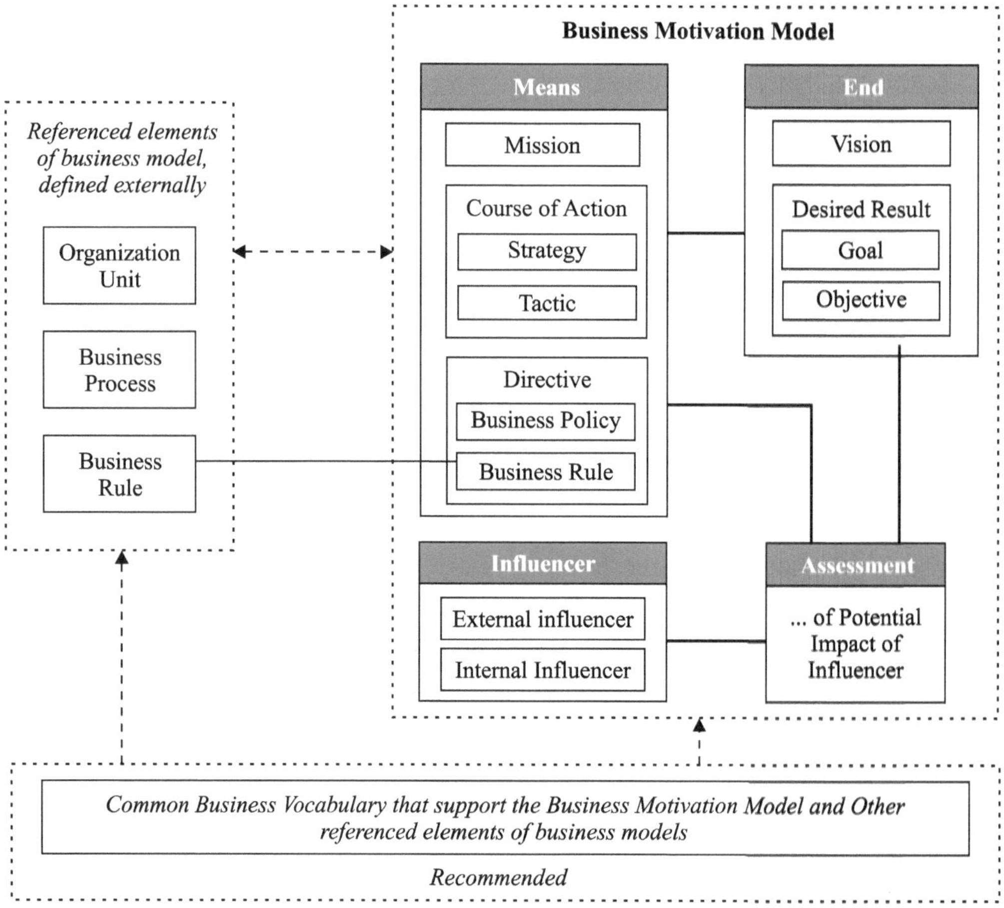

Source: Authors.

Especially, the implementation of business aspects and the bridging of technical and economical concepts will lead to a sufficiently described Enterprise Interoperability research. Therefore, in this chapter an initial proposal for an Enterprise Interoperability definition has been presented.

There are challenges in different aspects. First, there are no clear concepts that explain the diffusion of strategic decisions into new information systems as enabler of Enterprise Interoperability. Second, there is lack of concepts to explain the integration of business, process, and information system interoperability. To show that Enterprise Interoperability has to be treated as a holistic approach, the Enterprise Interoperability Framework was presented to get a complete and integrated understanding for Enterprise Interoperability.

The challenges exist in harmonizing the existing standards on the technical levels. Future research will show whether the standards BPMN 2.0 and BMM are appropriate to standardize the methods of collecting and specifying business requirements and to act as a basis for the technical implementation into service-oriented architectures and infrastructural components. This leads to the next research gap in business requirement modelling concerning the syntax and notation used. Especially the mapping of language concepts, information model types, and their coherent usage in communication are needed to enable a holistic interconnection of enterprises. Although Enterprise Interoperability is a state of potentially being able to do businesses, mechanisms for transferring potential into implementation have to be established. In the end, economic value is generated only by operating business, not by being perfectly prepared for.

REFERENCES

Becker J., et al. 2006. 'Konfigurative Referenzmodellierung mit dem H2-Toolset', in Becker J., et al. (eds) *Arbeitsbereiche des Instituts für Wirtschaftsinformatik*. Kompetenzzentrum: Referenzmodellierung, Münster.

Bendoly, E., A. Soni, and M.A. Venkataramanan. 2004. 'Value Chain Resource Planning: Adding Value with Systems beyond the Enterprise', *Business Horizons*, 47(2): 79–86.

Bendoly, E. and T. Schoenherr. 2005. 'ERP System and Implementation-process Benefits: Implications for B2B E-Procurement', *International Journal of Operations and Production Management*, 25(4): 304–19.

Bendoly, E., A. Citurs, and B. Konsynski. 2007. 'Internal Infrastructural Impacts on RFID Perceptions and Commitment: Knowledge, Operational Procedures and Information-Processing Standards', *Decision Sciences Journal*, 38(3): 423–49.

Chen, D. 2006. 'Framework for Enterprise Interoperability', in H. Panetto and N. Boudjlida (eds), *Interoperability for Enterprise Software and Applications*, pp. 77–89. ISTE.

Clark, K.B., R.H. Hayes, and S.C. Wheelright. 1988. *Dynamic Manufacturing: Creating the Learning Organization*. New York: The Free Press.

Davidsson, P. et al. 2008. 'The Concept and Technology of Plug and Play Business', in José Cordeiro, Yannis Manolopoulos, Joaquim Filipe, and Panos Constantopoulos (eds), Enterprise Information Systems: 8th International Conference, ICEIS 2006, Paphos, Cyprus, May 23–27, 2006, Revised Selected Papers (Lecture Notes in Business Information Processing).

De Groote, X. 1994. 'The Flexibility of Production Processes: A General Framework for the Relationship between Flexibility and Environmental Influences', *Management Science*, 40(7): 933–45.

Deelmann, T. 2007. *Geschäftsprozessmodellierung—Grundlagen, Konzeption und Integration*. Geschäftsmodellierung— Grundlagen, Konzeption und Integration, Berlin.

Fuchs, M. 1996. *Towards Full Automation of Deduction: A Case Study*. Kaiserslautern: Centre for Learning Systems and Application (LSA).

Gerst, M. and R. Bunduchi. 2006. 'The Analysis of Standardised Technology in the Automotive Industry', in P. Cunningham and M. Cunningham (eds), *Exploiting the Knowledge Economy: Issues, Applications and Case Studies*, Volume 3 Information and Communication Technologies and the Knowledge Economy, p. 255. IOS Press.

Gruber, T. 1993. 'Towards Principles for the Design of Ontologies used for Knowledge Sharing', in N. Guarino and R. Poli (eds), *Proceedings of the International Workshop on Formal Ontology in Conceptual Analysis and Knowledge Representation*. Padova: Institute for Systems Theory and Biomedical Engineering of the National Research Council.

Institute of Electrical and Electronics Engineers (IEEE). 1990. *IEEE Standard Computer Dictionary: A Compilation of IEEE Standard Computer Glossaries*. New York, NY: IEEE.

Jordan, W.C. and S.C. Graves. 1995. 'Principles of the Benefits of Manufacturing Process Flexibility', *Management Science*, 41(4): 577–94.

Lewerenz, J. 1999. *On the Use of Natural Language Concepts for the Conceptual Modeling of Interaction in Information Systems*. Cottbus: Computer Science Department, Brandenburg Technical University.

Lucke F. and J. Webering. 2003. 'Gegenwart und Zukunft von Online-Kooperationen', in M. Buttgen and F. Lucke (eds), *Online-Kooperationen—Erfolg im E-business durch Strategische Partnerschaften*, p. 5. Wiesbaden: Gabler Verlag.

Prahalad, C.K. and G. Hamel. 1990. 'The Core Competence of the Corporation', *Harvard Business Review*, 63(3): 79–91.

Roser, S. 2008. *Designing and Enacting Cross-organisational Business Process: A Model-driven, Ontology-based Approach*. Augsburg: Fakultat fur Angewandte Informatik.

Scheer, A.W. 1999, *ARIS—Business Process Frameworks*. Berlin: Springer.

Uption, D.M. 1994. 'The Management of Manufacturing Flexibility', *California Management Review*, 36(2, Winter), pp. 72–89.

Werth, D. 2006. *Kollaborative Geschäftsprozesse—Integrative Methoden zur Modellbasierten Deskription andKonstruction*. Berlin: Logos Verlag.

Werth, D. 2007. 'About the Nature of Collaborative Business Processes', in A. Arabinia and A. Bahrami (eds), *Proceedings of The 2007 International Conference on e-Learning, e-Business, Enterprise Information Systems, and e-Government*. Las Vegas: CSREA Press.

Ziemann, J., D. Werth, and T. Kahl. 2007. 'Using View Process Models in Collaborative Business Processes', in G.D. Putnik and M.M. Cunha (eds), *Encyclopedia of Networked and Virtual Organizations*. Hershey: IGI Global.

Websites

OMG: BPMN FTF final report. http://www.omg.org/cgi-bin/doc?dtc/2006-11-01. http://www.omg.org/cgi-
OMG: Business Motivation Model. http://www.omg.org/cgi-bin/doc?dtc/2006-08-03. http://www.omg.org/cgi-
OMG: Business Process Model Notation. http://www.omg.org/cgi-bin/doc?dtc/2006-11-01. http://www.omg.org/cgi-
W3C Semantic Web Activity. http://www.w3.org/2001/sw/
W3C Resource Description Framework Website. http://www.w3.org/RDF/
W3C: OWL Web Ontology Language Semantics and Abstract Syntax. http://www.w3.org/TR/owl-semantics/
Web Ontology Language—OWL, http://www.w3.org/TR/owl-feature/

3

Service-oriented Composite Applications: Enabling Enterprise Agility and Reuse

SUDEEP MALLICK

Principal Researcher, SETLabs
Infosys Technologies Ltd, Bangalore, India
E-mail: sudeepm@infosys.com

INTRODUCTION

Over the decades of adoption of automation software in enterprises, the enterprises having undergone an evolution in terms of their information technology (IT) architecture have accumulated a plethora of IT assets varied in terms of technology, architectural style, and adherence to open standards. The enterprise business architecture—business processes, rules, practices, business logic, etc.—are embedded in these legacy IT assets. These have stood the test of time, because they have survived and have undergone continuous, incremental modifications in order to respond to the business needs.

The changing market conditions and evolving technology maturity have changed the rules of the business. The cycle times of products and services have reduced drastically. It has become essential and possible to respond to changing market conditions more rapidly, by building the enabling IT automation layer more quickly, reliably, and efficiently than ever before. It is here that the legacy IT architecture, tools, and techniques are often found wanting. Inherent inflexibility in the architectural styles of legacy IT architecture (mainframes, legacy client server, legacy web applications, etc.), lack of adoption of open architectural standards, and traditional IT application development methodologies are some of the factors which hinder the responsiveness of these legacy systems.

The need of the hour for businesses, therefore, is to arrive at a scheme which balances both the mentioned factors. The scheme—IT architectural style, development methodology, and the enabling tools and standards—should be such whereby the business architecture embedded in the legacy IT architecture is reused to the greatest extent when responding to the new business needs, while at the same time being able to accomplish the maximum degree of responsiveness in the IT architecture.

Composite Application is an emerging paradigm of software systems engineering which is being seen as a potent answer to the aforementioned twin requirements thereby bringing about two key business benefits to the enterprise—agility and reuse. Business agility while responding to changing business needs is enhanced by rapidly creating IT applications (or systems), for automating new or re-engineered business processes. This is done out of pre-existing portfolio of enterprise IT assets (software systems, services, hardware, etc.) existing in various departments, divisions, and geographical units of the enterprise. Building IT applications from scratch is highly undesirable, inefficient, and wasteful having immediate adverse implications for IT asset return on investment (ROI) and total cost of ownership (TCO). Reuse, reconfiguration, redeployment, and re-engineering of IT architecture are the keys to survival. Composite application development based on the sound principles of Service Oriented Architecture (SOA) is being seen as an enabler of the enterprise in all these aspects, and is being rapidly adopted with great success in the most forward-looking enterprises today (Kinikin and Ramos, 2004; Rymer, 2005).

How is this magic combination of agility and reuse suddenly possible? This chapter will try to demystify this aspect. In short, however, the underlying capability that makes building composite applications possess such unique strengths is the ability to re-cast the legacy IT assets as context-based reconfigurable IT assets. These special assets could be adapted by reconfiguration to suit new business use cases and contexts. This leads us to the next question: What makes the legacy IT assets so reconfigurable and reusable? The answer lies in the application of sound architectural patterns and principles from service orientation and the capability of the composite application tools and methodologies to re-cast the legacy IT assets into reusable pieces and then being able to assemble these pieces after some reconfiguration, into larger pieces in an iterative manner, finally arriving at a full fledged new IT application (or systems).

AGILITY AND REUSE

AGILITY

Business agility is about being able to respond and evolve to changing business context (market dynamics, emerging competition, new regulations and compliance stipulations, inorganic business growth through mergers and acquisitions, supply chain dynamics, and so on) at a pace which will keep the business competitive. The lesser the cost, time, and risk (SYS-CON Media Inc., 2008) to engineer the response, the more competitive the business would be. The need for agility rises in the following forms:

- Ability to synergize and interoperate in multiple geographical regions having multiple currencies, regulations, consumers, and supplier contexts.

- Ability to take decisions based on as recent information as possible.
- Ability to take decisions based on full contextual information derived from multiple sources of data.
- Ability to change decision criteria and consume new information resources to make more informed decisions as called for by the changed circumstances.
- Ability to link supply chain partners smoothly and efficiently to exchange timely information and base decisions on accurate data.

REUSE

Reuse of enterprise assets has tremendous implications in terms of ROI and TCO. The enterprise assets could belong to the business architecture or IT architecture. Business architectural assets are business process, entity, role, responsibility, policy definitions based on some standardized definition language and semantics. IT architectural assets are reusable software components, IT systems, utilities, adapters, communication protocol handlers, runtime execution engines, software development lifecycle environment, executable business processes, executable data access systems, services, etc. Standards-based definition and careful design of these assets leads to reusability at various levels of granularity. New IT systems could be rolled out by assembling the reusable pieces akin to lego block assembly. IT has held out this promise for a long time without any visible results. However, emergence of concepts such as SOA, Enterprise Asset Management systems, and sophisticated MDA tools has led to reinvigoration of that promise. One of the core tenets of reusability of IT assets is context based re-configurability and customizability of the asset. This aspect would be discussed in detail in a later section.

Factors that inhibit agility and reuse are as follows:

- Inflexible business architecture:
  - Business processes: Inability to change business processes to accommodate new business policies, business rules, business process steps, establish process continuity with supply chain partners from the existing business processes, ability to respond to new business events [EDD paper on SET Labs Briefings Agility edition available at http://www.infosys.com/research/publications/setlabs-briefings/Pages/toc-platforms-enterprise-agility.aspx].
  - Information silos: Lack of availability of information in the right format to the right place at the right time. In the absence of correct, on-demand information availability there is latency is decision-making. Existence of data in disparate IT systems written using different technologies (due to evolutionary reasons) and having diverse semantics and structure inhibit smooth information flow.

■ Lack of existence of business policies, rules, roles, and responsibilities in a structured, codified form having uniformly understood semantics throughout the enterprise resulting into business architecture fragmentation. This hinders capability to roll out new policies, change existing ones in an agile manner.

- Inflexible IT architecture:

    ■ IT system silos and legacy applications: Monolithic legacy applications are not easy to modify or customize to enable them to respond to rapidly changing business needs. The lead times to implement these changes often exceed the relevant business lifecycle.
    ■ Time and cost to change: The time and cost of implementing new systems from scratch that would support new business processes or modify existing ones often inhibits agile adaptations.
    ■ The complexity of the IT architecture of an enterprise often limits adaptability. The IT systems silos having their own business data formats, messaging models, and communication protocols result into impedance mismatches between the systems.

        Inadequate linkage between the business and IT architecture. The lack of existence of codified business policies, rules, roles, responsibilities, events, processes into IT systems and databases in a manner that their life cycle governance, compliance monitoring could be automated, also results into inflexibility. Often these aspects exist in codified form in IT systems and databases but are outdated and no more reflect the current state of business architecture. Additionally it is possible that there are variations existing in different corners of the enterprise, which are isolated and exist in silos.

Factors that promote business agility and reuse are as follows:

- Adoption of the concept of business services: Business services (Jarman, 2007) embody a non-trivial piece of business logic that makes sense to the business domain expert, automates one or more steps of a business process, and could participate in multiple business processes and context. Getting employee details, creating purchase orders are examples. The concept of services leads to a virtualization of IT systems and enables their visibility and measurability in business relevant terms.
- Adoption of enterprise information architecture and strategy that makes information available at the right time in the right format to the business decision-makers. It also enables a uniform view of the information entities that are business critical across the entire enterprise. Availability of correct information in the desired manner enables a more efficient and effective decision-making process and engineering IT applications having the desired quality.
- Establishing a clear linkage between the business and IT architecture: Establishing a clear linkage between business services and IT services and the underlying IT systems is

very essential for being able to engineer a rapid response to the changes in the business architecture through automation.

- Codifying business architecture in clear and reusable terms: Business policies, rules, procedures, processes, and service level agreements (SLAs) in structured format (if possible in machine readable format) would enable reuse and customization of these business assets in multiple automation scenarios. This would lower the cost to adapt existing business processes (Hildreth, 2005).

- IT architectural styles, tools, and methodologies enable the right linkage between business and IT architecture by being able to capture critical pieces of the business architecture in reusable and reconfigurable chunks. They also enable use of these chunks to build new automation layers in unforeseen context having the right functionality and quality. Model Driven Development, Agile Development (Ambler, 2002) methodologies, Service Oriented Architectural principles, and Composite Applications are some of key enablers.

- Adoption of open standards for modeling the business and IT architecture enabling interoperability and uniformity in business semantics and ease of reuse across multiple IT technologies (Mallick, 2007b).

ADDRESSING AGILITY AND REUSE THROUGH COMPOSITE APPLICATIONS

REUSE DEPENDS UPON CONTEXT-BASED ADAPTATION

Composite application is all about encouraging reuse of legacy IT assets be it Graphical User Interfaces (GUIs), business process logic, business rules, business policies, or regulatory compliance enabling components. The success of the composite application approach lies a great deal on how the same 'piece' of a legacy IT asset could be reused in multiple different business contexts and scenarios. For example, a business service for calculating the interest payable on term deposits in a bank could have simple logic to do the calculations after making appropriate deductions based on existing income tax rules, prevailing bank policies, etc. For the case of a global bank spanning geographical boundaries and countries these rules and policies would vary. Moreover the rules and policies themselves are subject to change in the same country due to changing economic and market conditions. Hence, the logic embedded in the service would need to undergo minor or major changes to cater to these changing context and conditions. This clearly limits the reusability aspects and it also adversely affects the agility aspect.

A desirable situation would be such where the changes to the business service are minimal or even a better situation where the business service is configurable or 'tune-able' to change its behaviour depending on the context. This configurability or 'tune-ability' is vital to reuse of the same business service in multiple context and ultimately in rapid and reliable delivery of multiple composite applications (Mallick, 2007a). This is also sometimes accomplished by 'pushing out' the changeable portion of the logic in the business service into external 'portions' which are relatively easier to change. Modern Business Rules Management Systems (BRMS) allow externalization of such changeable business logic and easy configuration on-demand (Hildreth, 2005).

REUSE IS LIMITED BY ARCHITECTURAL MISMATCHES

As mentioned earlier, composite applications are literally IT applications built out of combining or compositing together multiple pre-existing IT applications. Each IT application would have a piece of the enterprise business architecture embedded in it in terms of business processes, policies, rules, data (or business entities), and events embedded in them. Due to an evolutionary reason different parts of the enterprise—geographical unit, business units, product lines, etc.—could have slightly varying business architecture. Hence, the IT applications automating the corresponding business architectures are not 'enterprise quality'. For example, each business unit or product line could have its own definition of a customer, differing in terms of constitution of the data items that constitute the definition of this important business entity as well as in terms of their meaning and representation. This difference is reflected in the corresponding IT applications using this data such as Customer Relationship Management (CRM) systems, Billing systems, and SFA systems. So an enterprise would end up having a portfolio of CRM systems, SFA systems, and so on, having differences in terms of features, embedded business architectures, and also a reasonable degree of overlap.

The enterprise might now wish to roll out a cross-functional business processes such as a new order-to-cash business process across the entire enterprise in order to streamline its customer order management function, give the customer a uniform experience, and also to synergize sales opportunities across product lines leading to cross sell opportunities. This would be a perfect case for engineering a composite application which would use portions of the automation logic existing in the multiple CRM systems, SFA, systems, Billing systems that the enterprise already has. These reuse portions could be such as creation of new customer records (functionality coming from CRM and Billing systems), application of discount and deferred payment schemes on purchases based on past customer purchase history (functionality coming from Billing, SFA, and CRM systems), and so on. Now these application portions to be reused would need to exchange data between them in order to execute. In case there are differences in formats and meanings it would create obvious interoperation bottlenecks. Hence, the enterprise-wide order-to-cash process would need to use a generic business service which will hide the complexity resulting out of these subtle differences.

One of important ingredients to building composite application is availability of reusable IT assets which hide the complexities arising out of such architectural mismatches among the enabling back end IT systems from which these reusable IT assets (or services in the SOA parlance) are harvested.

Composite applications tools and methodologies combined with the principles of Service Orientation and Model Driven Development motivate the creation of these reusable IT assets and finally the reuse through reconfiguration and customization of these reusable IT assets. In order to understand what makes the composite tools and methodologies so powerful we have to appreciate the fact that a composite application development platform is result of evolution of architectural styles, maturity of IT system development methodologies, tools and platforms, and the realization of the importance of reusability of enterprise architectural elements (Figure 3.1). It has also become a powerful paradigm of application development due to emergence of modern composite application development platforms which creates a synergy of concepts such as:

- Business Process Management (including modeling, re-engineering, simulation, lifecycle management, orchestration, and monitoring).
- Service Orientated Architecture (encouraging creation of Business and Technical Services (Jarman, 2007) and orchestration of these services into business processes).
- Business Rules Management Systems (enabling codifying of reusable and re-adjustable business rules and policies and their application to existing IT systems with minimal effort).

FIGURE 3.1
Reusability and Agility of IT Systems, Methodologies, and Architectures

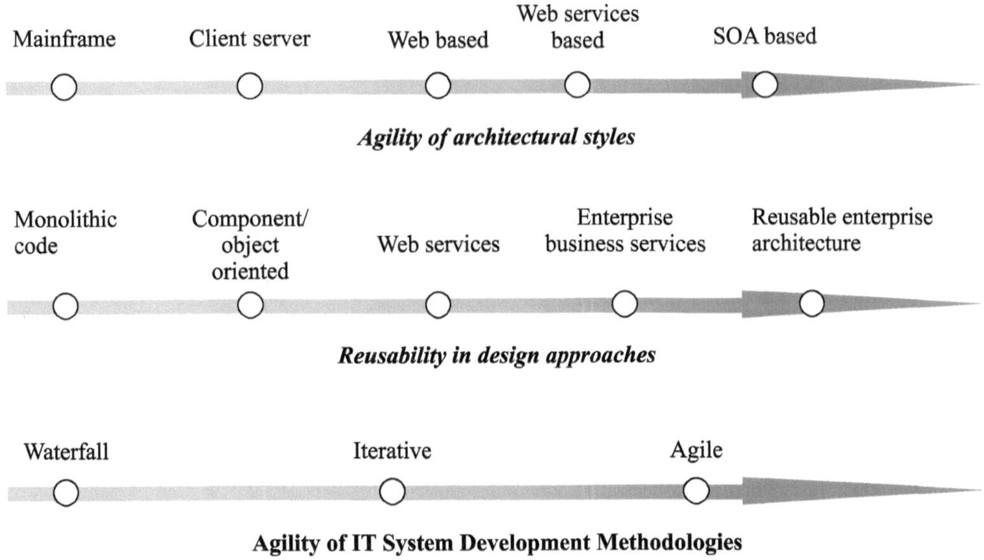

Source: Author.

- Model Driven Development (enabling automatic code generation for configurable aspects of an application).
- Enterprise Asset Management (encouraging lifecycle approach to reusable enterprise IT assets such as executable process models, business entity models, business services, etc.).
- Enterprise Integration (embodying best practices and patterns for enterprise application and data integration).
- Enterprise Portal and Dashboards (enabling creation of enterprise wide view of business critical data in the portal).
- CIM approaches and MDM techniques (enabling single view of business data from multiple sources on diverse platforms, architectures and formats).
- Knowledge management techniques (enabling availability of structured and unstructured information to the right user).
- Multi-channel delivery capabilities (enabling availability of data and access to transaction-oriented systems on multiple devices and over multiple communication channels such as the Internet, corporate intranet, mobile and hand-held devices, HTML pages, PDF forms, RIA gadgets, etc.).

Fundamental to all these concepts are the principles of service orientation which enables loose coupling, re-configurability, and, finally, reusability of automation pieces mined out of the existing portfolio of IT systems and platforms. This aspect will be discussed further in the later sections.

CONSTITUENTS OF A COMPOSITE APPLICATION

Composite applications are literally IT systems built out of existing portfolio of IT systems. As explained earlier business critical pieces of existing IT systems are carefully mined following principles of service orientation. The external interfaces to these pieces are designed in a manner which makes their applicability and reusability possible in multiple contexts through re-configuration and minimal customization. These 'pieces' are typically of the following nature (Figure 3.2):

- Executable business process definitions which comprise participating pieces from the other categories listed here.
- Executable business rules.
- Business entity definitions and access points.
- Business services each embodying business logic and implementing one or more business process steps.
- Metadata about business services, processes such as policies, user roles, and configuration properties.

FIGURE 3.2
Key Ingredients of a Composite Application Development Platform

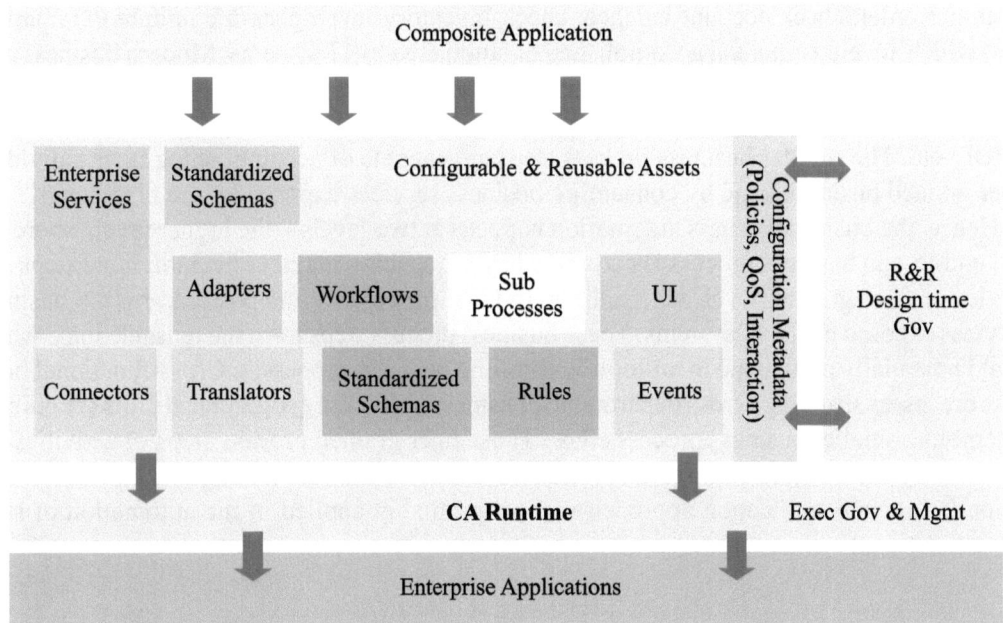

Source: Author.

- Adapters, bridges, and service busses enabling integration.
- Application portfolio.
- User interface components.
- Utility components enabling monitoring, reporting, auditing, etc.

Some of the critical pieces are explained further.

BUSINESS PROCESSES

Business process definitions defined in open standards based languages such as BPMN and BPML enable creation of reusable and executable (automated) business processes which are orchestrated by business process engines. The business processes comprises finer grained process steps or activities which have conditions defined for transitions between the steps. These conditions are business events such as arrival of customer purchase request, successful creation of purchase order, falling of inventory level below a limit, generation of invoice, filing of customer complaint, etc. Each business process activity such as creation of purchase order, ordering replenishment of inventory, etc., comprises of a series of finer grained steps (for a purchase order creation business process activity the finer grained steps could be validate customer order, check account balance, check inventory level, generate unique PO number, etc.) which are either manual accomplished or automated by IT systems. Modern business processes automation happens by codifying these business processes into executable business processes and human workflows defined in open standards based languages such as BPEL, XPDL, etc. The smaller business process steps are capable of accomplishing their individual finer grained business logic by consuming business services exposed by the IT systems.

Hence, the business process automation happens at two levels—the higher level, where the full end-to-end business process is automated by sequencing together the individual steps and the lower finer grained level, where the individual process step is powered by the business services exposed by the IT systems. These business process steps form the reusable logic which could potentially participate in multiple end-to-end business processes. Cross-functional business processes spanning across departments, business units, and geographical units are built by assembling smaller business process steps. These finer grained process steps or activities are powered by the services exposed from the IT systems owned and managed by the individual units. Composite application approach is most profitably applied in the automation of such cross functional business processes.

SERVICES

Composite applications are applications built out of reusable pieces of existing portfolio of applications (Figure 3.3). The key benefits of composite application are reuse of existing IT investments in new business scenarios and rapid time to market by following a composition approach. Composing stable, time tested legacy assets into a new composite application results into rapid reduction in delivery time as well as better reliability of the end product. Before these benefits of adopting a composite application could be realized the essential aspect of the composite application—reusable pieces of legacy IT assets—needs to be realized. SOA principles lie at the heart of creating such reusable assets. The concept of services with well-defined contract (or service interface) exposed to the external world enables exposure of pieces of existing IT systems into well-defined automation pieces with clearly defined behaviour.

The external world or the service consumer (in this case the larger composite application in which the piece would potentially participate) needs to just care about the 'what' part of the piece rather than bothering about the 'how' part. What this essentially means as long as the service interface or contract which defines the behaviour of the service satisfies the needs of the service consumer, it need not bother about how the service has been realized. It need not bother about which legacy application exposed (or enabled realization) the service, in which technology platform it is written. The service interface would determine the communication

FIGURE 3.3
Harvesting Services Out of Existing IT Systems for Reuse in the Automation of a New Business Process

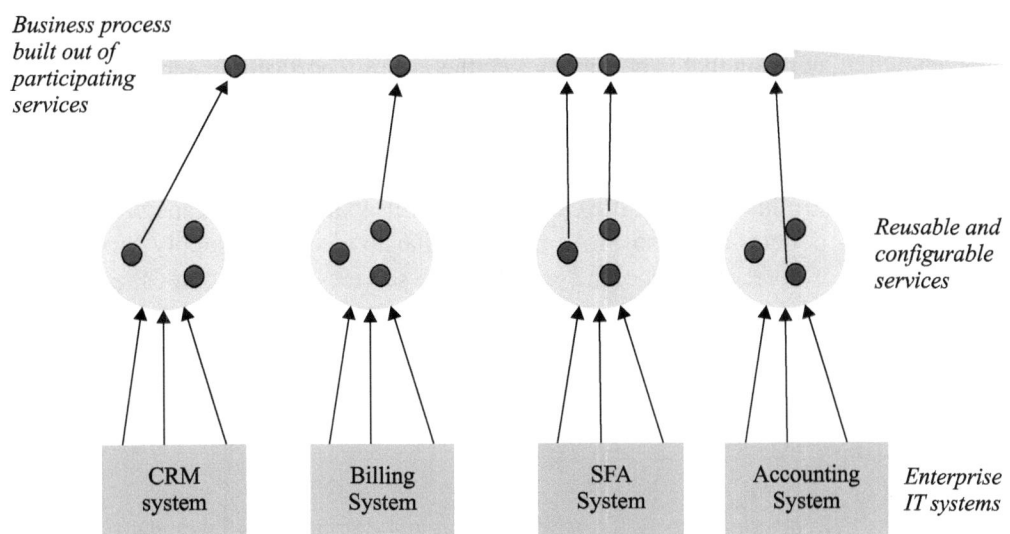

Source: Author.

protocol through which the service would need to be accessed and usually that is based on some open standards. Communication using open standards enhances interoperability.

Services can be extended and specialized to meet diverse contextual needs. Services are piece of automation logic having well-defined contract exposed to the external world. The contract details the functionality and behaviour of the enclosed logic of the service and also how a potential consumer should access and use the service. It does not mention anything about how the logic is implemented internally. This separation of the external contract from the internal implementation affords great advantages. The service consumer which is potentially another IT system or automation logic could be implemented using a different technology and yet would be able to consume another service implemented using a different technology. This also enables the service implementation to change to accommodate change in load conditions, audit requirements, and subtle changes in business logic without changing the external contract. Hence, the current and potential users of the service are presented with a stable interface using which they could continue their service consumption uninterrupted or plan for usage without undue worries about change-related impacts.

Of course, the service and its consumers would need to communicate with each other in order to exchange information for accomplishing their functionality and business transactions. This communication could happen in a language based on some open standards understood by both the parties.

The key to successful SOA based composite application is the breaking up of the envisaged functionality and behaviour of the composite application into smaller sized functionality and behaviour. The next key step is a mapping of this list of envisaged functionalities and behaviours with that of the business services already exposed from the existing legacy IT systems. The higher the percentage of mapping that is possible given the existing portfolio of services, the higher will be the percentage of reuse and degree of reliability and agility. The concept of business services is the key to this mapping process.

The concept of service has a few more unique connotations. Every service is provisioned by a service owner who administers its life cycle, plans for its load handling capacity, determines the service usage policies and also SLAs much similar to electricity supply service, parcel delivery service, or hotel room booking service. The services in the composite application development context could be categorized broadly into two types—business services and technical services.

Business Service

These services deliver complete, self-sufficient, and standalone units business functionality such as checking customer credit rating, raising purchase orders, registering customer complaints, etc.

Technical Service

These services are often termed as utility services or shared services which provide commonly used technology related services across the enterprise. Examples include security services, document management services, audit services, Business-to-Business (B2B) connectivity services, etc. These services are business domain agnostic and enclose technology-related features.

ADAPTERS AND BRIDGES

The reuse of legacy systems which embody much of existing business logic is possible by creating bridge code called adapters. These adapters bridge multiple technologies and platforms enabling interoperability. For example, a piece of logic in a SAP system could talk to another piece of logic embedded in IBM Mainframe system by using SAP provided adapter for IBM systems. Building of these adapters based on open standards affords further flexibility—akin to use of adapters between two standard voltage systems.

DATA

Often due to evolutionary reasons the same business entity such as customer, account, purchase order, etc., exists in multiple applications that an enterprise might have in slightly varying structure (format) and interpretations (semantics). This results in confusion as well as data maintenance redundancies having obvious implications from ROI or TCO point of view. This has a far greater ramification for agility and flexibility of the enterprise. Business processes of an enterprise often span across geographic boundaries, business units, etc. These business processes need to be powered with business logic created by the individual business units, divisions, geos, etc. Hence, an automated business process would need to communicate with multiple existing IT systems which have embedded business logic peculiar to the business unit or division or geo. Multiple data format and semantics embedded in these diverse participating IT systems could create inefficiencies, inflexibilities, and errors. Technology initiatives such as MDM and concepts such as DMTF's CIM enable creation of single, uniform view of business entities. These business entities are made available as something popularly known as shared data services.

PORTFOLIO OF APPLICATIONS

For example, in a manufacturing supply chain business process, the participating systems would be warehouse management systems (WMS), quality control, production planning, and control (PPC). These could be enterprise resource planning (ERP) systems from product vendors or built in house. Optimizing of raw material and semi-products inventory levels, optimizing on quality control checks for acceptable quality levels, customer order visibility, are some of the scenarios where information flow across different IT systems require accomplishing a business process or meeting a business performance indicator. Composite application approach would enable creation of the new enabling IT systems in an agile manner by re-using services exposed by the existing portfolio of IT systems. Modern day commercial off the shelf software (COTS) vendor products in the area of ERP, SCM, CRM, WMS, SFA, etc., come with their pre-built set of industry vertical related open standards based business process definitions, business data types, and the business services which implement the business process steps. These out of box services and components are amenable to configuration (simple change of property values) and customization (creation and modification of additional glue logic) enabling their use in creation of new composite applications. These COTS products also come with integration adapters for enabling rapid out of box communication with the COTS products from a plethora of other popular vendors in the domain. This rapid application integration capability is very vital for building composite applications.

BUSINESS RULES

Business rules codify changeable business policies and rules into IF-THEN-ELSE like statements such as IF the Customer is a Premium Customer THEN apply X per cent discount on sales ELSE apply Y per cent discount. Authoring and managing such rules in natural language like statements is simple yet powerful. Business Rules Management Systems (BRMS) allow creation, modification, management, selection, and application of such codified rules into existing IT systems. Business services and Business Process steps which are the essential reusable building blocks of composite applications could be configured to use one of more rules as applicable in the business context. This enables rapid creation of new business processes using new or existing business context specific rules in a very reliable manner.

UI COMPONENTS

Multi-channel delivery is an important enabler and often a unique proposition of the business to its customers. Multi-channel delivery include situations such as field sales executive of insurance companies needing to access customer and product information from remote locations over the Internet, marketing executives needing to receive real time alerts on critical business events on their mobile devices, production panning executives participating in business workflows from their mobile devices, customers needing to fill up electronic ADOBE© forms akin to hardcopy forms they are familiar with, etc. These situations demand that enterprise data, business processes, and workflows be available on different types of client devices having different form factors and characteristics (such as mobile phones, PDAs, laptops, and desktops), different delivery formats having different degrees of message handling capacities, message metadata, etc. (such as HTML, WML, XML, Java, and .NET) and over different communication protocols and channels having different latency and bandwidth characteristics (such as HTTP, HTTPS, and VPN). Pre-built customizable UI components and enabling UI infrastructure catering to most of these scenarios is essential for creating a composite application delivering multi-channel capabilities. Most modern composite application platforms enable out-of-box availability of such UI components or UI building capabilities. These UI components need to get integrated in an easy manner at appropriate steps in the end-to-end automated business process.

BUILDING COMPOSITE APPLICATIONS

Building a composite application is primarily about analyzing and breaking down the business requirements, identification of automation components from a readily available enterprise automation component portfolio that would satisfy these requirements through to assembly of these components into appropriate inter-relationships and validation of the resulting product. The crux of the composite application building methodology is related to the following aspects:

- Availability of a rich repository of business services and IT system components.
- Configuration and customization of the readily available components to suit the business context.
- Assembly of participating business services and other IT system components.

Agile and iterative IT system development methodologies are extremely relevant to composite application development. The amount of fresh development and programming work is expected to be minimal except for that glue code portion. The glue code enables:

- customization of the pre-existing components and
- bridging of the impedance mismatch (in terms of mismatch of data types, communication protocol, etc.) between two components that need to be connected together.

Composite applications are literally new applications built out of portions of existing IT systems (or applications). A composite application would usually have touch points with multiple pre-existing or legacy IT systems. Hence, testing and validating a composite application would imply testing whether the participating applications are being used or invoked by the composite application in the desired manner. Through the composite application a multiple number of hitherto siloed IT systems are getting integrated together albeit in a loosely coupled manner. This has tremendous implications in terms of ensuring that the execution of the composite application does not result into undesirable consequences or the corruption of the state of the participating applications in aspects such as data, security, transactions, and quality of service.

Once the first cut composite application is developed it undergoes iterative cycles of testing and validation to ensure that:

- there are no missing linkages and impedance mismatches between consecutive components;
- the execution of the business process being automated by the composite application is happening as desired—the activity steps are getting fired in the right sequences and there are no missing steps;
- the business events are getting generated and handled in the right order;
- the human–IT interaction is handled correctly by the UI components—the data input from the humans and the information display is happening as desired;
- the information flow between the participating applications is happening in the correct manner (these applications are participating in the composite application through the business services that they have exposed and which are in turn getting utilized in the composite application);

- the distributed business transactions are getting executed across the different participating applications in a desirable manner; and
- the execution of the composite application does not result into quality of service degradation of the participating applications resulting into a consequential overall degradation of the performance of the composite application.

The broad set of phases that go into the building of the composite application is (Figure 3.4):

- Requirements and analysis: This involves capturing of the business functionality requirements, non-functional requirements such as compliance, quality of service, and the IT system features through to analysis of the business use cases and alternative business scenarios. This phase is nothing specific to composite applications.
- Gap analysis: This involves identification of the reusable business services and IT system components that could potentially be used to realize the analyzed business functionality.

FIGURE 3.4
The Agile and Iterative Development Methodology of Composite Applications

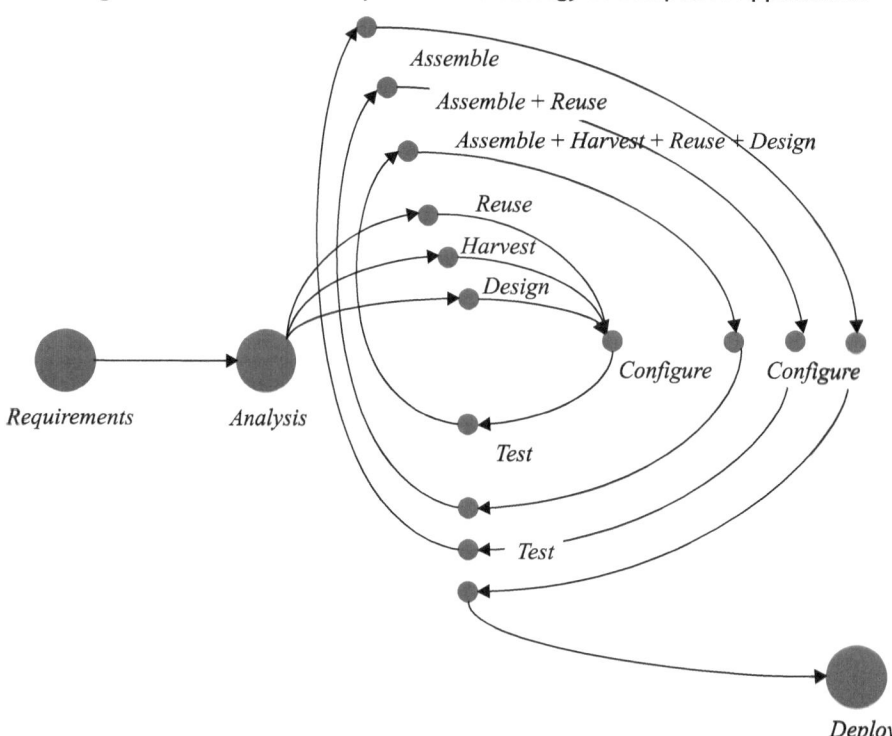

Source: Author.

This is a critical phase in the composite application development and would involve:

- Analyzing the existing repository to identify useful business services and components.
- Analyzing which of these services and components could be used as they are and which call for customization and configuration.
- Analyzing the configuration parameters.
- Identifying gaps in terms of business functionality and non-functional requirements that could not be satisfied from the existing service and component repository.
- Building a list of glue components and fresh services and components that would need to be created to plug the identified gaps.

- Realization of the services and components that would help fill the gaps. This would involve:

  - Analyzing and mining of existing portfolio of IT systems to identify possible opportunities of creation of new business services leading to reuse of pre-existing business functionality.
  - Creation of new services and components either from scratch or by exposing functionality pre-existing in the current portfolio of IT systems.
  - Testing and validation of these individual services and components.

- Assembly of the final set of services and components into the composite application. This would involve:

  - In some cases recursive composition of services into larger grained services.
  - Composition of participating services and components into larger grained business process steps.
  - Testing and validation of these larger grained services, components, and business process steps.
  - Final assembly of the participating process steps into the entire end-to-end business process.

- Once the entire business process is assembled it needs to be tested and validated for the various aspects identified earlier.
- Successful testing and validation is followed by final production release and deployment.

As can be seen, the stress on the composite application development is primarily on two aspects leading to an agile development process:

- Reuse of pre-existing services, components, and business functionality (deep inside IT systems that are not yet mined into reusable service format).
- Iterative assembly and testing of increasingly larger grained functionality until the entire end-to-end composition is tested from various aspects.

The typical constituents of a Composite Application development platform are:

- Business process modeling platform: This enables the business user or subject matter expert (SME) to visually compose the business process in various degrees of detail or identify existing process-mode segments that could be reused from the repository.
- Business entity modeling platform: This enables the SME to model the required set of data models and identify the existing data models that could be reused.
- User interface modeling platform: This enables the user, end user, and human–computer interaction experts to design the required set of user interfaces having the right set of data elements and usability.
- Workflow modeling platform: This enables the business user, SME, and composite application architects and designers to link together the user interfaces with the underlying business processes.
- Component reuse platform: This enables identification of components (business rules, policies, security components, monitoring components, etc.) and the services that could be reused from the existing repository to enable the business process or workflow being automated. It also enables linking of these components and services with the underlying process or workflow model and the user interface elements to make it an executable business process.
- Composite application testing and runtime platform: This enables the execution of the enabled business process or workflow as desired and testing for proper execution.

TYPES OF COMPOSITE APPLICATIONS

There are broadly two types of composite applications:

- Simple: This is the type mostly described in this chapter. It covers the set of composite application which is built by iteratively combining the participating pieces at various levels of granularity from pre-existing pieces in the enterprise repository. Most of the leading vendors such as SAP, Oracle, IBM, and Microsoft cater to this category.
- Complex: This is a very fascinating type and similar to a big bang approach to application development. The composite application in this flavour comes as a full product enabling a generic business process such as Project Management or Order Management which usually calls for interaction with multiple back end enterprise IT systems such as HR systems, Financial systems, etc. The composite application would come and sit on top of the existing enterprise IT application and interact with them through custom adapters. The business architecture embedded in the composite application is generic enough

and is amenable to customization based on a particular business's needs and context. Some of the large COTS product vendors such as SAP (xRPM product, etc.) have products in this space.

KEY BUSINESS BENEFITS AND DRIVERS

Enterprises' IT architectures have evolved over the last few decades resulting into assimilation of multiple technologies, standards, and architectural styles. Starting from the days of monolithic mainframe applications through to client server and web technologies, most Fortune 500 companies have seen the evolution of their IT landscape in terms of embracing these technology waves. Moreover, IT governance in these enterprises has undergone different organization styles—centralized and decentralized to federated. This has resulted into emergence of IT system or application silos, duplication, and redundancies of IT assets, existence of multiple interpretations, and format for business data, multiple instances of similar business processes having overlaps and functionality redundancies. Evolutionary reasons have resulted in burgeoning IT ownership and governance costs in these enterprises. Consequentially, during the past decade or so there has been a conscious effort by CIOs to adopt technologies and architectural styles which reduce the TCO of their IT assets and unlock the potential in IT assets.

Combined with the mentioned IT cost, ownership, and governance issues, the shortening of business cycles, emergence of new cool enabling technologies and gadgets, and the arrival of new electronic business models have made it imperative for the enterprise to adopt novel approaches to IT architecture and governance of IT assets. IT is not seen anymore as a support function but as a key business enabler. Multinational enterprises distributed in terms of geography, product lines, and operational styles need to function as a single entity in order to deliver a synergistic impact on the market and the competitor. Single view of the customer, quick roll out of cross functional business process spanning across business units and divisions, IT system ownership boundaries, and adoption of new regulatory compliance mechanism across the entire enterprise are examples of some of the key initiatives that determine the survival of the enterprise today. Critical success factors for the enterprise today are determined by their ability to swiftly capitalize on new business opportunities and play game changing roles in the market by harnessing the power of IT.

Some of the key IT capabilities that are essential for the survival of enterprise in this scenario are:

- Ability to reuse proven legacy assets in a flexible manner in novel business context.
- Ability to respond to new business requirements with utmost speed and agility.

The agility in responsiveness of an enterprise depends upon the agile methodologies it adopts to deliver new enabling IT systems as well as the flexibility of its existing IT assets in terms of its amenability in being used in novel business context. Adoption of SOA style of architecture and composite application development approaches to building of new IT systems are some of the prime enablers of the enterprise in this direction. The adoption of SOA based composite application development methodology results into the delivery of the following key business benefits to the enterprise:

- Ability to quickly build new IT systems from parts coming from pre-existing, stable, and proven IT systems resulting into combination of agility with reliability which is often the biggest challenge to meet.
- Ability to integrate multiple, siloed IT systems into new cross functional business processes with relatively greater ease and lower cost.
- Composite applications by their definition have touch points with multiple pre-existing enterprise IT systems. Engineering a composite application catering to an immediate business requirement provides business case for rolling out of long-term focused strategic business-IT initiatives. Such initiatives include adoption of uniform business semantics across greater part of the enterprise through streamlining of business models (process and data) existing in the multiple IT silos of the enterprise. These enterprise IT architectural initiatives of streamlining and standardization afford tremendous long-term benefit to the enterprise in terms lowering of TCO of IT assets, management transparency, single view of business entities such as customer data, product data, etc.
- The reuse of legacy IT assets (IT systems and infrastructure) gets a shot in the arm as the composite application development makes a clear business case for asset reuse. This in turn promotes a reuse culture in the enterprise leading to better reuse-oriented design of IT assets. All this has a long-term effect on the ROI of IT assets.
- Increasing maturity of composite application development methodologies and initiatives leads to a simultaneous maturity of the blueprinting of the enterprise IT architecture and emergence of a rich repository of reusable IT assets. This enables the enterprise to enter a virtuous cycle of reusability enabled business benefits.
- Composite applications reuse services and components from existing IT systems. A good design engineered by one particular IT system could be reused by another composite application in a hitherto unforeseen business context. For example, a new SFA system might have pioneered the adoption of mobile technologies in an enterprise. In case the SFA IT system owners and engineers expose the mobile technology-related IT infrastructural capabilities which the SFA system is using, in terms of reusable IT infrastructure services, then it could be reused by another composite application. The service could be made reusable by making it business context and technology platform agnostic.

COMPOSITE APPLICATION DEVELOPMENT APPROACH INCREASES IT AGILITY AND FLEXIBILITY

Composite application development comprises of the following key ingredients:

- A rich repository of:
  - Executable business process definitions.
  - Business services which are configurable.
  - IT services including infrastructural services, utility services.
  - Miscellaneous IT components such as UI builders, UI components, inter-IT system integration adapters, and bridges.

- A composite application development workbench which enables rapid composition of the executable business processes, services, and components in the right sequence and juxtaposition. The workbench comprises of a tool set which also enables configuration and customization of the services and components to suit the business context and development of any fresh glue code that is not addressed by the existing repository. It also takes care of iterative testing of the composites.
- A composite application runtime which breathes life into the developed composite. It enables execution of the composite application and communication with the back end supporting IT systems.
- A composite application development methodology which has a clearly defined set of artifacts, deliverables, steps, entry and exit criteria, roles, and responsibilities. The methodology addresses the concerns and has phases as explained in an earlier section.

The composite application development methodology based on agile and iterative techniques enables rapid composition and validation of pre-exiting pieces of business logic enclosed in the services by accessing them from the workbench. It also helps in quickly identifying the missing links and gaps unaddressed by the repository that could be filled by the glue code and new potential services. The product from the workbench could be seamlessly deployed on the runtime which takes care of the business process orchestration and seamless integration with the pre-existing set of IT systems at proper touch points through the participating services and components in the composite.

The rich repository of pre-built pieces and the methodology and tools that could exploit the repository is the key to enabling agile response to emerging business needs by rapidly creating new IT systems. The configurability and customizability of the participating services and components and capability of the workbench to model and engineer this capability is the key to accomplishing the desired degree of flexibility.

CHALLENGES

Key challenges in implementing composite application are in terms of enabling interoperability among the multiple participating IT systems with which it has touch points. These challenges manifest themselves in terms of the following:

- Synchronizing updates: Transactions started by the composite application might result into updates to multiple back end data bases of the participating IT systems. All the challenges of implementing a distributed transaction are present here.
- Disparities in information model: Multiple IT systems would likely have their information architecture (business entity definitions, database schema definitions, data security definitions, etc.). The composite application would need mechanism for implementation as well as governance to ensure that mapping of these diverse information architectures takes place smoothly and correctly.
- Composite testing and validation: As explained in the methodology section of this chapter, iterative, multiple rounds of recursive composition of IT assets takes place during the development of composite applications. Each of these intermediate level composites and the final composite application need to be verified and validated for functional and non-functional properties. The iterative and recursive nature of composition results into a higher degree of freedom and higher entropy for the entire composite system and poses its own challenges in terms of management and execution.
- Performance: Due to the reasons mentioned earlier (recursive composition and multiple degrees of freedom and higher entropy) prediction, measurement, and tuning of performance is more challenging. Additionally, the performance of the composite application depends upon the performance of the 'pieces' from the participating IT systems. While it may be possible to identify bottlenecks, tuning the performance has implications in terms of initiating modifications to the participating IT systems which have their respective owners, administrators, performance mandates, and roadmaps. This clearly makes the scope of performance tuning problem of a composite application much larger and more complex than it seems.
- Security propagation: Ensuring security of data and transactions is again challenging to the reasons cited earlier.
- Intrusive changes to existing applications: The functional and non-functional requirements of a composite application might imply changes to the identified participating IT systems as explained earlier. This increases the scope of project management work for composite application.
- Enterprise architecture: The degree and scope of standardization of an enterprise's architecture (business and IT architecture) determines to a large extent how smooth composite application initiatives could be rolled out and successfully accomplished. Often composite application development initiatives results into business case for incremental

standardization of enterprise architectures. Initiatives such as evolving a Common Information Mode (CIM) for the enterprise, MDM initiatives, adoption of B2B messaging standards, and creation of an SOA for the enterprise often are precursor or prerequisites to composite application development initiatives.

ROLE OF STANDARDS

Development of new IT systems in an agile manner through use of Model Driven approaches and reuse of pre-existing IT assets is the unique proposition of Composite Applications. Composite Applications have touch point with multiple back end IT systems as explained earlier. Each of these systems could have been implemented using different technologies, architectural approaches, and styles and have differences in their inherent business architectures (business semantics and format of data items, process definitions, role definitions, policy definitions, rule definitions, etc.). Given these aspects the role of business and technical standards in enabling interoperability is paramount. Business standards or industry domain standards enable interoperability of processes and data flow among the participating systems in a composite application. It also enables reuse of policy and rule definitions in the composite applications. Additional roles, policies, rules, data items, etc., might need to be created during the course of development of new composite applications. These new items in the business architecture of the composite application could have implications and touch points with the participating IT systems that the composite application needs to interoperate with. Use of some form of standards for definition of these new items (in terms of semantics and format) is essential to make them 'understandable' and usable during the exchange of information and transactions between the composite application and the participating systems. These business standards could be open industry wide standards such as ACCORD, SWIFT, HL7, and SCOR, which are usually meant for standardizing B2B interactions. An enterprise could adopt these open standards or evolve its own enterprise wide business semantics and structural standards whichever is deemed appropriate given the business context and IT strategy.

One of the key benefits of composite application platform is that it enables the business users and SMEs to work closely with the IT team (IT architects, designers, and developers). The MDD tools enable the business user to easily model and visualize business process definitions and semantics. The tools are steadily maturing and have reached a stage where to a limited extent it is possible for the business user to even identify the IT assets (such as the coarse grained business services) which could be useful for automating the proposed business process. This approach is not new and has been around from the days of BPR and ERP implementation initiatives. The SMEs who were to a reasonable degree familiar with a particular ERP COTS package could not only model the business process and understand business issues but also were able to identify the APIs and IT components from the ERP package which would need to be used and customized for implementing the business process under consideration. This approach to MDD has matured further and has inspired the modern composite applications. Use of open standards for business architecture modelling such as BPML, BPMN (for process modelling), UML (for business entity modelling), BPEL (for executable process modelling in terms of participating services), and WS-* set of standards (for specifying and implementing business and technical services) are some of key enabling standards that are supported by the emerging composite application platforms. WS-CAF, JBI, SCA, and SDO are another set of standards which are conceptualized specifically for standardizing composite application development platforms.

EXAMPLES OF COMPOSITE APPLICATION DEVELOPMENT PLATFORMS

Further is the list of some vendor platforms in this space. This list is not exhaustive and these names have been included to give the reader some representative examples:

1. *SAP eSOA*: SAP Composite Application Framework and Guided Procedures (CAF-GP) is a composite application development platform which allows consumption of SAP APIs from SAP packages, enterprise services from its own Enterprise Services Registry (ESR), it also allows workflow, and GUI modelling. It has adapters for communication with other technologies from IBM, Microsoft, etc.
2. *SAP xApps*: It is a model where the entire composite application embodying set of generic business processes is available out of box for deployment after configuration and customization over existing portfolio of enterprise IT systems.
3. *Oracle Fusion*: It provides out of box business domain specific functionality and adapters and bridges for interoperability with a number of other COTS products from SAP, Siebel, JD Edwards, etc.
4. *Sun JCAPs*: It is a composite application development platform which allows development and reuse of IT assets and sits on top of a powerful enterprise integration backbone which provides a suite of adapters and bridges for interoperability with platforms from multiple other vendor.
5. *IBM Business Services Fabric*: It is a composite application development platform built very closely in alignment with SOA principles. It provides a strong portfolio of out-of-box industry domain specific web services which could be used to build new composite application. The platform supports powerful agile and iterative composite application development methodology and interoperates with IBM's other workflow and BPM products such as Lotus Notes Domino, WebSphere AS, etc.
6. *Microsoft*: Office Business Applications are composite applications built through reusable service layers.

REFERENCES

Ambler, Scott W. 2002. *Agile Modeling: Effective Practices for eXtreme Programming and the Unified Process*. New York: John Wiley & Sons.

Hildreth, Sue. 2005. 'Rounding Up Business Rules', Computerworld, 23 May, pp. 24–26. Available online at http://www.computerworld.com.

Jarman, Peter. 2007. 'Viewpoint: SOA—Impact on Enterprise Architecture Service View', SETLabs Briefings, 5(1, January–March): 81–86. Available online at http://www.infosys.com/research/publications/setlabs-archive.asp

Kinikin, Erin and Laura Ramos. 2004. 'Packaged Composite Applications Emerge—Slowly', 2004 Giga Research, 22 January. Available at http://www.forrester.com/Research/LegacyIT/Excerpt/0,7208,33529,00.html (accessed January 2009).

Mallick, Sudeep. 2007a. 'Composite Apps, Paving the Way for Assembly Line SOA'. Available online at http://searchsoa.techtarget.com/tip/0,289483,sid26_gci1286977,00.html (accessed in December 2007).

———. 2007b. 'SOA and Open Standards Pave the Way for Composite Applications'. Available online at http://infosysblogs.com/soa/2007/11/soa_and_open_standards_paves_t_1.html (accessed on 16 November 2007).

Open SOA Architechture. 'Service Component Architecture Home'. Available online at http://osoa.org/display/Main/Service+Component+Architecture+Home

Rymer, John R. 2005. 'How Composite Apps will Change Enterprise Application Development', Forrester Trends, 20 July. Available at http://www.forrester.com/rb/Research/how_composite_apps_will_change_enterprise_application/q/id/36210/t/2 (accessed January 2009).

SYS-CON Media Inc., 2008. 'Business Agility: The Value Driver for SOA'. Available online at http://soa.sys-con.com/node/641256/print (accessed January 2009).

WEBSITES

SAP Composite Application Framework. https://www.sdn.sap.com/irj/sdn/develop-ca?rid=/webcontent/uuid/d8dbd703-0801-0010-c9bf-c04bc52f562f

WebSphere Business Services Fabric. http://www-01.ibm.com/software/integration/wbsf/

Sun JCAPS. http://www.sun.com/software/javaenterprisesystem/javacaps/index.jsp

Oracle Strengthens Commitment to Java Developers with Free Development Tool and Open Source Projects. http://www.oracle.com/corporate/press/2005_jun/06-28-05%20jdev%20free%20jsf.html

4

ES as Infrastructure for Analytics and Knowledge Management

GITA A. KUMTA

Professor and Head, Information Systems,
NMIMS (Deemed-to-be-University), Mumbai, India–400056
E-mail: gkumta@nmims.edu

INTRODUCTION

The competitive environment has forced organizations to reinvent themselves in order to survive which requires connecting people, processes, and information in real time. In a fiercely competitive environment, business strategy not only determines success, it governs business survival (Nah et al., 2001). The use of information technology (IT) in organizations has therefore moved from mere problem-solving to enterprise-wide IT strategies. IT is redefining the business model and creating major opportunities for companies positioned to take advantage. The IT infrastructure is now so intimately enmeshed with business processes that it effectively dictates the pace of change. There is a growing dependence of businesses on IT.

No longer is it adequate to simply get the system to run. Now, we must see the enterprise holistically as the implementation itself so it can be dynamically reshaped and redefined as the environmental change and complexity escalate (Zachman, 2000).

EVOLUTION OF ENTERPRISE SOLUTIONS

Corporate enterprises initially used technology for processing voluminous data or resolving a specific problem which was undertaken by the IT specialists. Understanding its potential management demanded management information system (MIS) to support its decisions. Each major function of the enterprise used IT to record transactions and provide information to the management. It was still restricted to a few individuals but responsibility predominantly remained with the technology people. Managers gradually felt the need to analyze data and look at multiple scenarios and decision support systems evolved as a result. A business activity framework is indicated in Figure 4.1.

FIGURE 4.1
Business Activity Framework

ENTERPRISE

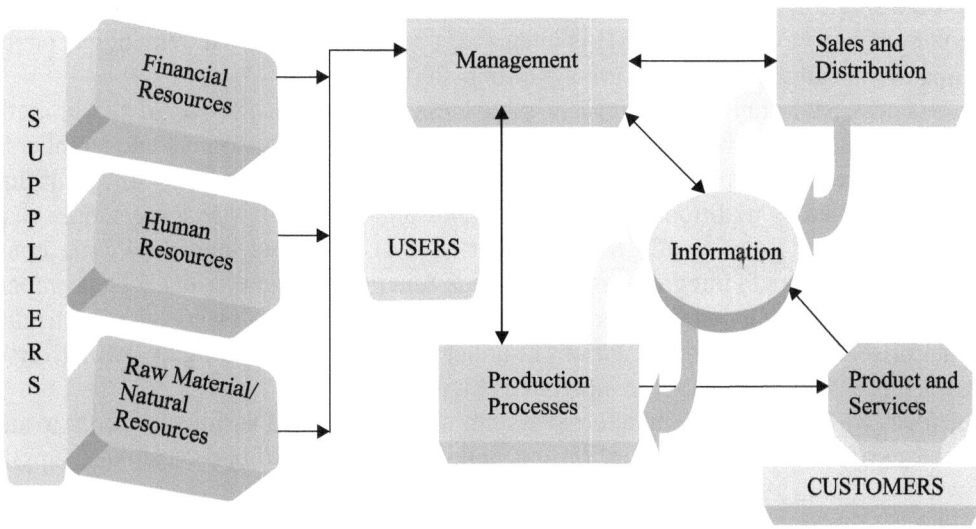

Source: Author.

At the enterprise level there was significant use of office automation tools. Data warehousing tools were developed to serve the needs of decision-making by integrating data from silos. The enterprise now had a network of computers with disconnected applications. The underlying IT infrastructure was fairly complex with servers, desktops, networks, and database management systems brought in for each application. There were two distinct groups—the 'IT people' and the 'business people'.

The focus of manufacturing systems moved from inventory management, production planning and control to Material Requirement Planning (MRP) systems which also focused on time-phased net requirements for the sub-assemblies, and planning and procurement of components and raw materials. Moving further the concept of Manufacturing Resources Planning (MRP II) evolved which was an extension of MRP to shop floor and distribution management activities.

However, businesses also managed other resources such as finance and people and there was an urgent need to integrate functions as the underlying data was common and multiple entry or owners of data created chaos. This resulted in ERP systems as a logical extension of the MRP II concept which integrated the data and processes of an organization into one single system with modules that support core business areas such as manufacturing, distribution, financials, and human resources to balance and optimize enterprise resources (Jacobs and Bendoly, 2003).

Enterprise resource planning (ERP) requires a powerful workflow component. Workflow that provides each member of the value chain, based on their roles and responsibilities, with a process-centric view of the business. This resulted in Transaction Processing Systems involving the operating level people in the whole process. IT by now had touched the whole enterprise. It runs off a single database so that the various departments can more easily share information and communicate with each other. This integrated approach can have a tremendous payback if companies install the software correctly (Koch, 2007).

As business environments changed to e-business, companies discovered the limitations of ERP systems and realized the importance of interfacing with customers and suppliers. As this might suggest, many new e-ventures had only tenuous links to the back-office fulfillment processes provided by traditional ERP systems (Harrington, 2001). Managing supply chains, devising Customer Relationship Management (CRM) strategies, and deploying content management solutions to integrate enterprise-wide functions became critical. The companies also required decision support and therefore data warehousing and MIS were other applications. The enterprise now had multiple solutions as indicated in the following figure, with diverse IT infrastructure which required to be integrated (Figure 4.2).

The focus was shifting from an internal system which integrated various functions to an external means of customer communication and market analysis. Customer's customer, supplier's

FIGURE 4.2
Application Framework of an Enterprise

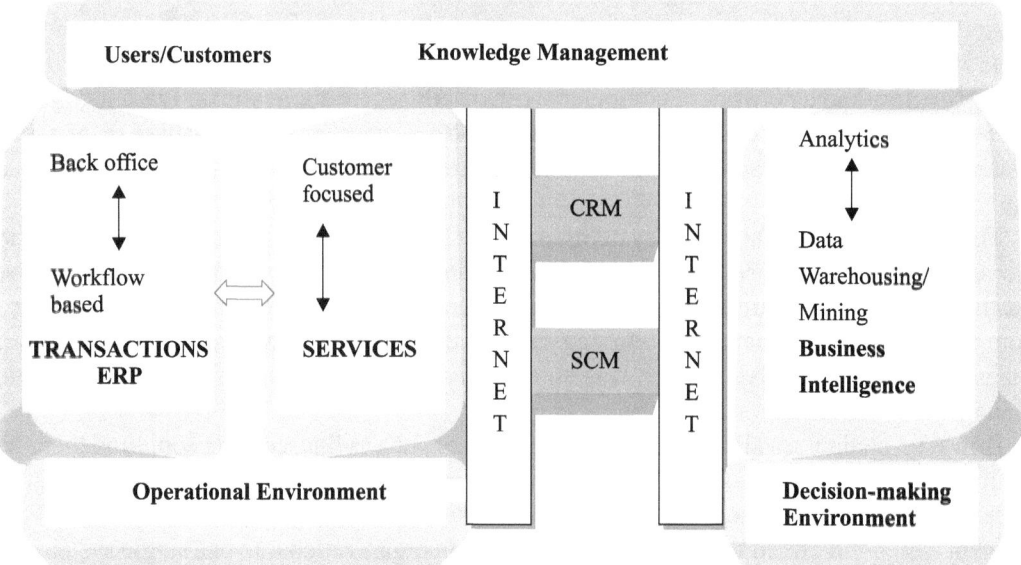

Source: Author.

supplier, and outsourcing service providers became part of the enterprise solution. Enterprise solutions therefore evolved into two components: *Enterprise Applications* focused on business and *Enterprise Service Architecture* as the IT infrastructure required to meet the business requirements of flexibility and innovation.

As indicated in the Figure 4.3, the user was at the core of these systems and had to be empowered with knowledge and analytics to be able to enhance performance. It was imperative to view the business as a system of interrelated components interacting to achieve a common goal. This system had multiple players and only IT could support this.

FIGURE 4.3
E-business Focus on Communication with External Stakeholders

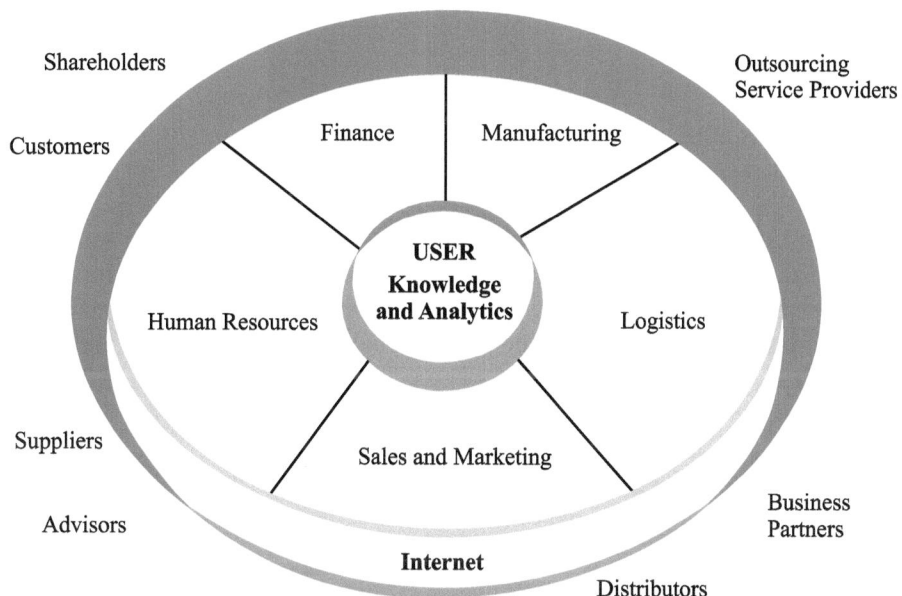

Source: Author.

This triggered off a dramatic transformation of business—from e-business to c-business where 'c' stands for collaboration. By the start of 2000, companies were transforming their ERP implementations into Internet-based applications. However, the high failure rate of ERP implementation called for a better understanding of its critical success factors (Somers et al., 2000). Aligning the business process to the software implementation was critical (Holland et al., 1999; Sumner, 2000).

A study of Markus et al. (2000) shows that many problems related to ERP implementation are related to a misfit of the system with the characteristics of the organization. This is consistent with the finding of Davenport (1998), who argues that ERP 'tends to impose its own logic on a company's strategy, culture, and organization' which may or may not fit with the existing organizational arrangements. Empirical evidence certainly seems to suggest similar fit concerns (Bendoly and Jacobs, 2004; Bendoly et al., 2009). ERP implementations therefore were (and still remain) not just replacement of technology but called for an organizational change process.

Enterprise Applications

Organizations implemented multiple solutions to address the changing needs of the businesses. Some of these were:

- Office automation
- Groupware and intranets
- Websites
- MIS
- Enterprise resource planning systems
- Data warehousing and data mining

Every organization had infrastructure to support word processing and spread sheets. The desktops were then connected to facilitate interdepartmental communication through e-mail and groupware. Intranets also provided facility to create repositories of information for sharing. MIS collated data from functional systems and provided the management with reports of the various aspects of business viewed from different perspectives such as location, time, products, etc.

Internet brought in the concept of website which became the gateway to the external world. Communication to the external world became easier with the e-mail facility. This also required good internal systems to respond to customers faster than through the traditional communication facility. Integration became the need of the hour.

Enterprise Resource Planning

The standalone functional systems in finance, HR, manufacturing, stores, procurement and sales, and distribution were replaced by a single unified software package divided into software modules that can serve all those departments' particular needs. These systems were called ERP systems which attempted to integrate all departments and functions across a company onto a single computer system which runs off a single database with client machines for every desk. This facilitated sharing of information across the organization.

Initially ERP was developed as a tightly integrated monolith, but later most solution providers came up with a modular design so that only required modules could be implemented by the organizations. Subsequently supply chain management and customer relationship management assumed importance and these systems were implemented as add-ons. Internet-based applications were built to facilitate customer or supplier interaction with the system.

In spite of various technologies organizations had trouble in accessing and understanding corporate data. Questions therefore persist about how corporations can consolidate and use their storehouses of information to deliver better products and services, while maintaining profit margins. Business analytics and knowledge management were no more stand-alone applications but required to be integrated in the enterprise solution.

BUSINESS ANALYTICS

Large deployment of enterprise IT or information system (IS) systems created huge volumes of data. As the consequence of non-stop business operations, enterprise repositories may store terabytes of data per year. Unstructured data and information collection levels have risen but only a tiny fraction of the enterprise repository content is effectively used. Enterprise data redundancy is very high (up to four times) (Delic, 2009).

Traditionally data warehouses compiled data from functional applications to provide reports to the managers with drill down and other analytical facilities. The lifecycle of a data record through enterprise analytics starts with a business event taking place. Data acquisition technologies deliver the event record to the data warehouse. Analytical processing helps turn the data into information, and a business decision leads to a corresponding action. To approach real time, the duration between the event and its consequent action needs to be minimized. Typically, it is the data acquisition process that introduces majority of the latency (GoldenGate Software, 2004).

Transaction systems, such as ERP can provide excellent snapshots on business activity, such as status reports on inventory levels or order backlogs. Managers have more information at hand about their business environment than ever before. There has been a power shift not only within the enterprise but also beyond the enterprise as the customers have access to the same information as the enterprise (Toffler, 1990). Today, more companies are working hard to make their data warehouses active at the operational level. Data warehousing technologies have moved from mere reporting of analysis to predictive support. Tools and techniques such as business analytics and data mining enable the manager to transform performance data into actionable business intelligence, thereby providing timely, actionable intelligence, deeper visibility, and empowered decision-making.

High-performing enterprises are now building their competitive strategies around data-driven insights that in turn generate impressive business results. Business intelligence (BI) provides the ability for businesses to look back and examine how well the organization has worked to achieve such goals as meeting customers' expectations for price, quality, or service (Sun). Key business intelligence elements which are required at operational levels can be identified as data visualization, decision-making, alerts, and reporting. Data warehousing supports business intelligence solutions and both are an essential part of information lifecycle management (ILM). The implementation of data archiving for data warehousing and other enterprise systems tends to raise the level of an enterprise's information agility, especially when accomplished in the context of a coherent approach to ILM (Agosta, 2008).

BI is moving from an inactive environment answering questions like what happened to a proactive intervention seeking answers to what is happening so as to change the strategies online. Today they need to be integrated into business at operational level. Data created from ERP is now beginning to be used for managing operational performance. An important requirement is to enable lowest possible latency in which new data is delivered to the data warehouse, ideally in real time.

KNOWLEDGE MANAGEMENT

People—the employees, customers, and suppliers—are at the core of any enterprise and are the main players in the enterprise. Every organization is a complex network of processes. In spite of documented standard processes, there is inherent variability due to the execution and interpretations by the various players based on their experience and insights. Knowledge is therefore defined as 'a fluid mix of framed experience, values, contextual information, expert insight and grounded intuition that provides an environment and framework for evaluating and incorporating new experiences and information' (Davenport and Prusak, 1998). In a 'global world', knowledge is crucial. It provides the basic framework to connect, collaborate, coordinate, and communicate in a highly complex and competitive market place (Seshachala, 2006).

Like information is distilled out of data, past experiences, insights, and others' expertise when applied to information generates knowledge, which helps in making better decisions for the future. Data leads to information, and experience when applied to information gives knowledge. Knowing what went wrong and what was effective will help the organizations use their resources optimally, thereby contributing to business excellence. Lessons are learned but not shared. Knowledge gained through failures is often undervalued. Events that caused a delay in the project completion or those that affected sales adversely are often forgotten. One tends to repeat past mistakes due to lack of knowledge or the inaccessibility to learning from failures. Due to lack of sharing culture and facilitation, best practices of a group do not get embedded into the organization's procedures.

In spite of all the tools, employees are unable to find critical existing information whenever required. This results in employees using incomplete information or reinventing the wheel. Information about a study conducted in a particular area, if found easily, will help reduce the time in initiating a study in another similar area and estimate the effort more realistically. Organizations often do not know what they already know (Bendoly, 2003, Bendoly et al., 2009).

Very often individuals who have valuable information are not tracked in the organization and this knowledge moves with them with no benefit to the organization.

In the knowledge-based economy survival depends on the best possible response to a multitude of challenges primarily using the knowledge gained through past experience. Knowledge can therefore be classified as:

- Explicit which is information that can be articulated or documented and exists in some form within the organization, and
- Tacit which can not be articulated easily and is characterized by experience and insights.

Knowledge Management can therefore be defined as the ability to create value by leveraging know-how, judgement, intuition, and experience within the organization by capturing and facilitating the sharing of existing knowledge. Kirk Klasson elucidates, 'Knowledge management is the ability to create and retain greater value from core business competencies' (Tiwana, 2002). It is a process by which an organization converts information to 'actionable' information.

As discussed earlier knowledge is generated through a combination of information and thinking. Knowledge Management therefore is a combination of information systems and the human systems. This has been brought out clearly by Richard McDermott in his article 'Why Information Technology Inspired but Cannot Deliver Knowledge Management' where he opines that 'while the knowledge revolution is inspired by new information systems, it takes human systems to realize it' (McDermott, 1999).

The knowledge management process needs to assess two major components:

- *Business processes*: Do these help or hinder knowledge management?
- *Infrastructure*: Does the organization have the infrastructure to store and retrieve the actionable information as and when required?

An organization's corporate imperatives, application environment, and cultural readiness along with the existing infrastructure dictate the starting point for a knowledge management strategy (Satyadas, 2003). ERP systems have already put the basic infrastructure in place.

BUSINESS PROCESS DESIGN AND MANAGEMENT

It is therefore not incorrect to conclude that at the core of enterprise solutions are two main components—business processes and the underlying basic data. In a typical business process one will find that business interaction is about events that occur and how businesses respond to such events. 'Organizations need to be able to look at both a specific event as it happens as well as look at it in the context of what has happened historically,'says Holly Hayes, pro-gramme director for Information Integration at IBM's Silicon Valley Lab in San Jose, California (Griffin, 2004).

In 2002, Gartner Group first identified the need for monitoring the different activities in-volved in business processes, as a form of business intelligence usage called Business Activity Monitoring (BAM). The next-generation BAM initiative, called process-driven BI, begins with a simple design notion: decision-making is a fundamental aspect of any operational business process. As such, decision-making capabilities and analytics should be embedded into the design of a process. With this type of intelligent process design, the need for decision-making is anticipated as an integral part of each process, resulting in business processes that work smarter in improving business efficiency and performance. As an event occurs and travels through its lifecycle within the enterprise, a business process will generate many possible outputs to each event, enabling people or other processes to take action as required. A 'smart' business process is the result of combining business intelligence with process design (iway Software, 2006).

Today's business leaders need information to be more readily accessible. They want real-time views into their businesses so that decisions can be made when they need to be, without the added time of tracking data and generating reports. Managers want to monitor key metrics in real-time to actively track the health of their business (Exact Software America, 2005). Combining BI with process design is critical to the success of businesses today. The system needs to anticipate the need for decision-making and supply just the right infor-mation to support those decisions during real-time operations (Information Builders Inc., 2006).

Process-driven BI takes reporting to a higher level by aligning business intelligence with decision-making more tightly than ever before. Now one can define the precise events or con-ditions that trigger the need for a report right into the business process. The emerging business process framework is a real-time integration of transaction, analytics and content as depicted in Figure 4.4.

In a dynamic business environment, organizations need to be able to adapt their processes rapidly and effectively. They need to be able to analyze problems and execute solutions accordingly. Organizations therefore require the full integration capabilities to orchestrate and leverage cross-functional business processes that are used over multiple systems, divisions, people, and partners.

THE ESSENCE OF ENTERPRISE ARCHITECTURE

Transforming core business processes to create strategic advantage increasingly involves people, processes, and information across multiple organizations and systems. IT today plays

FIGURE 4.4
Emerging Business Process Framework

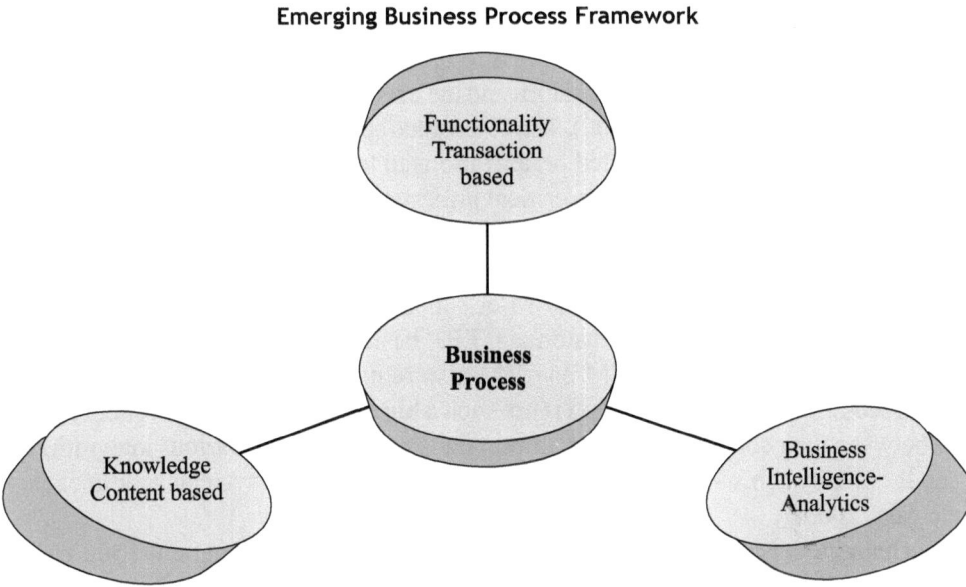

a larger role than ever in driving business success by enabling organizations to adapt rapidly to evolving business needs. However, today, IT portfolio in organizations is dominated by a mix of packaged enterprise suites, best-of-breed applications, and the legacy systems. With multiple acquisitions and mergers and outsourcing of processes, the IT infrastructure has become a web of disparate, stand-alone systems requiring to be integrated in order to implement simple business processes. This requires 'stitching' together processes spanning different functional units, different systems, and external service providers.

'True integration starts with the underlying data. Organizations must not only bring together data from multiple systems, but assimilate and standardize the different data types and formats,' says Darren Taylor, Vice-President of the Information Access Division, Blue Cross and Blue Shield of Kansas City (BCBSKC) (2008). By integrating and standardizing their enterprise data, they have shifted from transactional to strategic organizations and improved overall processes, operations, and patient care (Hewlett Packard Development Company, 2008). Organizing functionality and content into a structure that people are able to navigate intuitively does not happen by chance. Organizations must recognize the importance of information architecture or else they run the risk of creating great content and functionality that no one can ever find (Barker, 2005).

According to Griffin, true enterprise—wide information integration—requires an information strategy that combines the concepts of business process management, time-driven business intelligence, and information integration concepts into an architecture that spans the enterprise in business-time. Information Architecture that enables the common view of diverse data is business-time information architecture (BTIA). The concept of business time recognizes that users' needs are not always covered by access to the most current data (Griffin, 2004).

'Information Technology is both the culprit and the traffic cop for this knowledge management process' (Bukowitz and Williams, 2000). The IT-enabled services and workflows have generated too much of information which has led organizations to look for IT solutions capable of helping them in retrieving and renewing the critical information to support the business objectives. The role of IT has now changed from just repositories of information and MIS reports to its ability to support collaboration and communication.

Tight integration between ERP and CRM or supply chain management (SCM) systems is critical to gain a complete view of customers. ERP basically works on an online transaction processing (OLTP) process and SCM or CRM also requires an online analytical processing (OLAP) process. These days integration is not such a big issue because most vendors offer connectors between their solutions. 'What is important is to consider the various integration points between the two systems—how, when and how often will the two systems talk to each other' (Sirsalewala, 2003).

In the changing business environment approaches to integration can be viewed from three perspectives—business process, applications, and enterprise integration for delivering services. All three are needed for the business to be flexible and responsive to changing needs.

ENTERPRISE APPLICATION INTEGRATION (EAI)

There is a definite trend among enterprises towards integrating their existing applications as they find themselves having to merge with other enterprises, reorganize their internal structure, and adopt new technologies and platforms to remain competitive. All organizations at some time face the problem of integrating different applications and database systems. Organizations need to establish a web presence and make their business services available to web users. At the same time, they cannot afford to discard its existing systems and applications.

Success in e-business is driven by an organization's ability to integrate existing applications and make its business data accessible to others, from internal employees to external partners, suppliers, and customers through web-based access. Application Integration provides high performance and fine-grained control of process services that span applications. EAI enables an organization to integrate its existing applications and systems and add new technologies and applications to the IT portfolio. EAI facilitates integrating applications and data sources so that the organization can easily share business processes and data.

However, EAI has proven to be costly to implement and even harder to change over time. Enterprise Services Architecture will move IT architectures to higher levels of adaptability and help companies move closer to the vision of the real-time enterprise.

Enterprise Integration

Enterprise Integration is achieved through the Service Oriented Architecture (SOA) which has emerged as a potentially attractive solution for helping enterprises to become more agile and achieve the vision of a collaborative and process-centric organization. Designed from a services perspective and implemented as a set of loosely coupled systems, SOA can help enterprises integrate disparate applications.

The fundamental premise is the abstraction of business activities, modelled as 'enterprise services', drawn from the functionality of the applications. These services can be developed rapidly deployed easily across heterogeneous landscapes, and adapted quickly and efficiently as business needs change. SOA changes the way solutions are built and deployed, moving away from the hardwired one-to-one integrations to the flexible assembling of a service in the new business scenario.

Enterprise Architecture

Enterprise Integration has two major components: applications systems covering business processes and data and IT infrastructure covering various platforms, technologies, and tools. Next generation business application 'stack' would cover the following applications, all on one integrated platform:

- Transaction-based applications such as ERP, SCM, and CRM.
- Enterprise Business Intelligence.
- Enterprise knowledge creation and usage framework.
- Integration through portals and application servers.
- One point user interface covering employee, customers, and suppliers.

Enterprise Architecture is of critical importance for the future of businesses. An enterprise can be viewed as having three distinctive layers:

- Overall business model covering processes and functions.
- Data and information sets embedded in applications.
- Technology, tools, and techniques.

Each of these has different goals, capabilities, and constraints. The aim is to make these three layers collaborate and talk to each other. Most enterprises have self-grown architecture that works, but solutions and practices are typically not documented. Choice of data and information modelling practice and software development methods should align with technology choices and top enterprise architecture goals (Delic, 2009). Web services make up a connection technology. It is a way to connect services together into a service-oriented architecture. Primary elements of web services are repository, messaging, and service.

The organization has most of the basic infrastructure in place with the implementation of applications like office automation, intranet, e-mail, and ERP systems. Both Business Intelligence and Knowledge Management need to build upon the enterprise solution infrastructure to create the Enterprise Architecture. The Knowledge Management Architecture is built upon the structured and unstructured components of the Enterprise Applications (Figure 4.5).

FIGURE 4.5
Enterprise Knowledge Management Architecture

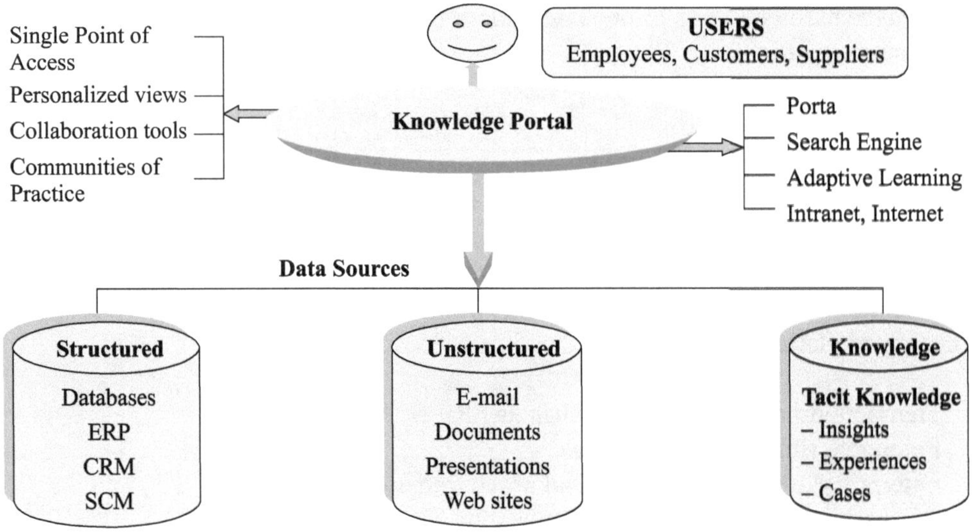

Source: Author.

The Business Intelligence Architecture also requires the basic data from the enterprise applications such as ERP, CRM, and SCM. This data then passes throughes an ETL process to create a data warehouse on which the Business Intelligence analytical engine is built. The BI Architecture is indicated in Figure 4.5. The challenge now is to integrate knowledge and analytics at the OLTP stage so as to improve the performance.

EMERGENCE OF ERP II

Enterprise systems are evolving because organizations are changing. Global supply chains mean inter-organizational systems that span different cultures and countries. This brings in even greater challenges due to cultural differences and legal issues. ERP focuses on trying to integrate departments and functions throughout a company. It attempts to integrate everything into a single system that can serve every department's needs. ERP broken down simply is an application/system that both small and large companies are using today in order to streamline and integrate operation processes.

With the historic growth from ERP as a monolithic application to ERP II which needs an open architecture and a vertical-specific functionality, enterprises have recognized the need to have a solid foundation on which all applications can run. This has been termed as the Information, Integration, and Collaboration (IIC) framework. ERP II is defined as an application and deployment strategy that expands out from traditional ERP functions to achieve integration of an enterprise's key, domain specific internal and external collaborative, and operational and financial processes. Although a clearer term has been proposed as 'Value Chain Resource Planning' by notable authors such as Bendoly et al. (2004), ERP II is likely to continue to be used in reference to these strategic extensions (and is likely unfortunately to generate the same misleading implications that MRP II engendered).

Regardless of nomenclature, it is clear that there is movement away from client–server system to Internet-based architecture. The principle for ERP II or Value Chain Resource Planning (VCRP) is that it is a back-office kernel that all the other products bolt onto. So it may not matter whether SAP manages to develop its own front end or not, or whether it partners with Clarify or Siebel. At bottom, they will always need each other, and the future is between these two groups working together.

CONCLUSION

As the time required for making business decisions decreases, BI solutions are evolving from historical analysis to real-time event-driven tools. The line between transactional systems and analytics is blurring. Traditional back-office ERP systems are important in this process, but the real differentiators are in the front-end personalization, content management, and customer tracking side of an operation.

The technology backbone and the people environment has set the stage for a truly collaborative enterprise solution involving all stakeholders and technologies covering ERP, analytics, and knowledge management. Going live is not the end of the ERP journey. ERP provides a backbone to further extend functionality through bolt-ons and other solutions. ERP delivers significant tactical and bottom-line strategic results. An ERP implementation is, at its core, a people project.

Workflows have to be redefined to ensure that assigned tasks are completed, or escalated if required. This requires alert management technology to identify potential problems in the value chain so as to take proactive action and improve the quality of service. Workflow processes have to be updated as needs change which may result in changing the code and requires intervention of the IT function. It is therefore necessary to provide business managers with technology that can facilitate them to define and modify their workflow through configuration of the system.

The competitive strategy in today's business environment is to create a virtual company resulting in organizational redesign, integrate processes giving a single experience to the customer, and build learning and agile organizations. The only facilitator in addition to good leadership is a robust and flexible technology.

Complexity and high rates of change are the challenge of the information age enterprise, and neither can be accommodated without Enterprise Architecture. Enterprises are simply too complex to expect simplistic solutions. The systems are no longer discretionary support to the enterprise. They are mandatory. Zackman (2000) emphasises the need to perceive 'systems as the enterprise; the design of the system is the design of the enterprise; and if the system can't change, the enterprise can't change!'

REFERENCES

Agosta, L. 2008. 'Data Warehousing Meets Data Archiving in Information Lifecycle Management', *Data Strategy Adviser,* Information Management Online, 17 April.

Barker, I. 2005. *What is Information Architecture?* May, in KM column. Available online at http://www.steptwo. com.au/papers/kmc_whatisinfoarch

Bendoly, E. 2003. 'Theory and Support for Process Frameworks of Knowledge Discovery and Data Mining from ERP Systems', *Information & Management,* 40(7): 639–47.

Bendoly, E. and F.R. Jacobs. 2004. 'ERP Architectural/Operational Alignment for Order-processing Performance', *International Journal of Operations and Production Management,* 24(1): 99–117.

Bendoly, E., E. Rosenzweig, and J. Stratman. 2009. 'The Efficient Use of Enterprise Information for Strategic Advantage: A DEA Analysis', *Journal of Operations Management,* 26(4): 310–323.

Bendoly, E., A. Soni, and M.A. Venkataramanan. 2004. 'Value Chain Resource Planning: Adding Value with Systems beyond the Enterprise', *Business Horizons,* 47(2): 79–86.

Bukowitz, W.R. and R.L. Williams. 2000. *The Knowledge Management Fieldbook.* UK: Financial Times/Prentice Hall.

Davenport, T.H. 1998. 'Putting the Enterprise into the Enterprise System', *Harvard Business Review,* 76(4): 121–32.

Davenport, T.H. and L. Prusak. 1998. *Working Knowledge: How Organizations Manage What They Know.* Boston: Harvard Business School Press.

Delic, K.A. 2009. *Enterprise Models, Strategic Transformations and Possible Solutions* Enterprise Solutions/ Enterprise Models, Strategic Transformations and Possible Solutions. Available at http://www.acm.org/ubiquity/ views/k_delic_2.html (accessed January 2009).

Exact Software North America. 2005. 'Making ERP Deliver on its Promise to the Enterprise', A White Paper by Exact Software, MAS1600, 4/26/2005. Available online at www.exactamerica.com

Griffin, J. 2004. 'Building a Better Mousetrap—The Business–Time Information architecture', *DM Review,* Information Management Online, May.

GoldenGate Software. 2004. 'Real-Time Data Warehousing', White Paper, August. Available at http://www.oracle. com/technology/products/warehouse/pdf/goldengate (accessed January 2008).

Harrington, A. 2001. 'Gartner Touts the ERP II Vision', Management Consultancy, January. Available online at http://www.managementconsultancy.couk

Hewlett Packard Development Company. 2008. 'From Transactional to Strategic Use of Data', *Transforming Your Enterprise Magazine*, Spring. Available at http://h20338.www2.hp.com/enterprise/cache/598618-0-0-225-121. html (accessed January 2009).

Holland, C.P., B. Light, and N. Gibson. 1999. 'A Critical Success Factors Model for Enterprise Resource Planning Implementation', in J. Pries-Heje, C.U. Ciborra, K. Kautz, J. Valor, E. Christiaanse, D. Avison, and C. Heje (eds), *Proceedings of the 7th European Conference on Information Systems*, 1: 273–87. Copenhagen: Copenhagen Business School.

Information Builders Inc. 2006. 'Process-Driven Business Intelligence: Building Smarter Business Processes', White paper, November. Available online at http://productfinder.infoworld.com/infoworld/search/viewabstract/85776/ index.jsp

Iway Software. 2006. 'Process-Driven Business Intelligence a White paper on Building Smarter Business Processes With iWay Technology and WebFOCUS'. Available online at www.informationbuilders.com

Jacobs, F.R. and E. Bendoly. 2003. 'Enterprise Resource Planning: Developments and Directions for Operations Management Research', *European Journal of Operational Research*, 146(2): 5–12.

Koch, C. 2007. 'ABC: An Introduction to ERP Getting started with Enterprise Resource Planning (ERP)'. Available online at http://www.cio.com/article/40323/ABC_An_Introduction_to_ERP

Markus, M.Lynne, Sheryl Axline, David Petrie, and Sheryl Cornelis Tanis. 2000. 'Learning from Adopters Experiences with ERP: Problems Encountered and Success Achieved', *Journal of Information Technology*, 15(4): 245–65.

McDermott, R. 1999. 'Why Information Technology Inspired but cannot Deliver Knowledge Management', *California Management Review*, 41(4, Summer).

Nah, F.F., J. Lee-Shang Lau, and J. Kuang. 2001. 'Critical Factors for Successful Implementation of Enterprise Systems', *Business Process Management Journal*, 7(3): 285–296.

Satyadas, Antony. 2003. *Growing a Practical KM System*, 3 March. Available at www.DestinationKM.com (accessed January 2009).

Seshachala, S. 2006. 'How to Build a Global Knowledge Management System', February. Available online at http://www.rediff.com/money/2006/feb/10km.htm.

Sirsalewala, M. 2003, 'Where ERP is Going', *Network Magazine*, Indian Express Newspapers (Bombay) Limited, Mumbai, India, October.

Somers, T.M., K. Nelson, and A. Ragowsky. 2000. 'Enterprise Resource Planning (ERP) for the Next Millennium: Development of an Integrative Framework and Implications for Research', *Proceedings of the 2000 Americas Conference on Information Systems (AMCIS)*, 10–13 April, Long Beach, California.(PDF).

Sumner, Mary. 2000. 'Risk Factors in Enterprise-wide/ERP Projects', *Journal of Information Technology*, 15(4): 317–27.

Taylor, Darren. 2008. 'Transforming Your Enterprise Magazine' http://h20338.www2.hp.com/enterprise/ cache/598618-0-0-225-121.html (accessed January 2009).

Tiwana, Amrit. 2002. *The Knowledge Management Toolkit: Orchestrating IT, Strategy and Knowledge Platforms* (2nd edition). UK: Prentice Hall (Pearson Education Asia).

Toffler, A. 1990. *Powershift*. New York: Bantam.

Zachman, J.A. 2000. 'Enterprise Architecture: The Past and the Future', *DM Direct*, Information Management Online, April.

5

Towards Service-oriented Enterprise Systems: A Business Intelligence Perspective

Jayanthi Ranjan
Institute of Management Technology,
Ghaziabad, Uttar Pradesh, India
E-mail: jranjan@imt.edu

B.S. Sahay
Director and Professor of Supply Chain Management,
Management Development Institute, Gurgaon, Haryana, India
E-mail: bssahay@mdi.ac.in

INTRODUCTION

The worldwide emergence of information revolution affects every enterprise. The value of a given piece of information increases with the square root of the number of users who can access that information, multiplied by the number of business areas in which users work (Hammond and Liautand, 2001). The path to business insight as described by Rogalski Shari and Fisher Dan (2003) follows the process of integration of data from disparate internal and external data sources, applying analysis tools and techniques to understand the information within the data, making decisions, and taking actions based on this gained insight. Despite a huge amount of information stored in enterprises, one can rarely exploit its full potential in leveraging tactical and strategic decision-making.

Firms are experiencing environmental changes resulting from the new economics of information (D'Aveni, 1994; Evans and Wurster, 2000) and the increasingly dynamic and global nature of competition. Therefore, organizational survival depends on the construction and integration of knowledge fostering the adaptation to the environment as well as stimulating environmental changes through the firm's knowledge and practices (Dijksterhuis et al., 1999).

Enterprise Service Oriented Architecture (SOA) aims at leveraging the established aspects of SOA like its strong link to established standards for the enterprise as a whole. It does not remain in the technology domain but takes SOA to the core of the business. It aims at connecting the business domain with technology domain in a holistic and consistent manner. Service oriented enterprises (SOEs) deploy service-oriented solutions. Building these solutions covers the entire spectrum of service-oriented definition, analysis, and design—from higher-level business focus to the lower-level information technology (IT) focus. This IT focus is primarily the service infrastructure with concerns focusing on integration performance, reliability, and security. In terms of the systems that are built, IT is also focused on maintainability, software lifecycle, and overall productivity of the development team to meet business demands.

Business focus, on the other hand, typically starts top down with goals and objectives driven by business requirements. Businesses set goals often measurable objectives and then attempt to align the implementation of the various projects to meet these objectives and goals. It is not uncommon to find IT enabled projects targeting business objectives that have incurred delays and cost overruns. Service orientation (SO) starts as a powerful technical idea to operationalize the goal of rapid enterprise change by allowing business processes to negotiate diverse systems. This offers a technical advantage as it becomes easier to integrate systems and to reposition existing capabilities for new purposes. Silos of technology that were hidden in arcane interfaces become reusable components that are accessible through transparent standards.

But an organization that only adopts SO as a technical architecture is missing the true potential of the concept. The SO revolution will fully empower organizations that apply it to both their technology and their culture. Applying a service oriented approach to the management of business performance will change the fundamental dynamics of a business.

Business intelligence or BI (Nicholls, 2006; White, 2006) is a business management term used to describe applications and technologies which are used to gather, provide access to and analyze data and information about an enterprise, in order to help them make better informed business decisions. BI technologies include traditional data warehousing technologies such as reporting, ad-hoc querying, and online analytical processing (OLAP). More advanced BI tools that include data-mining, predictive analysis using rule-based simulations, web services and advanced visualization capabilities. BI includes several softwares for extraction, transformation, and loading (ETL), data warehousing, database query and reporting (Berson and Smith, 2001; Hall, 1999), multidimensional or OLAP data analysis, data mining, and visualization.

In this chapter enterprise SO is explained from BI point of view that is necessary to make it possible a seamless integration of technologies into a coherent BI environment, thus enabling simplified data delivery and low-latency analytics. Service-oriented approach is also provided and the BI view in SOEs is illustrated. The rest of the chapter is organized as follows. Section 2 describes an overview of BI and its importance and relevance in business. Section 3 explains the SOA. Section 4 explores the Enterprise SOA. Section 5 emphasizes on SOBI. Section 6 concludes the chapter.

BUSINESS INTELLIGENCE

According to Adelman et al. (2002), BI is a term that encompasses a broad range of analytical software and solutions for gathering, consolidating, analyzing, and providing access to information in a way that is supposed to let an enterprise's users make better business decisions. Malhotra (2000) describes BI as something that facilitates the connections in the newly formed organization, bringing real-time information to centralized repositories, and supporting analytics that can be exploited at every horizontal and vertical level within and outside the firm. BI describes the result of in-depth analysis of detailed business data, including database and application technologies, as well as analysis practices (Gangadharan and Swamy, 2004). BI is technically much broader, potentially encompassing knowledge management, Enterprise Resource Planning (ERP), decision support systems, and data mining (Gangadharan and Swamy, 2004).

The main key to successful BI system is consolidating data from the many different enterprise operational systems into an enterprise data warehouse. Very few organizations have a full-fledged enterprise data warehouse. This is due to the vast scope of effort towards consolidating the entire enterprise data. Berson et al. (2002) emphasizes that in view of emerging highly dynamic business environment, only the most competitive enterprises will achieve sustained market success. The organizations will distinguish themselves by the capability to leverage information about their market place, customers, and operations to capitalize on the business opportunities. Moss and Atre (2003) describe BI as seamless integration of operational front-office applications with operational back-office applications. Gangadharan and Swamy (2004) define BI as an enterprise architecture for an integrated collection of operational as well as decision support applications and databases, which provides the business community easy access to their business data and allows them to make accurate business decisions.

SERVICE-ORIENTED ARCHITECTURE

There is no single standard definition of SOA that has been agreed upon by enterprises. Instead, several definitions were published by different groups, portals, vendors, and business analysts. These definitions range from a high-level view of what SOA does for a business to definitions that focus on the technical aspects of SOA-based solution.

As per World Wide Web Consortium (www.w3.org), SOA is a set of components which can be invoked, and whose interface descriptions can be published and discovered. The CBDI [(http://www.cbdiforum.com/ (accessed in January 2009)] defines SOA as the policies, practices, and frameworks that enable application functionality to be provided and consumed as sets of services published at a granularity relevant to the service consumer. These services can be invoked, published, and discovered, which are abstracted away from the implementation using a single, standards based form of interface. Gartner [(www.gartner.com (accessed in December 2008)] defines SOA as a client/server software design approach in which an application consists of software services and software service consumers (also known as clients or service requesters). SOA differs from the more general client/server model in its definitive emphasis on loose coupling between software components, and in its use of separately standing interfaces. IBM [http://www.ibm.com/in/en/ (accessed in December 2008)] defines SOA as follows: An SOA is an enterprise-scale IT architecture for linking resources on demand. These resources are represented as business-aligned services which can participate and be composed in a value-net, enterprise, or line of business to fulfill business needs. The primary structuring element for SOA applications is a service as opposed to subsystems, systems, or components. Before explaining SOA lets have an idea of what an Enterprise Architecture (EA) may provide.

EA framework is provided in Figure 5.1. The framework established by Ibrahim and Long (2007) is used to facilitate the development and implementation of the EA consists of several architecture domains.

From Figure 5.1 it can be comprehended that the business directions and investments are very much critical for this EA. The architecture domains that need to be modelled as part of the EA are business architecture, application architecture, information architecture, and technology architecture. EA deals with application frameworks and enterprise applications, while SOA's scope is only on service modelling. EA deals with enterprise-level infrastructure including servers, databases, and so on, while SOA focuses on the infrastructure that supports services, namely, the enterprise service bus. EA addresses enterprise integration patterns and when they should be used, including point-to-point integration, file transfer, and other traditional application integration approaches. SOA provides an integration approach based on using services. Though the SOA approach to integration may prove to be the most flexible and recommended approach, one should consider it as one of the approaches EA needs to define and support. There are many differences between a SOA and EA frameworks. The main focus is the business process in SOA and the main focus is business architecture in EA. The applications architecture mainly consists of services and components in SOA whereas EA's domain focuses on application architecture only. The SOA focuses on data architecture while the EA framework is information architecture enabled.

However, it is also obvious that the SOA domains are a subset of EA domains. For example, SOA is not concerned with the development of business architecture. Instead, it uses the outcome of business processes and other business architecture artefacts, such as component business modelling as input to identify business services. In contrast, EA is concerned with the development of business architecture, including business processes and component business modelling among others. Similarly, from an application architecture point of view, SOA is concerned with the modelling and development of services and the components that realize them, while EA architecture deals not only with SOA-specific artefacts, but with other components, packages, and systems for the whole enterprise. When analyzing the technology architecture, the SOA enterprise service bus is just one of many integration mechanisms an EA may

FIGURE 5.1
Enterprise Architecture

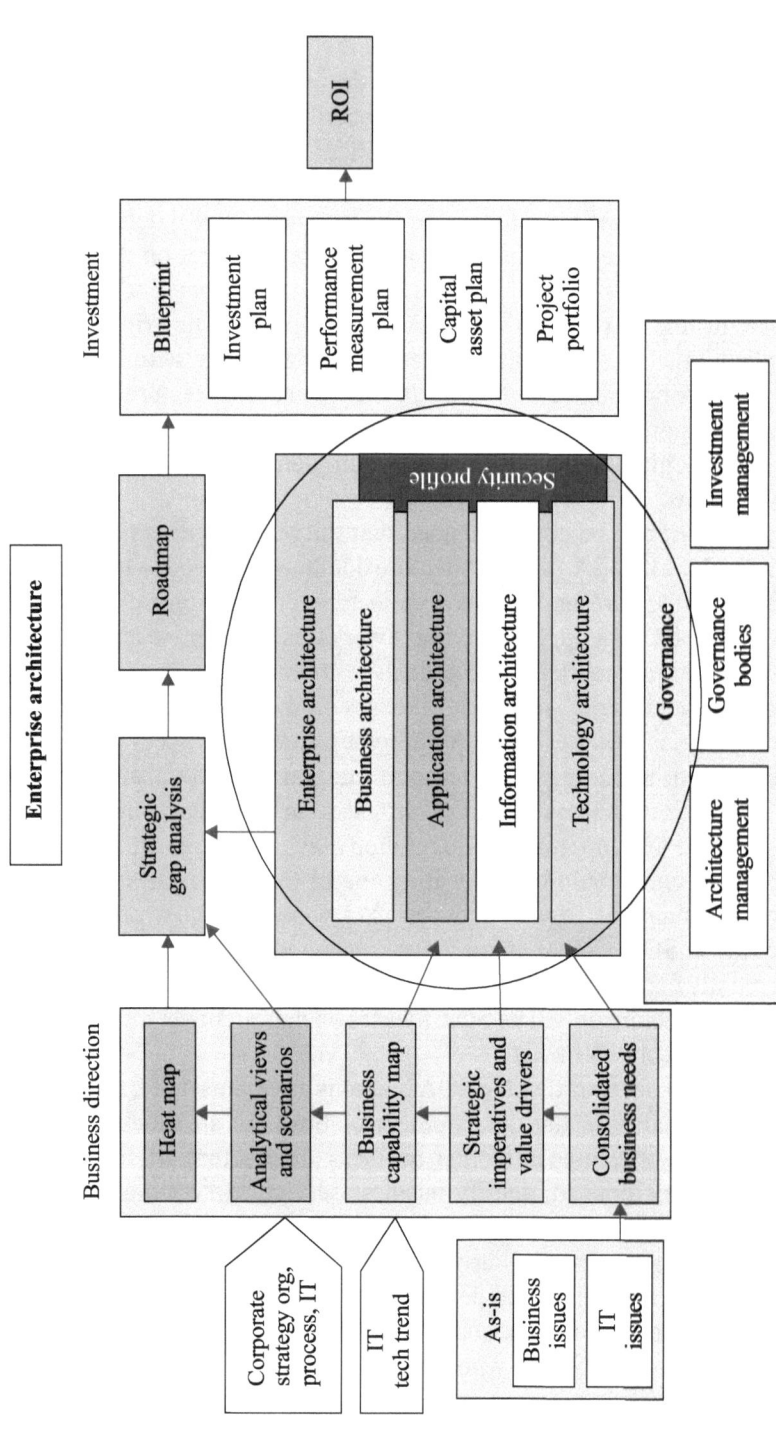

need to address. It should also be noted that SOA does not address content management archi-tecture, while EA does. Another area of overlap is security and service management. In fact, SOA security is a special case of the total security that EA must specify, and SOA service man-agement and monitoring is a subset of systems management that EA must deal with.

Ibrahim and Long (2007) specified SOA and EA domains. SOA and EA share many simi-larities like sharing of address similar architectural domains. Both are intended to closely align IT with business. Both require similar strategies and planning activities. While the focus of the EA architecture domains is on the macro level, the SOA architecture domains work on a micro level. EA focuses on defining business components, while SOA focuses on business services. A service-oriented architecture provides a standardized, flexible approach to enterprise busi-ness process integration and role-based access to process activities, information (including BI), business transactions and collaboration tools. An SOA is used to separate processes from appli-cations and to create on-demand and event driven information, application, and collaborative services that can be invoked in an industry standard way. These services can then be rapidly assembled into composite applications associated with individual process activities in an industry standard way.

An SOA is effectively a blueprint for integrating all aspects of enterprise computing to sup-port business integration. It, therefore, should support several types of services including:

- Business process services (whole processes published as services).
- Operational application services.
- BI services.
- Content (documents, web content, digital media) services.
- Collaboration (e-mail, web chat, instant messaging, net conference rooms, calendar, etc.) services.
- Data integration services.
- Common services (e.g., security, search, business rules).

There are many reasons why companies are investing in SOA initiatives at present. The obvious one is that SOA reduces operational costs and increases efficiency, improves effectiveness, and increases collaboration. Improving efficiency is typically achieved by standardizing common business processes that have been separated from applications and then integrating and automating them by mapping process activities to applications within the enterprise and across businesses. An SOA can be used to improve effectiveness by leveraging BI everywhere in order to guide employees during every performed activity so that everyone contributes to strategic objectives and executes on a common business strategy (Allen, 2006). It is also possible to monitor events to automatically detect/predict problems and opportunities for rapid response and business (re-)optimization. Improving collaboration allows employees, partners, customers, and suppliers with access to team workspaces where they can share information and services. With collaboration services, people can also be located rapidly and communication can be in real time.

SERVICE-ORIENTED ENTERPRISES

SOEs are not just about technology or a framework for building systems. Technology is important and necessary (Khoshafian, 2007). To fully realize the potential of SO, enterprises need to develop the corporate culture of service. SOEs leverage technology to service and to serve many communities. It is this culture of serving and focusing on the needs of others that will best leverage the infrastructures of SO. Therefore, the SOE is a new standards-based integration paradigm (Erl, 2004). It is a new way of building enterprises that are extended, virtual, real-time, and resilient. It is a new way of thinking about applications, partnerships, and outsourcing. SOEs provide a framework that narrows the chasm between IT and business owners. Finally, the elusive business–technical rapprochement becomes a reality under the umbrella of a service culture.

SOEs are a new approach in professional dealings—in business. Each party or participant in SO sees herself as a service provider as well as a service consumer, in an increasingly well-connected global economy. Actually there is nothing new here. Businesses have been serving their clientele (well, at least claiming to do so) since time immemorial. But SO is different in two essential ways. First, culturally, organizations are realizing that best productivity could be achieved if they focus on serving the needs of the parties with whom they interact and serve: their customers, yes, but also their employees, trading partners, shareholders, government, and communities. This is often characterized as servant leadership, and without this essential cultural shift much of what goes under the banner of SO is hollow. The cultural shift to focus on and to serve the various target communities of the SOE helps the enterprise realize the full potential of the underlying service-oriented infrastructures and technologies. The second change, of course, is the emergence of SO as a new enabling technological trend. Building primarily on the success of the Internet as well as on a much better understanding of how business policies and processes could be automated, today, we are witnessing the emergence of robust service-oriented platforms. These platforms are reflected in three essential layers: an enterprise performance layer (also called business performance management and corporate performance management), a business process management layer, and the underlying service oriented architecture infrastructure.

Haentjes et al. (2007) provided the complete SOA for enterprises. The enterprise SOA blueprint provided by them shows how these building blocks facilitate innovation, enable business network transformation, and achieve operational excellence in an cost efficient way. Any given enterprise-level scenario does not need to use all of the capabilities that reside in these building blocks; different scenarios will use different capabilities and the facilitating platform will enable the incremental adoption of more capabilities to ensure flexibility and innovation.

SO provides the ability to loosely couple applications, trading partners, and organizations and to invoke them via service calls. The coupling is often achieved through discovery. Furthermore, independent services can be composed in processes to provide even greater value than the sum of component services. SO enables internal applications as well as external trading partners to participate in straight-through processing involving internal as well as partner procedures, policies, and applications.

The enterprise service bus is a key layer used in the service discovery, management, and request–response brokering. Business process management extends and leverages the service bus. A process provides the information as well as controls sequencing between services. Processes also involve human participants. More importantly, processes include simple as well as complex decision-making. Business rules guide and control the processes.

To guarantee the required quality of service (e.g., performance, reliability, security, compliance), enterprises need to enact service level agreements, which involve response-time constraints. But they can also involve much more complex constraints (e.g., handling exceptions or faults) on the exchanges between the internal applications or trading partners.

Each of the terms in this very basic definition of SO contributes to the productivity and agility of the SOE. In other words, SOEs use SO throughout their enterprise architectures. This helps the organization produce and consume services through a uniform paradigm.

SERVICE-ORIENTED BUSINESS INTELLIGENCE (SoBI)

Service-oriented Business Intelligence (SoBI) is the synergy of BI and SO paradigms and describes patterns and architecture to accomplish this synergy by providing a best practice implementation framework, the ability to integrate at the most appropriate architectural level, the data modelling of a BI project within the SO strategy of leaving the source systems in place, and a common implementation for data transformations and data logic: data to data, data to service, service to data, and service to service. SO is a means of building distributed applications; at its most abstract, SO views everything as a service provider: from applications, to companies, to devices. The service providers expose capabilities through interfaces. These interfaces define the contract between the caller of the service and the service itself (Gordon et al., 2006). The consumer of a service does not care how the service is implemented, only what the service does and how to invoke the service. The services themselves are the building blocks of service-oriented applications. Services encapsulate the fundamental aspects of SO, namely, the separation between interface and implementation. SO is essential to delivering the business agility and IT flexibility promised by web services. These benefits are delivered not just by viewing service architecture from a technology perspective or by adopting web service protocols, but also by requiring the creation of a service-oriented environment that is based on specific key principles.

BI has been around for years; its practices are well established, and people are comfortable with the concepts involved in delivering a BI solution. To many, BI is simply the presentation of information in a timely manner through a sophisticated client interface. To those involved with the delivery of BI solutions, this aspect of the overall BI solution is the tip of the iceberg. Under the covers is a huge exercise in data quality improvement and data integration among disparate corporate applications and systems and the consolidation of that data in a data warehouse. The integration of data is predominantly the biggest cost on a BI project.

SO is best suited to application-to-application integration and well suited to low-volume, high-frequency events, while BI is best suited for data-to-data integration and able to handle large data volumes. SO provides an operational platform, tightly defines data formats and structures, and encapsulates and abstracts functionality. BI provides a combined model of the enterprise data and provides foundation for business decisions and the ability to ask any question of the data. SO supports reuse of enterprise components and allow agile change in business processes.

Until recently, as described by Sean Gordon et al. (2006) SO has had little or no part to play in the world of BI, primarily because the SO approach to data integration seemed laborious and overly complex to a community used to moving data of any volume around by connecting directly to the source system at database level. In BI, data integration is accomplished through the extract, transform, load (ETL) process, which is the keystone of every BI solution, and BI solutions tend to look for the most direct and efficient way of accomplishing it. Enterprise application integration (EAI), like BI, has been around for many years. It is a common problem encountered within an enterprise where systems have been introduced or grown in an organic manner. EAI itself can be defined as the sharing of both process and data between applications within the enterprise. Specifically, when the term EAI is used, it refers to the integration of systems within the enterprise, e.g., application, data, and process integration.

Michael Horne and Rob Grigg (2005) discussed various issues on data and services in SoBI. They explored various issues on integration of systems. Application-to-application integration refers to the exchange of data and services between applications within the enterprise. Notably, this form of integration is often between applications that reside on different technology platforms, based on differing architectures. EAI is often difficult, and typically it requires the connectivity between heterogeneous technology platforms, involves complex business rules and processes, involves long-running business processes where logical units of work may span days or weeks as they move through different processes within the organization, and is generally driven by the need to extend or enhance an existing automated business and process or introduces an entirely new automated business process.

BI systems need to deliver the right information to the right consumers at the right time. Since the source information can potentially come from many different and non-integrated sources, data has to be processed before it is effectively delivered to the end user. There are many data flows existing in any BI system.

In most deployed BI environments, multiple BI systems—each with their tools, processes, and data architectures—can be found across multiple business units and divisions of the enterprise. These non-integrated BI systems (whether built in-house or acquired) result in high component redundancy, inconsistent knowledge information, proprietary, non-open standard integration interfaces, and highly maintained point-to-point integration that ultimately increase the cost of development and prevent the achievement of a single version of truth across the organization. For BI to deliver on its promises of real time, zero latency information delivery and closed loop processing, technologies and techniques have emerged or have been introduced. One such evolution is the transformation of traditional BI architectures into service-oriented, component-based ones. Moving from our belief that SOA (Erl, 2004) technology has great potential for delivering enhanced BI, we present an approach to architecting BI systems using a service-oriented approach.

Although SOAs and BI architectures have evolved separately and include technologies and disciplines specific to their own individual architectural aims, many of the technologies that they utilize overlap. There is also a clear mapping between the concepts used, with each able to view the other in their own terms.

From a BI perspective, it is possible to view an SO application as a collection of data sources and event sources. There are two primary modes in which a service can operate as a data source in a BI context: service as the provider of data upon request and service as the publisher of events that are of interest. In both scenarios, the message sizes are small. The solution for large-scale data transfer and transformation will still be through the normal data warehouse import techniques such as ETL. Such physically large messages are not the normal domain of SO. From the SO viewpoint, BI can be seen as a collection of services. From an SO perspective, a data source can readily be exposed as a service with the introduction of a simple façade layer that receives the service request from the service bus and calls the appropriate query.

The SoBI architecture makes BI data in the data warehouse available as a service to other applications within the architecture. This availability gives applications a clean way of accessing consolidated data to support the requirements of BI. In this way, BI architecture becomes an integrated component of SO application architecture. It should be noted that there will be occasions when the type of data that is required from the system is purely of a BI nature, such as large-scale data export. In these scenarios the service interface approach will not be suitable.

Azvine et al. (2007b) discuss the issues and problems of current BI systems and then outlines our vision of future real-time BI. In large organizations, IT departments have had to gather information from multiple databases (heterogeneous databases) such as those in accounting programmes and ERP applications and normalize it into a single view in a time-consuming, frequently manual process.

When it comes to extensive data analysis, BI is used to produce the information that is necessary to decide and take appropriate actions. Addressing this, real-time decision support gained great attention. Concepts such as active warehousing, real-time analytics (Brobst and Ballinger, 2000; Raden, 2003), and real-time warehousing became hot topics of interest to firms. Real-time decisions support provides suggestions of how to speed up the flow of information in order to achieve competitive advantage.

From a BI perspective, a service can readily be exposed as a data source with the introduction of a simple façade layer that provides a mapping between the BI interface and the interface exposed by the service. The façade then transforms the results of the call from the data schema used on the service bus to the data format expected by the BI platform and returns the results to the caller. Some services expose information through events that are published when an interesting change occurs in the service. Other services and applications within the organization can subscribe to the events published by services. Integrating event-publishing services into a BI platform is achieved through the use of an agent that collates the subscribed events and periodically transfers them in bulk to the BI platform.

One of the challenges in the development of SoBI was to find an approach that leveraged the core strengths of each architecture and identified the area where the integration caused challenges. Some of the main challenges inherent in implementing BI in an SO manner will be looked at. These challenges generally arise because of the specific requirements that each architecture was developed to address.

Nguyen et al. (2005) proposed an approach to real time BI based on SOA. As organizations seek to incorporate intelligence into business operations, a robust infrastructure is necessary to meet mission-critical requirements for high scalability, availability, and performance (Nguyen et al., 2005). Azvine et al. (2007a) proposed a real-time BI architecture for an adaptive enterprise. BI solutions are tightly coupled to the data sources that feed the data warehouse and to the applications that use it. BI has evolved from a batch-centric environment where ETL is used as the means to directly consume and consolidate large amounts of source system data on a known schedule for population of the data warehouse.

Pradipa Kabhari (2005) discussed various SOA trends with respect to BI. SO is the architectural approach for application integration where as BI is the single version of the truth for BI data. SO will provide application to application integration by providing some event feed to the data warehouse; SO also describes the services provided and the messages passed; BI will provide an open access to data services, support ad hoc analysis, and support management reposting besides consolidating data. One should note that BI and SO will not become a dumping ground for all data, will not be used by every instance, and replace data import interfaces; both will not be the default data source to other applications. For example, in a BI environment that is interested in the analysis of health and safety incidents, SoBI would allow factual detail of each incident to be moved to the data warehouse, i.e., the fact that an incident happened, where it happened, and the classification of that incident, that would allow all appropriate aggregation and analysis to be performed as expected of the BI platform.

Where SoBI wins is that it provides a means to still access the transactional detail in the system of record, e.g., the free-format text that accompanies the incident, which describes the circumstances surrounding the event in detail (Gordon et al., 2006). This access is commonly referred to as 'drill through' or 'drill to detail' in BI, and to accomplish it all data relevant to the requirement is traditionally moved into the data warehouse. In fact, this may not be allowed (such as for data protection reasons) or preferred (it increases the ETL burden and the storage requirements of the data warehouse to hold data, which, by definition, is operational in nature), and it has the potential to add additional pressure on the BI platform by becoming the de facto source for all incident data even though it is never up to date.

The combination of the enablement of real-enough-time BI and the ability to leave operational data in place gives us the opportunity to build a rich service around the SoBI framework that would not be possible if working within only one of the component architectures. Consider a system detecting retail fraud. In BI we have the tools to build an analytical engine capable of mining the potentially huge amounts of transactional data for patterns resulting in a list of suspicious credit cards. The adoption of SO principles allows us to offer a service providing the details of credit cards in use in our store as they are swiped. The SoBI architecture allows this service to be consumed by the BI component of the platform and analyze it against the known list of suspicious cards, and, therefore, to respond immediately should a potentially suspicious transaction be detected.

IMPLICATIONS

In today's competitive global markets, firms are under constant pressure to achieve high performance through improved productivity, faster time to market, greater flexibility, and a more effective workforce. Achieving these goals requires them to use state-of-the-art SoBI solutions posing huge challenges for chief executives to deliver simpler, more flexible systems at a lower cost of ownership. This must be accomplished despite the fact that corporate information systems are heterogeneous, with multiple products across multiple platforms.

SOA is a services-based approach for designing and building flexible IT solutions, easily combining legacy and new technologies. It enables business process components to be assembled and orchestrated efficiently and rapidly, giving businesses the agility to respond to changing business conditions, and delivering distinctive business services. SoBI attempts to solve problems of integration in an enterprise of disparate systems. It attempts to provide a common data transformation mechanism for operational and management information both.

An SOA enabled BI can answer query with the use of business rules such as, 'list those items if this specific customer service call has been processed by the service center in due time and list the precise logic of what "in due time" means in this context'.

Because of SoBI, more and more end-users will demand access to relevant BI information and flexible BI tools in the future. Business systems and non-enterprise data sources will be refined with orderliness among all information sources to meet constantly growing needs to support all kinds of offered services, including SoBI services.

By improved processes of SoBI, managers can gain new insights about customers, suppliers, and the market, e.g., explain and discover long-term methods for strategic purposes like fusions or which products are to be provided in ten years. SoBI also accomplishes daily decision support.

CONCLUSIONS

One question everybody would like to know the answer is will technologies, solutions, and companies based on SO lead to the next bubble? It is not difficult to remember how bubbles occurred during the dot-com era. One may ask that will emerge SOEs result in another bubble? Perhaps it may happen. Some would argue that SOAs have not delivered at least so far. But equating SOEs with SOAs especially web services is an exception.

One should clearly understand that SO is best suited to application-to-application integration and well suited to low-volume, high-frequency events, while BI is best suited for data-to-data integration and is able to handle large data volumes. In this chapter SO is discussed and how SO provides an operational platform. It is also explained how BI provides a combined model of the enterprise data and provides foundation for business decisions and the ability to ask any question of the data.

REFERENCES

Adelman, Sid, Moss Larissa, and Barbusinski Les. 2002. 'I Found Several Definitions of BI', *DM Review*. Available online at http://www.dmreview.com/article_sub.cfm?articleId=5700 (accessed on 17 August 2002).

Allen, Paul. 2006 *Service Orientation: Winning Strategies and Best Practices*. Cambridge, UK: Cambridge University Press.

Azvine, B., Z. Cui, D.D. Nauck, and B. Majeed. 2007a. 'Real Time Business Intelligence for the Adaptive Enterprise', The 8th IEEE International Conference on and Enterprise Computing, E-Commerce, and E-Services, San Francisco, USA, 26–29 June.

Azvine, B., Z. Cui, B. Majeed, and M. Spott. 2007b. 'Operational Risk Management with Real-time Business Intelligence', *BT Technology Journal*, 25(1): 154–67.

Berson, Alex and Stephen Smith. 2001. *Data Warehousing, Data Mining, and OLAP*. New York: McGraw Hill International Edition.

Berson, Alex, Stephen Smith, and Kurt Thearling. 2002. *Building Data Mining Applications for CRM*. New York: Tata McGraw Hill.

Brobst, S. and C. Ballinger. 2000. 'Active Data Warehousing', White paper, NCR Corporation, EB–1327. Available online at http://strattech.com/pubs.htm (accessed in January 2009).

D'Aveni, R.M. 1994. *Hyper Competition*. New York: The Free Press.

Dijksterhuis, M.S., F.A.J. Van den Bosch, and H.W. Volberda. 1999. 'Where do New Organizational Forms Come From? Management Logics as a Source of Co-evolution', *Organization Science*, 105: 569–82.

Erl, T. 2004. *Service-Oriented Architecture: A Field Guide to Integrating XML and Web Services*. Prentice-Hall Publishers.

Evans, Philip and Thomas S. Wurster. 2000. *Blown to Bits*. Boston: Harvard Business School Press.

Gangadharan, G.R. and N. Swamy Sundaravalli. 2004. 'Business Intelligence Systems: Design and Implementation Strategies', Proceedings of 26th International Conference on Information Technology Interfaces, Cavtat, Croatia.

Gordon, S., Horne M. Grigg, and S. Thurman. 2006. 'Service-Oriented Business Intelligence', *The Microsoft Architect Journal*. Available online at http://msdn.microsoft.com/en-us/library/bb245659.aspx (accessed in April 2007).

Haentjes, Volker, Hans-Joachim Odlozinski, and Volker Stiehl. 2007. 'Enterprise SOA: An Introduction from Technology Point of View', SAP Technical Article. Available online at https://www.sdn.sap.com/irj/sdn/go/portal/prtroot/docs/library/uuid/70cb113e-a3d8-2a10-c2ad-e2888166e7cd (accessed on 15 April 2007).

Hall, Curt. 1999. 'Data Warehousing for Business Intelligence'. Available online at http://www.cutter.com/itreports/RP68E.pdf (accessed on 20 March 1999).

Hammond, M. and B. Liautand. 2001. *E-Business Intelligence, Turning Information into Knowledge into Profit*. New York: McGraw-Hill.

Horne, Michael and Rob Grigg. 2005. 'Service Oriented Business Intelligence SoBI'. Available online at www.microsoft.com (accessed on 15 June 2007).

Ibrahim, Mamdouh and Gil Long. 2007. 'Service-Oriented Architecture and Enterprise Architecture, Part 1: A Framework for Understanding how SOA and Enterprise Architecture Work Together', IBM SOA report. http://www-306.ibm.com/software/solutions/soa/ (accessed on 23 April 2008).

Kabhari, Pradipa. 2005. 'SOA Trends: Service Oriented Business Intelligence'. Available online at http://www.technologyexecutivesclub.com /Articles/webservices/silvertrainsoatrends.php (accessed on 15 April 2007).

Khoshafian, Setrag. 2007 'Service Oriented Enterprises'. Available online at www.auerbach-publications.com (accessed on 15 April 2007).

Malhotra, Y. 2000. 'Information Management to Knowledge Management: Beyond "Hi-Tech Hidebound" Systems', in T.K. Srikantaiah and M.E.D. Koenig (eds), *Knowledge Management*. New Jersey: Medford.

Moss, Larissa T. and Shaku Atre. 2003. *Business Intelligence Roadmap: The Complete Project Lifecycle for Decision Support Applications*. Boston: Addison Wesley Longman.

Nguyen, Tho Manh, Josef Schiefer, and A. Min Tjoa. 2005. 'Data Warehouse Design 2: Sense & Response Service Architecture (SARESA): An Approach towards a Real-time Business Intelligence Solution and its Use for a Fraud Detection Application', Proceedings of the 8th ACM international workshop on Data warehousing and OLAP, Bremen, Germany, 4–5 November.

Nicholls, C. 2006. 'BI 2.0—How Real Time Business Intelligence is Irrevocably Changing the Way that we do Business—In Search Insight'. Available online at www.seewhy.com (accessed on 14 August 2006).

Raden, N. 2003. 'Exploring the Business Imperative of Real-Time Analytics', Teradata white paper. Available online at http://www.hiredbrains.com/teradata.pdf (accessed in January 2009).

Rogalski, Shari and Fisher Dan. 2003. 'Business Intelligence: 360" Insight: Insight: A Powerful Combination of Capabilities', DM Review. Available online at http://www.dmreview.com/toc.cfm?issueid=350 (accessed on 23 February).

White, C. 2006. 'Business Intelligence Network—The Vision for BI and Beyond'. Available online at from www.b-eye-network (accessed on 23 September 2007).

6

Enterprise Tomography: An Efficient Application Lifecycle Management Approach Supporting Semi-automatic Localization, Delta-tracking, and Visualization of Integration Ontologies in VLBAs

JORGE MARX GÓMEZ
University Oldenburg
Ammerländer Heerstr. 114-118, 26129 Oldenburg, Germany
E-mail: jorge.marx.gomez@uni-oldenburg.de

JAN AALMINK
University Oldenburg,
Ammerländer Heerstr. 114-118, 26129 Oldenburg, Germany
E-mail: jan.aalmink@sap.com

INTRODUCTION

In Enterprise Software Industry, development and maintenance of Very Large Business Applications (VLBAs) and Enterprise Platforms are getting more and more complex. Large and distributed teams are involved, teams are changing, and division of labour proceeds. Enterprise Systems Engineering requires efficient development and maintenance means for software and business data evaluation.

Without knowing the semantic integration of enterprise software it is inherently difficult to control and orchestrate large scaled development, maintenance, and configuration processes. Domain-specific enterprise integration knowledge, coded in enterprise software, is normally not instantaneously available for involved teams. Lack of precise knowledge of integration concepts in development and maintenance phases results in erroneous software, is risky, and might have negative business impact for both, the software manufacturer and the consumer.

In this chapter a semi-automatic environment for Application Lifecycle Management of VLBAs and Enterprise Platforms based on enhanced standard scientific algorithms is outlined. In accordance with medicine diagnostics, the metaphor Enterprise Tomography is used for scanning, indexing, identifying, visualization, and delta visualization of enterprise integration knowledge containing in enterprise software. Based on the results of the Enterprise Tomograph the operating teams are in the position to make decisions efficiently and have a reliable foundation for incremental steps of the development and maintenance lifecycle.

The Enterprise Tomograph represents a central ecosystem for sharing domain specific integration knowledge across the development teams. Because of sharing and socializing of integration knowledge across the operating teams, the Enterprise Tomography approach can be incorporated in the Enterprise 2.0 initiative.

Figure 6.1 outlines the Enterprise Tomography approach in the context of cross-organizational VLBAs and Cloud Computing. The Enterprie Tomograph crawler extracts integration ontology forests from VLBAs, Enterprise Platforms, and databases. In-memory indices and delta indices are created in a Cloud. Via search user interface (UI) a full domain-specific search is possible.

FIGURE 6.1
Enterprise Tomography for Cross-organizational VLBAs and Enterprise Platforms

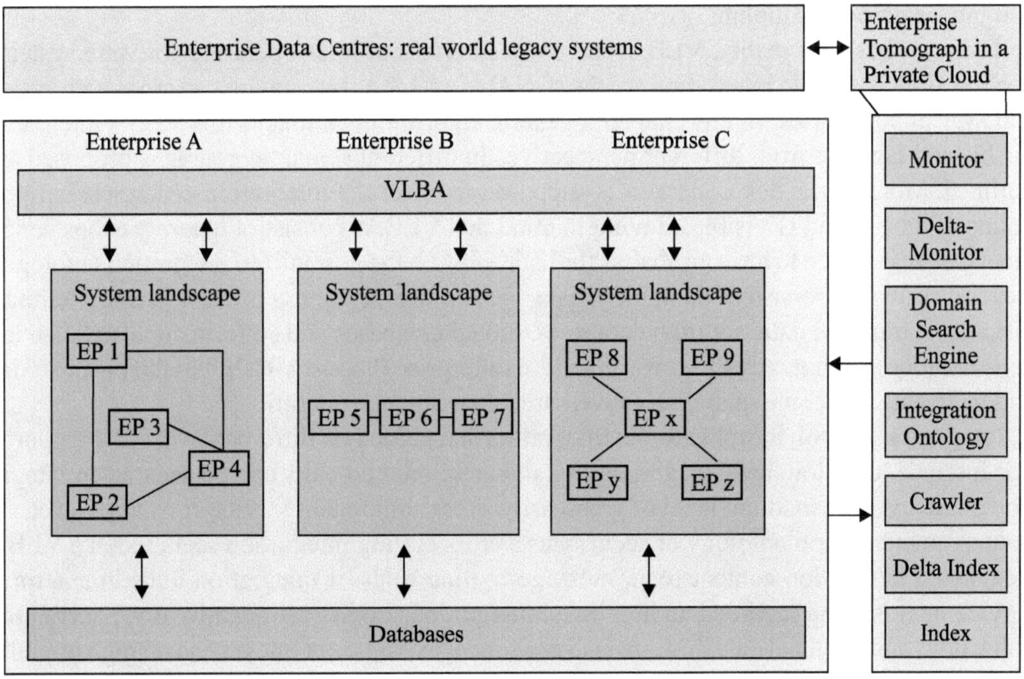

Source: Authors.
Note: EP: Enterprise Platform.

In the Delta Monitor changes of integration concepts can be traced. In this scenario the algorithms of the Enterprise Tomograph have to comply with the interfaces exposed by the cloud provider. With several MapReduce instances in a sequence combined with a distributed file system it is possible to process large datasets. The cloud provider divides the workload (Map phase) and executes the work items on a dynamic allocated resource pool. The results are postprocessed (Reduce phase). Index data is organized on a distributed file system. With a Search UI (Web Interface) the tomograms are ubiquitous available for diagnostic purposes.

In the research area where VLBA is located within business informatics, Application Lifecycle Management is the centre of attention (Grabski et al., 2007). A real life VLBA, in dimension time, is in a permanent flux: gradual development to meet business requirements; continuous improvements to exploit innovation; continuous maintenance to keep consistent business processing; horizontal connection of software systems to scale data processing and to extend business scope; recombination of loosely coupled services to exploit new business functionality; re-configuration and personalization; data evolution resulting from service calls; and business transactions and background processing, just to name a few.

VLBAs are not usually built from scratch and deployed in an immutable stadium. VLBAs are not monomorphic. Some of the characteristics of VLBAs are as follows: complexity, a long lifecycle, huge continuous development and maintenance efforts, large user groups, and inter- and intra-enterprise coupling.

Today, in business reality, VLBAs are conglomerates of inter-operating software systems. Technical and semantic integration are the 'DNA' of a VLBA. Integration can cross both system and system boundaries. In this chapter a generic algorithm that makes this VLBA integration visible and tangible from different perspectives in different semantic genres is proposed and outlined. Moreover, a delta operator is supposed to make the integration difference between points of time t0 and t1 visible. Having in mind that VLBAs consist of heterogeneous constituents, there is a need to have an abstract holistic view on the normalized integration ontologies. Beyond software, persistent data, meta data, system logs, business process activity journals, virtual and transient data, solution databases, model databases and so forth are also taken into consideration. So, not only the software of the Enterprise Platform itself, but the business data and meta data and contextual data as well are taken into consideration.

Integration is a polymorphic topic. Integration is regarded on different levels of granularity. For instance, on a low level of granularity, dynamic method calls can be seen as an integration ontology. On a medium level of granularity, cross component service consumption can be seen as an integration ontology or security as a cross cutting integration scattered in a VLBA. Registered integration content (e.g., message routing rules of integration hubs in enterprise service bus) is to be regarded as high level integration. Logistical quantity flow, accounting value flow, and financial data flow are also prominent examples of integration on high granularity level. Workflow, Webflow, and Process Integration can be regarded as integration on high granularity level as well.

RESEARCH FINDINGS

ENTERPRISE TOMOGRAPHY IN THE CONTEXT OF ENTERPRISE SYSTEMS ENGINEERING

Developer teams and maintenance teams have different perspectives on VLBAs in their daily work. Developers are primarily assembly focused (bottom up), whereas maintainers have the inverted the top down view on a VLBA: Maintainers are thinking rather in error symptoms and ontologies provoking the error symptoms (Panchenko, 2007; Tiun et al., 2001). For example, they need to find out for a given (inconsistent) production order id, the involved coding and meta data, the header and items in the persistency layer, material consumption, confirmation items, models, relevant documentation, etc. In this example integration is regarded as a semantic join between those concepts. It is valuable information to see the delta of this semantic join between points of time t0 and t1. So one can track the evolution of the integration of a VLBA. A comparison of VLBAs (e.g., modified code clones) will be possible with our algorithm as well. So it might be very interesting to evaluate the software Add-On between two releases or the delta in the business data.

In accordance to tomography in medical diagnostics, a similar metaphor is utilized: the Enterprise Tomograph. It is supposed to diagnose integration ontologies of a complex VLBA, perform indexing of all scanned information, and provide time efficient access to the assembled scanned data from different semantic perspectives. Especially the integration ontology delta is supposed to be made available for large maintenance and service teams. Based on this information, maintenance teams can locate real error symptoms in a VLBA more easily. They are also in a better position to assess the consequences of any change in the VLBA software and therefore mitigate the risk of inconsistent data processing.

In the scope of this chapter it is assumed that in an enterprise software factory the construction procedure of a VLBA is very similar to that of the building industry. The first step is requirement specification, architecture modelling, review and acceptance, construction, and, finally, continuous maintenance. The construction procedure in both industries is quite similar: If architecture models are in place, the construction procedure starts bottom up—beginning from the foundation and ending in the construction of the roof, not vice versa.

Traditional top down model-driven approaches of Software Engineering do not necessarily meet the needs of service and maintenance teams in the context of VLBAs adequately. Models are important, but usually those models are not linked to the VLBA software. To bridge this technical gap, the Enterprise Tomograph comes into place with multiple phase iteration. The Enterprise Tomograph knows three phases. The first phase in concerned with scanning of the VLBA, the intermediate phase constructs and prepares indices for efficient access, and the third phase provides access to integration data.

During the time-consuming scanning procedure (parallel crawling of VLBA), the Enterprise Tomograph orchestrates concept mining algorithms. The mining algorithms extract models, software fragments, links of software fragments, business objects, technical objects, meta data, solution databases, and transforms those to standard ontology representations that are grammar compliant (Abels et al., 2005). The resulting ontology is the integration knowledge representation. A subset of the ontology representation standards into is taken into consideration: The concept mining algorithms are supposed to map the integration ontology to rooted unordered labelled trees. The set of rooted unordered labelled trees are to be indexed and stored in PAT Arrays (PAT Array as a space efficient and access optimized data structure of Patricia Tries and suffix trees; PAT Arrays are well known in genetic engineering and information retrieval).

One theme of the Enterprise Tomograph will be the Enterprise Introspector. It generically calculates the footprint of a business transaction execution in the persistency layer, the footprint of a service call or the footprint of a message choreography process instance between t0 and t1, or the delta between two database schema in a specific domain area. The basis algorithm of the Enterprise Tomograph is a modified DC3-algorithm (difference cover modulo 3 known in information retrieval) (Dementiev, 2006; Kärkkäinen et al., 2006). It constructs PAT Arrays and stores textual suffixes in a compressed manner. The set of resulting PAT Arrays are organized in a genre-layered tenancy concept allowing independent user groups working on the global index and updating it in a concurrent polychronic way. A quasi algebra will be defined on the set of PAT Arrays: delta operator, plus operator, pseudo inverse operator.

For instance the plus operator merges two indices (PAT Arrays) resulting in one encompassing PAT Array. Integration deltas are determined by modified tree distance algorithms (Lu et al., 2001) and displayed in a structured textual manner. Typically, integration concepts are best known by individual developers and maintainers of the VLBA community. They may want to register additional concept mining algorithms to the integration ecosystem of the Enterprise Tomograph. In this way the integration knowledge of a few integration experts can be shared across the community. The Enterprise Tomograph provides a domain-specific search UI and displays the integration ontologies. The output can be iteratively refined and may serve as input or workload for the Enterprise Engineer for further processing. For example, refactoring, navigation, semantic tagging, search and replace within integration genres, multiple breakpoints, code and data compare, and undo. The Enterprise Tomograph itself is dedicated for service enabling and can be hosted in a VLBA side-by-side mode. It provides highly efficient logarithmic access to integration concepts of a VLBA in the space time continuum. Enterprise Tomography is a proposed collaborative index-snapshot based and domain-specific approach for efficient incremental development and maintenance of VLBAs in the enterprise software industry.

For deeper understanding Figure 6.2 displays a VLBA in an abstract space-time continuum. A vector in this space represents a dendrogram node index at a point of time. The x-axis represents the instances of the VLBA software and its business data persistency at different points of time. The y-axis enumerates the locations of the VLBA software within the software landscape. The z-axis enumerates the domains of the dendrogram path beginning from root node to leaf node.

FIGURE 6.2
Data Universe in Enterprise Software System

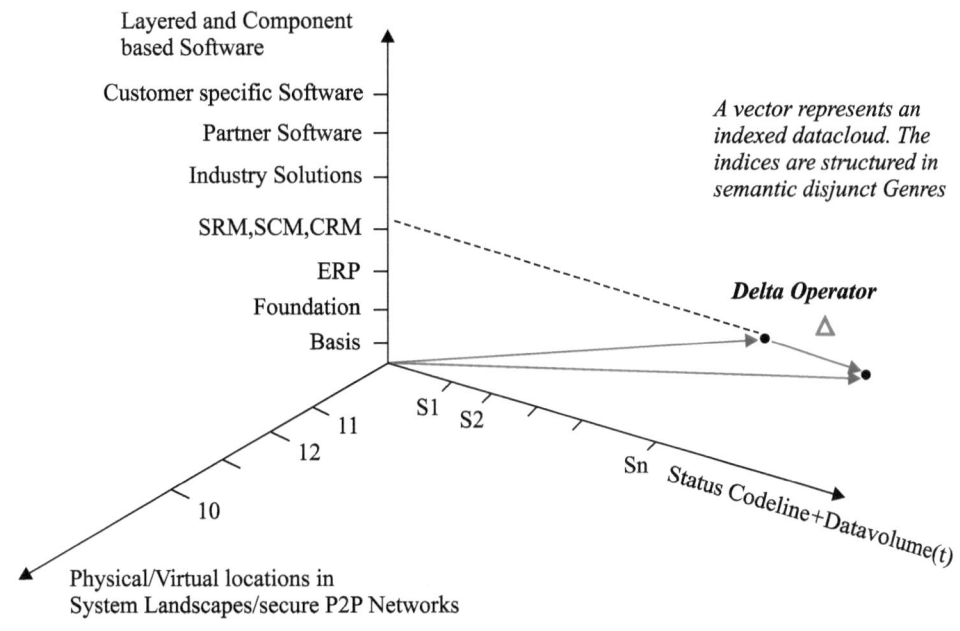

VLBA Data Universe in Space-Time Continuum

A vector represents an indexed datacloud. The indices are structured in semantic disjunct Genres

Source: Authors.

The difference of the two vectors is calculated by the Enterprise Tomograph Delta Operator. In our example we see the difference of SCM (coding + data at different points of time) on a fixed location. Another use case is the comparison of a VLBA at different locations on the y-axis. For example the difference of a VLBA in a development system and in a production system can be determined. This means we compare code clones. In this regard the difference of configuration data in different software locations is valuable information as well.

BUILDING BLOCKS AND DATA FLOW

The Enterprise Tomograph is divided in building blocks for time consuming tasks (data extraction and data organization) and building blocks for time efficient tasks like querying, index merging, and visualization. Figure 6.3 illustrates the anatomy and high level architecture of the Enterprise Tomograph. First of all the VLBA dendrogram is determined. Based on a dendrogram the Enterprise Tomograph starts the VLBA crawling for containing nodes. For each node and for each semantic genre an Ontology Mining Algorithm is executed. It supplies

FIGURE 6.3
Anatomy and High Level Architecture of Enterprise Tomograph

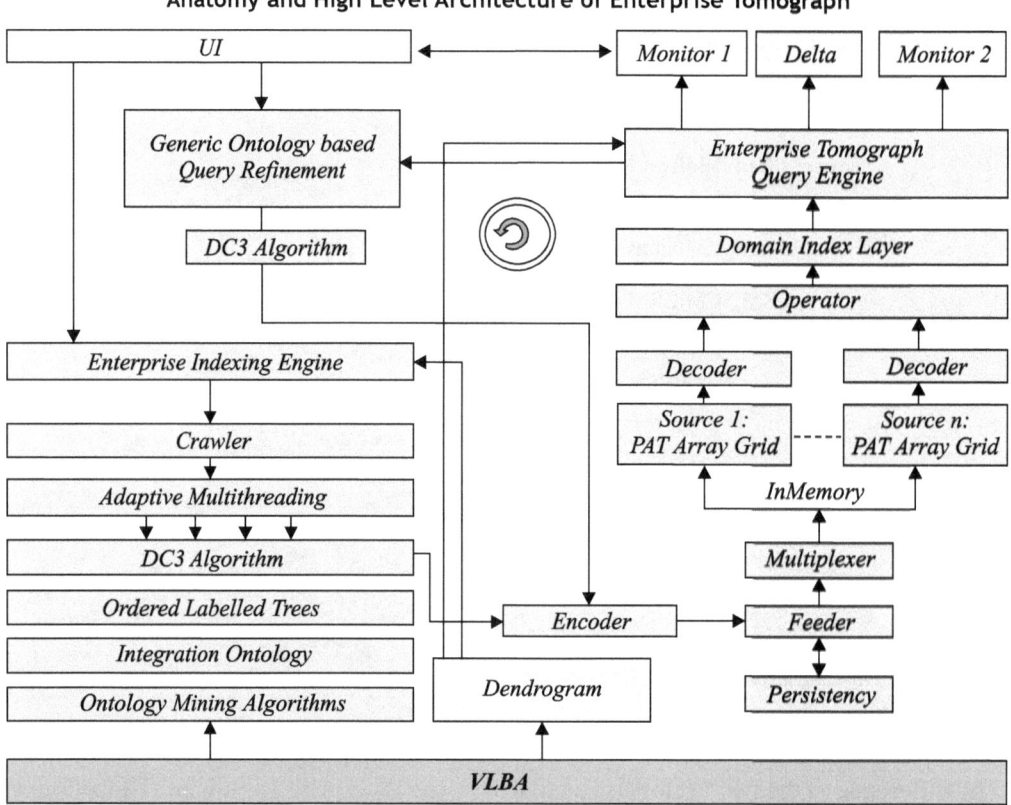

Source: Authors.

rooted unordered labelled trees. Those trees are sequenced. The skewed algorithm DC3 (or difference cover modulo 3) is performed on the sequenced data. The resulting index and the original sequenced data is compressed and in-memory organized in an two-dimensional node-genre grid. Each element of this grid points to a compressed PAT Array and its associated sequenced data. Based on a VLBA dendrogram this procedure can be repeated for different data sources, i.e., for different VLBA locations or for different point of times. Later on the data sources can be compared with the Enterprise Tomograph Delta Operator.

When the developer needs to perform a search in a domain, he selects a dendrogram node. The node sub-tree is exploded and all node-associated PAT Arrays together with sequenced data are decoded. The PAT Arrays are merged. The results are published in the Domain Index Layer. A Query Engine executes queries based on the domain index. Monitor 1 visualizes the search results. Now the developer may want to refine the search results. The search results are sequenced and re-indexed with DC3 Algorithm. A new PAT Array comes into being, is coded, and placed into a data source which is published to the Domain Index Layer again. The Query Engine searches for the new search pattern and the refined results are displayed again in Monitor 1. This search-refinement round-trip is depicted in Figure 6.3 with the circular arrow. The phases of the refinement round-trip can be started asynchronously: While the user is evaluating search results on Monitor 1, the time consuming PAT Array construction via DC3 can be started in parallel as preparation for the next refinement query. In this way the user is not aware of interruptions of subsequent time consuming index construction.

In delta mode of the Enterprise Tomograph, delta calculation is performed on two data sources. As explained later in more detail, domain indices of source 'm' and source 'n' are merged with watermark data. Delta trees of both tree sets are determined. Monitor 1 serves for displaying of delta trees of source m in full version whereas Monitor 2 displays delta trees of source n in full version. The edit scripts of the delta trees are visualized in Delta Monitor.

The main part of the VLBA crawling mechanism is the ontology mining algorithm as outlined in Figure 6.4. Basically for a given dendrogram node and a semantic genre a forest of rooted unordered labelled trees is determined. The VLBA data universe serves as the input. Data extraction takes place with subsequent stemming algorithms for filtering significant information relevant to the integration context. According to rule sets, ontologies are calculated and normalized. The resulting trees are annotated with tree hash values and with tree node hash values as labels.

FIGURE 6.4
Integration Ontology Mining

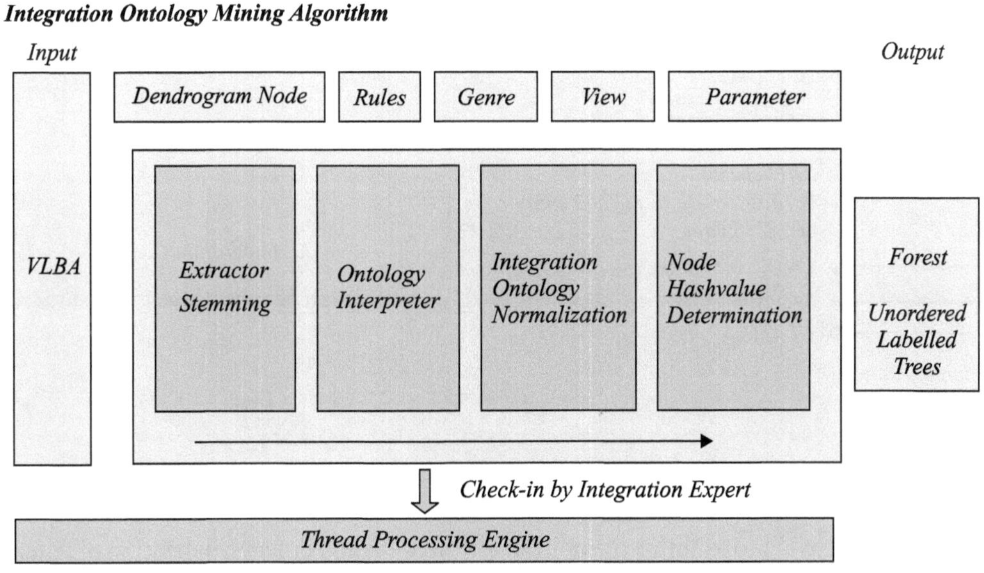

Source: Authors.

The view projects tree nodes to the node set of interest. With parameter the behaviour of the ontology mining algorithm is influenced. Ontology Mining Algorithms reside in a framework and are orchestrated according to the Inversion of Control Design Pattern. Integration ontology mining algorithms can be registered by integration experts.

Rooted unordered labelled trees are used for representing integration concepts. An exemplary integration ontology instance is displayed in Figure 6.5. Here the business object instance relations, coding fragments, data persistency, and application programming interface (APIs) amongst others are highlighted. Trees containing the integration concepts are sequenced to textual data, which is indexed with DC3 algorithm.

FIGURE 6.5
Example of Integration Ontology

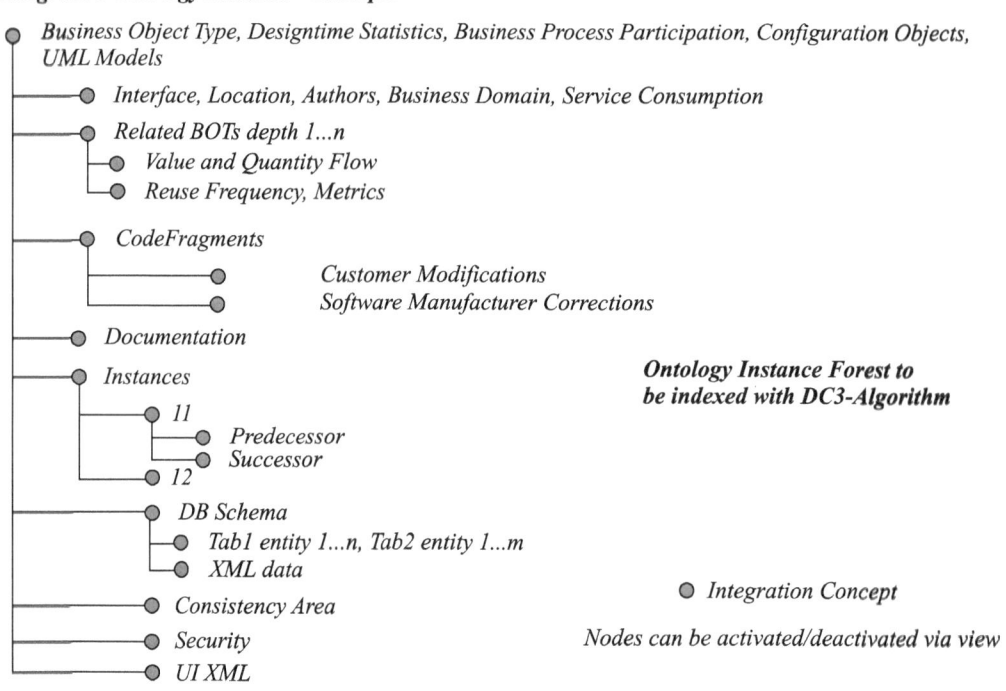

Integration Ontology Instance – Example

Business Object Type, Designtime Statistics, Business Process Participation, Configuration Objects, UML Models

Interface, Location, Authors, Business Domain, Service Consumption
Related BOTs depth 1...n
Value and Quantity Flow
Reuse Frequency, Metrics

CodeFragments

Customer Modifications
Software Manufacturer Corrections

Documentation

Instances
11
Predecessor
Successor
12
DB Schema
Tab1 entity 1...n, Tab2 entity 1...m
XML data
Consistency Area
Security
UI XML

Ontology Instance Forest to be indexed with DC3-Algorithm

● *Integration Concept*

Nodes can be activated/deactivated via view

Source: Authors.

DELTA OPERATOR

In this chapter we want to examine the delta determination and delta visualization of enterprise integration ontologies. Tree distance algorithms generated considerable interest in the research community within the last years. Assuming there are two ontology trees originating from different data sources as depicted in Figure 6.6. Each node is annotated with a label, i.e., with a hash value calculated by the ontology mining algorithm mentioned before. Now the question that arises is which minimal set of operations need to be performed on tree 'F' to retrieve tree 'G'. This minimal set of operations is called edit script. The minimal number of edit operations is called edit distance. The edit script serves as a basis for visual mapping of tree 'F' into tree 'G' in the Enterprise Tomograph Delta Monitor.

FIGURE 6.6
Delta Visualization with Tree Distance Algorithm

Tree Distance Algorithm – Delta Determination of Integration Ontologies

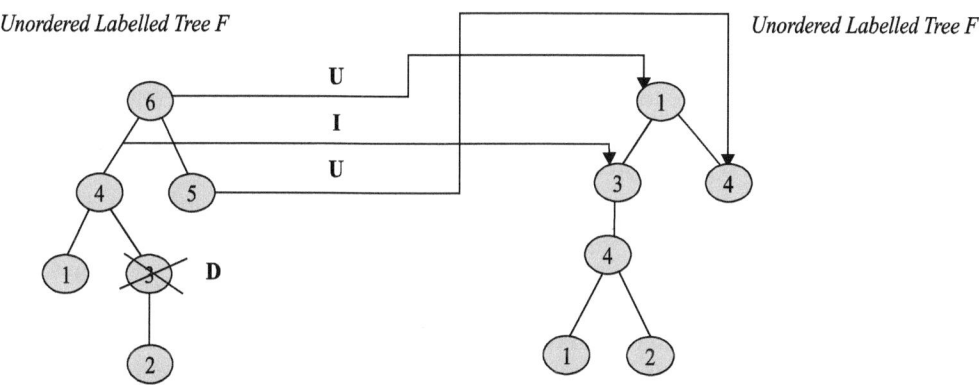

Edit Script(F,G)

- *Delete 3*
- *Insert 3*
- *Update 6 to 1*
- *Update 5 to 4*

Edit Tree Distance(F,G) = min {#operations in Edit Scripts(F,G)}

Distance = #operations => Distance = 4

Edit Script as a visual abstraction of Integration Delta

Source: Authors.

It is worth noting that as of today delta determination for rooted unordered labelled trees is considered as NP-complete. Delta determination of ordered labelled trees is much more efficient. Because of paging in the Delta Monitor, it is not mandatory to determine all tree deltas at a time. Although extremely time consuming procedure for large trees, delta determination for reasonable sized unordered labelled trees can be performed efficiently on demand at visualization time.

In contrast to the original definition of labelled trees (Zhang et al., 1992), we take non-unique labelled trees into consideration. It is assumed that delta determination for unordered non-unique labelled trees is a relaxative or similar problem in comparison to delta determination for unique labelled trees. A proof for this can be made with Simplex Algorithm known in Dynamic Programming (Bille, 2005). This issue is not detailed in this chapter.

In this section the skewed DC3 algorithm for PAT Array construction is being discussed. PAT Array construction means an indirect lexicographical sort of semi-finite suffixes of a given string. In Abouelhoda et al. (2005) it is proven that this construction consumes linear operations. The DC3 Algorithm is a skewed divide and conquer algorithm. A detailed pseudo algorithm and a concrete implementation of DC3 is given in Abouelhoda et al. (2005).

PAT Arrays are space efficient data structures containing indirect hierarchical lexicographic sort order according to Patricia Tries. Extended PAT Arrays accelerates the search procedure. Longest Common Prefix (LCP) can be skipped during search (Abouelhoda et al., 2005). A drawback of the extension is the additional space consumption in PAT Array.

PAT Arrays in the context of Enterprise Tomograph are advantageous because PAT Arrays can be merged in linear time.

A PAT Array is the basis for logarithmic indirect search. Assuming all semi-finite suffixes with prefix equal to searchstring are to be identified. A' points to semi-finite suffixes. A' is divided in two intervals: [left bound ... medium] and [medium ... right bound]. Medium serves as a basis for indirect comparison: if search string is lower than semi-finite suffix of medium then the new right border : = medium, otherwise new left border : = medium. The new medium is determined in the middle of the new interval. This procedure is reiterated until border convergence.

All lexicographical neighbours can be found in a row direct behind the location identified previously via indirect logarithmic search. The Delta Operator of the Enterprise Tomograph is concerned with detecting Delta Trees of two forests originating from different data sources. The intersection represents integration ontologies existing in both Data Sources A and B. A subset of this intersection is delta integration ontologies and needs to be identified and visualized according to Figure 6.6. The delta identification algorithm is explained in the next section in more detail.

The basic idea for identifying delta trees is to integrate watermarks into the sequenced forest text content. A watermark is assembled of a four fixed-length tuple with hash value of TreeID, hash value of tree, the location of the tree, and the offset of the sequenced tree. Watermark integration is done for all trees in both Forests A and B. PAT Array construction is done for the textual content of A and B each. The resulting PAT Arrays are merged. On this constructed PAT Array a binary indirect search is performed for the tag <WATERMARK>. Watermark neighbours can be found in a sequence. Iterating over this sequence trees located only in A, only in B, trees in A and B, and delta trees in A and B can easily be determined. Delta trees have a common prefix '<WATERMARK>Hash Value TreeID' with different hash value tree in consecutive PAT Array positions.

With this approach PAT Array algorithms can be reused for negative doublet recognition of trees, i.e., delta tree detection. Of course, the administrative data integrated in the textual content must not be part of any visualized search result. Appropriate measures can suppress these occurrences.

Generic Operators for Maintenance Networks in Enterprise Clouds

Enterprise software manufacturers normally provide maintenance services for their customers. They are granted access to their individual customers for detailed root cause analysis. In fact, the code bases of the individual deployed enterprise software may be modified or enhanced. Such individual changes may result in error symptoms. To make modifications and enhancements visible, the Inter-Delta Operator of the Enterprise Tomograph comes into place. For example, enterprise software manufacturer provides an encoded index of a domain of its Enterprise Platform (reference index) into a Peer-to-Peer (P2P) network. The customer can calculate the delta of its changed enterprise software and the decoded reference index. In semantic genres the modifications and enhancements are listed. Now the maintainer semi-automatically can assess and estimate, if the error symptom relates to modifications and enhancements made by the customer.

Another meaningful operator in maintenance networks is the align operator. Assuming the enterprise software manufacturer wants to deploy a best practice. This best practice (delta) can be added to customers' configuration. In this case, adding a delta is equivalent to aligning configuration in a domain. The align operator can also be applied for code bases. In this way updates of enterprise software can be provided.

The locate operator performs concept location in integration ontologies. This operator can be iteratively applied for refinement purposes. Based on the result, other orthogonal operators can be applied, e.g., multiple break-point operator, launch operator, and modify operator. The locate operator is the basis for refactoring purposes. In the P2P network the sender of the encoded domain index is the owner of the key. Enterprises knowing this key are able to decrypt and use the domain index only. The domain index is divided into n fragments. These fragments are redundantly encoded and the resulting amount of encoded fragments $m = n + k$ is distributed to the peers of the network. The retrieval of the encoded index happens according to an implementation of a distributed hash table (DHT).

With Reed Solomon Codes, retrieval of arbitrary 'n' of 'm' fragments suffices for reconstruction of the original domain index (Grolimund, 2007). The basics behind is the fundamental theorem of algebra (Korner, 2006). If a fragment is damaged, or not transmitted consistently, the retrieval of an additional encoded fragment may be triggered ('n' different consistent encoded fragments are necessary for reconstruction of the original domain index). The independent fragment retrieval approach ensures an efficient upload and download of large Enterprise Tomograph domain indices because 'n' ('n' of 'm') arbitrary encoded fragments can be retrieved in parallel (Grolimund, 2007) for reconstructing the original domain index.

In addition, with Reed Solomon Codes (RS-Codes), damaged or not, consistently transmitted encoded fragments can be reconstructed with high reliability. Encoded fragments contain attached redundant information (polynom). With polynom division the correctness can be evaluated. With help of RS erasure codes damaged fragments can be repaired (Forward Error Correction).

CONCLUSIONS

Enterprise Tomography is an efficient approach for application lifecycle management of VLBAs and Enterprise Platforms. It supports development and maintenance teams to track incremental changes of integration concepts in VLBA software, business data, and contextual data. Full domain-specific search of integration concepts, refinement search, and delta search and its visualization is realized with enhanced standard scientific algorithms. Interchangeable enhanced PAT Arrays, PAT Array-based delta tree recognition, tree distance algorithms, and tree mappings based on dynamic programming are the main algorithms used in Enterprise Tomography. Complexity calculation for Enterprise Tomography can easily be derived from complexity of the individual involved enhanced standard algorithms.

REFERENCES

Abels, S., L. Haak, and A. Hahn. 2005. 'Identification of Common Methods used for Ontology Integration Tasks. Interoperability of Heterogeneous Information Systems', Proceedings of the first international workshop on Interoperability of Heterogeneous Information Systems, Bremen, Germany, pp. 75–78.

Abouelhoda, M.I., S. Kurtz, and E. Ohlebusch. 2005. 'Replacing Suffix Trees with Enhanced Suffix Arrays', *Journal of Discrete Algorithms*, 2: 53–86.

Bille, P. 2005. 'A Survey on Tree Edit Distance and Related Problems', *Theoretical Computer Science*, 337(1/3): 217–39.

Dementiev, R. 2006. 'Algorithm Engineering for Large Data Sets', Doctoral Thesis, University of Saarland, Saarbrücken, pp. 151–56.

Grabski, B., S. Günther, S. Herden, L. Krüger, C. Rautenstrauch, and A. Zwanziger. 2007. 'Very Large Business Applications', *Informatik-Spektrum*, pp. 259–63. Berlin, Heidelberg: Springer Verlag.

Grolimund, D. 2007. 'Wuala—A Distributed File System, Dominik Grolimund', 30 October, Caleido AG, ETH Zuerich. Online Publication in Google Research, Google TechTalks.

Kärkkäinen, J., P. Sanders, and S. Burkhardt. 2006. 'Linear Work Suffix Array Construction', *Journal of the ACM*, 53(6): 918–36.

Korner, T.E. 2006. 'On the Fundamental Theorem of Algebra', *Journal Storage*, 113(4): 347–48.

Lu, C.L., Z.Y. Su, and C.Y. Tang. 2001. 'A New Measure of Edit Distance between Labeled Trees', in *Computing and Combinatorics*, 7th Annual International Conference, Cocoon 2001, Guilin, China, pp. 338–48.

Panchenko, O. 2007. 'Concept Location and Program Comprehension in Service-Oriented Software', Proceedings of the IEEE 23rd International Conference on Software Maintenance, Doctoral Symposium, ICSM, Paris, France, pp. 513–14.

Tiun, S., R. Abdullah, and T.E. Kong. 2001. 'Automatic Topic Identification Using Ontology Hierarchy', Proceedings of Computational Linguistic and Intelligent Text Processing, Second International Conference CICLing, Mexico City, Mexico, Springer, pp. 444–53.

Zhang, K., R. Statman, and D. Shasha. 1992. 'On the Editing Distance between Unordered Labeled Trees', Information Processing Letters, 42: 133–39.

7

The Paradoxical Impact of Enterprise-wide Integration on Flexibility

Judy E. Scott

Associate Professor, Information Systems Program,
University of Colorado, Denver, USA
E-mail: judy.scott@ucdenver.edu

INTRODUCTION

Even as business environments in many industries have become hypercompetitive requiring organizational agility and flexibility (Sambamurthy, 2000), a double revolution, driven by Enterprise Resource Planning (ERP)[1] software packages and the Internet, along with emerging technologies such as web services (WS),[2] has changed the landscape of corporate business throughout much of the world. One critical aspect of the change is the evolution of enterprise-wide integration (EWI).

The motivation to integrate applications on an enterprise-wide scale is high. First, EWI increases versatility with new business capabilities such as effective forecasting and available-to-promise functionality (Bhattacherjee, 2000). Second, EWI facilitates faster responsiveness by eliminating redundant data entry in unconnected systems, increasing productivity, reducing errors, and streamlining processes (Barki and Pinsonneault, 2005; Bhattacherjee, 2000; Khoumbati et al., 2006; Malone and Crowston, 1994; Ross and Vitale, 2000). EWI also enhances responsiveness in strategic decision-making and customer service by providing real-time global inventory visibility (Goodhue and Wybo, 1992; Markus, 2000; Ross and Vitale, 2000). Third, EWI increases the availability of organizational knowledge, facilitating cross-functional and inter-organizational collaboration (Barki and Pinsonneault, 2005; Christiaanse, 2005; Elmes et al., 2005), user learning, and adaptability to change (Robey et al., 2002).

---

[1] ERP systems often encompass core data-processing applications and most of the enterprise's key data in a common database (Duncan, 1995). They contribute to infrastructure capability and integrate organizational processes in human resources, logistics, financials, customer relationship management and supply chain management.

[2] WS rely on modularity to semantically encapsulate discrete functionality in loosely coupled, reusable software components that are distributed and programmatically accessible using interoperability standards.

On the other hand, EWI may introduce constraints. First, organizations conforming to embedded 'best practices' in EWI software forgo versatility and idiosyncratic business capabilities that provide competitive advantage (Gosain, 2004; Nonaka, 1994; Orlikowski, 1992). Second, organizations relinquish the capability to respond quickly because EWI technology becomes a 'black box' that is difficult to change, and implementation and upgrade delays are common (Aerts et al., 2004; Allen and Boyton, 1991; Duncan, 1995; Pozzebon, 2001; Schilling, 2000). Third, with EWI imposed routines, organizations become inertial and less capable of the organizational learning, and they need for adaptability to strategic and operational change (Fan et al., 2000; Gosain, 2004; March, 1991; Sitkin, 1992).

This paradox that EWI could both empower and constrain flexibility (Elmes et al., 2005; Pawlowski et al., 1999; Sia et al., 2002) indicates a need for theoretical explanations (Robey et al., 2002). Despite the current concern of practitioners, most information technology (IT) research on EWI focuses on frameworks and models oriented around ERP implementation (Markus and Tanis, 2000; Robey et al., 2002; Ross and Vitale, 2000; Scott and Vessey, 2000, 2002) rather than a theoretical study of flexibility from EWI that extends beyond software packages.

This study attempts to fill this gap by explaining the paradox that EWI could both empower and constrain flexibility. Many ambiguities are removed by decomposing the integration and flexibility constructs and examining them in depth to improve our understanding of the conditions for EWI effectiveness in organizations. The chapter proposes a model and eight propositions that include aspects of integration: reach, range and modularity, and dimensions of flexibility—versatility, responsiveness, and adaptability.

In the next section, flexibility, EWI, and related terms are defined. In the third section, theory development, a model, and eight propositions are focused upon. The concluding section has a summary of the findings and implications and suggestions to further develop theory, which explains the relationship between flexibility and EWI.

DEFINITIONS AND ASSUMPTIONS

Very little information system (IS) research has focused on either flexibility or integration. This section defines terms associated with flexibility and EWI.

FLEXIBILITY

Flexibility is a polymorphous concept that varies with context (Evans, 1991). It refers to 'a blend of capabilities and attributes that facilitate adjustments to change' (Bahrami, 1992). Capabilities include: *(a)* versatility—the ability to do a variety of things; *(b)* responsiveness—the ability to react quickly to change; and *(c)* adaptability—the ability to reposition or adjust to a new environment (Bahrami, 1992; Evans, 1991; Golden and Powell, 2000).

Strategic flexibility 'is the ability of an organization to respond to changes in the environment in a timely and appropriate manner with due regard to the competitive forces in the marketplace' (Das and Elango, 1995). 'High-flex' firms have honed these capabilities both externally through suppliers, alliances, and multinational operations, and internally through manufacturing flexibility, modular product design, employee flexibility, and organizational structure. Agility, which is often used interchangeably with strategic flexibility, is defined as the ability to detect and seize market opportunities with speed and surprise (Sambamurthy et al., 2003). It is a critical capability for enabling 'time-based' competition, facilitating rapid response, and the ability to move rapidly, changing course to take advantage of an opportunity, or to cope with a threat (Bahrami, 1992).

In prior IS literature, flexibility is the ability: *(a)* to adapt to new circumstances and uncertainty (Lucas and Olson, 1994)[33], *(b)* to respond rapidly to changing market conditions enabled by information architecture (Allen and Boyton, 1991) and *(c)* to generate options for end product diversification based on IT infrastructure flexibility (Duncan, 1995).

ENTERPRISE-WIDE INTEGRATION

Integration is a multidimensional concept, which describes the combination, coupling, linking and coordination of interdependent units to function as a unified unit (Markus, 2000; Tushman and Nadler, 1978). EWI is defined as as the combination, coupling, linking, and coordination of interdependent units at the enterprise level and beyond. Systems theory explains coupling as the combination between a system's components (Schilling, 2000). The degree to which a system's components can be separated and recombined is its modularity. Modularity is a strategy for 'building a complex product or process from smaller subsystems that can be designed independently yet function together as a whole' (Baldwin and Clark, 1997).

EWI characteristics depend on the organization's IT architectural stage and competencies (Ross, 2003). High distinctiveness and high responsiveness between interdependent units is typical of loose coupling and modular IT architectures (Orton and Weick, 1990; Ross, 2003). Also, the more integrated the system, the greater its reach to stakeholders and range of information for sharing (Weill et al., 2002). Immature IT architectures have locally optimized application silos with little or no coupling, which limit reach and range. More mature IT architectures adopt enterprise technology standards and a shared infrastructure. Standardized data and processes using ERP systems or Enterprise Application Integration (EAI) software[3] enable seamlessly shared information throughout (or beyond) the enterprise. The most mature modular architecture stage leverages loose coupling, such as WS, that facilitates rapid inter-organizational linking (Ross, 2003).

---

[3] The term EAI refers to the plans, methods, and tools (such as asynchronous event or message transport, transformation engines, and integration brokers), aimed at consolidating, integrating, and coordinating the computer applications within an enterprise (McKeen and Smith, 2003).

Table 7.1 summarizes integration measures based on process reach, range, and modularity for immature and mature IT architectures. Transition stages, into which most organizations' architectures fall, are omitted for clarity.

TABLE 7.1
Integration Measures

Integration process measures	Immature IT architecture	Mature IT architecture	Example
Reach represents the (internal or external) locations to which integration extends (Weill et al., 2002)	Local reach limited by locally optimized application silo	Reach extends to global locations, across organizations or industries	Elemica integration hub enables global reach for firms in chemical industry (Christiaanse, 2005)
Range of information for sharing (Weill et al., 2002)	Local range of information for sharing limited by locally optimized application silo	Commonality and standardized technology enable cross functional or inter-organizational information sharing	Geneva supply and demand information sharing enables better forecasting (Bhattacherjee, 2000)
Modularity or coupling is the extent of distinctiveness and responsiveness (Orton and Weick, 1990)	Locally optimized application silos have little or no coupling and no responsiveness between subunits	Modular Web services provide loose coupling, high distinctiveness, and high responsiveness	Dell shares real time information with vendor managed hubs using loosely coupled WS (Hagel, 2002)

Source: Author.

THEORY DEVELOPMENT

Given that the impact of IT on flexibility is mixed (Lucas and Olson, 1994), an interesting and controversial question that arises is whether EWI enables or inhibits flexibility. The research literature notes the paradox and tradeoff between efficiency and flexibility (Adler et al., 1999; Volberda, 1996). Coordination theory models the tradeoff using production costs, coordination costs, and vulnerability costs (Malone and Crowston, 1994). Information processing theory and transaction cost theory explain how IT coordinates inter-dependencies and enables faster transactions and lower transaction costs (Tushman and Nadler, 1978). On the other hand, IT may increase the time, effort and cost to change: *(a)* systems and *(b)* work flows and organization structures (Lucas and Olson, 1994). It is proposed that the paradox between efficiency and flexibility is also applicable to EWI. While EWI increases efficiency and lowers transaction, production, and coordination costs, vulnerability costs may rise due to inertial forces.

Organizational learning theory explains inertia in terms of efficiency tradeoffs. While exploitation is efficient, without exploration organizations become inertial and self-destruct in the long term (March, 1991). Similarly, although single-loop learning is relatively efficient, without double-loop learning, organizations do not change established processes and question norms in the organization (Argyris and Schon, 1978). ERP facilitates exploitation rather than exploration if organizations converge on adopting embedded best practices which produce inertial forces that hinder flexibility.

Several arguments and counter-arguments for EWI enabling flexibility along the dimensions of versatility, responsiveness, and adaptability moderated by industry stability and modularity (Figure 7.1) are discussed next.

FIGURE 7.1
Relationship between EWI and Flexibility

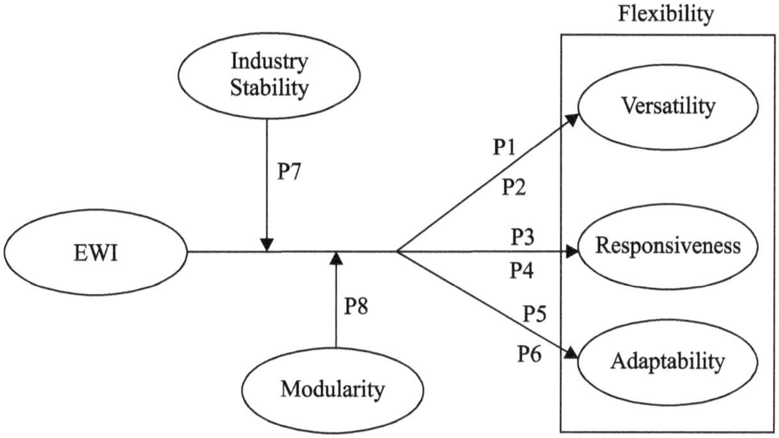

Source: Author.

VERSATILITY FROM EWI

Versatility refers to the ability to do a variety of different things and apply different capabilities depending on a wide range of scenarios (Bahrami, 1992; Evans, 1991; Golden and Powell, 2000). Coordination mechanisms reduce uncertainty and increase information processing capacity (Goodhue and Wybo, 1992; Tushman and Nadler, 1978). EWI through coordination, standardization, and enterprise information visibility enable capabilities, such as forecasting, planning, fulfillment, and strategic decision-making to be applied to a wide range of scenarios, such as geographic, temporal, and product specific.

At Geneva and Nestle, forecasting and planning decisions no longer depend on intuition because EWI of supply and demand enable them to readily adjust their production plans to different scenarios (Bhattacherjee, 2000; Worthen, 2002). Organizational capabilities to exploit EWI technological opportunities increase options for satisfying customers (Khoumbati et al., 2006; Shang and Seddon, 2002). Patients' perception of the quality of care at NWE-HOSPITAL improved after an EAI implementation (Khoumbati et al., 2006). At Elf Altochem EWI functionality provides available-to-promise feedback to customers (Davenport, 1998).

EWI provides global information visibility, multiple languages, and currencies so that organizations gain versatility in providing country-specific reporting and better strategic decisions (Ross and Vitale, 2000). Oracle gained such versatility when it replaced multiple disparate local websites and ERP customizations with a single global central source run in multiple languages and standardized prices and discounts globally (Ghoshal and Gratton, 2002). Similarly, Nestle leveraged global decision-making by standardizing on an enterprise part number and price for vanilla instead of business units paying 29 different prices to the same vendor (Worthen, 2002). This leads to the following:

Proposition1: Organizations with more enterprise-wide integration gain versatility.

Constraints on versatility

EWI software, such as ERP, has embedded 'best practices', which constrain the range of processes available to organizations. Best practices function as norms and institutionalize processes in the organization (Gosain, 2004; Orlikowski, 1992). Institutional theory explains that routines, social structures, and norms can restrict the variety of activities available to organizations (DiMaggio and Powell, 1983; Gosain, 2004). ERP systems confine knowledge creation and other organizational learning because the embedded models limit what can be known (Baskerville et al., 2000), reduce the requisite variety (Nonaka, 1994), and discourage exploration (March, 1991).

Since parameter settings in ERP systems offer a much more limited range of choices than tailor-made systems (Pawlowski et al., 1999), users may perceive functionality loss and less versatility (Robey et al., 2002). EWI limits choices to enterprise-wide standards, which forces highly differentiated subunits to lose autonomy, compromise on their local requirements, and forfeit aspects of local specialization and intra-subunit efficiency to gain overall efficient solutions (Aerts et al., 2004; Gattiker and Goodhue, 2005; Goodhue and Wybo, 1992).

ERP systems require well-structured processes, data, and roles which can reduce the number of alternatives. 'Users not only lose a measure of control over their jobs, but also lose flexibility necessary to handle various exceptions that arise in their daily tasks' (Strong et al., 2001). As a result, users may create workarounds that support their local needs (Soh et al., 2000, 2003), while adversely affecting other groups by ignoring task inter-dependencies created by process integration (Elmes et al., 2005; Strong et al., 2001). This suggests:

Proposition 2: Organizations with more enterprise-wide integration lose process versatility.

Table 7.2 summarizes how EWI enables and constrains the versatility flexibility dimension.

Responsiveness from EWI

Streamlined processes from EWI enable organizations to respond faster. IT enables faster processes and transactions with quick response (Lucas and Olson, 1994) and coupling enhances

TABLE 7.2
Impact of EWI on Versatility

	Versatility gain	*Versatility loss*
Strategic level	EWI functionality from standardization and enhanced sharing dependencies facilitates capabilities for a wide range of new products and services	EWI limits business processes to embedded 'best practices' so organization relinquishes competitive idiosyncratic business capabilities
Operational level	EWI provides new functionality for users' tasks	EWI introduces constraints on processes and the range of users' tasks

Source: Author.

responsiveness (Orton and Weick, 1990). Information processing theory recognizes the role of IS to speed up information flow (Tushman and Nadler, 1978) and coordination theory explains how IT facilitates flow dependencies (Malone and Crowston, 1994). Several sources acknowledge the improvements in time-based performance as a result of EWI (Davenport, 1998; Ross and Vitale, 2000). In fact time-based benefits tend to exceed original expectations. IBM Storage Division benchmarked processes before and after implementation of ERP and found dramatic benefits. For example, Material Requirement Planning (MRP) runs that used to take a day complete in less than an hour, credit checks took three seconds instead of 20 minutes and the time to reprice all of its products reduced from five days to five minutes (Davenport, 1998). Many firms close their books more promptly with EWI (Ross and Vitale, 2000). Nibco's ERP helps it close its books in two to three days instead of two to three weeks (Brown and Vessey, 2001).

Speeding up the flow of information enables faster decision-making. An EAI implementation at NWE-HOSPITAL facilitated doctors receiving X-ray and lab test results in 24 hours instead of eight days (Khoumbati et al., 2006). Enterprise visibility of real-time inventory globally lets an organization provide products where they are needed (Markus, 2000) and enterprise visibility of headcount improves human resources management. For example, EWI enables Oracle to know the real-time number of its employees worldwide (Ghoshal and Gratton, 2002). It no longer needs to access 60 differently formatted databases and consolidate the outdated numbers. This suggests the following proposition:

Proposition 3: Organizations with more enterprise-wide integration gain strategic responsiveness.

Constraints on responsiveness

Because of the complexity of implementing EWI and even upgrades, organizations become constrained on how quickly they can respond to change. For large organizations, it often takes years to configure their ERP system and change business processes to fit 'best practices' embedded in the software.

In the stabilization phase following ERP implementation, delays delivering products are partly due to increased difficulties circumventing EWI systems than less integrated legacy systems (Davenport, 1998). Organizations are reluctant to make quick changes to the system after it has stabilized because of the risk that business will be disrupted. The complexity and interdependence of processes means that even a small change could trigger unpredictable results and the need for thorough testing and training. Persistence is exacerbated by complex interdependencies that are difficult to understand (DiMaggio and Powell, 1983). Organizational routines are often embedded in information systems, which are not well documented or understood. Because there is a time–space discontinuity between the design and use of technology, people forget its malleable nature (Pozzebon, 2001). When the interpretive flexibility of technology is very low, people tend to abandon any attempt to change it and rhetorical closure is reinforced in the interpretive scheme of organizational members, vendors, and consultants. The system may become a black box.

Tightly coupled, integrated systems are constrained and inflexible because the parameters need to be consistent across the sub-systems (Pawlowski et al., 1999). In a global implementation, imposed enterprise standards constrain local responsiveness, and force tradeoffs for multisite implementations (Markus et al., 2000). Although providing reconfiguration without programming (Shang and Seddon, 2002), adopters often do not know the business implications of different configurations and find thousands of tables of system parameters confusing. Modular systems theory explains the synergistic specificity of components to a particular configuration in software that forfeit flexibility to achieve synergy and functionality (Schilling, 2000). This suggests:

Proposition 4: Organizations with more enterprise-wide integration lose responsiveness.

Table 7.3 summarizes how EWI enables and constrains the responsiveness flexibility dimension.

Adaptability from EWI

Adaptability, a flexibility dimension, is the ability to reposition or adjust to a new environment (Evans, 1991). EWI facilitates cross-functional and inter-organizational collaboration

TABLE 7.3
Impact of EWI on Responsiveness

	Responsiveness gain	*Responsiveness loss*
Strategic level	EWI functionality from streamlined processes and enterprise data visibility facilitate capabilities for faster strategic response	EWI introduces constraints on faster strategic response from complex technology which cannot be changed quickly
Operational level	EWI provides new functionality for faster operational response	EWI introduces constraints on technological response

Source: Author.

(Barki and Pinsonneault, 2005; Christiaanse, 2005; Crowston; 1997; Malone and Crowston, 1994), user learning, and adaptability to change (Robey et al., 2002). The expanded access and scope of information available enables employees to respond to problems and opportunities more directly and effectively with greater flexibility in day-to-day operations and in doing their jobs through expanded individual awareness, influence, creativity, and innovation (Pawlowski et al., 1999). EWI empowers by shifting the control of information flow between information creators and information users, who make decisions that were formally referred upwards or to other departments due to a lack of information (Elmes et al., 2005; Pawlowski et al., 1999; Sia et al., 2002; Volkoff et al., 2004). '[C]aches of organizational memory formerly guarded by division managers become transparent' (Robey et al., 2002).

The embedded knowledge repository of EWI 'best practices' encourages organizational learning as adopters reflect on their own way of doing things and fundamentally rethink their own processes (Sasovova et al., 2001). The reusability of WS components promotes the concept of a knowledge repository from which the organization can leverage prior learning and learn from each small WS project using an incremental approach (Hagel, 2002). This suggests:

Proposition 5: Organizations with more enterprise-wide integration gain adaptability.

Constraints on Adaptability

EWI constrains organizations' adaptability to change at both the strategic and operational levels. Routines and business processes embedded in an EWI system impose its own logic on a company and limit adaptability in a dynamic business environment (Fan et al., 2000). Persistence may occur at the expense of adaptability (Sitkin, 1992). Organizational learning and institutional theories explain that organizational inertia results from the tendency for routines to persist because they are perceived as allowing efficient coordinated action (Gosain, 2004; March, 1991; Schilling, 2000; Sitkin, 1992). Nevertheless, organizations need to experiment and overcome resistance to change for long-term success because routines may become inappropriate or suboptimal over time (Sitkin, 1992).

In dynamic industries, EWI constrains mergers, acquisitions, outsourcing, and compliance (MAOC) (Markus, 2001). Cardinal Health struggled to integrate 11 different order entry systems (with different product numbering schemes) during the merger of 12 different business entities. EWI problems might trigger the need for disintegration of systems (Markus, 2001; Sasovova et al., 2001). For example, Mobil Europe (Davenport, 1998) and Alpha Ltd abandoned their ERP systems and many new processes following mergers (Larsen and Myers, 1999).

EWI also negatively impacts adaptability at the operational level when users perceive EWI software as a misfit that does not meet their requirements (Larsen and Myers, 1999; Lee and Lee, 2000; Soh et al., 2000, 2003; Strong et al., 2001). Users cannot adapt if they perceive the business rules associated with the ERP reference models conflict with the existing culture, values, and norms of the organization (Lee and Lee, 2000; Soh et al., 2000).

Information processing theory explains adaptability and misfits such as how highly differentiated subunits lose autonomy and flexibility when EWI forces them to compromise on their requirements (Gattiker and Goodhue, 2005; Goodhue and Wybo, 1992). Conflicting interests among business units need to be resolved before integrating their knowledge. Users perceiving loss of power, discretion or autonomy resist EWI and cling to legacy systems. At Nestle there was 'rebellion in the ranks' and 'nobody wanted to learn the new way of doing things' (Worthen, 2002). Adaptability problems result in high turnover (Baskerville et al., 2000). For example, at Nestle, turnover reached 77 per cent for employees who forecast demand and were unwilling to replace their spreadsheets with complex enterprise models (Worthen, 2002). This suggests:

Proposition 6: Organizations with more enterprise-wide integration lose adaptability to change.

Table 7.4 summarizes how EWI enables and constrains the adaptability flexibility dimension.

TABLE 7.4
Impact of EWI on Adaptability

	Adaptability gain	*Adaptability loss*
Strategic level	EWI facilitates inter-organizational collaboration for strategic adaptability	EWI restricts organizational change; organization routines persist constraining strategic adaptability
Operational level	EWI's expanded access and scope of information empowers users' operational adaptability	Misalignment between EWI and business processes introduces constraints on operational adaptability

Source: Author.

Moderating the flexibility dimensions are industry stability and the extent of modularity of the EWI technology.

Industry Stability

Stable industries find exemplary procedures embedded in EWI systems as 'best practices' provide standard operating procedures and rules for: *(a)* routinization processes that build capabilities and *(b)* coordination mechanisms that cope with low environmental uncertainty (Tushman and Nadler, 1978). They improve customer service and facilitate speed, responsiveness, agility, and efficiency. However, 'best practices' are likely to be short-lived in dynamic industries which value versatility, responsiveness, and adaptability for dynamic capabilities to address rapidly changing environments (Eisenhardt and Martin, 2000). Moreover, organizations are often reluctant to forfeit their idiosyncratic business processes, especially if they are essential for competitive advantage (Sambamurthy et al., 2003). Aerogroup abandoned its SAP implementation when it perceived critical processes could not be supported (Soh et al., 2003). This suggests:

Proposition 7: Industry stability moderates the affect of enterprise-wide integration on versatility, responsiveness, and adaptability.

IT modularity

Modularity is a mechanism for supporting the upgrading and reuse of existing functions or components (Aerts et al., 2004). A modular 'plug and play' approach with software components frees customers from dependence on one vendor (Aerts et al., 2004; Schilling, 2000) and enables more flexibility than traditional package modules based on functional areas (Duncan, 1995). There is a tradeoff between modularity offering flexibility and integration offering performance optimization (Aerts et al., 2004; Schilling, 2000). Modular software architectures leverage loosely coupled software components such as WS (Ross, 2003) to reconfigure organizations from hardwired models to much more loosely coupled dynamically reconfigured models (Hagel, 2002). Such independent systems for smaller units with defined simple interfaces between them enable flexibility. In contrast, integrated software packages gain overall efficient solutions by subunits forfeiting local specialization and intra-component efficiency.

At the strategic level, modular technology facilitates flexibility such as responsiveness and adaptability to MAOC (Schilling, 2000). Loosely coupled modular systems enable dynamic industries with flexible cultures to consider more possibilities, have a broader range of alternatives and have heterogeneous demands with a diversity of perspectives. In the dynamic electronics industry, e2open facilitates constantly changing Business-to-Business (B2B) collaboration with WS. Similarly, in the chemical industry, Elemica enables transactions between multiple suppliers and customers with its B2B integration hub (Christiaanse, 2005).

At the operational level, flexibility is needed to respond to changing user requirements. The tighter the coupling, the more difficult it is to change and maintain the link. WS, with its machine-to-machine execution of loosely coupled business processes, can be invoked when needed, offering just-in-time integration of applications and flexibility. This suggests:

Proposition 8: Modularity will moderate the relationship between EWI and versatility, technological responsiveness, and adaptability.

IMPLICATIONS AND CONCLUSION

The relationship between EWI and flexibility is complex. In this study flexibility has been decomposed into the versatility, responsiveness, and adaptability dimensions and EWI into tight versus loose coupling. Drawing on information processing, coordination, organizational learning, and institutional theories, propositions that support a positive and negative relationship for each of the three dimensions of flexibility have been developed. It becomes apparent that, with some exceptions, tightly coupled EWI enables strategic flexibility and constrains operational flexibility. Because management acquires more control while users lose discretion, ERP systems have been accused of being an iron cage and a medium for administrative evil (Dillard et al., 2005; Gosain, 2004). While management gains versatility from new EWI functionality, users lose versatility from standardization. Similarly, management gains responsiveness from real-time monitoring and by leveraging best practices (in stable industries), while users lose responsiveness from 'black box' technology lock-in. Also management gains adaptability from cross-functional and inter-organizational collaboration (Barki and Pinsonneault, 2005; Christiaanse, 2005; Crowston, 1997), while users lose adaptability from the misalignment of their requirements with embedded 'best practices' (Soh et al., 2000, 2003).

Two propositions explain the moderating effects of industry type and modularity. Dynamic industries have more stringent requirements for flexibility, along dimensions of versatility, responsiveness, and adaptability, than stable industries (Eisenhardt and Martin, 2000). Our model suggests that in dynamic industries tight coupling constrains MAOC at the strategic level and user requirements at the operational level. On the other hand, the logic in our model finds that loosely coupled EWI, although risky due to its relative immaturity, does not constrain flexibility at either the strategic or operational level.

This study probes the theoretical and empirical findings on both the EWI construct and the flexibility construct to explain the contradictory findings on the relationship. Our model posits that EWI is multi-faceted and in particular could be measured by reach and range (Broadbent et al., 1996), and the extent of modularity (Orton and Weick, 1990; Schilling, 2000). Similarly, flexibility is polymorphous (Evans, 1991) and has multiple attributes and multiple potential levels of analysis (Golden and Powell, 2000). Of particular relevance to this study is the examination of flexibility at both the strategic and operational level. At the strategic level, it is proposed that flexibility be measured for process versatility (Bahrami, 1992; Golden and Powell, 2000), enabling responsive strategic decisions (Goodhue and Wybo, 1992) and technological responsiveness to MAOC (Markus, 2001). At the operational level, it is suggested that flexibility be indicated by facilitation of user learning adaptability (Baskerville et al., 2000) and adaptability to user requirements (Soh et al., 2000, 2003).

IMPLICATIONS FOR RESEARCH

The propositions and model presented in this chapter clarify several ambiguities associated with the relationship between EWI and flexibility. This study advances theory development in the topic and offers practical applicability following criteria specified by experts (Dubin, 1978; Sutton and Staw, 1995) Eisenhardt and Martin (2000), and Robey et al. (2002). It focuses on a topic that is of contemporary interest to a broad audience of both researchers and practitioners; it does not ignore conflicting findings on EWI's impact on flexibility; it builds on strong theoretical findings and lays the foundation for empirical research; and it makes assumptions explicit and follows recommendations for completeness, thoroughness, and non-superficial propositions.

Minimal IS research has focused on either flexibility or integration. Although there are streams of research on IS architecture and infrastructure flexibility (Allen and Boyton, 1991; Broadbent et al., 1996; Duncan, 1995; Ross, 2003; Weill et al., 2002), IS capabilities (Sambamurthy et al., 2003), and ERP implementation (Markus and Tanis, 2000; Robey et al., 2002; Ross and Vitale, 2000; Scott and Vessey, 2000, 2002), IS literature has largely skirted the relationship between flexibility and integration. This study shows how these research streams can converge to address an important contemporary problem that is relevant to IS practice.

Further research can potentially convert the propositions in this study into testable hypotheses, moving us closer to a rigorous theory of EWI. The propositions could be operationalized by measures suggested earlier. Future research might improve our model by making it more parsimonious. With increased knowledge from empirical testing, researchers should be able to fine-tune the constructs and hypotheses for specific situations such as hypercompetitive markets.

IMPLICATIONS FOR PRACTICE

Practitioners perceive flexibility as critical at both the strategic and operational levels. At the same time, EWI is usually considered essential and becoming widespread with the availability of ERP, EAI, WS, and other integrating technologies. Fast paced industries benefit from loose integration in that links can be quickly formed and discarded. More stable industries take advantage of best practices modeled in tightly integrated enterprise software.

Although most managers covet EWI to enable them to compete in their industries, the optimal degree of EWI will vary according to a firm's resources, its industry, and its history. A more complete understanding of the EWI process will enable practitioners to make better decisions on integration software selection, integration architecture planning, business value assessment from EWI, and determination of the appropriate degree of EWI for their organization. Understanding theoretical aspects of EWI is particularly relevant for organizations in hypercompetitive industries where flexibility is a critical dynamic capability for facilitating versatility and strategic decisions such as MAOC.

REFERENCES

Adler, P.S., B. Goldoftas, and D.L. Levine. 1999. 'Flexibility versus Efficiency? A Case Study of Model Changeovers in the Toyota Production System', *Organization Science*, 10: 43–68.

Aerts, A.T.M., J.B.M. Goossenaerts, D.K. Hammer, and J.C. Wortmann. 2004. 'Architectures in Context: On the Evolution of Business, Application Software, and ICT Platform Architectures', *Information and Management*, 41: 781–94.

Allen, B.R. and A.C. Boyton. 1991. 'Information Architecture: In Search of Efficient Flexibility', *MIS Quarterly*, 15: 435–45.

Bahrami, H. 1992. 'The Emerging Flexible Organization', *California Management Review*, 34: 33–52.

Baldwin, C.Y. and K.B. Clark. 1997. 'Managing in an Age of Modularity', *Harvard Business Review*, 75: 84–93.

Barki, H. and A. Pinsonneault. 2005. 'A Model of Organizational Integration, Implementation Effort, and Performance', *Organization Science*, 16: 165–79.

Baskerville, R., S. Pawlowski, and E. McLean. 2000. 'Enterprise Resource Planning and Organizational Knowledge: Patterns of Convergence and Divergence', in *Proceedings of the Twenty-first International Conference on Information Systems*, pp. 396–406. Atlanta, GA, USA: Association for Information Systems.

Bhattacherjee, A. 2000. 'SAP R/3 Implementation at Geneva Pharmaceuticals', *Communications of AIS*, 4: 1–38.

Broadbent, M., P. Weill, T. O'Brien, and B.S. Neo. 1996. 'Firm Context and Patterns of IT Infrastructure Capability', in Sirkka L. Jarvenpaa and Ananth Srinivasan (eds), *Proceedings of the Seventeenth International Conference on Information Systems*, 16–18 December. Cleveland, Ohio, USA.

Brown, C.V. and I. Vessey. 2001. 'Nibco's Big Bang', *Communications of the AIS*, 5: 1–41.

Christiaanse, E. 2005. 'Performance Benefits through Integration Hubs', *Communications of ACM*, 48: 95–100.

Crowston, K. 1997. 'A Coordination Theory Approach to Organizational Process Design', *Organization Science*, 8: 157–75.

Das, T.K. and B. Elango. 1995. 'Managing Strategic Flexibility: Key to Effective Performance', *Journal of General Management*, 20: 60–75.

Davenport, T.H. 1998. 'Putting the Enterprise into Enterprise Systems', *Harvard Business Review*, 76: 121–31.

Dillard, J.F., L. Ruchala, and K. Yuthas. 2005. 'Enterprise Resource Planning Systems: A Physical Manifestation of Administrative Evil', *Accounting Information Systems*, 6: 107–27.

DiMaggio, P.J. and W.W. Powell. 1983. 'The Iron Cage Revisited: Institutional Isomorphism and Collective Rationality in Organizational Fields', *American Sociological Review*, 48: 147–60.

Dubin, R. 1978. *Theory Building*. New York, NY: Free Press.

Duncan, N.B. 1995. 'Capturing Flexibility of Information Technology Infrastructure: A Study of Resource Characteristics and their Measure', *Journal of Management Information Systems*, 12: 37–57.

Eisenhardt, K.M. and J.A. Martin. 2000. 'Dynamic Capabilities: What are they?' *Strategic Management Journal*, 21: 1105–121.

Elmes, M.B., D.M. Strong, and O. Volkoff. 2005. 'Panoptic Empowerment and Reflective Conformity in Enterprise Systems-enabled Organizations', *Information and Organization*, 15: 1–37.

Evans, S. 1991. 'Strategic Flexibility for High Technology Manoeuvres', *Journal of Management Studies*, 28: 69–89.

Fan, M., J. Stallaert, and A. Whinston. 2000. 'The Adoption and Design Methodologies of Component-based Enterprise Systems', *European Journal of Information Systems*, 9: 25–35.

Gattiker, T.F. and D.L. Goodhue. 2005. 'What Happens after ERP Implementation: Understanding the Impact of Interdependence and Differentiation on Plant-Level Outcomes', *MIS Quarterly*, 29: 559–85.

Ghoshal, S. and L. Gratton. 2002. 'Integrating the Enterprise', *Sloan Management Review*, 44: 31–39.

Golden, W. and P. Powell. 2000. 'Towards a Definition of Flexibility: In Search of the Holy Grail?' *Omega*, 28: 373–84.

Goodhue, D.L. and M. Wybo. 1992. 'The Impact of Data Integration on the Costs and Benefits of Information Systems', *MIS Quarterly*, 16: 293–311.

Gosain, S. 2004. 'Enterprise Information Systems as Objects and Carriers of Institutional Forces: The New Iron Cage?' *Journal of AIS*, 5: 151–82.

Hagel, J. 2002. *Out of the Box: Strategies for Achieving Profits Today and Growth Tomorrow through Web Services*. Boston: Harvard Business School Press.

Khoumbati, K., M. Themistocleous, and Z. Irani. 2006. 'Evaluating the Adoption of Enterprise Application Integration in Health-Care Organizations', *Journal of Management Information Systems*, 22: 69–108.

Larsen, M.A. and M. Myers. 1999. 'When Success Turns into Failure: A Package-driven Business Process Re-engineering Project in the Financial Services Industry', *The Journal of Strategic Information Systems*, 8: 395–417.

Lee, Z. and J. Lee. 2000. 'An ERP Implementation Case Study from a Knowledge Transfer Perspective', *Journal of Information Technology*, 15: 281–88.

Lucas, H.C. and M. Olson. 1994. 'The Impact of Information Technology on Organizational Flexibility', *Journal of Organizational Computing*, 4: 155–76.

Malone, T.W. and K. Crowston. 1994. 'The Interdisciplinary Study of Coordination', *ACM Computing Surveys*, 26: 87–119.

March, J.G. 1991. 'Exploration and Exploitation in Organizational Learning', *Organization Science*, 2: 71–87.

Markus, M.L. 2000. 'Paradigm Shifts—E-Business/Systems Integration', *Communications of the AIS*, 4(1): 1–45.

———. 2001. 'Reflections on the Systems Integration Enterprise', *Business Process Management Journal*, 7: 1.

Markus, M.L. and C. Tanis. 2000. 'The Enterprise Systems Experience—From Adoption to Success', in R.W. Zmud (ed.), *Framing the Domains of IT Research: Glimpsing the Future through the Past*. Cincinnati, OH: Pinnaflex Educational Resources, Inc.

Markus, M.L., C. Tanis, and P.C.V. Fenema. 2000. 'Multisite ERP Implementations', *Communications of the ACM*, 43: 42–46.

McKeen, James D. and Heather A. Smith. 2003. *Making IT Happen: Critical Issues in IT Management*. John Wiley Series in Information Systems.

Nonaka, I. 1994. 'A Dynamic Theory of Organizational Knowledge Creation', *Organization Science*, 5: 14–37.

Orlikowski, W.J. 1992. 'The Duality of Technology: Rethinking the Concept of Technology in Organizations', *Organization Science*, 3: 398–427.

Orton, J.D. and K.E. Weick. 1990. 'Loosely Coupled Systems: A Reconceptualization', *Academy of Management Review*, 15: 203–23.

Pawlowski, S., M. Boudreau, and R. Baskerville. 1999. 'Constraints and Flexibility in Enterprise Systems: A Dialectic of System and Job', in W. Haseman and D. Nazareth (eds), *Proceedings of The Fifth Americas Conference on Information Systems*, pp. 791–93. Milwaukee, Wisconsin: Association of Information Systems.

Pozzebon, M. 2001. 'Demystifying the Rhetorical Closure of ERP Packages', in V. Storey, S. Sarkar, and J.I. DeGross (eds), *Proceedings of the Twenty-Second International Conference on Information Systems*, pp. 329–337. Atlanta: AIS. Available online at aisel.isworld.org

Robey, D., J.W. Ross, and M.C. Boudreau. 2002. 'Learning to Implement Enterprise Systems: An Exploratory Study of the Dialectics of Change', *Journal of Management Information Systems*, 19: 17–46.

Ross, J. 2003. 'Creating a Strategic IT Architecture Competency: Learning in Stages', *MIS Quarterly Executive*, 2: 31–43.

Ross, J.W. and M.R. Vitale. 2000. 'The ERP Revolution: Surviving versus Thriving', *Information Systems Frontiers*, 2: 233–41.

Sambamurthy, V. 2000. 'Business Strategy in Hypercompetitive Environments: Rethinking the Logic of IT Differentiation', in R.W. Zmud (ed.), *Framing the Domains of IT Research: Glimpsing the Future through the Past*. Cincinnati, OH: Pinnaflex Educational Resources, Inc.

Sambamurthy, V., A. Bharadwaj, and V. Grover. 2003. 'Shaping Agility through Digital Options: Reconceptualizing the Role of Information Technology in Contemporary Firms', *MIS Quarterly*, 27: 237–63.

Sasovova, Z., M. Heng, and M. Newman. 2001. 'Limits for Using ERP Systems', in *Seventh Americas Conference on Information Systems (AMCIS)*, pp. 1142–47. Boston, MA: AMCIS.

Schilling, M.A. 2000. 'Toward a General Modular Systems Theory and its Application to Interfirm Product Modularity', *Academy of Management Review*, 25: 312–34.

Scott, J.E. and I. Vessey. 2000. 'Implementing Enterprise Resource Planning Systems: The Role of Learning from Failure', *Information System Frontiers*, 2: 213–32.

———. 2002. 'Managing Risks in Enterprise Systems Implementations', *Communications of the ACM*, 45: 74–81.

Shang, S. and P.B. Seddon. 2002. 'Assessing and Managing the Benefits of Enterprise Systems', *Information Systems Journal*, 12: 271–99.

Sia, S.K., M. Tang, C. Soh, and W.F. Boh. 2002. 'Enterprise Resource Planning Systems as a Technology of Power: Empowerment or Panoptic Control?' *Data Base for Advances in Information Systems*, 33: 23–37.

Sitkin, S.B. 1992. 'Learning through Failure: The Strategy of Small Losses', *Research in Organizational Behavior*, 14: 231–66.

Soh, C., S.S. Kein, and J. Tay-Yap. 2000. 'Cultural Fits and Misfits: Is ERP a Universal Solution?' *Communications of the ACM*, 43: 47–51.

Soh, C., S.K. Sia, W.F. Boh, and M. Tang. 2003. 'Misalignments in ERP Implementation: A Dialectic Perspective', *International Journal of Human-Computer Interaction*, 16: 81–100.

Strong, D.M., O. Volkoff, and M.B. Elmes. 2001. 'ERP Systems, Task Structure and Workarounds', in *Seventh Americas Conference on Information Systems (AMCIS)*, pp. 1049–51. Boston, USA: AMCIS.

Sutton, R.I. and B.M. Staw. 1995. 'What Theory is Not', *Administrative Science Quarterly*, 40: 371–84.

Tushman, M. and D. Nadler. 1978. 'Information Processing as an Integrating Concept in Organizational Design', *Academy of Management Review*, 3: 613–24.

Volberda, H.W. 1996. 'Toward the Flexible Form: How to Remain Vital in Hypercompetitive Environments', *Organization Science*, 7: 359–74.

Volkoff, O., M.B. Elmes, and D.M. Strong. 2004. 'Enterprise Systems, Knowledge Transfer and Power Users', *Journal of Strategic Information Systems*, 13(4): 279–304.

Weill, P., M. Subramani, and M. Broadbent. 2002. 'Building IT Infrastructure for Strategic Agility', *Sloan Management Review*, 44: 57–65.

Worthen, B. 2002. 'Nestle's ERP Odyssey', *CIO magazine*. Available online at www.cio.com accessed on 15 May 2002).

8

Building Knowledge-intensive Customer-centric Supply Chain Organizations

MINWIR AL-SHAMMARI
Department of Management and Marketing
College of Business Administration, University of Bahrain, P.O. Box 32038, Kingdom of Bahrain
E-mail: minwir@yahoo.com

INTRODUCTION

Future business environments are expected to witness accelerating rates of change and uncertainty, a shift towards a reactive mode of change and towards knowledge-based customization of products or services. The basic notion of the chapter holds that organizations respond to environmental changes through organizational response activities that seek to diffuse existing pressures, exploit existing opportunities, or create new opportunities. As a response to environmental drivers, customer knowledge management (CKM) has been introduced as an integrative knowledge-based customer-centric strategic business model that intends to create value for customers and develop long-term loyal and profitable relationships through development of products and/or services that meet customer preferences.

EXTERNAL ENVIRONMENT

This part of the chapter discusses basic concepts related to organizational environments and the relationship between organizations and their environments. It explains the main concepts such as the general environment, task environment, and environmental scanning.

THE GENERAL ENVIRONMENT

Organizations' environments include external drivers that affect business delivery of products or services, and, in turn, customer satisfaction. Business external environments are becoming increasingly dynamic, competitive, and complex, carrying with them both challenges and opportunities. Adaptability to environmental conditions is becoming a key prerequisite to survival and success in today's turbulent environments.

The 21st-century corporations face unprecedented complex and dynamic business environments and develop newly emerging organizational characteristics. New ways of doing business coupled with fast paced markets and continuous information generation require knowledge-based skills to be consistently utilized and improved in order to achieve Supply Chain Advantage (Bontis, 2004). Conducting a PESTIL analysis may identify general environmental conditions that impact a business. PESTIL is an acronym for political, economic, social, technological, international, and legal conditions. Major environmental conditions in today's marketplace include increased power of customers, growing competition, globalization of business, technological advancements, and government interventions.

THE TASK ENVIRONMENT

In this section, a low-level new classification of environments is provided, namely, the task environment. Because the impact of the general environment sometimes is vague, imprecise, and long term, most organizations tend to focus their attention on their detailed and observable task environment. The task environment includes five components: competitors, customers, suppliers, strategic partners, and regulators. The task environment provides useful information to the organization more readily because managers can identify environmental factors of specific interest to the organization, rather than having to deal with the high-level and more abstract dimensions of the general environment (Griffin, 2005).

ENVIRONMENTAL ANALYSIS MODEL

Some writers try to explain the concept of organizational change based on the notion of the environment as an objective entity *per se* that pressurizes organizations to change. Organizations in dynamic and complex business environments need to continue to monitor feedback from their environments and make appropriate adjustments in order to avoid decline or even failure. Inaccurate perceptions of the environment as an objective entity may occur when the environment is *objectively* stable, but managers perceive it as turbulent and take unnecessary actions (Type I error), or when managers threaten the survival of their firms by failing to take actions as they perceive their environment as stable when it is *objectively* turbulent (Type II error) (Boyd et al., 1993; Sull, 1999).

Forces for and against change, for instance, are not purely contingent upon objective environmental events but upon images of these events held by chief executive officer (CEO) and senior management. This implies that organizational change actions will take place only when perceived forces for change exceed those against it, and it also implies that 'brainpower' will have a profound impact on setting future directions of organizations, as manifested in the planning, design, and development of change programmes (Boyett and Boyett, 1995).

The purpose of environmental scanning is to develop a complete understanding of the three dimensions of environments, known as the 'environmental scanning trilogy'. Environmental scanning involves a four-dimensional dynamic and creative macro level analysis of opportunities and threats in business environments that include three components (Figure 8.1)—dynamism, diversity, and differentiation:

1. Dynamism (static versus dynamic): It refers to the fact that environmental conditions are relatively dynamic and are subject to constant changes at different degrees of pace, volume, and intensity.
2. Diversity (similar versus diversified): It refers to the fact that there are multiple diverse or identical PESTIL factors that exist in the environment and challenge business organizations to respond.
3. Differentiation (old versus new): It relates to the evolving and renewable nature of diverse and dynamic environmental conditions. For instance, new socio-economic or technological conditions could emerge while old ones are subject to decline or even demise.

FIGURE 8.1
A Four-dimensional Environmental Analysis Model

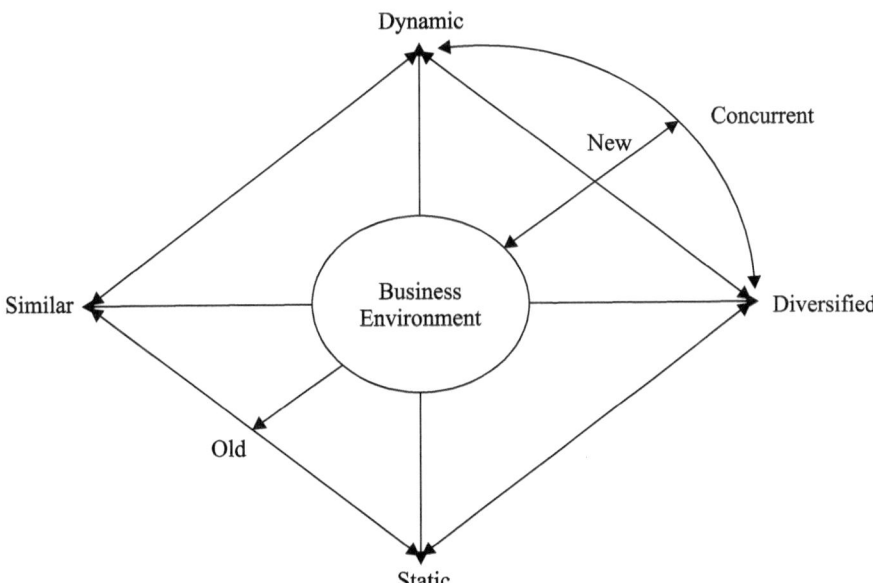

Source: Author.

CKM: A HOLISTIC CHANGE MODEL

Organizational change and its management may be analyzed from partial or total change perspectives. A partial change perspective takes one particular type of intervention, i.e., technology, people, or processes. On the other hand, holistic change takes a pluralistic approach to change that is based on simultaneous utilization of multiple sources of intervention. Comprehensive understanding of change and its management will not come from a single discipline (Hughes, 2006). Burnes (2004) suggested that change management is not a distinct discipline with rigid and clearly defined boundaries that the theory and practice of change management draws on a number of disciplines.

The 21st century's economy has witnessed a shift from focus on products to focus on services for both manufacturing and service organizations. Customer service can be considered as a competitive battlefield, and the process to deliver customer service can be considered as a weapon for competition. Companies recognized that it is more appropriate to concentrate on serving the customer rather than producing the product. Some of the organizational requirements to continue to be competitive are (Burlton, 2001):

- To adopt a customer and product focus, not a product focus only.
- To design customizable modules of products that can evolve and change.
- To use adaptable technologies wherein rules and workflows can be changed without getting programmers involved.
- To focus on the continuous enhancement of the knowledge of workers.
- To build flexible, responsive processes.

One of the most popular business approaches in responding to external environmental drivers is to support knowledge-intensive customer processes required for the transformation towards customer-centric organizations. The model does not try to sell too much too soon, rather, a number of steps need to take place in between, each of which requires permission to move to the next step. Finalizing a sale requires building confidence and trust, and then moving up through higher levels of permission to strike a deal. Such a task requires offering knowledge to customers in order to create familiarity and trust, as well as infusion of knowledge into business processes to make it easy for customers to buy and interact with sellers.

This chapter proposes CKM as a knowledge-intensive holistic business model for supply chain (SC) organizations. CKM is a total strategic change business model for building long-term profitable and loyal relationship with customers in order to face highly competitive and dynamic business environments. The undertaking of CKM as an integrative business solution requires a complete transformation from product-centred and hierarchical to customer-centric and networked organization. CKM is a holistic business model that integrates the aforementioned organizational change programmes.

The major planned change programmes that may be undertaken by organizations are: strategic information systems (SIS); total quality management (TQM); just-in-time (JIT); knowledge management (KM); organizational learning (OL); business process re-engineering (BPR); customer relationship management (CRM); and electronic business (e-biz) (Currie, 2000; Turban et al., 2002). The CKM strategic change lies in the heart of the change programmes and represents a holistic business model that integrates all of the previously mentioned change programmes.

STRATEGIC INFORMATION SYSTEMS (SIS)

Strategic systems provide organizations with advantages that enable them to increase their market share, better negotiation with suppliers, or to prevent competitors from entering their territory (Callon, 1996). An example is Federal Express's overnight delivery system. The system enables tracking of the status of every individual package.

TOTAL QUALITY MANAGEMENT (TQM)

TQM is a corporate-wide quality effort concerned with improving competitiveness, effectiveness, and flexibility. The core of TQM is about improving relationship with customers and suppliers (Currie, 2000).

JUST-IN-TIME (JIT)

JIT is a comprehensive production scheduling and inventory control system that attempts to reduce costs and improve workflow by scheduling materials and parts to arrive at a workstation exactly when they are needed. JIT minimizes machine downtime, in-process inventories, wastes, and storage space. JIT is a philosophy that can be applied not only to inventory to many business areas such as production management methods and techniques, total quality assurance, total preventive maintenance, customer–supplier relationships, technology or innovation strategies, flexible working practices, and machine performance (Currie, 2000).

KNOWLEDGE MANAGEMENT (KM)

KM tells us how to create, store, process, and use knowledge efficiently and effectively. KM is best interpreted as complex, multilayered, and multifaceted (Blackler, 1995). Effective KM methods and systems are needed to store, access, navigate, and probably use the vast amount of information to generate knowledge. Examples of knowledge-based systems are Data Mining (DM) and neural network (NN) systems. Recently, many companies have incorporated KM policies and practices into their corporate strategies and systems (Davenport et al., 1998).

Organizational Learning (OL)

The concept of OL has become a popular organizational change programme from the late 1970 to the early 1990s. OL occurs through shared insights, knowledge, and mental models, and build on past knowledge and experience. Some writers even emphasize the learning organization and its advantage to business (Senge, 1990).

Business Process Reengineering (BPR)

BPR is a 'clean sheet' redesigning or streamlining of work processes to increase efficiency, improve quality, and reduce costs. Technological, human, and structural dimensions of an organization may all be changed in BPR (Hammer and Champy, 1993, Peppard and Rowland, 1995).

A somewhat similar approach to BPR, is process innovation, was proposed by Davenport (1993). Process innovation encompasses the envisioning of new work strategies, the actual process design activity, and the implementation of change in all complex technological, human, and organizational dimensions (Davenport, 1993).

Customer Relationship Management (CRM)

Due to the increased power of customers and stiff competition, companies are increasingly becoming more customer-oriented. In addition to the traditional activities of customer service, companies are finding it necessary to pay more attention to preferences of customers, and so they are redesigning themselves to meet customers' demands (Turban et al., 2002).

Electronic Business (E-biz)

Doing business electronically is the newest and perhaps most promising strategy that many firms can pursue (Turban et al., 2002). E-biz is another form of organizational response to business pressures. E-biz is an expansion of electronic commerce by adding computer applications for business transactions such as e-CRM, Enterprise Resource Planning (ERP), Supply Chain Management (SCM), e-procurement (integrates ordering, fulfillment, and payment), and Business Intelligence (BI) Applications such as, Date Warehousing or Mining and KM technologies (Kalakota and Robinson, 2001).

CKM FOR SUPPLY CHAIN ORGANIZATIONS

An SC is a network of facilities and distribution options that performs the functions of procurement of materials, transformation of these materials into intermediate and finished products, and the distribution of these finished products to end customers. SCM is a systems approach to managing the entire flow of information, materials, money, and services from upstream suppliers through internal transformations of factories/service providers and downstream intermediaries to the end customer. Traditionally, marketing, distribution, planning, manufacturing, and the purchasing organizations along the SC operated independently, and as a result, no single, integrated plan exists for the organization. SCM is a strategy that provides the mechanism through which these different functions can be integrated together.

ERP FOR SUPPLY CHAIN AUTOMATION, INTEGRATION, AND COLLABORATION

ERP systems have frequently been used for automating internal business transactions through the creation of an integrated database of storing and viewing data across the enterprise (Figure 8.2). However, new forms of organizational relationships and technological advancements, especially the Internet and electronic commerce, have brought SCM and its systems to the forefront of management attention. SCM has emerged as the new key to improve value-added inter-organizational processes of manufacturing and service enterprises. Companies traditionally used ERP systems to support management of an enterprise. However, major ERP companies are now offering SC solutions as a major extended feature of their ERP packages.

Electronic value-added SC may be achieved when customers and suppliers are successfully linked to the business external value chain system (Figure 8.3). SCM is based on a series of linked, planned–source–make–deliver–and–return processes (Fawcett et al., 2007) that aims at promoting inter- and intra-enterprise integration and collaboration of people, systems, processes, and information across the enterprise, including business partners and end customers. SCM systems seek to improve visibility of what is happening upstream and downstream through process automation and collaboration between trading partners.

SCM helps organizations know where they can add value to their customers or suppliers. The e-SC integrates front-office with back-office transactions and improves the efficiency of processing purchase orders by cutting down on product or process cycle time and by enabling

FIGURE 8.2
Typical ERP System Components for SCM Processes

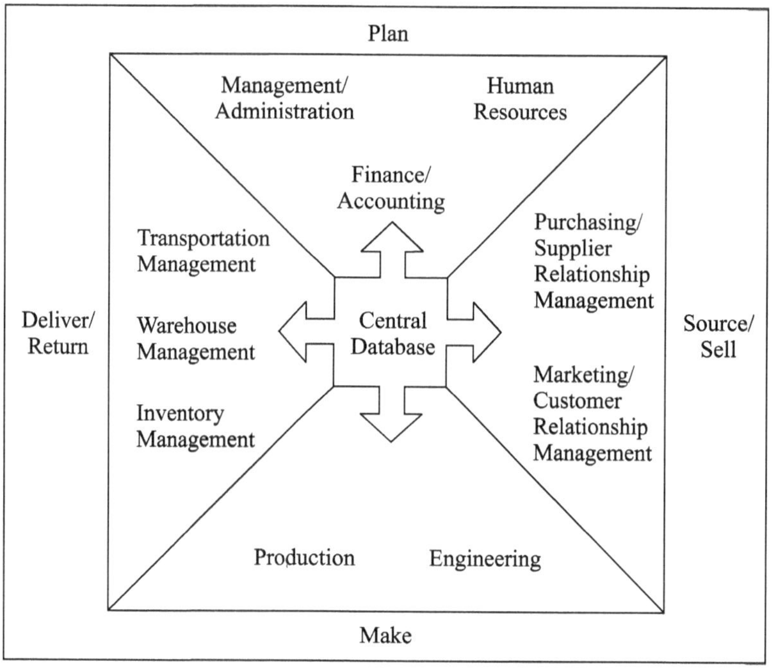

Plan

Management/
Administration

Human
Resources

Finance/
Accounting

Transportation
Management

Purchasing/
Supplier
Relationship
Management

Deliver/
Return

Warehouse
Management

Central
Database

Source/
Sell

Inventory
Management

Marketing/
Customer
Relationship
Management

Production   Engineering

Make

Source: Fawcett et al. (2007).

FIGURE 8.3
External Business Value Chain Model

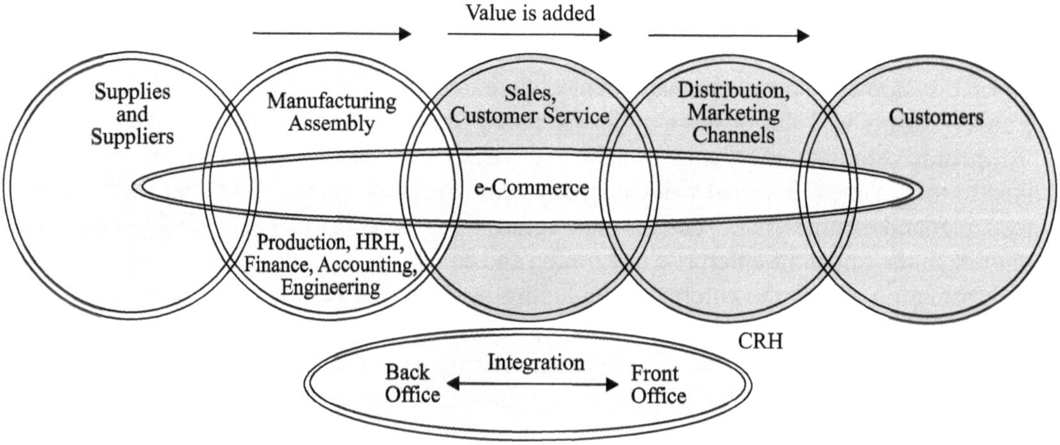

Value is added

Supplies
and
Suppliers

Manufacturing
Assembly

Sales,
Customer Service

Distribution,
Marketing
Channels

Customers

e-Commerce

Production, HRH,
Finance, Accounting,
Engineering

CRH

Back
Office

Integration

Front
Office

Source: Turban et al. (2008).

retailers to check on available sock before placing orders. The e-SC also gives manufacturers a competitive advantage as customers are electronically linked to the order entry system find it easier to place orders through the networked system of certain manufacturer than with others.

A Proposed SCM Model for Integrating CRM, ERP, SRM, and BPR

An effective enterprise's value chain for competing in a particular industry is embedded in a larger stream of knowledge-based market activities that may be referred to as the 'external value chain' or 'SC' that includes suppliers and distribution channels. Achieving sustainable competitive advantage requires that synergies of a firm's SC be leveraged as a system rather than as a collection of separate parts.

Cooper and Ellram (1993) compare SCM to a well-balanced and well-practiced relay-race team. Such a team is more competitive when each player knows how to be positioned for the hand-off. The relationships are the strongest between players who directly pass the baton, but the entire team needs to make a coordinated effort to win the race. Optimizing the performance of individual links within a SC is of limited value if these links have little or no visibility or integration with what is happening upstream and downstream as the strength of the SC is judged by its weakest link. Therefore, information and information and communication technology (ICT) systems are essential for decision-makers to be able to respond to unexpected deviations and secure higher organizational performance. Mansor and Bahari (2008) have studied the integration of ERP systems and the Balanced Score Card (BSC) in Malaysian firms and found that such integration is significant in driving performance management. Such a study could also help to link ERP systems with strategic information systems and BPR.

The CKM value chain model seeks to bring organizations together and by their synergies and shared values produce as a group in excess of their individual capacity. The value chain model once applied to SC may be operationalized through:

- Adoption of a knowledge-intensive process-based inter-organizational orientation.
- Formulation of a customer-centric business strategy.
- Development of a networked organization structure.
- Development of a networked ICT infrastructure in order to enable reconfiguration of knowledge-based customer-centric SC processes.
- Development of a team working spirit that allows knowledge sharing culture.

In addition to the mentioned infrastructural requirements, CKM, as a holistic change strategy, promotes an end-to-end SCM integration from point of manufacture to consumers by tying together the following components in order to secure effective flow management in SC (Figure 8.4): *(a)* CRM, *(b)* ERP, *(c)* SRM, and *(d)* BPR.

FIGURE 8.4
A Proposed SCM Model that Integrates SRM, ERP, CRM, and BPR

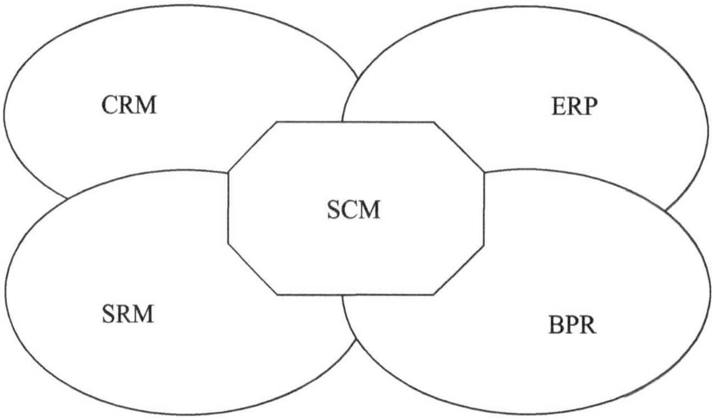

Source: Author.

Customer Relationship Management (CRM)

CRM is a combination of business processes and technology that seeks to understand customers multiple perspectives to competitively differentiate products and/or services. The goal of CRM is to 'increase the opportunity by improving the process to communicate with the *right* customer, providing the *right* offer (product or service), through the *right* channel, at the *right* time' (Swift, 2001: 14). The focus of CRM is to integrate processes in order to build relationships, improve customer satisfaction, loyalty, and revenues in the face of stiff competition, globalization, high customer turnover, and growing customer acquisition costs (Tiwana, 2001). The key CRM processes that take place between an enterprise and its customers downstream in the SC are marketing, selling, order management, and customer service.

Enterprise Resource Planning (ERP)

ERP systems represent the backbone of SCM and automate internal processes such as strategic planning, demand planning, supply planning, fulfillment, field service. ERP systems must be strongly integrated with CRM processes (Chopra and Meindl, 2007).

Supplier Relationship Management (SRM)

The SRM strategic choice for securing flow of raw materials, parts, components, or subassemblies is 'relationship' rather than 'ownership'. SRM processes focus on the interaction between the enterprise and upstream SC suppliers and there is expected to be a natural fit between SCM and SRM processes. Key SRM processes include design collaboration, source, negotiate, buy, and supply collaboration (Chopra and Meindl, 2007).

Business Process Reengineering

By coordinating and integrating, and reengineering value chain activities through strategic systems, e.g., ERP, an enterprise should be able to reduce transaction costs, reduce cycle time, gather better information for control purposes, and substitute less costly operations in one activity for more costly ones elsewhere. Therefore BPR is becoming increasingly important for gaining sustainable competitive advantage. In this situation, ICTs play a crucial role in enabling value chain revamp (removal of business mediators such as wholesalers, distributors, and retailers). Manufacturers sell directly to the customer (e.g., Dell Co.). Values achieved include higher efficiency (lower cost due to elimination of non-value adding processes), product customization, reduced time, and higher flexibility. Re-intermediation is possible through new intermediaries (e.g., infomediaries, e-retailers, aggregators, and portals) introduced at the downstream SC processes related to delivering the products to final customers or consumers.

In order to secure efficient transaction and information flow and to realize full benefits of standard ERP system, companies could make changes to their processes before implementing ERP or implement ERP systems and then make process changes. Conducting reengineering of business processes, i.e., eliminating or simplifying non-value adding activities for the customer, before ERP implementation may benefit from leveraging the capabilities of modern ICT systems and learning 'best learned lessons' from other organizations. In this option, the organization may not develop world-class business processes, but its employees would develop a good sense of process orientation and ownership. On the other side, when companies customize their ERP systems to suit existing business processes, their employees would lack process ownership and orientation. This option entails that ERP systems should be flexible enough, so that changes in business processes are easily automated and executed through changing ERP systems.

CONCLUSION

The only constant in life is change, and business organizations are not different. The 21st-century organizations live in a world of constant dynamic and complex change. Key business environmental drivers of change are changing nature and power of customers, increased competition, globalization of business, proliferation of the ICTs, as well as government regulations or deregulations have been discussed. Survival and success in the new wave of business changes depend entirely on the organization's ability to adjust to changing environmental conditions.

Therefore, environmental forces make organizations respond to competitive environments through change programmes like SIS, TQM, JIT, KM, CRM, OL, BPR, and e-biz. The aim of organizational responses is to create value adding propositions, i.e., quality, speed, timeliness of development, and delivery in order to satisfy customers.

As the focus of the world's economy has made changes in rules of competition as evidenced by a shift from products to services, and a shift in power from producers to customers, many companies have started looking for their distinctive core competencies, i.e., knowledge, as a non-depleting resource to achieve sustainable competitive advantage. For SC organizations that tend to be adaptive and successful, a knowledge-intensive customer-centric transformation strategy is inevitable in order to reduce order cycle times, lower inventory levels, improve accuracy and efficiency, lower costs, and improve customer service and satisfaction.

The chapter proposes a four-tier SCM model to combine upstream and downstream processes into a virtual SC network. The components of the model are CRM, ERP, CRM, and BPR. In order to maximize the performance of value chain organizations, SC may be revamped through elimination of a domestic distribution network and inventory and material handling, which in turn allows organizations to attain lower selling prices and a higher level of order fulfillment.

REFERENCES

Blackler, F. 1995. 'Knowledge, Work and Organizations: An Overview and Interpretation', *Organization Studies*, 16(6): 16–36.

Bontis, N. 2004. 'National Intellectual Capital Index: A United Nations Initiative for the Arab Region', *Journal of Intellectual Capital*, 5(1): 13–39.

Boyd, B.K., G.C. Dess, and A.M.A. Rasheed. 1993. 'Divergence between Archival and Perceptual Measures of the Environment: Causes and Consequences', *Academy of Management Review*, 210(2): 204–26.

Boyett, J.H. and J.T. Boyett. 1995. *Beyond Workplace 2000: Essential Strategies for the New American Corporation*. New York: Dutton.

Burlton, R.T. 2001. *Business Process Management: Profiting from Process*. Indianapolis, Indiana: Sams Publishing.

Burnes, B. 2004. *Managing Change*, 4th edition. Harlow: FT/Prentice-Hall.

Callon, J. 1996. *Competitive Advantage through Information Technology*. New York: McGraw-Hill.

Chopra, S. and P. Meindl. 2007. *Supply Chain Management: Strategy, Planning, and Operation*, 3rd edition. Upper Saddle River, New Jersey: Pearson/Prentice-Hall.

Cooper, M.C. and L.M. Ellram. 1993. 'Characteristics of Supply Chain Management and the Implications for Purchasing and Logistics Strategy', *The International Journal of Logistics Management*, 4(2): 13–24.

Currie, W. 2000. *The Global Information Society*. Chichester, England: John Wiley.

Davenport, T.H. 1993. *Process Innovation: Reengineering Work through Information Technology*. Boston, MA: Harvard Business School Press.

Davenport, Thomas H., David W. De Long, and Michael C. Beers. 1998. 'Successful Knowledge Management Projects', *Sloan Management Review*, 39(2, Winter): 43–57.

Fawcett, S., L. Ellarm, and J. Ogden. 2007. *Supply Chain Management: From Vision to Implementation*. Upper Saddle River, New Jersey: Pearson/Prentice-Hall.

Griffin, R. 2005. *Management*, 8th edition. Boston: Houghton Mifflin Company.

Hammer, M. and J. Champy. 1993. *Reengineering the Corporation: A Manifesto for Business Revolution*. New York: HarperCollins.

Hughes, M. 2006. *Change Management: A Critical Perspective*. London: CIPD Publications.

Kalakota, R. and M. Robinson. 2001. *e-Business 2.0: Roadmap for Success*. Boston, MA: Addison-Wesley.

Mansor, N. and A. Bahari. 2008. 'Integrating Enterprise Resource Planning Systems and the Balanced Score Card in Performance Management', *Proceedings of the International Conference on Business Globalization in the 21st Century*, University of Bahrain Press, Bahrain, pp. 136–51.

Peppard, J. and P. Rowland. 1995. *The Essence of Business Process Re-Engineering*. Upper Saddle River, NJ: Prentice-Hall.

Senge, P.M. 1990. *The Fifth Discipline: The Art and Practice of the Learning Organization*. New York: Doubleday.

Sull, D.N. 1999. 'Why Good Companies Go Bad', *Harvard Business Review*, 77(4): 42–52.

Swift, R.S. 2001. *Accelerating Customer Relationships: Using CRM and Relationship Technologies*. Upper Saddle River, NJ: Prentice-Hall.

Tiwana, A. 2001. *The Essential Guide to Knowledge Management: E-Business and CRM Applications*. Upper Saddle River, NJ: Prentice-Hall.

Turban, E., E. McLean, and J. Wetherbe. 2002. *Information Technology for Management: Transforming Business in the Digital Economy*, 3rd edition. New York: John Wiley.

Turban, E., D. Leidner, E. McLean, and J. Wetherbe. 2008. *Information Technology for Management: Transforming Organizations in the Digital Economy*, 6th edition. New York: John Wiley.

Section 2

Enterprise Systems—Implementation and Management

9

The 'Six Imperatives' Framework for the Evaluation of an ERP Project

MARIA ARGYROPOULOU
Brunel Business School
Brunel University, Uxbridge, Middlesex UB8 3PH, UK
E-mail: maria.argyropoulou@brunel.ac.uk

GEORGE IOANNOU
Management Science Laboratory
Athens University of Economics and Business, Evelpidon 47 a, Athens 113-62
E-mail: ioannou@aueb.gr

DIMITRIOS N. KOUFOPOULOS
Brunel Business School
Brunel University, Uxbridge, Middlesex UB8 3PH, UK
E-mail: dimitrios.koufopoulos@brunel.ac.uk

JAIDEEP MOTWANI
Seidman College of Business
Grand Valley State University, 401 West fulton, Suite 409C, Grand Rapids, MI 49504, USA
E-mail: motwanij@gvsu.edu

INTRODUCTION

After over a decade of applications, the implementation of Enterprise Resource Planning (ERP) systems is still considered a complex project with many problems concerning budgets and expected benefits. In spite of the inherent qualities and advantages of ERP systems, some problems can be identified through the different stages of ERP deployment. The type of problems and issues that arise from the implementation of ERP systems range from specific issues and problems that can come up during the installation of an ERP to behavioural, procedural, political, and organizational changes, that manifest themselves once the system is installed (Appleton, 1997; Benson and Rowe, 2001; Verville and Halingten, 2003). The results of the article by Verville and Halingten (2003) prove, contrary to the wide-standing belief that IT acquisitions are done routinely and fairly simply, that acquisitions of this nature (for ERPs) are complex, involved, demanding, and intensive. These findings coincide with those of Peterson et al. (2001), who claimed that ERP systems are complex software; consequently, implementations are difficult, long, and expensive. For these reasons, the business objectives are sometimes not even reached a year after the implementation.

Given the possibility for success and failures, it is reasonable to expect that organizations should be able to assess the implications of the ERP adoption on their overall performance. However, very few multi-disciplinary studies have been conducted in an attempt to conclude on the impact of ERP system on organizational performance. Moreover, the topic of assessing the benefits of ERP systems has not been fully addressed mainly because the justification process is a major concern for organizations investing in information technology (IT), and managers are unable to evaluate the holistic implications of adopting new technology, both in terms of benefits and costs (Gunasekaran et al., 2006). Questions like how do we define a successful ERP project have not yet been answered.

ERP System Implementation and SMEs

Existing literature suggest that small and medium enterprises (SMEs) may be differentiated from larger enterprises by a number of key characteristics such as personalized management, severe resource limitations, flat and flexible structures, etc. (Berry, 1998; Burns and Dewhurst, 1996; Huin, 2004; Marri et al., 1998). Another major characteristic of SMEs is the absence of proper and formal information system (IS) practices and skills. In the present era of globalization, it is obvious that the survival of SMEs will be determined by their ability to understand and acknowledge the importance of IS and their accessibility to the right information at the right time (Sharma and Bhagwat, 2006). Thus far, ERP adoption has been attempted by larger organizations, thereby consulting and implementation methodologies are specified for their operations. Following a study in 150 Italian SMEs, Morabito et al. (2005) concluded that the risks associated with investments in ERP software are many and resellers should be able to offer end-to-end business management solutions addressing specific requirements before and after implementation of the solution. According to Sun et al. (2005) few SMEs have the resources to adequately address every Critical Success Factor (CSF) as they should and they are forced to make implementation compromises according to resource constraints, subsequently putting the success of their ERP project at risk. Thus to improve the increased use of ERP systems and the overall business performance necessitates suitable ERP project management strategy. With limited financial resources and in most cases insufficient managerial and technical skills SMEs need a simple and comprehensive methodology to evaluate ERP implementation throughout the whole ERP lifecycle. Although there is no company to accept or justify an unsuccessful investment, it is obvious that large companies can afford the damages better than SMEs as they have more resources available. It is imperative for smaller companies to embrace ERP projects with great care (Argyropoulou et al., 2007; Argyropoulou, Ioannou, Soderquist, and Motwani, 2008).

This study provides a framework for the evaluation of the impact of an ERP system on SMEs organizational performance.

The organization of the chapter is as follows: Section 2 reviews the related literature on ERP adoption and performance measures. Section 3 discusses the theoretical background of the recommended framework, as well as the methodological deployment describing the proposed performance metrics. Then, the case study findings are discussed and the chapter finishes with a discussion, limitations, and future research directions.

LITERATURE REVIEW

ERP Adoption and Organizational Benefits

Until recently most ERP researchers and practitioners generally talk about ERP CSFs and implementation models based on CSFs that address key implementation issues (Holland and Light, 1999; Motwani et al., 2005; Umble et al., 2003). Top management involvement, business plans, vision, vendor support, change readiness, teamwork, team composition, and communication were found to be critical factors to ensure a smooth introduction for successful ERP implementation (Ramayah et al., 2007).

ERP provides two major benefits that do not exist in non-integrated departmental systems: *(a)* a unified enterprise view of the business that encompasses all functions and departments and *(b)* an enterprise database where all business transactions are entered, recorded, processed, monitored, and reported. Moreover, it enables companies to achieve their objectives of increased communication and responsiveness to all stakeholders. This is the most important point raised when it comes to the ERP systems as they can support information sharing along company value chain and help companies achieve operating efficiency (Ngai et al., 2008). Shang and Seddon, (2000) introduced a framework which classified the types of benefits that organizations can achieve by using ERP systems. The authors explained that the expected benefits can be gained on five dimensions: operational, managerial, strategic, IT infrastructure, and organizational.

As Sumner (2005: 4) argues that an ERP achieves a number of important objectives, including maximizing throughput of information, minimizing response time to customers and suppliers, pushing decision-making down to the lowest appropriate level, and providing timely information to decision-makers. Moreover, according to the author, an ERP system integrates information throughout the supply chain. The key underlying idea of ERP is using information technology to integrate company operations. ERP systems impose 'an integrated systems' approach by establishing a common set of applications supporting business operations (Sumner, 2005: 3).

Motivated by the ERP benefits concept and considering the ERP system as the tool for internal supply chain integration, in this chapter it is suggested that ERP success is achieved when the organization is able to perform all its operations better and when the integrated information system can support the performance increase of the company. This comprises of the benefits that the company has reaped from the implementation of the ERP or the achievement of ERP objectives. This is often called benefits management (Willcocks, 1994) and is defined as 'the process of organising and managing such that potential benefits arising from IT are actually realized'. According to Colleman and Jamieson (1994) benefits management encourages manager to focus on exactly how they will make the system pay off and contribute to the business objectives.

Supply Chain Performance Measures

The literature review on the area of supply chain performance measures revealed three important frameworks: *(a)* the Supply Chain Operations Reference (SCOR) Model, developed by the Supply Chain Council (SCC) in 1996; *(b)* the Oliver Wight ABCD checklist; and *(c)* the Balanced Scorecard for Supply Chain Management (SCM) evaluation (Bhagwat and Sharma, 2007). The SCOR model provides a common process oriented language for communicating among supply-chain partners in the following decision areas: plan; source; make; and deliver. It contains 12 metrics which fall into four categories: *(a)* delivery reliability metrics; *(b)* flexibility and responsiveness metrics; *(c)* cost metrics; and *(d)* assets metrics. The Oliver Wight ABCD 20 point checklist, on the other hand, is a guide used by manufacturing professionals to improve their company's performance. It addresses the following business areas: strategic planning; people and team systems; product development; continuous improvement; planning; and control. Both frameworks do not cover every area of ERP performance, but they give an indication about the company's overall business performance. In a recent study Bhagwat and Sharma (2007) propose a balanced approach for SCM performance evaluation. The authors used the Balanced Scorecard or BSC (Kaplan and Norton, 1992) four perspectives and developed a new framework structurally similar to BSC with corresponding metrics that reflect SCM strategy and goals.

IS Performance Measures

Many researchers focused on measuring IS performance (Cha-Jan Chang and King, 2005; DeLone and McLean, 1992, 2003; Jiang and Klein, 1999; Mirani and Lederer 1998; Pitt et al., 1995; Saarinen, 1996; Sharma and Bhagwat, 2006; Torkzadeh and Doll, 1999). All these studies have substantially contributed, in that they advocate the importance of performance measurement for the improvement of business activities and they identified a number of metrics for the IS function.

However, most of them have developed and tested general survey instruments, which measure IS performance without focusing on a specific system being evaluated and its purpose.

ERP Systems Performance Measures

The review of recent literature covering the particular area of ERP systems impact on overall performance allowed us to identify the following significant papers: *(a)* Wieder et al., (2006) who conducted a field study to find the impacts of several aspects of ERP adoption using IT measures, business process performance measures, and firm performance and *(b)* Chand et al., (2005) who carried out a case study research where a BSC-based framework for valuing the strategic contributions of an ERP system was applied. Motivated by these two researchers but mainly by the Information Systems Functional Scorecard (Cha-Jan Chang and King, 2005), Argyropoulou, Ioannou, Soderquist, and Motwani (2008) and Argyropoulou, Ioannou, Koufopoulos, and Motwani (2008) introduced a new framework called the 'six-imperatives' framework which provides a solid methodology for the identification and incorporation of the necessary metrics for ERP system post implementation review. The framework was used to measure and compare the impact of the ERP implementation project on two Greek SMEs.

The next section describes briefly the theoretical background as well as the methodological deployment of the 'six-imperatives' framework, for the readers to comprehend the rational of the case study analysis that follows.

THE 'SIX-IMPERATIVES' FRAMEWORK—THEORETICAL BACKGROUND

The theoretical background of the framework is based mainly on two previously developed methodologies: The Information Systems Functional Scorecard developed by Cha-Jan Chang and King (2005) and the 'six-imperatives' framework for ERP system selection and evaluation developed by Argyropoulou, Ioannou, Soderquist, and Motwani (2008) and Argyropoulou, Ioannou, Koufopoulos, and Motwani (2008). Both these frameworks are briefly described in the remainder of this section (detailed theoretical information can be found in Argyropoulou, Ioannou, Soderquist, and Motwani, 2008 and Argyropoulou, Ioannou, Koufopoulos, and Motwani, 2008).

The Information Systems Functional Scorecard (ISFS)

The Cha-Jan Chang and King (2005) scorecard is based on the model suggested by Pitt et al. (1995), and has been designed to measure the performance of the entire IS function. The authors developed an instrument consisting of three major dimensions: systems performance, informa-tion effectiveness, and service performance. These dimensions constituted the basic constructs for their field study research. These are briefly discussed in the next paragraph, whereas the ISFS sub-constructs are presented in Table 9.1.

TABLE 9.1
Sub-ISFS Constructs

Systems performance	Information effectiveness	Service performance
Impact on job	Intrinsic quality of information	Responsiveness
Impact on external constituencies	Contextual quality of information	Reliability
Impact on internal processes	Presentation quality of information	Service provider quality
Effect on knowledge and learning	Accessibility of information	Empathy
Systems features	Reliability of information	Training
Ease of use	Flexibility of information	Flexibility of services
	Usefulness of information	Cost/benefit of services

Source: Cha-Jan Chang and King (2005).

Systems performance: Measures of the systems performance assess the quality aspects of the system such as reliability, response time, ease of use, and so on, and the various impacts that the systems have on the user's work.

Information effectiveness: Measures of the information effectiveness assess the quality of information in terms of the design, operation, use, and value provided by information as well as the effects of the information on the user's job.

Service performance: Measures of service performance assess each user's experience with the services provided by the IS function in terms of quality and flexibility.

THE SIX IMPERATIVES FRAMEWORK FOR ERP SYSTEM IMPLEMENTATION

According to Figure 9.1, the ERP system's evaluation should commence well before imple-mentation, during the selection process, where necessary ERP objectives are identified, and determined (Argyropoulou, Ioannou, Soderquist, and Motwani, 2008). Any SME that wishes to implement an appropriate ERP system should primarily conduct an in-depth analysis of their strategy and needs based on six imperatives which represent the building pillars on which the investigation is actually performed and are critical for implementation and operative success. These are analyzed briefly in the following paragraph, to draw attention to the main activities, issues, dynamics, and complexities involved in the ERP project implementation cycle (detailed analysis in Argyropoulou et al., 2007; Argyropoulou, Ioannou, Soderquist, and Motwani, 2008).

FIGURE 9.1
**Synthesis of the 'ISFS Scorecard' and the 'Six Imperatives' Framework for
the Assessment of an ERP Project**

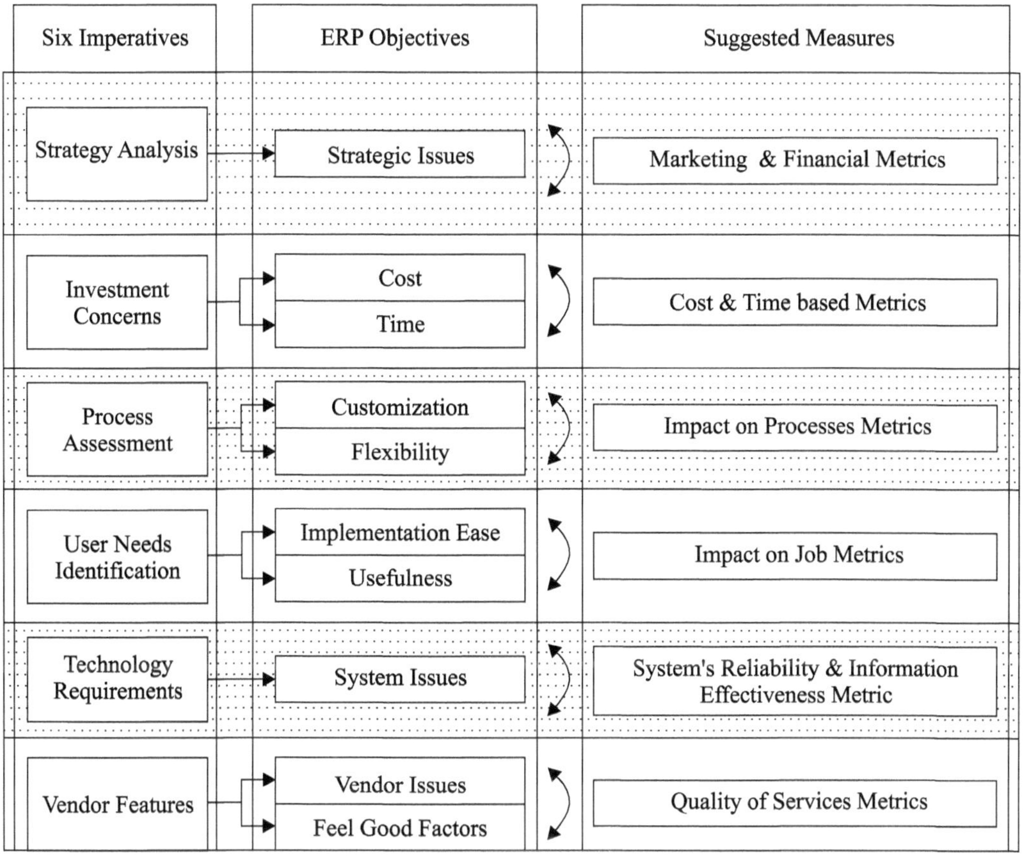

Six Imperatives	ERP Objectives	Suggested Measures
Strategy Analysis	Strategic Issues	Marketing & Financial Metrics
Investment Concerns	Cost / Time	Cost & Time based Metrics
Process Assessment	Customization / Flexibility	Impact on Processes Metrics
User Needs Identification	Implementation Ease / Usefulness	Impact on Job Metrics
Technology Requirements	System Issues	System's Reliability & Information Effectiveness Metric
Vendor Features	Vendor Issues / Feel Good Factors	Quality of Services Metrics

Source: Argyropoulou, Ioannou, Koufopoulos, and Motwani (2008).

The strategy analysis imperative implies that companies should look for ERP implementation options and objectives concerning the package's alignment with the corporate strategy and competitive priorities such as expansion, alliances, or other competitive priorities. The investment concerns imperative emphasizes the importance of investment justification in an ERP project and the two associated objectives are: *(a)* adherence to time schedule and *(b)* contingency budgetary planning which can reduce the issues relating to increased financial expenses that may label the project as a 'black hole' or failure.

The process assessment imperative suggests that the ease of customization and systems functionality should constitute the basic ERP objectives because a better fit between packaged software functionality and user organization requirements leads to successful implementation and usage. The user needs identification imperative recommends that the future system should be designed to support business processes based on the needs and capabilities of the current and future users. The ERP objectives stemming from this imperative are the development and communication of an easy system, which fulfils a range of specific user needs, and expectations that will be covered under the term 'usefulness' of the system.

The technology requirements imperative considers the technical characteristics as well as the system's integration with other information technologies within the supply chain. Moreover, it implies that the ERP must produce the required information when needed, and that control over both the information and the information systems is maintained. The vendor features imperative commands an effective supplier relationship management (SRM) by implementing specific supplier selection practices.

An organizational analysis based on the these imperatives leads to a number of ERP objectives to be achieved, which integrate all the expected benefits pursued in order to derive value from the new system (Figure 9.1). The specific objectives, that are determined pre-project, can serve as a guidance tool throughout the whole ERP lifecycle and especially for post-implementation review (Argyropoulou, Ioannou, Soderquist, and Motwani, 2008; Nicolaou, 2004). Combining the Sub-ISFS Constructs (see Table 9.1), and the 'six-imperatives' framework, (Argyropoulou, Ioannou, Soderquist, and Motwani, 2008) provided a set of performance metrics which can actually measure to which extent the pre-determined ERP objectives have been achieved (see Appendix).The strategy analysis and the investment concerns measures were drawn from the recent literature (i.e., Hunton and Bieler, 1997; Irani, 2002; Poston and Grabski, 2001, and the SCOR model as it was used by Weider et al., 2006). The remaining metrics were based on the ISFS sub-constructs (see Table 9.1). At this point it should be mentioned that any organization might choose amongst a number of metrics available in the literature. The important issue is their direct relationship to the ERP implementation objectives and the degree to which the latter have been achieved.

METHODOLOGY

TESTING THE 'SIX-IMPERATIVES' FRAMEWORK

This section describes a practical example of the use of the 'six-imperatives' framework for measuring the impact of an ERP project in a Greek SME. The original 'six-imperatives' framework for ERP evaluation and implementation had been applied in NR SA, a Greek company of the aquaculture sector (Argyropoulou, Ioannou, Soderquist, and Motwani, 2008). In this chapter, the same framework is used to measure the impact of ERP on organizational performance after two years of its adoption.

The 'action research' strategy has been followed as the whole project focused on action, promoting change in the company (Cunningham, 1995; Marsick and Watkins, 1997) and involved academics with a genuine concern for the expected findings (Eden and Huxham, 1996: 75).

COMPANY BACKGROUND

The company is one of the most dynamic and rapidly expanding Greek enterprises in the aquaculture industry. In 2006, the company had successfully implemented an ERP system following top management's strategy to reengineer and automate some of their complex processes. Two years later, top managers decided to conduct a post-implementation review of their ERP system. They retained the services of the same project team (comprising academics and consultants) for the post-implementation review activities to measure the actual performance of their ERP system.

DATA COLLECTION

The measures were provided to the IT manager one week prior to the scheduled interview allowing them to look for answers not readily available. These people were fully aware of the ERP system's impact on their operations and they found it rather is to give us the results which are presented in Table 9.2 whereas a brief explanation is discussed in the next section.

ANALYSIS OF RESULTS

COMMENTS ON 'STRATEGY ANALYSIS' MEASURES

The pre-project 'strategic goals' were the optimization of business processes, the standardization of operations flow, the establishment of customer-centric policies, and the support of operations in the whole group. These were translated into financial and marketing measures which indicated that there was a 10 per cent reduction of cost of goods sold (COGS) or revenues mainly due to a reduction in production costs. For NR SA inventory costs and labour hours were significantly reduced due to a more effective production schedule that followed ERP implementation. NR SA also reported that the percentage of missed orders or total orders reduced from 4 per cent before ERP to 2 per cent after ERP adoption because of the specific marketing or sales module implementation. The delivery time was also improved by 10 per cent as the data warehouse application for in-bound and out-bound logistics had been in use for the last 12 months.

TABLE 9.2
Actual Performance Measures

Imperative	Measure	Difference between the 2005 measures and the year end 2007 (pre-project and post-implementation)
Strategy analysis		
Financial	% reduction of COGS/revenues	10%
Marketing	% reduction of missed orders/total orders	50%
	% reduction of delivery time	10%
Investment concerns		
Time-based	Processing time along critical path	6 months
Cost-based	Direct project costs	Within budget
	Indirect human costs	10%
	Indirect organizational costs	N/A
Process assessment		
Impact on internal processes	Reduction in order fulfilment time	5%
	Reduction of order cost	12%
User needs		
Impact on job	% of errors per function/department	50% improvement
Ease of use	Number of training hours per user	90 days
	Number of consultant days per user	N/A
Impact on knowledge/ learning	productivity	40% increase
Technology requirements		
Systems reliability	Number of restoration hours	N/A
	Number of maintenance hours	as projected
Information effectives		
Accessibility	Number of hours that the information was not received in timely manner.	
Accuracy	Number of errors in reports	Limited
Flexibility	Number of hours for parameterization customisation	4 man months
Vendor Features		
Service Responsiveness	Response time and maintenance fees	As projected

Source: Authors.
Note: COGS: Cost of goods sold.

COMMENTS ON 'INVESTMENT CONCERN' MEASURES

The pre-project objectives concerned specific time and budget limits. NP reported that the project had been successfully completed within the time limits. The new system was to be up and running in six months. They had replaced their legacy systems almost immediately, following a two-month period of preparatory training. Indirect human costs exceeded budgets by 10 per cent due to additional training and motivation schemes. Indirect organizational cost overruns were not reported as all organizational restructuring had already been planned during the pre-implementation needs analysis.

COMMENTS ON 'PROCESS ASSESSMENT' MEASURES

The ERP objectives before adoption concerned reduction of order fulfilment time and order cost. Two years later the managers of NR SA reported a 5 per cent reduction in order fulfilment time and a 12 per cent reduction in order fulfilment cost. They explained that that the new system had been easily customized which was very important for their unique processes and competitive priorities. Additional attention had been paid to the unique business processes of the aquaculture sector (long lead times for fish production, live product with dynamic development, sensitivity to external factors, multiple plants with various capacities, perishable inventories, etc.).

COMMENTS ON 'USER NEEDS' MEASURES

The pre-project objectives concerned a useful system (with the following characteristics: ease of learning, usability of interfaces, quality of training programmes) and an easy system (i.e., available in the desired time frame, easy to administer, and efficient in terms of technical support required). The managers of NR SA were enthusiastic to report that most employees were able to perform after a 90-day training period (the training had started right after the system selection phase at the vendor's premises). The productivity index which was calculated as labour hours or total orders had been decreased from 0.28 to 0.185 which resulted in a 40 per cent increase in productivity. As far as the impact on the job is concerned they explained that errors (measured as a percentage of returns) had been improved to 0.2 per cent from 0.4 per cent.

COMMENTS ON 'TECHNOLOGY REQUIREMENTS' MEASURES

The original decision concerned a gradual replacement of all legacy systems and a new information system with a number of requirements concerning installation, reliability, and information effectiveness. The installation requirements were: (*a*) centralized administration and control scheme, according to which all data management procedures, application administration, and network operation and management would be handled at the Headquarters (HQ); (*b*) remote site equipment which would be mainly used for capturing data and providing access to all applications; *(c)* infrastructure that could support remote monitoring and control functions; and *(d)* architecture which could allow other supply chain software solutions and web-based integration systems reliability was measured by the number of maintenance and restoration hours. The managers of NR SA explained that the 2007 maintenance hours were according to projections; restoration hours were not reported as the system was rather new for breakdowns.

Information effectiveness was measured in terms accessibility, accuracy, and flexibility. The managers said that it took them four man-months for parameterization and data loading which, however, had been projected in the first months of the system's design. The original project schedule involved six months for the system to be up and running and most of it concerned data migration. There were no delays for data transfer-data re-entry. In addition information effectiveness measures compared the quality of information before and after implementation and it became apparent that the reporting system had been significantly upgraded: the reports were produced in a timely manner comprising the necessary information for the recipients.

COMMENTS ON 'VENDOR FEATURES' MEASURES

The managers of NR SA explained that the choice of the suitable vendor might have been the most important factor for the system's success. The lack of sufficient in-house knowledge of the inherent intricacies could have caused many problems—even failures. However, the supplier had been willing to cooperate and the expertise had been imparted to end-users smoothly and effectively. Finally, the vendor responded immediately to all the encountered problems and challenges.

CONCLUSIONS AND FUTURE DIRECTIONS

This research reports on a case study of a Greek SME that implemented an ERP system. Using established approaches in the literature of IS performance measurement, in this chapter, a previously developed model was tested for the evaluation of an ERP project. The 'six-imperatives' framework consists of six key components, each of which containing a set of metrics, expressed in measurable units, or percentages. The holistic approach of the framework is simple and can be used by managers. The suggested metrics can be objective, and can provide SMEs with valuable information in a fast and accurate way, to ensure the comprehensiveness in their decision-making which in most cases can strengthen their competitive position. The 'six-imperatives' framework for ERP performance measurement contributes to the ERP evaluation literature because it integrates the necessary factors to be considered in this process.

Conclusively, this framework illustrates the critical factors or issues that need to be addressed at all three phases of the implementation process: pre-implementation or setting-up phase, implementation, and post-implementation or evaluation phase. Future research might compare the 'six-imperatives' framework with the balanced scorecard and/or other performance measurement frameworks. Moreover, it can be further expanded and used as an instrument for field study research.

APPENDIX

Methodological Deployment of the Six-Imperatives Framework

Imperative	Measure	Relevant literature
Strategy analysis		
Financial	% reduction of COGS/revenues	Net benefits proposed by DeLone and McLean (2003)
	% reduction of inventory holding cost	SCOR model
	% reduction in logistics costs	SCOR model
Marketing	% reduction of defects	Total Quality Management Theory
	% reduction of lead time	SCOR model
Investment concerns		
Time-based	Processing time along critical path	Project management theory
Cost-based	Direct Project Costs	Irani et al. (1997); Irani (2002)
	Indirect Human Costs	Irani et al. (1997); Irani (2002)
	Indirect Organizational Costs	Irani et al. (1997); Irani (2002)
Process assessment		
Impact on internal processes	Reduction in process time	Cha-Jan Chang and King (2005)
	Reduction of process cost	Cha-Jan Chang and King (2005)
User needs		
Impact on job	Number of errors per function/ department	Cha-Jan Chang and King (2005)
Ease of use (Cha-Jan Chang and King, 2005)	Number of training hours per user	Cha-Jan Chang and King (2005)
	Number of consultant days per user	Cha-Jan Chang and King (2005)
Impact on knowledge/learning	Rate of sick leave, or staff turnover	New
	% increase in employees' productivity	SCOR model
Technology requirements		
Systems reliability	Number of restoration hours	New
	Number of maintenance hours	New

(*Appendix continued*)

(*Appendix continued*)

Imperative	Measure	Relevant literature
Information effectives		
Accessibility	Number of hours that the information was not received in timely manner	Cha-Jan Chang and King (2005)
Accuracy (Cha-Jan Chang and King, 2005)	Number of errors in reports	Cha-Jan Chang and King (2005)
Flexibility (Cha-Jan Chang and King, 2005)	Number of hours for customization and enhancements	Cha-Jan Chang and King (2005)
Vendor Features		
Service Responsiveness	Response time and maintenance fees	Cha-Jan Chang and King (2005)
Service Flexibility	Response time and maintenance fees	Cha-Jan Chang and King (2005)

Source: Authors.
Note: COGS = Cost of Goods Sold.

REFERENCES

Appleton, E.L. 1997. 'How to Survive ERP', *Datamation*, 43(3): 50–53.

Argyropoulou, M., G. Ioannou, and G.P. Prastacos. 2007 'ERP Implementation at SMEs: An Initial Study of the Greek Market', *International Journal of Integrated Supply Management*, 3(4): 406–25.

Argyropoulou, M., G. Ioannou, K.E. Soderquist, and J. Motwani. 2008. 'Managing ERP System Evaluation and Selection in SMEs using the 'Six-imperatives' Methodology', *IJPM V1*, 4: 430–52.

Argyropoulou M., G. Ioannou, D. Koufopoulos, and J. Motwani. 2008. 'Performance Drivers of ERP Systems in Small and Medium-sized Enterprises', *International Journal of Enterprise Network Management*, 2(3): 333–49.

Benson, P. and F. Rowe. 2001. 'ERP Project Dynamics and Enacted Dialogue: Perceived Understanding, Perceived Leeway, and the Nature of Task-related Conflicts', *Database for Advances in Information Systems*, 32(4, Fall): 47–66.

Berry, M. 1998. 'Strategic Planning in Small and High Tech Companies', *Long Range Planning*, 32(3): 455–66.

Bhagwat, R. and M.K. Sharma. 2007. 'Performance Measurement of Supply Chain Management: A Balanced Scorecard Approach', *Computers and Industrial Engineering*, 53: 43–62.

Burns, P. and J. Dewhurst. 1996. *Small Business and Entrepreneurship*, 2nd edition. London: Macmillan Press.

Cha-Jan Chang, J. and W.R. King. 2005. 'Measuring the Performance of Information Systems: A Functional Scorecard', *Journal of Management Information Systems*, 22(1): 85–115.

Chand, D., G. Hachey, J. Hunton, V. Owhoso, and S. Vasudevan. 2005. 'A Balanced Scorecard Based Framework for Assessing the Strategic Impacts of ERP Systems', *Computers in Industry*, 56: 558–72.

Colleman, T. and M. Jamieson. 1994. 'Beyond Return of Investment', in L. Willocks (ed.), *Information Management: The Evaluation of Information Systems Investments*, pp. 189–205, Chapter 10. London: Chapman & Hall.

Cunningham, J.B. 1995. 'Strategic Considerations in Using Action Research for Improving Personnel Practices', *Public Personnel Management*, 24(2): 515–29.

DeLone, W.H., and E.R. McLean. 1992. 'Information Systems Success: The Quest for the Dependent Variable', *Information Systems Research* 3(1): 60–95.

———. 2003. 'The DeLone and McLean Model of Information Systems Success: A Ten-year Update', *Journal of Management Information Systems*, 19(4): 9–30.

Eden, C. and C. Huxham. 1996. 'Action Research for Management Research', *British Journal of Management*, 71(1): 75–86.

Gunasekaran, A., E.W.T. Ngai, and R.E. McGaughey. 2006. 'Information Technology and Systems Justification: A Review for Research and Applications', *European Journal of Operational Research*, 173(3): 957–83.

Holland, C.P. and B. Light. 1999. 'A Critical Success Factors Model for ERP Implementation', *IEEE Software*, 16(3): 30–35.

Huin, S.F. 2004. 'Managing Deployment of ERP Systems in SMEs Using Multi-agents', *International Journal of Project Management*, 22(6): 511–17.

Hunton, J.E. and J.D. Bieler. 1997. 'Effects of User Participation in Systems Development: A Longitudinal Field Experiment', *MIS Quarterly*, 21(4): 359–88.

Irani, Z. 2002. 'Information Systems Evaluation: Navigating through the Problem Domain', *Information and Management*, 40(1): 199–211.

Irani, Z., J.N. Ezingeard, and R.J. Grieve. 1997. 'Integrating Costs of Manufacturing IT/IS Infrastructure into the Investment Decision-making Process', *Technovation*, 17(11/12): 695–706.

Jiang, J.J. and G. Klein. 1999. 'User Evaluation of Information Systems: By System Typology', *IEEE Transactions on Systems Man and Cybernetics*, 29(1): 111–16.

Kaplan, R.S. and D.P. Norton. 1992. 'The Balanced Scorecard—Measures that Drive Performance', *Harvard Business Review*, (January–February): 71–79.

Marri, H., A. Gunasekaran, and R. Grieve. 1998. 'An Investigation into the Implementation of the Computer Integrated Manufacturing in Small and Medium Sized Enterprises', *International Journal of Advanced Manufacturing Technology*, 14: 935–42.

Marsick, V.J. and K.E. Watkins. 1997. 'Case Study Research Methods'. in R.A. Swanson and E.F. Holton (eds), *Human Resource Development Research Handbook*, pp. 138–57. San Franscisco, CA: Berret-Koehler.

Mirani, R. and A.L. Lederer. 1998. 'An Instrument for Assessing the Organisational Benefits of IS Projects', *Decision Sciences*, 29(40): 803–38.

Morabito, V., S. Pace, and P. Previtali. 2005. 'ERP Marketing and Italian SMEs', *European Management Journal*, 23(5): 590–98.

Motwani, J., R. Subramanian, and P. Gopalakrishna. 2005. 'Critical Factors for Successful ERP Implementation: Exploratory Findings from Four Case Studies', *Computers in Industry*, 56: 529–44.

Ngai, Eric W.T., Chuck C.H. Law, and F.K.T. Wat. 2008. 'Examining the Critical Success Factors in the Adoption of Enterprise Resource Planning', *Computers in Industry*, 59(6): 548–64.

Nicolaou, A. 2004. 'Quality of Post Implementation Review for Enterprise Resource Planning Systems', *International Journal of Accounting Information Systems*, 5(1): 25–49.

Peterson, W.J., L. Gelman, and D.P. Cooke. 2001. 'ERP Trends', Conference Board, New York, NY.

Pitt, L.F., R.T. Watson, and C.B. Kavan. 1995. 'Service Quality: A Measure of Information Systems Effectiveness', *MIS Quarterly*, 19(2): 173–85.

Poston, R. and S. Grabski. 2001. 'Financial Impact of Enterprise Resource Planning Implementations', *International Journal of Accounting Information Systems*, 2(4): 271–94.

Ramayah, T., M.H. Roy, S. Arokiasamy, I. Zbib, and Z.U. Ahmed. 2007. 'Critical Success Fctors for Successful Implementation of Enterprise Resource Planning Systems in Manufacturing Organisations', *International Journal of Business Information Systems*, 2(3): 276–97.

Saarinen, T. 1996. 'An Expanded for Evaluating Information Systems Success', *Information and Management*, 31(2): 103–18.

Shang, S. and B.P. Seddon. 2000. 'A Comprehensive Framework for Classifying the Benefits of ERP Systems,' Paper presented at the Americas Conference on Information Systems (AMCIS), Long Beach, CA, 10–13 August.

Sharma, M.K. and R. Bhagwat. 2006. 'Performance Measurements in the Implementation of Information Systems in Small and Medium-sized Enterprises: A Framework and Empirical Analysis', *Measuring Business Excellence*, 10(4): 8–21.

Sumner, M. 2005. *Enterprise Resource Planning*. Upper Saddle River, New Jersey: Pearson Education, Inc.

Sun, A.Y.T., A. Yazdani, and J.D. Overend. 2005. 'Achievement Assessment for Enterprise Resource Planning ERP System Implementations based on Critical Success Factors CSFs', *International Journal of Production Economics*, 98(2): 189–203.

Torkzadeh, G. and W.J. Doll. 1999. 'The Development of a Tool for Measuring the Perceived Impact of Information Technology on Work', *Omega—The International Journal of Management Science*, 27(3): 327–39.

Umble E., R. Haft, and M. Umble. 2003. 'Enterprise Resource Planning: Implementation Procedures and Critical Success Factors', *European Journal of Operational Research*, 146(2): 241–57.

Verville, J. and A. Halingten. 2003. 'A Six-stage Model of the Buying Process for ERP Software', *Industrial Marketing Management*, 32(7): 585–94.

Wieder, B., P. Booth, Z.P. Matolcsy, and M.L. Ossimitz. 2006. 'The Impact of ERP Systems on Firm and Business Process Performance', *Journal of Enterprise Information Management*, 19(1): 13–29.

Willcocks, L. 1994. 'Introduction of Capital Importance', in L. Willcocks (ed.), *Information Management: The Evaluation of Information Systems Investments*, Chapter 1, pp. 1–27. London: Chapman & Hall.

10

Enterprise Resource Planning Systems Implementation: A Practical Approach

MANOJ JHA

Senior Consultant,
HRMS, Aricent Technologies

ABSTRACT

The successful adoption process of an enterprise system has been of significant importance for the successful progress made by enterprise systems over last few decades.

A number of research have been carried out since the early 1990s to analyze the process of adoption of enterprise system by organizations of different sizes and across different industries and identify and enlist critical success factors of the adoption process.

While Enterprise Resource System vendors have gone through the process of incorporating technological advances and business process enhancements, the organizations adopting these solutions and the consulting companies helping them in the process have also modified and optimized the processes over these years.

This chapter describes a success story of Enterprise Resource System making efforts to highlight the 'Critical Success Factors' that could be generalized and adopted for replicating this success. The author has also introduced a new 'Seven Stage Enterprise System Adoption Model' using seven stages of an ERP adoption process.

INTRODUCTION

This chapter provides an overview of implementation of Enterprise Resource Planning Human Resource Management System (ERP HRMS) solution for a reputed industry leading organization. Even though HRMS involves only human resource (HR) related processes and modules, the adoption initiatives actually have all the elements of an ERP module, consist of similar challenges, need similar approach, have the same success factors, and, in every way, could be treated as any typical Enterprise Solution Adoption Project. The examples used in this chapter are from large and reputed organizations. They represent live examples for sole purpose of learning.

The author has introduced a new 'Seven Stage Enterprise System Adoption Model' using seven stages of an ERP adoption process (Figure 10.1).

1. Expectation management stage
2. Foundation stage
3. Business process review and streamlining
4. Implementation stage
5. Data exploitation stage
6. Extension stage
7. Innovation stage

This case study has been written in a narrative format moving from one stage of adoption to the other, moving back and forth in time horizon to highlight the real-life adoption experience.

FIGURE 10.1
Seven Stages of ERP Adoption Model

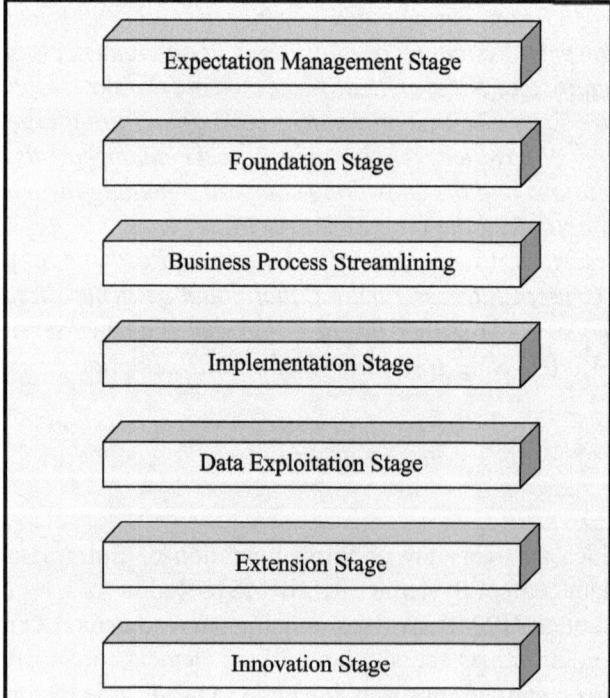

Source: Author.

Finally, a quick literature review of Enterprise Resource adoption process and critical success factors has been provided. The author has also briefly introduced his own 'Seven Stage Adoption Model' and 'Critical Success Factors' in this section.

ES Adoption: A Real Success Story

This section of the chapter attempts to apply the 'Seven Stage Adoption Model' to the story of ERP adoption of a world-class organization, a leader in application of technology and development, and implementation of innovative solutions using technology. The model is still being developed by the author as part of his research on ERP adoption process.

The story dates back almost to the beginning of the new millennium and describes the ERP adoption process in HR and payroll areas over a period of almost a decade. The company is being named 'Company X' for referring in this chapter.

Some of the facts and figures have been suitably altered in order to maintain confidentiality of the organization keeping the academic relevance of the story.

Background

Technology adoption and implementation in an organization as well as the maturity of governance processes around their information technology (IT) plays extremely critical roles in the foundation stage. In Company X, the organization was fairly matured in the usage of IT and its IT governance process. This made the task of setting the right expectations as well as correct priorities.

Information Technology

Company X prides itself as a pioneer in integration of technology with business. Ever since its inception, the organization earned a name for introducing innovative solutions and managed to receive numerous industry accolades confirming its status as one of the industry leaders.

The use of information and communication technology (ICT) has been at the forefront of business strategy. IT has been used in both operational and strategic levels. They have been consistently spending on development and upgradation of applications that provide them operational efficiency as well as convenience and competitive advantage.

The Head of IT always said, 'IT is as core to our business as our core equipments.'

The IT division of Company X not only boasts of an experienced employee strength having considerable industry experience to augment their understanding of technology. Most of the processes were IT-enabled and having developed industry leading software in key business process areas and a host of other custom-built IT solutions that give them a leading edge, their IT division is a highly regarded set-up in the industry.

A study of the progress of the company powered by ICT indicates that Company X has had a DUAL Focus. The executive team of the company was aware of the potential of technology and considered it as a strategically important factor to achieve targeted growth. As one of the senior executives of the company said, 'We can sustain double digit growth and continued reduction of our unit costs only through innovative integration of Information Technology into our processes and by including Self-Service wherever feasible.' It only confirms the statement made by their head of IT, 'IT is as strategically important for us' (Figure 10.4).

A review of business cases of Company X and their top five (value-wise) initiatives reveals the expected return on IT investments cover both increased market share as well as improved bottom line. IT is seen both as the tool to improve offerings and bring efficiency gains.

IT Governance

IT governance is extremely important in deciding the role IT can practically play in delivering competitive advantages. The IT projects were driven by business focus and the responsibilities of delivering business benefits was optimally balanced between the business and IT project managers. Most of the projects have a project management team comprising of business and IT specialists.

Project Management methodology was provided by 'their own standards', which is a blend of Project Management Institute's Project Management Standards and Prince II methodology.

As recommended by Jeanne Ross and Peter Weill (2002), the organization was following the policy of business executives who were made responsible for IT projects. This ensured accountability. The IT and business team responsible for the project met regularly to review the progress. Business managers have been responsible for determining the measurable success factors, plan for enhancements, training, and business support. The ERP implementation team comprised of the business project manager and the IT project manager. On completion of the project, the business project manager was made the head of Business Support Group (BSG) who took full responsibility for managing user training, analysis, and business impact of new releases and development of Standard Operating Procedures (SOP). They have achieved a reasonably high level of success in ERP implementation and have been one of the reference customers for their ERP vendor.

There are teams of business analysts on the IT side and BSG executives who develop long-term relationship and understanding of IT vision. These specialists work together effectively to deliver IT projects, anticipate business IT needs and are 'Relationship Asset' (Piccoli and Ives, 2005) for the organization (Figure 10.2).

FIGURE 10.2
Composition and Focus of Project Team

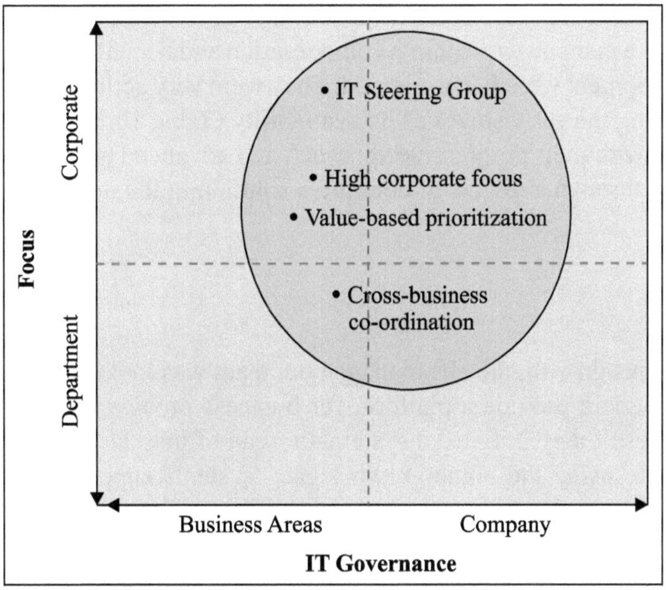

The decision regarding IT projects was taken by the IT Steering Committee, which kept the corporate focus. The IT Steering Group consisted of top executives from business units and the head of IT. It was responsible for budget approvals, major project reviews, prioritization, and major resource allocations. Since senior executives from various business units were part of this group, it helped in ensuring the group was able to prioritize projects based on quality and strength of business cases. The Head of IT provided necessary technology inputs and ensured a consistent set of projects that were in line with medium and long-term IT focus are taken up, while business representatives maintained business focus.

IT projects maintained files that contained details of lessons learnt which were later referred by new projects. Risk analysis was carried out in the beginning of the projects and a risk file was maintained by the project manager throughout the project life cycle.

HR Department

Company X had a matured and well-established HR department. The policies and procedures were well developed and applied to the whole organization in a uniform way. In spite of being a conglomerate of different businesses, the HR department adopted a blend of centralized and decentralized functions to ensure efficient application of HR principles.

The HR department was very efficient in the use of IT with implementation of efficient applications including self-service functions in critical areas of leave management, performance appraisal, information query, and update.

The processes like manpower planning, compensation and benefit management, recruitment, training, and development were fairly matured. They were very active in adoption of computer-based training during the early stages of its availability (Table 10.1).

Keeping in line with their progressive approach and advanced usage of IT, it is no surprise that they had gone through a review of enterprise solution in the mid-1990s.

Need for Change

As part of continuous growth, the HR management team was looking for a world-class packaged solution that could provide a platform for business process integration within the HR department. As a result they initiated a systematic scan of market for the available packaged solution. They were using the home-grown legacy systems supported by various modules developed over the years. The legacy system was creaking. 'The original design did not allow us to implement new changes as required. The transactions generated are also ever increasing in size and managing the database is becoming an issue,' said Faizal (name changed),[1] the IS manager handling HR Systems.

After a failed attempt to evaluate and implement an enterprise solution in the mid-1990s as a short-term measure, oracle database was built and data was being transferred at various frequencies, depending upon business needs and technological feasibility, from legacy system, but it had an added overhead of data transfer and maintainability.

However, by the end of the 1990s, the need to change was being felt again. The need could be summarized as follows:

- Technology restrictions
- Functionality limitations
- Integration issues
- Inter-operability of modules
- Maintainability
- Availability of support/maintenance staff
- Availability of competent enterprise solutions

The existing system was developed using an old technology.

---

[1] Names of the company and its employees have been changed to maintain confidentiality. Only issues relating to the implementation model have been discussed in detail in this chapter.

The tremendous rise in the volume of data handled was also putting pressure on the existing legacy system. There was minimal or no current support for key HR and training business functions such as planning, recruitment, and overseas operations for having a consolidated database for better controls.

There was little or no support for strategic HR management initiatives such as increased devolution, succession planning, career progression or planning, new structures (matrix), and more complex performance tracking and remuneration.

Self-service and workflow initiatives could not work due to lack of technology integration.

Online interfacing and interaction with other oracle-based applications was also not possible. This resulted in inconsistencies in data across various systems.

A senior executive from the HR department of the company said:

Our existing system has a future of about 2 years due to increase in staff strength [80K transactions are updated on a monthly basis, the database was never designed to handle such volumes], system complexity and increasing integration and change issues. A number of business changes, had to be curtailed and such problems will only increase.

The senior executive also said:

We want a suit of application that reduces over dependence on IT department for our day-to-day needs. We want to empower our HR Service employees, provide Line Managers with most up to date information regarding their employees and increasingly use self service for routine data maintenance.

FOUNDATION STAGE

Evaluation of HRMS

A further evaluation cycle was initiated when the proposed ERP package was put forward in Quarter 3 of 1999 as a possible complete solution to the HR, Finance, and Procurement business areas.

Even though there was a general feeling of satisfaction regarding the HRMS and its related suite of products, a comprehensive evaluation process was initiated. 'We want to learn more about the product through our investments in evaluation process,' said the senior executive leading the evaluation process at Company X.

Two senior managers from HR and IT departments were sent to the ERP vendor's office for complete training on all the modules of the HRMS product suite. The new version was in the pipeline, but this training was primarily aimed at 'understanding the heart and soul of HRMS and getting a first hand feel of what the product offers to us'.

A task force consisting of members from all HR and IT departments was prepared for formal evaluation. A comprehensive document of requirements were prepared and sent to the vendor's local office.

A series of presentations and demo sessions were organized, but something was still missing. 'I am not getting convinced with the efforts being put by the consultants running the demo. Get me a consultant who understands the product inside out,' demanded the project manager.

Finally, a two-week session covering critical features was organized at one of the implementation partners' office. Through the demos and workshop, it became clear that, like other ERP solutions, HRMS is a very generic product, which without defining rules cannot be mapped against given requirements and the detail functionality cannot be seen without taking up a full implementation phase. Again, it was not possible to do a product evaluation without seeing our core must-see functionality.

A consulting organization was given the necessary briefing regarding the must-see business rules and was asked to do a mini implementation so that effective evaluation of HRMS functionality could be carried out.

TABLE 10.1
Requirement and Fit Assessment of Various Functional Modules

Module	Importance	Requirement fit	Vendor recommended fit
HR	30%	82%	87%
Payroll	30%	78%	83%
Training	18%	76%	84%
Recruitment	18%	74%	76%
Other Functions	4%	76%	81%
Overall		78.04%	83.04%

Source: Author.

There were some gaps identified during the evaluation process, but the team was convinced that the product meets the overall objective of an integrated solution within HR departments with a potential to integrate with financial modules, which were very likely to follow suit. An overview of 'solution architecture' was drawn at this stage which indicated that they will have to build their own attendance module, retain the existing performance appraisal system, and online information distribution system.

The flexibility offered by the legacy system to make changes in employee records at any stage and integration of the attendance management module with payroll calculation engine provided a great strength to the payroll department in carrying out 'what if scenario analysis', while processing termination-related payments. A plan, while implementing the HRMS modules, was drawn to ensure these in-house developed systems be made 'custom modules' to augment the core modules.

Vendor Selection

Once the product was selected, the next task was negotiating the best commercial deal with the vendor in terms of licencing costs, support during implementation, any additional support, and implementation partner selection (Figure 10.3).

FIGURE 10.3
Implementation Partners

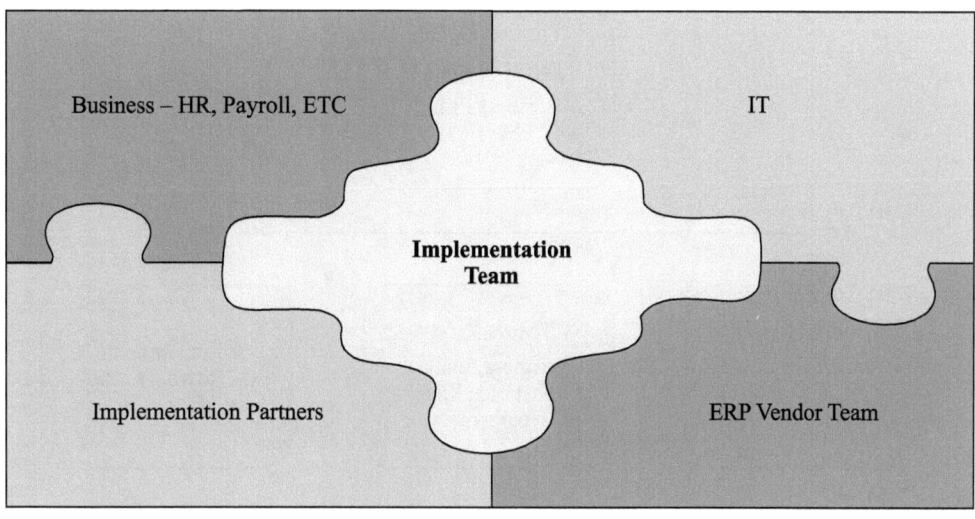

Source: Author.

Some preliminary scanning was done with regard to availability of consulting organizations with expertise in HRMS. The exorbitantly high costs of consultants also made the decision of partner relatively simpler and straight-forward. The implementation partner had a small team and the only implementation they had on HRMS was in a small African country. Hence, in order to mitigate the risk, expert management advice was contracted from the vendor's UK office. This subsequently proved to be a very good move as it opened up doors of the vendor's development lab and, in subsequent stages, experts from the vendor's corporate office were coming at regular stages to guide the project team.

IMPLEMENTATION STAGE

Team Selection

A team consisting of full-time members from HR Services, Payroll, and Training Administration departments was put together. All the team members were assigned to the project team on a full time basis. Other experts were available on a as-and-when-needed basis, but due to top management support, availability of such experts was never an issue. However, full-time members had 'implementation of HRMS' as their key objective for their performance reviews.

A business project manager was appointed by the HR department to be fully responsible for the implementation. Its IT department also appointed their 'HR systems manager' as the

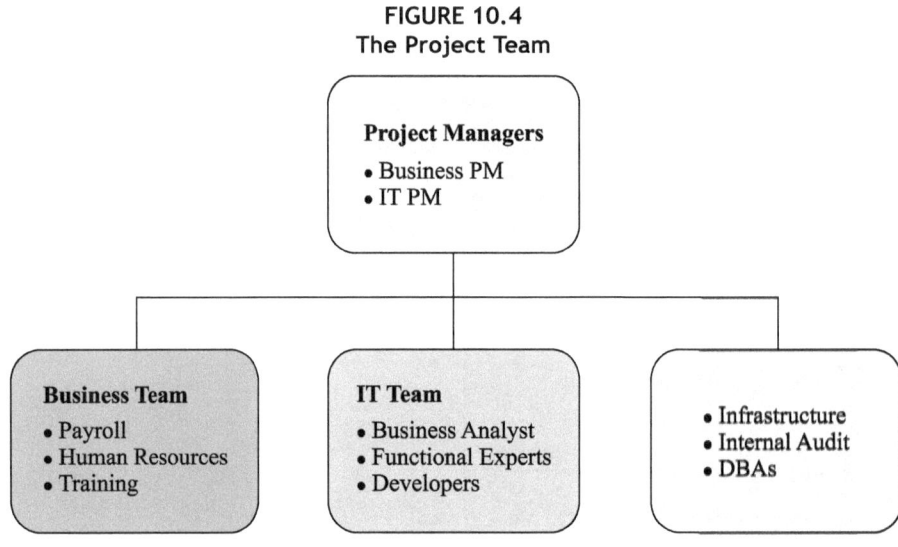

FIGURE 10.4
The Project Team

Source: Author.

project manager. A team of business and IT experts were carefully chosen to ensure the project team had an adequate mix of experience and vision.

Representatives from Internal Audit and Infrastructure divisions were also put on the project team. The idea was to address any system security and infrastructure incompatibility issues during early stages of the project.

The team was divided on functional lines. An external expert was assigned to each of these functional teams. They were primarily responsible for their own process areas. The processes cutting across these functional areas were discussed in a joint meeting managed by the Senior Business Analyst, Rakesh, who was also doubling as support to Faizal in managing project planning and control.

The team first focused on handling key decision areas like 'work structure' and 'chart of accounts' (finance-related). Once these decisions were taken, the teams worked fairly independently and met as the project team once a week where progress and plans were discussed.

Project Kick-off

The project initiation was done with the kick-off meeting addressed by the chief director of Services and Operations at Company X, sending a clear signal of top management support. In his key address, he stressed the need of keeping the focus on achieving the main objective of implementation by adopting the 'Keep it Simple' philosophy. This session was also attended by the regional director of the ERP vendor indicating the importance attached to this implementation. This was in process of being the first major implementation of HRMS in the region.

The kick-off session was followed by a short phase where project planning was initiated by the Project Management Team consisting of the business project manager, IT project manager, vendor project manager, and the senior business analyst. A simplified implementation methodology, which was a mix of ETVX model, Vendor's Own Implementation Model, and the implementation partner model, was selected. This methodology focused on completion and reviewing of each phase before the initiation of the next phase (Figure 10.5).

FIGURE 10.5
Implementation Methodology

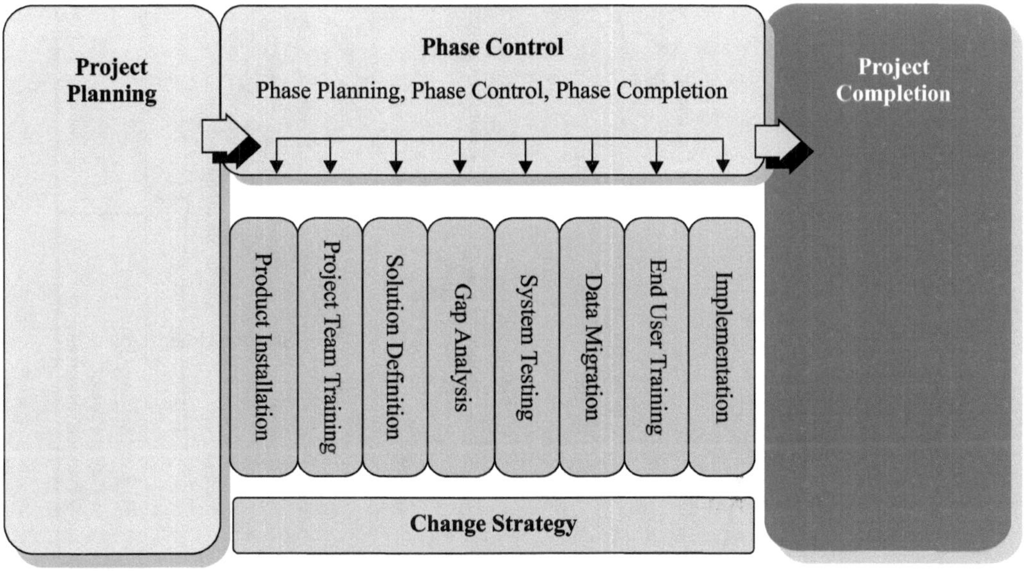

Source: Author.

Immediately after the kick-off meeting, the full working group met to reflect on what they called 'Blue Sky Discussions'. The objective of such a discussion was to brainstorm what the long-term vision of HR was so that the project could focus on aligning itself with the vision.

Project Charter was also subjected to a very detailed discussion ensuring it reflected and included all aspects of project objectives, governance, and controlling processes.

A detailed 'brainstorming session' to identify the risks associated with the massive implementation project also took place around this time. Within 10–15 days all aspects of project management, project plan, and project management plan were ready to revalidate within the team.

'Free and fair discussions' were encouraged to ensure all aspects and views were considered before the plan was finalized.

'We have to live by our Project Charter for the duration of this project. Hence, it is extremely important it covers all our discussions and decisions,' said Albert, who was very excited about the project as he knew he was moving in the right direction (Figure 10.6).

FIGURE 10.6
Project Overview

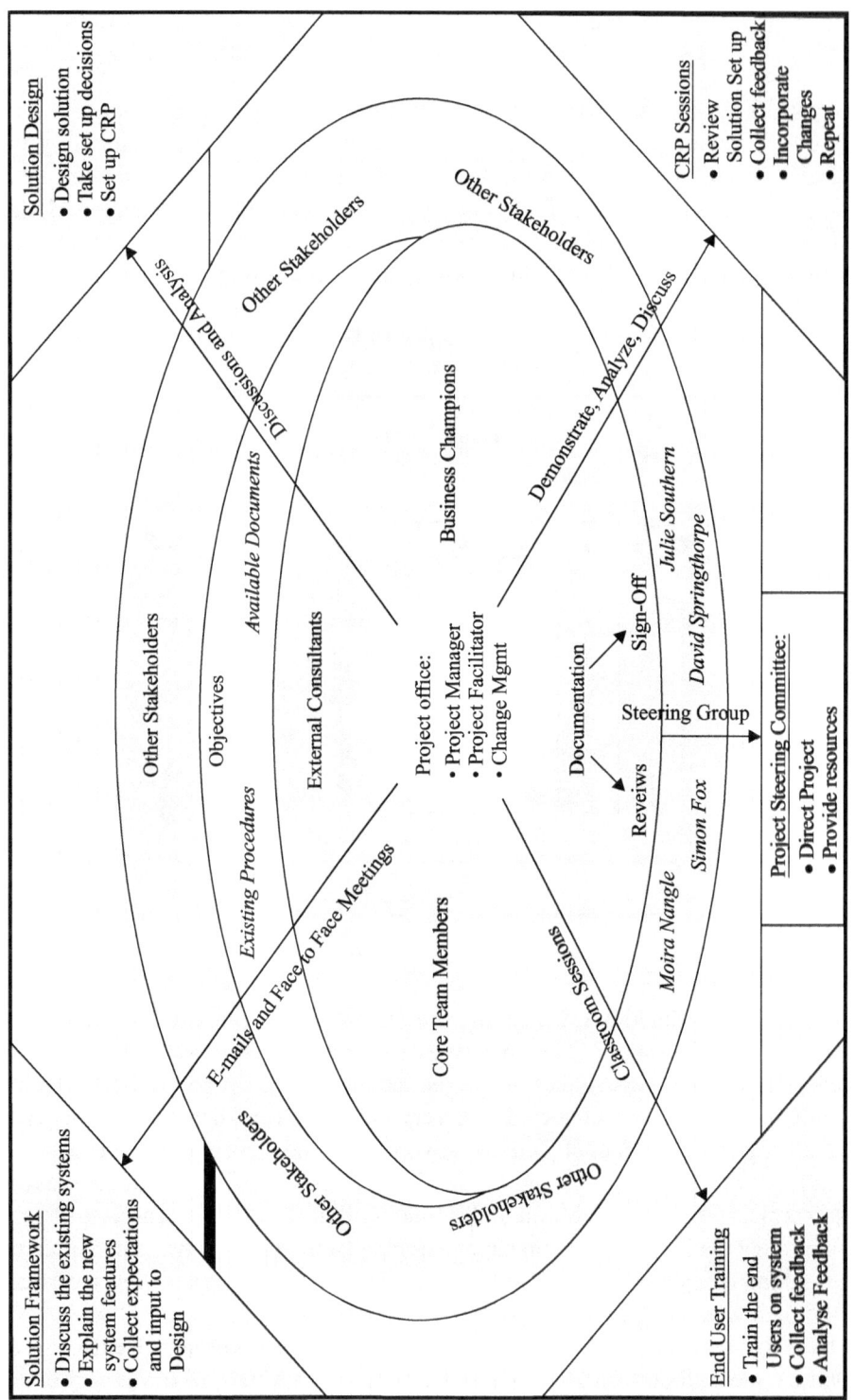

Source: Author.

Project Management Approach

Project management approach could be summarized as follows:

- Continuous review.
- Iterative approach in key areas.
- Complete involvement of all stakeholders.
- Appropriate and timely decision-making.
- Top management support.
- Integrated working group consisting of:

  - IT
  - Top business leaders
  - HR
  - Finance
  - Procurement

Albert was involved in the project almost full-time, which was a clear sign and result of top management interests in the project. What made the project even more important was the view taken by the Finance department which said that they will follow suit with the implementation based on how HRMS implementation goes.

Discussions were encouraged all the time. The Project Team consisting of HR, IT, and external consultants were co-located in the project office. The atmosphere in the project office was entirely different and people were encouraged to become more and more informal with the target-focused approach.

The Project Review Group met every week and Albert himself presented in these review meetings.

Decision-making was largely divested in the business project managers (PM) and IT PM. Any escalation used to be handled very quickly. At no point of time, any decision remained pending for over a week. The Steering Group met once a month and largely focused on project progress and issues escalated to them such as:

- Vanilla implementation of ERP applications.
- No customization to the base product.
- Continuous business team commitment.
- Effective leadership and Steering Group.
- Phased/staged approach.
- Continuous review of objectives.

Vanilla implementation was the main slogan in the project office and any changes were discussed at great length to ensure no changes to product were made if any closely fitting work around was available.

The HRMS did not have a global payroll engine and they needed to build a dummy localization layer to handle payroll requirement. This was developed by the implementation partner and was primarily a copy of UK legislation.

The project team was trained on complete suit of HRMS products by ERP vendor at their local office. The training was aimed at ensuring that the project team is able to take an informed, involved, and appropriate decision during their Conference Room Pilot (CRP) stage.

At its peak strength, the project had 30 full-time members working on core implementation, interface development, and other custom development.

Top Management Support

Top management support was unflinching and complete to this project. Decision-making was largely decentralized to the project team.

The top management was extremely involved through the senior executive of HR, who, at one stage, would spend days together deliberating on project issues with the project team.

The Steering Group used to meet once a month and primarily focused on progress made and issue resolutions, if any. The kick-off meeting was addressed by the chief director, Services, who requested things to be kept simple. Even from the vendor's side there was tremendous level of support available. The head of the local region was present during the meeting and, from time to time, experts from the UK flew in to guide the project team. No decisions were pending for more than a week during the project and this was clearly one of the key success factors.

Even the core project team had a large level of representation from the middle-level management from the HR, which indicates top management support.

HRMS implementation project progress was regularly discussed in the weekly HR review meetings.

User Involvement

The project was run as a user-driven initiative. It consisted of a business project manager and the project team consisted of nearly 60 per cent members from the user community.

Even the project location was at the office headquarters on the same floor as the HR service centre.

Apart from the 'full-time members' in the project team, the project team had access to 'business process champions'. The success of the project was largely due to complete involvement of 'these business process champions' as they were called.

Even the 'working group' consisted of a 'payroll manager', 'training and administration manager', and 'senior recruitment manager' apart from the business project manager and HR services manager.

Approach to Training

The system was the new 'electronic nervous system' for the HR division and its 12,000 employees and managers. Delivering integration across processes and 'single version of truth' and empowering all the employees was the main objective.

But all the efforts of the project team hinged on how successfully the system was adopted. Hence, training the user community was extremely critical.

They adopted the following three approaches:

- Adopt the 'Train the Trainer' approach to ensure a continuous presence of 'application champions' at each strategic location. The idea was to empower these champions to help others in their location.
- Classroom training for the core HR employees.
- 'Auditorium sessions' were also organized to ensure 'generic features' are explained to larger audience to increase awareness.

The key focus areas for training were the add-on attendance module, which was to be used to handle flexible attendance management for the group. It was to be used by 500-plus users across various sections to enter 'attendance exceptions'.[2]

E-Learning was at its initial stages and even though it was discussed, it was not used as a training strategy.

Reporting Strategy

ERP was not found to be very strong in meeting the reporting needs and hence an 'Analytics Delivery Team' was formed immediately after the CRP stage was over. The team went through all existing reporting needs and validated it with the user community.

Reports were then developed in parallel to 'technical development'. This ensured that sufficient number of reports meeting all key functional requirements were ready in time for the cut-over. The team utilized their expertise and available infrastructure of D2K reports to handle the reporting requirements.

Reports delivery team was augmented towards end of the project phase and it continued its work even after the cut-over.

---

[2] Attendance was entered only by exception. For example, if some one is absent, an absent entry would be made. Absence of any entry meant the employee worked as per the 'Roster'. All employees including administrative staff were on rosters.

Cut-over Strategy

Implementing a system of this magnitude is always a challenge. Hence, a very careful approach was adopted. A change management team was formed consisting of representatives from all the major business units.

Three months of representative data testing was carried out and results were verified with the production system. The sample base for carrying out this test was carefully chosen so that representative employees were picked up from every business unit.

The results were analyzed and documented. Only after the successful completion of this stage, the team moved to the 'production parallel' run stage. This was almost like a production run.

The payroll run was on the old system which was then shut down for all data entry activities. The data was migrated carefully to the new system and a thorough verification exercise was carried out. Data was verified element by element for completeness and accuracy. The team had already done several 'dummy runs' of data migration and verification and, therefore, was aware of sensitive points. Balances were tallied and once the base data was 'signed off', the parallel run process was initiated. Payroll was the key process and parallel run was primarily focused on payroll run and verification.

The results on legacy system and new system were subjected to detailed verification. Wherever there were variations, they were either resolved or explained. After two cycles, the comparison looked acceptable and management gave a go ahead.

Other add-on modules were started one after the other, followed by the release of the new system for data entry and updates.

The group had an ERP after 18 months from the formal project kick-off.

BUSINESS PROCESS STREAMLINING AND EXPLOITATION

Being in the project office was a tough experience. Hectic activities were on to resolve issues to ensure the new system is accepted and used.

Setting up a 'support structure' was a key task. The BSG primarily consisting of 'project team members from business' was formed.

A membership of vendor's user group was obtained.

By now, they had a close relationship with the vendor, they were made member of Customer Advisory Board (CAB) and were also included on the Industry Special Interest Group. Memberships of these organizations ensure being up-to-date in terms of product development and also being able to influence some of the product changes.

Release of consultants from partner organization was another challenge. But the approach of 'Shadow IT Employee'[3] proved very useful. By the time the product was implemented, the

---

[3] Every external consultant had an IT member shadowing with him or her.

IT team had a bunch of ERP experts made out of original D2K experts. This helped them keep the cost of support to a very manageably low level.

The expertise acquired during the implementation was also potentially beneficial to the sales and market development team which was keen on adding 'ERP implementation services to industry customers' into their portfolio of offerings (Figure 10.7).

FIGURE 10.7
HRMS Functionalities

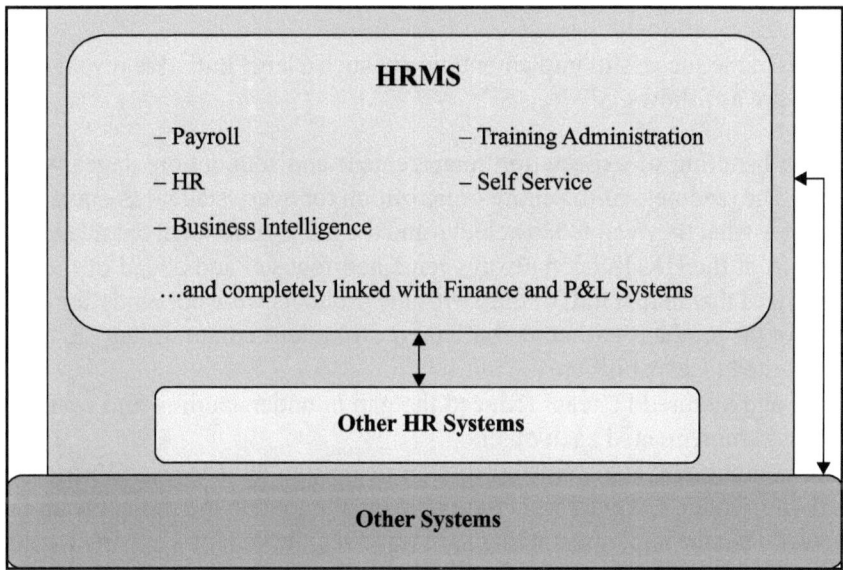

Source: Author.

DATA EXPLOITATION AND EXTENSION STAGES

They started building data warehouses using data from ERP system and other legacy systems. This gave them enormous advantage in terms of reporting and consolidation.

Development of additional online systems like 'payslip enquiry', 'leave and absences', and 'salary review process' gave them the benefit of online interaction with employees.

'Our employees are always connected to us and they get up to date information whenever they need and wherever they need it', says the head of HR at Company X.

The integration of HRMS database and online performance appraisal system enables them to conduct performance review session for always mobile staff members.

The company has gone though two cycles of version upgradation in seven years of ERP utilization. They have implemented the financials, e-Procurement and built seamless interfaces with a number of systems the organization uses. Their journey with enterprise systems continues.

The IT department is happy to share experiences with others in the industry and even leverages its expertise by offering consultancy on enterprise system adoption to other organization in the industry.

The next stage for them would be the innovation stage which will run concurrently with this stage.

CRITICAL SUCCESS FACTORS

A brief analysis of the successful implementation of such a large initiative reveals many factors. Some of them are as follows:

- Effective handling of expectation management and foundation stages was the key to success. The readiness of the entire organization for every stage was managed very well. They knew what they wanted to achieve and the cross-functional team lead by the senior leadership of the HR division always remained focused and ahead of the game. When they realized that in first half of the 1990s the products were not ready for adoption, they waited for the products to mature, built their own intermediate strategy to bridge the gap, and exploited IT capabilities.
- Capable and matured IT team reduced the gap in understanding and users and IT team members complemented each other.
- Vendor commitment also contributed significantly to the success. Whenever there was a need, the vendor's experts were available on-site to help the project team in all stages. Even well after the implementation phase was over, the vendor's experts would be present for database fine-tuning and performance analysis. This ensured a healthy partnership developed between them. The business analysts and enterprise system experts were also available to reciprocate by assisting the vendor in their sales efforts to industry prospects.
- Vanilla implementation of ERP modules to ensure subsequent upgrades could easily be incorporated in the implemented solution. This ensured continued flow of benefits of ERP over a longer time.
- The business team's continuous commitment was a key to the success of the implementation as they were accountable for ensuring that business case benefits were realized. They were driving the implementation ensuring that technology-savvy IT specialists do not lose focus of business benefits and that technology is used for meeting business objectives.
- Effective leadership: The Steering Group provided continuous support and quick decisions. Any changes in business practices were approved on priority basis and change management team was managed by one of the senior HR managers.
- A staged/phased approach ensured risk mitigation and step-by-step adoption of modules. HR modules were implemented by finance modules. Head office operations were implemented before overseas operations.

- Continual re-balancing to achieve objectives was done as suggested by Prince II methodology. The Project Team was empowered to review and propose changes in agreed processes.
- Integration with other initiatives was achieved through regular project bulletins. Monthly IT meetings of senior IT executives ensured every one was aware of the progress and dependencies were handled through the Interface Management Team. Interfaces were not changed as much as possible to make ERP implementation as far transparent as possible.
- Delivery of pre-requisites was ensured through coordination committee working under the umbrella of corporate project office. This ensured smooth transition and integration.
- Proper alignment with business objectives was achieved through detailed requirement document consisting of current practices and vision about the future.
- Effective change management was a key factor. ERP implementation changes the way business is conducted and results in restructuring and realignment of job responsibilities. The Change Management Team was fed with the impending changes to manage the related aspects in a proactive manner. A full-time Change Management Team was a very significant factor behind smooth transition.
- Continuous review of progress was made at agreed intervals as documented in the Project Charter. There were two significant international events during the implementation—the 9/11 bombings and the SARS outbreak. Due to clear set objectives and continuous review processes, everyone was aware of what is expected and, hence, the project progressed smoothly. Even a delay of two months from the original plan was very smoothly handled as everyone was fully on board and knew the reasons and benefits.
- Complete involvement of all members by having full-time and dedicated resources working on the project was also important to keep the focus during challenging and difficult times. Part-time members tend to shift focus during such demanding times.
- Iterative approach in key areas meant there were no inhibitions in revisiting decisions before they were implemented if they meant improved product delivery and stakeholder satisfaction.
- Encourage discussions throughout the project. Discussions ensured best possible options were always chosen.
- Quick and timely decisions made by the Steering Group and other senior stakeholders was also an important factor.
- An integrated working group was established to handle inter-department and division process flows. They consisted of senior managers from the respective departments who provided guidance to the project teams. Many potential problems were avoided as this group met at a regular interval and was fully aware of what was happening.
- Strong project management methodology made its own contributions towards successful outcome. ETVX model of starting and ending phases (stages) was adopted. This ensured that every stage had a pre-agreed entry and exit criteria and clearly delineated tasks and responsibilities.

LITERATURE REVIEW

ERP systems are integrated systems with mechanisms based on planning and forecasting, which support the management of the entire enterprise and integrate all its activities. The effective implementation of such a system can bring about many benefits, such as enterprise management and information flow enhancement. Consequently, improvement of economic indicators is achievable, which finally leads to an increase in enterprise profitability.

However, the achievement of these aforementioned benefits depends upon the effective implementation of the full functionality of the ERP system, which is quite difficult. There are a great many implementation projects that do not bring about the planned effects, or even end up in project abandonment. The duration and budget of the implementation projects significantly exceed initial estimates, and the planned scope of the implementation is limited (Parr and Shanks, 2000). Therefore, conducting research seems crucial in order to explore the conditions having an influence on the project outcome.

ERP IMPLEMENTATION MODELS

On the one hand, researchers and practitioners have proposed various implementation models such as those by Wallace and Kremzar (2001), Markus and Tanis (2000), and Parr and Shanks (2000). Majority of these models include the technical activities involved in the implementation as well as change management and organizational factors [a good description of these technical activities is given in Markus and Tanis (2000) and Miller (2000),—ASAP implementation—etc.]. The models proposed by practitioners tend to be prescriptive in nature, and the model proposed by Kremzar and Wallace (2000) is also prescriptive. The normal implementation is proposed in 18 months, while an accelerated implementation model is proposed in 18 weeks.

The model proposed by Parr and Shanks (2000) also uses the project management phases for the implementation such as planning, project management, and enhancement. The authors also recommend that the model be merged with the process model of ERP implementation by Markus and Tanis (2000). The design phase is broken up into sub-phases of set-up, reengineer, design, configuration, and testing and installation phases. Each of these phases has a set of critical success factors for guiding the practitioner as to the desired and undesired activities.

The process model of Markus and Tanis (2000) has a process-based approach to ERP implementation. Earlier work of the authors has identified the three phases to value of any IT project, viz. the 'IT conversion process', the 'IT use process', and the 'competitive process'. They argue that all three phases are important to the 'success' of any IT implementation.

Based on these phases, the model then proposes the four phases as shown in Figure 10.8, viz., 'project chartering' comprising the activities of developing the business case and the solution constraints in terms of manpower, timeline and budgets, 'project rollout' involving the activities of configuring the system, getting the system and users up and running (training), 'shakedown' in which the concentration is on elimination of bugs, legacy data transfer and cleaning, and getting to normal operations, and 'onward and upward' in which system maintenance, user support, getting results, and upgrading are the main activities.

FIGURE 10.8
Enterprise System Implementation Cycle

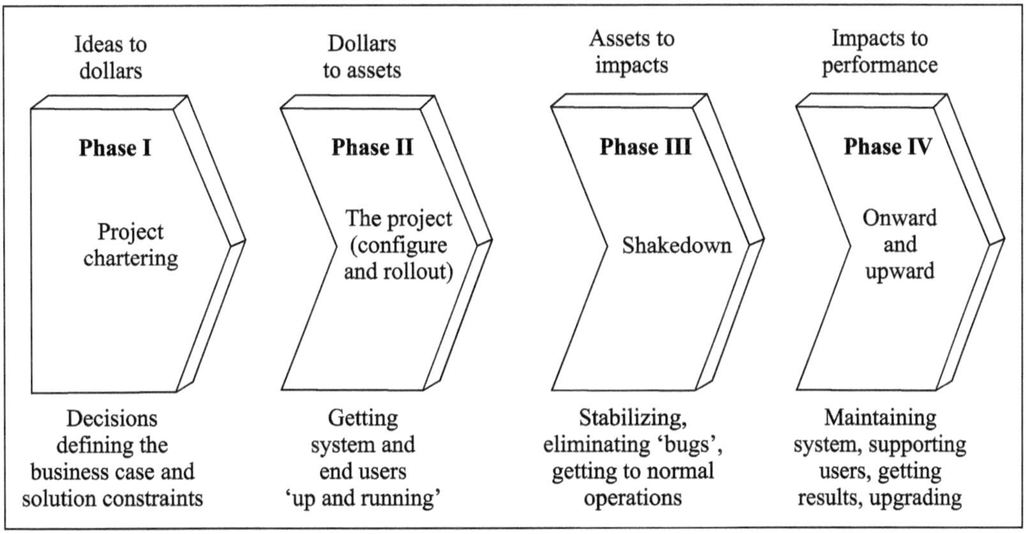

Ideas to dollars	Dollars to assets	Assets to impacts	Impacts to performance
Phase I	**Phase II**	**Phase III**	**Phase IV**
Project chartering	The project (configure and rollout)	Shakedown	Onward and upward
Decisions defining the business case and solution constraints	Getting system and end users 'up and running'	Stabilizing, eliminating 'bugs', getting to normal operations	Maintaining system, supporting users, getting results, upgrading

Source: Markus and Tanis (2000).

Bajwa et al. (2004) propose an ERP implementation model incorporating business constructs such as external and internal stakeholders, technology constructs, business integration, and technical efficiency constructs, and show how they become effective in the main steps of ERP implementation such as specific package selection, as-is and to-be states in process mapping, implementation, and going live steps.

Metaxiotis et al. (2005) suggest a goal-directed project management methodology for ERP implementation where the project goals drive the selection of the activities of planning, organization, and control. The authors claim that this methodology helps to focus the activities of the project and thus reduce the time for implementation and also conserve the resources being used in the project.

Karakanian (1999) suggests the use of nine factors such as drivers of ERP implementation, resources, package functionality fits, the modules to be implemented, existing technology platforms and budgets, etc., to suggest an ERP implementation strategy. This strategy would help in choosing the minimum resources in terms of personnel and the time phasing strategy of the ERP implementation project to match with the other constraints of the implementation, so that the overall ERP implementation is in sync with the available actors.

The seven stage model as seen from Figure 10.1 could be effectively used to understand the process of adoption of enterprise solution in an organization.

The overall success of enterprise solution is greatly dependent on successful management of each of these stages by various stakeholders.

The Identification of ERP Implementation Success Factors

Researchers and practitioners have used the critical factors approach to draw up an implementation plan for successful implementation of ERP systems. ERP system implementation is a process of great complexity, with a great many conditions and factors potentially influencing the implementation. These conditions could have a positive effect on the outcome of ERP project, while their absence could generate problems during implementation. The results of some major research on ERP implementation success factors have been described ahead.

Burns et al. (1991), while researching critical success factors in Material Requirements Planning (MRP) implementation, suggested dividing potential factors into environmental and methodological factors. Environmental factors include, apart from those describing enterprise activity, the product technology level and the organization's willingness to change. The methodological factors are connected with the implementation approach incorporated. On the basis of 504 survey responses, most of the methodological factors were identified as being associated with Manufacturing Resources Planning (MRP II) success, while only two of the environmental factors were found to be connected with implementation success—product technology and organization willingness to change.

In another research, Parr and Shanks (2000) turned to experts participating in many implementation projects. The research sample consisted of 10 experts who had participated in a total of 42 ERP implementation projects, mainly as project managers. Based on interviews with these experts, 10 candidate factors necessary for successful implementation of ERP systems were identified. These factors were divided into groups related with management, personnel, software, and project. Of these 10 candidate factors, three are of paramount importance. They are management support of the project team and of the implementation process, a project team that has the appropriate balance of business and technical skills, and commitment to change by all the stakeholders.

Holland and Light (1999) presented a number of potential success factors in ERP implementation and suggested their division into strategic and tactical factors. The model was illustrated on a sample of two ERP implementation projects. Among 12 factors, the authors highlighted the critical impact of legacy systems upon the implementation process and the importance of selecting an appropriate ERP strategy. However, they did not formulate conclusions regarding factors' ranking.

Esteves and Pastor (2000) suggested a unified ERP implementation critical success factors model. This model is based on the analysis of considerable research regarding implementation success factors. The authors indicated that factors should be categorized into strategic and tactical factors from organizational and technological perspectives.

Similarly, the research of Nah et al. (2001) was based on literature review and yielded a model of 11 critical success factors. These models were fitted into the four stages of ERP implementation identified by Marcus and Tanis (2000). This model was next verified on the basis of the opinions of 54 chief information officers (CIOs) implementing ERP into their organizations (Nah et al., 2003). The five most critical factors identified by the CIOs were: top management support; project champion; ERP teamwork and composition; project management; and change management programme and culture.

Somers and Nelson (2001) described the importance of critical success factors across the stages of ERP implementations using the responses from 86 organizations implementing ERP. From their broad list of 22 critical success factors for ERP implementation in overall ranking, the most important are: top management support; project team competence; inter-departmental cooperation; clear goals and objectives; project management; and inter-departmental communication.

Al-Mashari et al. (2003) presented taxonomy of ERP critical factors where 12 factors were divided into three dimensions related to the stages of ERP project, which are: setting-up; deployment; and evaluation. The taxonomy presented emphasizes that a clear vision and business director is fundamental for the success of ERP system implementation. It also highlights the importance of business process management and suggests that the evaluation and performance monitoring of ERP system's implementation can lead to the achievement of all desired business goals and objectives. Finally, the authors conclude that the most essential element of success and the pre-requisite for successful and effective ERP implementation is leadership and commitment.

Brown and Vessey (2003), on the basis of their research, concluded that there are five success factors for ERP projects and illustrated their significance with the use of three successful ERP implementations case studies. The resulting factors are: top management is engaged in the project, not just involved; project leaders are veterans, and team members are decision-makers; third parties fill gaps in expertise and transfer their knowledge; change management goes hand-in-hand with project planning; and a 'satisficing' mindset prevails.

The results of the mentioned researches on ERP implementation success factors illustrate the problem complexity and the variety of approaches.

Some of the key success factors of Enterprise Resource Implementation project are as provided in Table 10.2.

The success of implementation stage is impacted by the following key stakeholders:

- Implementation consultants
- Internal contributing team
- Senior management
- Enterprise system vendor

TABLE 10.2
Critical Success Factors for ERP Implementation

Area	High/Low	Probability of success
Degree of readiness	↑	↑
Top Management Support	↑	↑
Product Functionality Fit	↑	↑
Degree of Customization	↑	↓
Consultant Capabilities	↑	↑
Strength of Business Case	↑	↑
Team Commitment	↑	↑
Organizational Awareness	↑	↑
Swiftness of Decision Making	↑	↑
Organizational Maturity on Project Management	↑	↑
Change Management Capabilities	↑	↑

Source: Author.

- Key user group
- Change management team

One of the key differentiators is the presence of experienced members in the above team. This means having members who have been previously involved in successful enterprise system adoption process. Such members are generally provided by the implementation partner organization. Therefore, selection of the right vendor partner is extremely important.

High degree of commitment of the internal team is also critical. The commitment comes from the usual high profile associated with such an implementation. Organizations are advised to pick up the best for this kind of transformational projects.

Since implementation is a transformational project, senior management commitment at various stages contribute towards the success of the adoption process.

REFERENCES

Al-Mashari, M., A. Al-Mudimigh and M. Zairi. 2003. 'Enterprise Resource Planning: A Taxonomy of Critical Factors', *European Journal of Operational Research*, 146: 352–64.

Bajwa, D.S., T. Mooney, and J.E. Garcia. 2004. 'An Integrative Framework for the Assimilation of Enterprise Resource Planning Systems: Phases, Antecedents and Outcomes', *The Journal of Computer Information Systems*, 44(3, Spring): 81–90.

Brown, C.V. and I. Vessey. 2003. 'Managing the Next Wave of Enterprise Systems—Leveraging Lessons from ERP', *MIS Quarterly Executive*, 2(1): 65–77.

Burns, O. Maxie and David Turnispeed. 1991. 'Critical Success Factors in Manufacturing Resource Planning Implementation', International Journal of Operations & Production Management, 11(4): 5–19.

Esteves, J. and J. Pastor, J. 2000. 'Towards the Unification of Critical Success Factors for ERP Implementations', paper presented at 10th Annual BIT Conference, Manchester.

Holland, C. and B. Light. 1999. A Critical Success Factors Model for ERP Implementation, *IEEE Software*, (May/June): 30–5.

Karakanian, M. 1999. 'Choosing an ERP Implementation Strategy', Year 2000 Practitioner, 2(7, July): 1–6.

Markus, M.L., S. Axline, D. Petrie, and C. Tanis. 2000. 'Learning from Adopters' Experiences with ERP: Problems Encountered and Success Achieved', *Journal of Information Technology*, 15(4): 245–65.

Markus, M.L. and C. Tanis. 2000. 'The Enterprise Systems Experience: From Adoption to Success', in R.W. Zmud (ed.), *Framing the Domains of IT Research: Glimpsing the Future through the Past*, pp. 173–207. Cincinnati, Ohio: Pinnaflex Educational Resources Inc.

Metaxiotis, Kostas, Ioannis Zafeiropoulos, Konstantina Nikolinakou, and John Psarras. 2005. 'Goal Directed Project Management Methodology for the Support of ERP Implementation and Optimal Adaptation Procedure', *Information Management and Computer Security*, 13(1).

Miller, E. 2000. 'ERP expands to serve engineering', *Computer-aided Engineering*, 19(7): 34–6.

Nah, Fui-Hoon, Fiona, Janet Lee-Shang Lau, and Jinghua Kuang. 2001. 'Critical Factors for Successful Implementation of Enterprise Systems', *Business Process Management Journal*, 7(3).

Nah, Fui-Hoon, Fiona, Kathryn M. Zuckweiler, and Janet Lee-Shang Lau. 2003. 'ERP Implementation—CIOs Perceptions of CSFs', *International Journal of Human-Computer Interaction*, 16(1): 5–22.

Parr, A. N. and Graeme G. Shanks. 2000. 'A Model of ERP Project Implementation', *Journal of Information Technology—Regular Paper*, 15(December): 289–303.

Piccoli and Ives. 2005. 'IT Dependent Strategic Initiatives', *MIS Quarterly*, 29(4, December).

Ross, Jeanne and Peter Weill. 2002. 'SIX IT Decisions your IT People shouldn't Make', *Harvard Business Review*, November.

Somers, T. and K. Nelson. 2001. 'The Impact of Critical Success Factors Across the Stages of Enterprise Resource Planning Implementations, In Proceedings of the 34th Hawaii International Conference on System Sciences (HICSS), Hawaii.

Wallace, Thomas F. and Michael H. Kremzar. 2001. *ERP: Making it Happen: The Implementers' Guide to Success With Enterprise Resource Planning*. New York: John Wiley & Sons, Inc.

11

A Model for ERP Systems Management: An Exploratory Study in Companies Using SAP R/3

CESAR ALEXANDRE DE SOUZA
University of São Paulo, Brazil
E-mail: calesou@usp.br

RONALDO ZWICKER
University of São Paulo, Brazil
E-mail: rzwicker@usp.br

INTRODUCTION

ERP systems have become the main and vital component of corporate information systems of many companies. This takes place at a time when information technology (IT) staffs are under great pressure to ensure the capacity of response and adjustment of their systems to business needs and constant changes (Agarwal and Sambamurthy, 2002; Feeny and Willcocks, 1998). The Enterprise Resource Planning (ERP) system is a critical component of the integrated management of diverse company areas and of supply chain management, which demands compliance with extreme availability and performance requirements. In principle this describes the meaning and the importance of managing such systems.

According to Souza and Zwicker (2005) this management encompasses the set of actions undertaken to ensure meeting the business needs, the performance, availability, and control of the maintenance and operation costs. The authors present a model for the study of ERP systems management which includes the activities of development (implementation and evolution of the system), operation (keep the system operation within the specified parameters of performance and availability), and support (user services). As actors the model includes the IT area, the system's supplier, the user areas, and outside consultants. The present text initially carries out a revision of the model proposed by these authors based upon the concept of core capabilities of the IT area as proposed by Feeny and Willcocks (1998). Next, the aspects covered in the revised model are analyzed through a survey conducted at 85 companies using the SAP R/3 system in Brazil.

CORE CAPABILITIES MODEL

According to Feeny and Willcocks (1998) and Willcocks and Feeny (2006), to reach sustainable competitiveness using IT, companies must pay attention to three issues: *(a)* focus on utilization of systems that support business opportunities; *(b)* development and management of effective strategies for the high quality and low cost IT service delivery; and *(c)* choice of a technical platform or IT architecture on which services will be made available. The authors regard as premise that the current trend is the outsourcing of an extended range of IT services. In this way, the issue becomes one of outlining the internal capabilities which should be kept and to which maximum of attention should be given. Included are the core capabilities which the IT area must have internally, independent from the type of sourcing it elects to adopt. The rationale is that core capabilities ensure that the current and future capability of the business to benefit from IT is not jeopardized, and that they provide adequate support to the three listed issues. According to the Feeny and Willcocks (1998) model the core capabilities are: *(a)* leadership, or the capability to integrate IT efforts with the business objectives and activities; *(b)* business systems thinking, or the capability to discern new procedures made possible by the technology; *(c)* relationship building, or the capability to achieve a constructive engagement of the user areas with IT matters; *(d)* architecture planning, or the capability to create a consistent technology platform to meet current and future requirements; *(e)* making technology work, or the capability to quickly solve unexpected problems and keep up delivery of IT services; *(f)* informed buying, or the capability to set up and manage a fitting sourcing strategy for business; *(g)* contract facilitation, or the capability to manage the day-to-day of sourcing contracts to avoid interruption problems; *(h)* contract monitoring, or the capability to guarantee that the current and future position of the company is protected in the sourcing contracts; and *(i)* vendor development, or the capability to identify the potential of reaching value by means of IT based upon the current and future services offered. The relationship between these nine core capabilities and the three issues of IT management is illustrated in Figure 11.1.

The relationship between the core capabilities model and the implementation of ERP systems is examined by Willcocks and Sykes (2000). The need of systems thinking and the capability of building relationships to achieve an effective integration of the procedures promised by the ERP systems are enhanced. Furthermore, the implementation effort requires preservation of the internal capability to solve problems to meet the company's specific situations and qualification for the vital activities related to outsourcing including informed buying, contract facilitation, and monitoring.

FIGURE 11.1
Core Capabilities Model

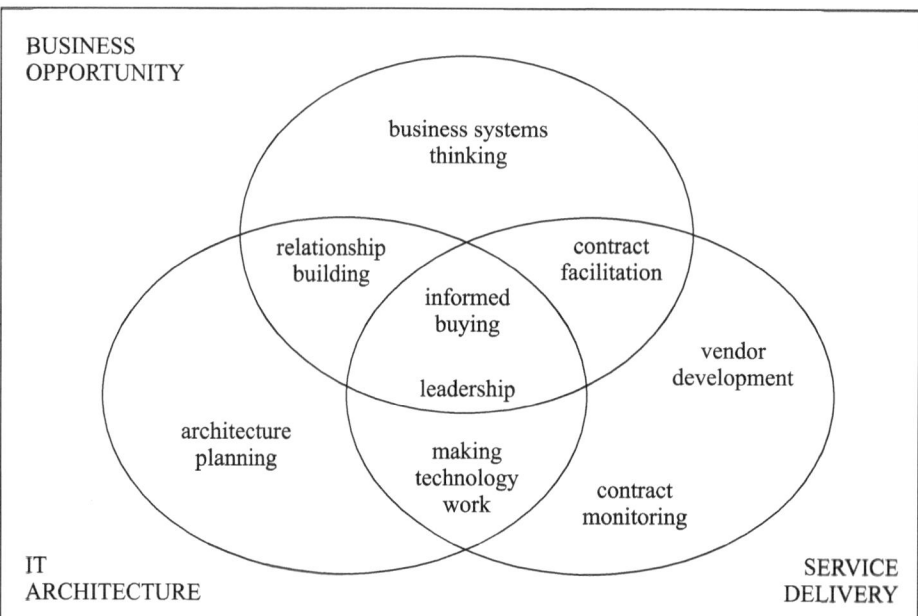

Source: Feeny and Willcocks (1998).

One of the issues not addressed by the authors is the issue of IT governance, that is to say the perspective of sharing decision-making responsibility on diverse aspects that involve the IT area, business areas, and users themselves. In addition, as the model is strictly built according to the 'total' outsourcing of the IT area, no consideration has been given to environments that combine outsourcing with activities conducted internally. Finally, details specifically related to ERP systems management, such as the level of proficiency to manage projects of the user areas and relationship with other companies that use the same ERP system, were not considered by the cited authors.

MANAGEMENT OF ERP SYSTEMS

Most models of IT management emphasize two aspects that pervade this process: *(a)* provide for business needs, in the sense of strategic alignment of IT with company business and *(b)* technological response in the sense of the support architecture and portfolio of applications. With respect to these aspects, IT management involves decisions about what must be done, characterized as IT governance, as well as decisions on how it should be done, characterized as IT management (Starre and Jong, 1998). Inherent to IT management is the quick evolution of technology and the growing pressure to justify IT investments worth and effective contribution to company productivity and competitiveness. This is the context of the challenge to respond to company business needs. To equate this response is a wide ranging problem which, among other things, must consider aspects as the company strategy, the knowledge of current and future technology, and the suitable relationship between the IT area and other business areas. From the previous discussion the aspects that may be considered relevant for the study of ERP systems management are shown consolidated in Figure 11.2. This figure states the model of the components of ERP systems management that was used to develop the survey presented next.

In Figure 11.2 the diagonal dotted line produced two 'spaces': the space of the business needs in the upper right triangle and the space of the technological response in the lower left triangle. These are spaces for the action of different actors and where specific abilities are demanded from the internal actors of the company. In the space of business needs appear those involved with IT governance, the user areas, and owners of the same system that likewise seek to achieve

FIGURE 11.2
Model of the Components of ERP Systems Management

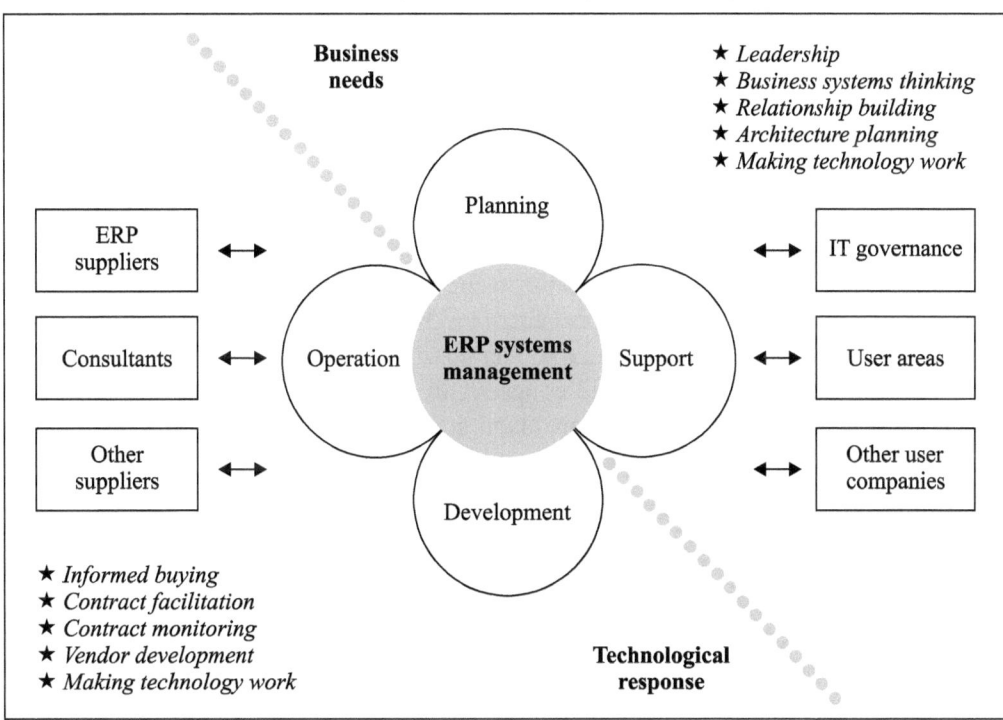

Source: Authors.

solutions for their needs. In the space of technological response emerge the vendors of the ERP system, the consultants, and the remaining vendors, all of which are involved with the technological architecture defined for the company. Arrows in the figure represent the actors' participation in the managerial process.

The performance of the IT area is expressed by the activities related to ERP systems management found in the centre of Figure 11.2. To the managerial activities previously shown was added the planning activity, in order to consider the medium- and long-term evolution of these systems from the point of view of IT and business. Planning and support activities are preferentially located in the space of business needs, while the development and operational activities are preferentially found in the space of technological response.

In each of the spaces were allocated the core capabilities for the company's positive performance in the domain of management of its ERP system. In the business needs space are the capabilities regarding relationship and strategic alignment of the system and technology architecture, while in the technological response space are the capabilities regarding the achievement of solutions. Note that the capability of making technology work is essential in the two spaces. The model of Figure 11.2 consolidates the core capabilities under the perspective of Souza and Zwicker (2005) of the users' participation on the management of ERP system and under the perspective of Feeny and Willcocks (1998) on the management challenges brought about by outsourcing.

RESULTS OF THE SURVEY

The survey was carried out by sending a questionnaire in July 2004 to the members of ASUG Brasil, the association of Brazilian SAP users. In early 2006 it had 460 members who corresponded to 56 per cent of the companies using SAP R/3 in Brazil. The return comprised 85 questionnaires considered valid (24 per cent of the 350 members at the time, and about 17 per cent of the companies using R/3 in Brazil). The questionnaire was completed by companies participating in the association's yearly congress, by means of their IT managers, business analysts, and key users. The questions were elaborated based on the professional experience of the authors relative to ERP systems management and encompassed more than 100 operational and managerial aspects of the ERP routine of the companies. The questionnaire may be requested from the authors (in Portuguese).

Figures 11.3 and 11.4 show some results that characterize the sample obtained. The sample may be considered representative of the population of companies that are associated to ASUG Brasil. Most companies belong to the industrial sector and are medium- and large-sized companies with some of them highly representative of Brazilian economy. The median of invoicing of the sample companies for the year of 2003 was $ 500 million and the median of the number of employees was 1,500.

FIGURE 11.3
Sector of Activity

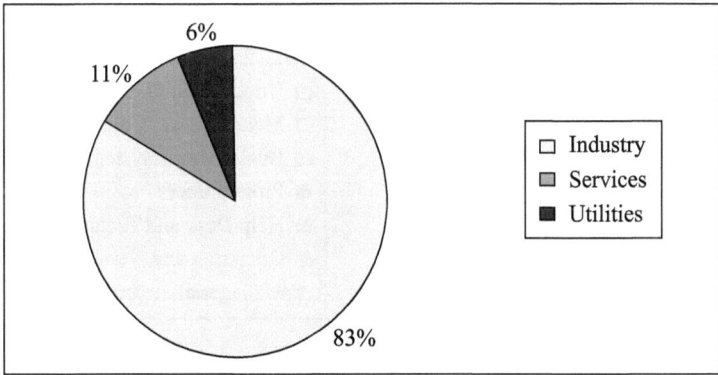

Source: Authors.

FIGURE 11.4
Nationality of the Companies

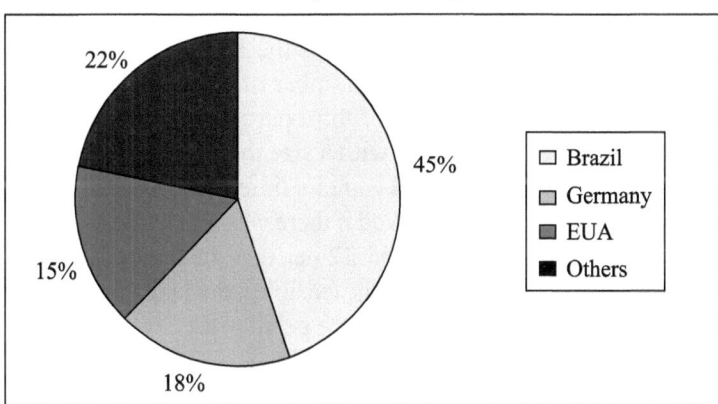

Source: Authors.

HUMAN RESOURCES OF IT AREAS

Figure 11.5 shows the mean number of employees (internal and external) of the IT area of the companies in the sample. On the average IT areas have 31 persons, but the median is around 17 people with a larger number occupying the functions of business and system analysts. Also significant is the number of help desk people, although their time dedicated to the ERP is relatively short. The percentage of the professionals' time dedicated to the R/3 discloses that it is rather high for programmers and analysts, which shows that these professionals are almost

FIGURE 11.5
Mean Number of Employees in Each Function

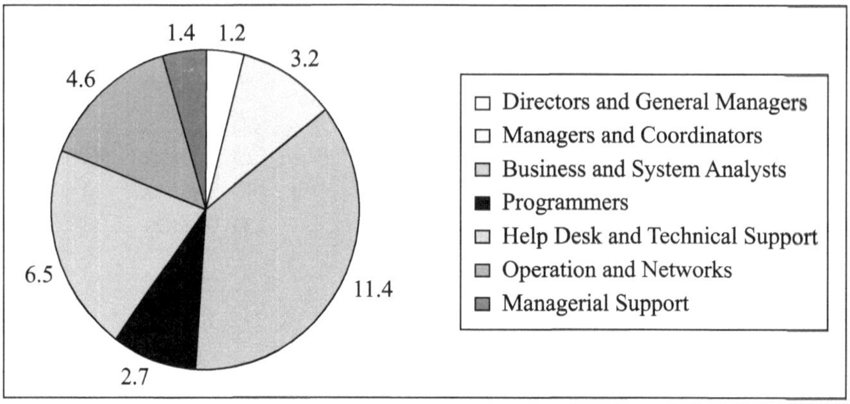

Source: Authors.

solely dedicated to project and develop applications tied to the ERP. This suggests that system's architecture and the effort of IT areas are significantly focused on ERP on these companies.

Table 11.1 shows statistics related to the size of the IT area. 'SD' indicates the standard deviation of the sample and 'N' relates to the number of companies that supply information considered valid. The number of employees of third parties in the IT area is small suggesting that companies indeed keep their own staffs with a size that may also be considered small. On an average the R/3 uses 51 per cent of the IT area's time, which again shows its importance within the company. Companies were also asked if there was a separate area in the IT department exclusively dedicated to the ERP system and 32 per cent of the companies gave a positive reply. This finding discloses that separation is feasible and takes into account the peculiar proficiencies of the development and maintenance personnel.

TABLE 11.1
Statistics of IT Human Resources

Description	Mean	SD	Median	N
Total of employees in the IT area	25.8	27.3	14.0	70
Total of third party people in the IT area	5.3	14.9	0.0	70
Total of people in the IT area	31.0	36.5	17.5	70
Percentage of time dedicated to the R/3 in the IT area	51%	24%	52%	70
Number of IT users per person in the IT area	31.8	20.6	26.7	35
Number of R/3 users per person in the IT area	26.2	75.5	14.1	68
Percentage of persons in the IT area coming from user areas	65%	–	–	85
Number of persons in the IT area coming from user areas	6.2	7.2	3	55
Percentage of separated areas dedicated to the R/3	32%	–	–	85

Source: Authors.

Another indicative aspect is that 65 per cent of companies reported currently having in their IT staff people coming from user areas, especially key users. In these companies the average of people coming from user areas is about six persons, that is to say they comprise some 20 per cent of the IT area. This apparently indicates a change of view of the IT areas that begin to seek knowledge and proficiencies dedicated to processes. It also may point to an IT management strategy to consolidate the relationship with user areas that begun during the implementation projects.

PERCEIVED ERP CONTRIBUTIONS TO THE COMPANY

Figure 11.6 displays the evaluation of respondents on the ERP system contribution to the company's business according to a ranking from 1 (very low) to 5 (very high). The main contribution perceived is the integration of information between departments while, contrary to the initial expectation of many projects, decrease of IT expenses and increase of the level of outsourcing of IT were viewed as lesser contributions. Respondents were also queried if expectations related to the original implementation project were met by the ERP system and the results are shown in Figure 11.7.

ASPECTS OF THE COMPONENTS MODEL

Each company informed by means of its respondent about the effort in activities related to the day to day management of its ERP system according to a ranking ranging from 1 (very low)

FIGURE 11.6
Contributions of the ERP System to Business

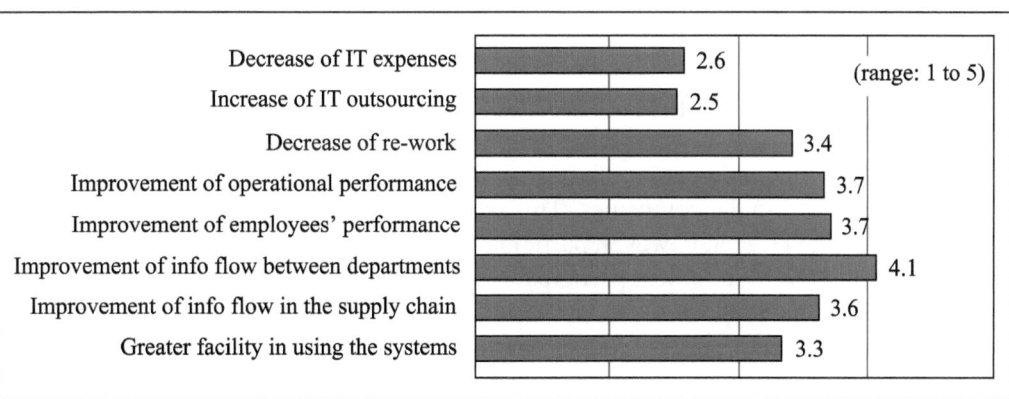

Source: Authors.

FIGURE 11.7
Fulfillment of the Original Expectations

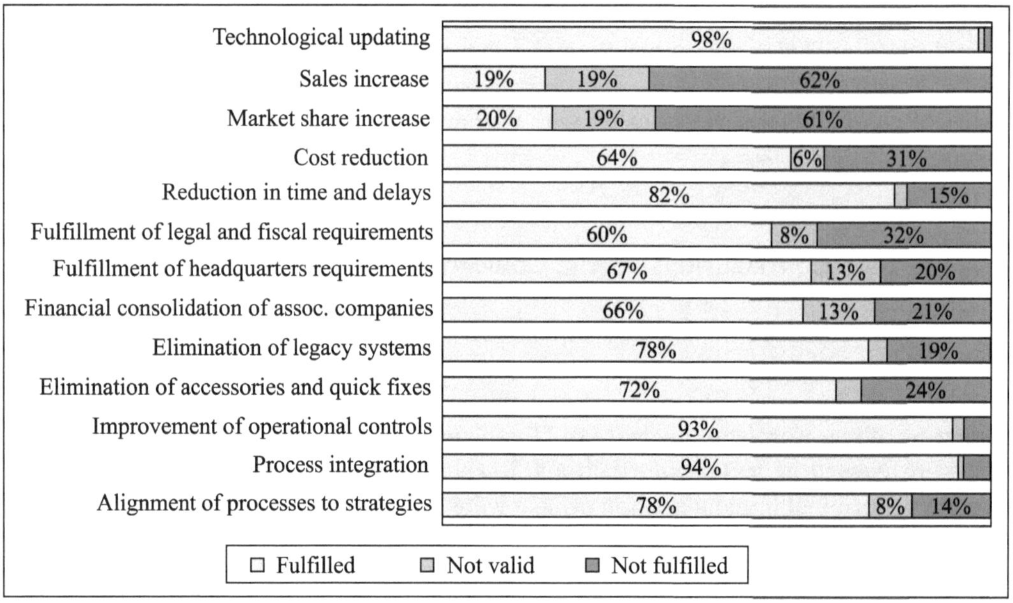

Source: Authors.

to 5 (very high). Figure 11.8 shows the means reported indicating that they concentrated efforts in all activities and mainly in what is directly related to the users. It should be noted that negotiation with vendors and third parties does not seem to be too demanding which is in agreement with the relatively little importance given to this capability by companies' IT areas (according to Figure 11.21). More results of the survey regarding aspects of the model of components of ERP systems management are presented next.

IT Governance and Planning

Figure 11.9 shows the participation of six sets of people responsible for the definition of objectives related to R/3 in the companies. This responsibility is in general shared between top management and the IT area; however, participation of the user areas seems quite remarkable. The Users Committee has a limited participation in the definition of objectives, but it must be taken into account that it appears only in half of the companies in the sample (Figure 11.11). Apparently, the Committee has the role of strengthening the relationship between the area of IT and User Community that it played during the ERP implementation process. The Committee does not always share the responsibility for management of the ERP system and therefore cannot be viewed as a formal instrument of IT or ERP governance in the companies.

FIGURE 11.8
Effort Dedicated to Management of the ERP System

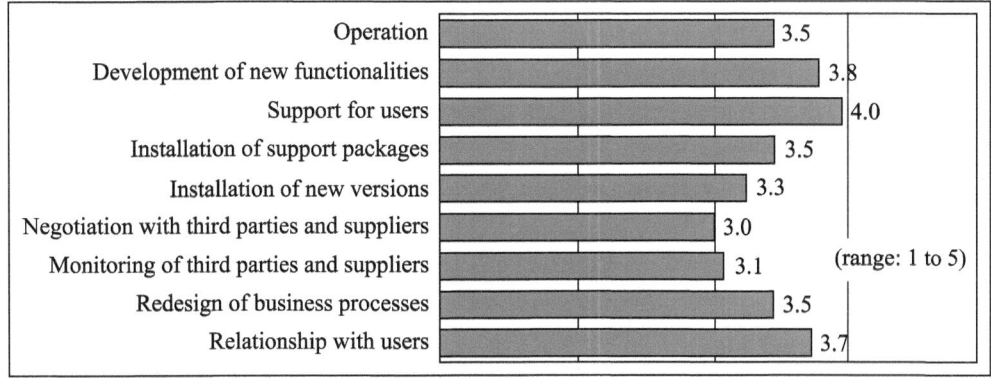

Source: Authors.

FIGURE 11.9
Who Sets the Objectives Regarding the R/3

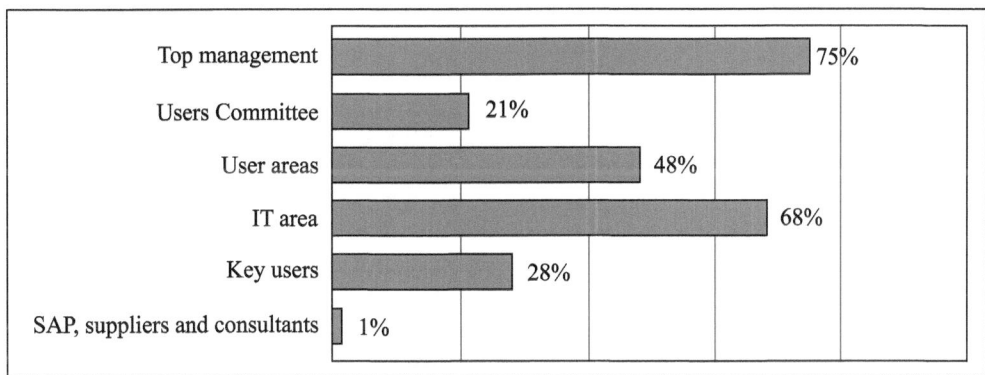

Source: Authors.

The results presented in Figure 11.10 show that the IT area considers that it has the power to carry out changes in user areas, which fulfils the need for integration of processes by technology and is consistent with the perception of the IT areas that their participation is relevant in the redesign of the company processes. The ERP context is definitely a vital operational support for business and, in this sense, participation of the IT area is understood as significant. The results in Figure 11.10 also corroborate the participation of user areas in decisions on R/3.

These results are consistent with the finding presented in Figure 11.12 that the IT area normally has a participation in the leadership of projects involving R/3. But it is interesting to note that in about 25 per cent of companies' leadership belongs exclusively to the user areas. Possibly, in most companies ERP systems are viewed as technology and not as business solutions.

FIGURE 11.10
Participation of the IT Area and User Areas

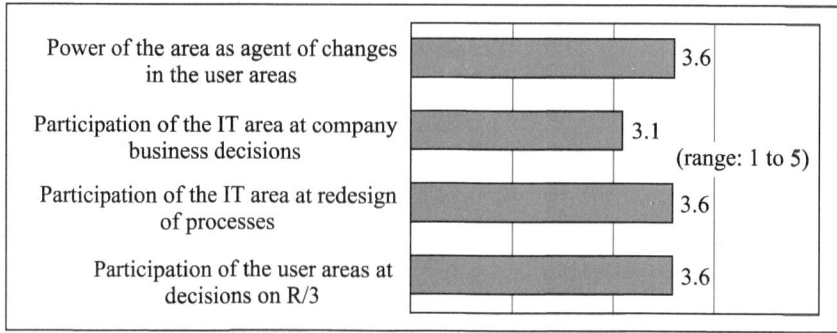

Source: Authors.

FIGURE 11.11
Users Committee (of the ERP)

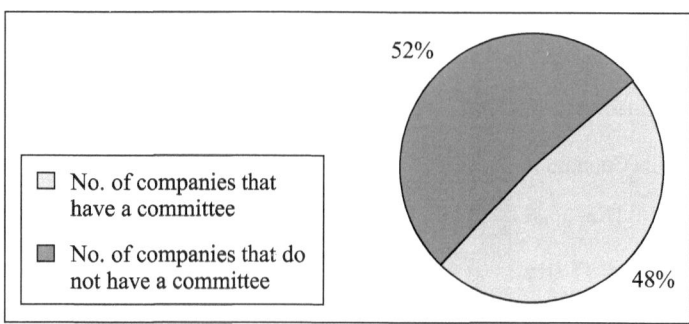

Source: Authors.

FIGURE 11.12
Leadership of R/3 Projects

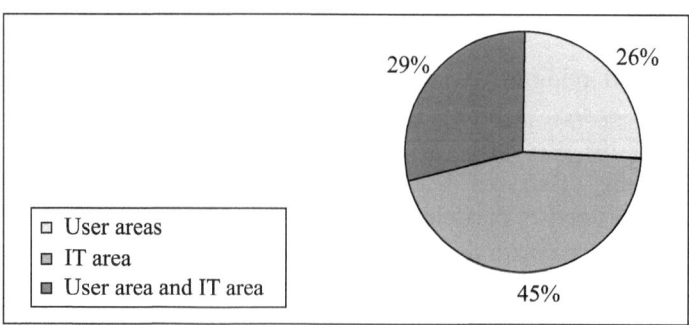

Source: Authors.

In principle, it would be expected that in more companies user areas would be the exclusive holders of the new applications projects under the perspective of ERP being indeed a business solution. The issue can also be ascribed to the user areas' difficulty to manage projects, a fact that not takes place in IT areas.

USER AREAS

Key users play an important role in various activities. They are involved in the system's maintenance, testing corrections and new versions, participate in disseminating knowledge on the system when training users, and solve doubts and problems of other users and contribute to the system's evolution when collaborating with the specification and implementation of new functionalities. The dimension of such involvement is registered in Figure 11.13 which also shows that centralization of contacts with the IT area through key users is not adopted by companies as a rule. Few companies report that users developed 'quick fixes', in general in the form of accessory spreadsheets, to by-pass ERP restrictions. Nevertheless, it becomes evident that development of 'quick fixes' is a recognized fact in at least 20 per cent of companies.

Figure 11.14 portrays the level of satisfaction and cooperation that prevails among the user areas and IT area. Results mirror the IT area's point of view, since it provided the replies in a ranking from 1 (very low) to 5 (very high). The IT area considers that users are relatively satisfied with the area, while it is rather less satisfied with them. Cooperation with the user areas is to some extent brought into evidence and the role of key users is acknowledged by the IT area. Overall satisfaction with the SAP system is evidenced.

FIGURE 11.13
Participation of Key Users

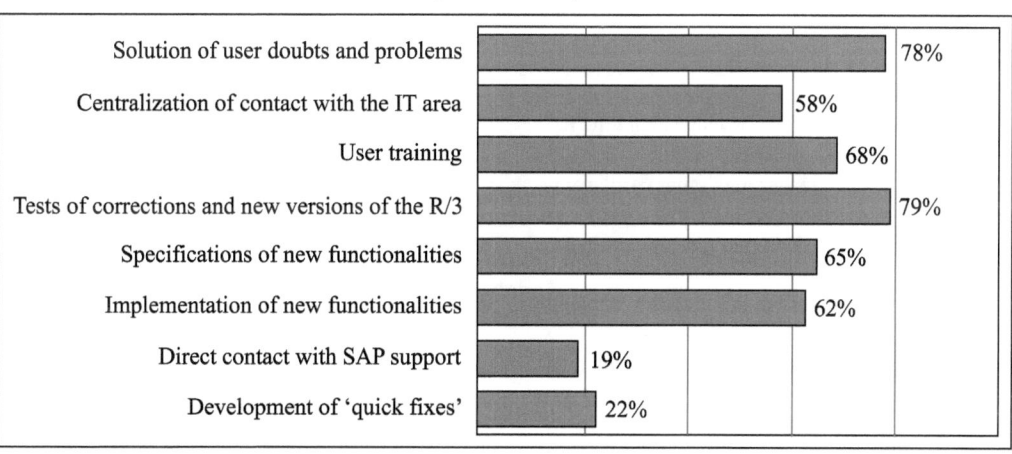

Source: Authors.

FIGURE 11.14
Satisfaction of User Areas and IT Area

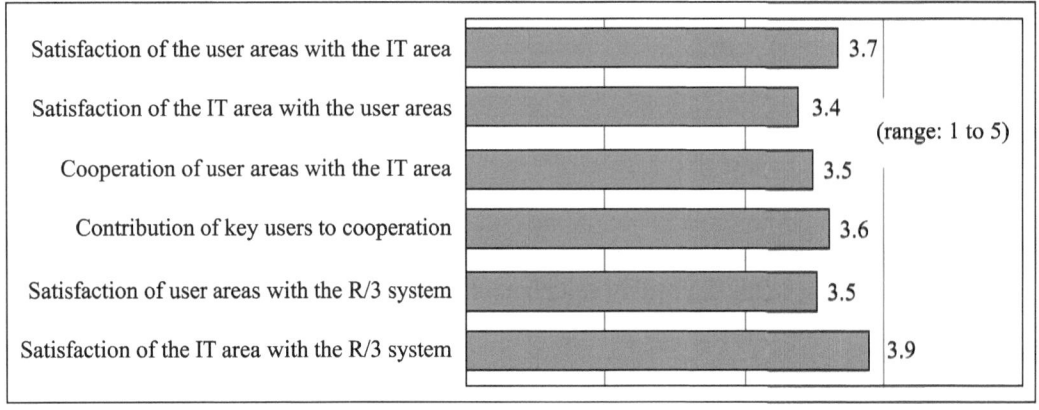

Source: Authors.

OTHER USER COMPANIES

Other companies using the R/3 system also seek to achieve solutions for their problems. Sharing of these problems and of eventual solutions may take place through associations or groups of users. Figure 11.15 presents mean scores of the evaluation of companies related to the issue of the role played by the SAP users' group (ASUG Brasil). Note that the group is considered important for exchange of experiences with other participants, but is of little importance regarding protection of the companies' interests when facing the system vendor.

FIGURE 11.15
Role of the Group of SAP Users

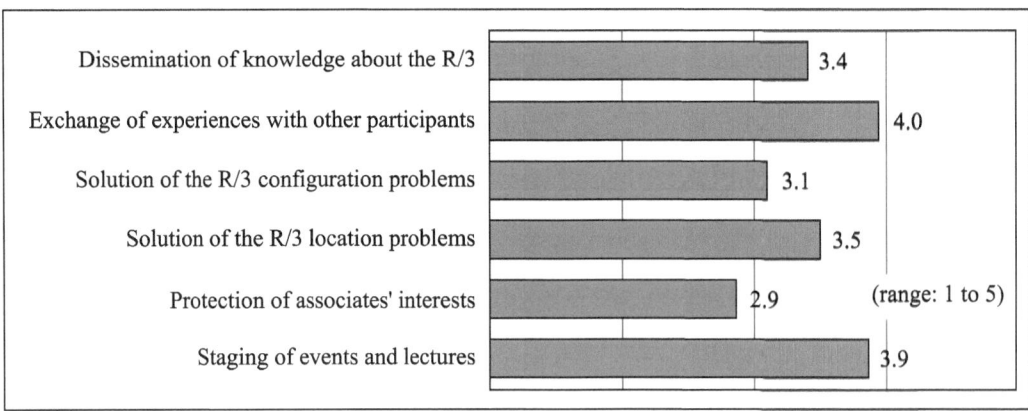

Source: Authors.

CONSULTANTS

Figures 11.16 to 11.18 list results of the issues on outsourcing, consultants and service supply. As previously noted, the level of outsourcing of various activities connected to management of the R/3 system may be considered low. The IT area tends to carry out with the internal personnel mostly activities not directly related to the R/3 technology. Consultants are in charge of the system's configuration, customization, and programming in ABAP, the R/3 language. The main reason for utilizing consultants is that they have a better knowledge, specifically on the R/3 technology; however, the results they supply are not well assessed. This is probably why few companies adopt an explicit policy on outsourcing. It should be noted that contrary to expectations, consultants are understood as not being of great help for redesign of processes.

FIGURE 11.16
Level of Outsourcing of Activities Related to the R/3

Activity	Value
Planning of technology infra structure	2.2
Analysis and redesign of processes	1.9
Configuration of the R/3	2.7
ABAP customizing and programming	3.2
Support to users and help desk	2.5
Training	2.2
Operation, BASIS and tuning	2.4
Data Center	2.1
ASP	1.7

(range: 1 to5)

Source: Authors.

FIGURE 11.17
Motive for Consulting and Outsourcing

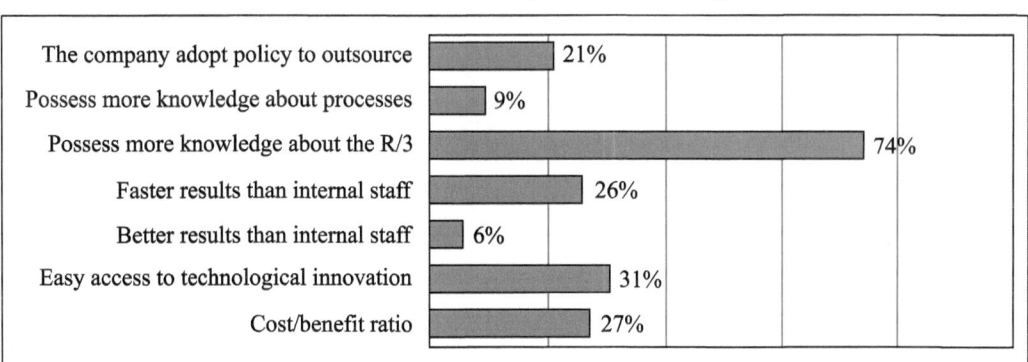

Motive	Value
The company adopt policy to outsource	21%
Possess more knowledge about processes	9%
Possess more knowledge about the R/3	74%
Faster results than internal staff	26%
Better results than internal staff	6%
Easy access to technological innovation	31%
Cost/benefit ratio	27%

Source: Authors.

FIGURE 11.18
Relationship with Third Parties

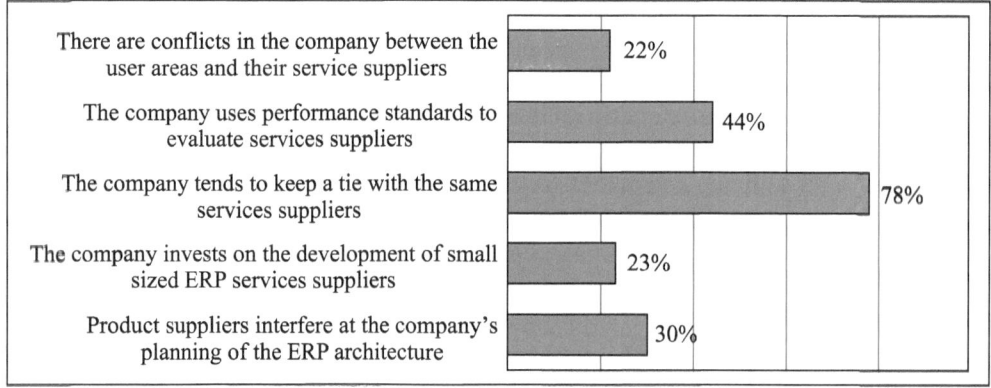

Source: Authors.

Companies surveyed seek to establish long-term relationships with the service suppliers and performance assessment of these suppliers is not representative. The companies tend to use large-sized suppliers what is coherent with the severe dependence of the company from their ERP system. There is also a certain degree of conflict between user areas and service suppliers. The nature of this conflict must be more closely investigated and is possibly related with the finding that almost a third of the companies stated that consultants and suppliers interfere in the management of the company's technological architecture.

Figure 11.19 shows that the IT area has exclusive responsibility for monitoring outsourcing services related to the R/3. Greater participation of the user areas in this monitoring was expected, based upon the argument that more consulting activities were carried out in the ambit of process redesign. This further corroborates the finding that centralization of the contact with

FIGURE 11.19
Responsibility for Monitoring of Third Parties Linked to the R/3

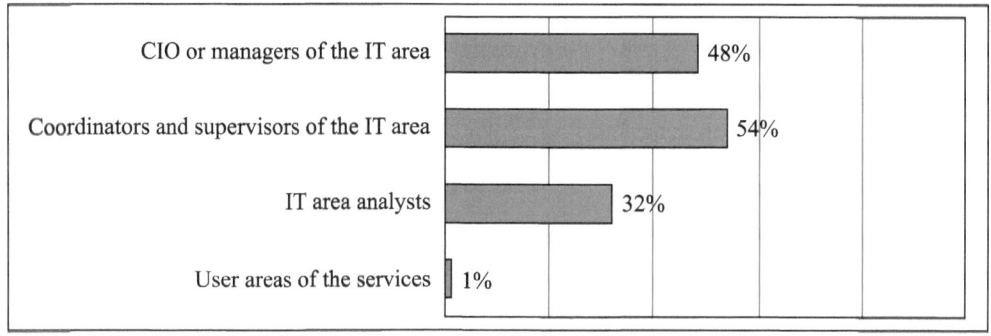

Source: Authors.

consultants and with the ERP vendor, by the IT area, may represent the area's endeavour to retain power and responsibility over evolution and management of the ERP system.

RELATIONSHIP WITH THE ERP VENDOR

The company's relationship with the ERP vendor is outlined in Figure 11.20, which describes the company's satisfaction with various tasks that would be within the vendor's scope according to a ranking from 1 (very dissatisfied) to 5 (very satisfied). In general, companies are satisfied with the SAP support and with the quality of new versions of the system. Dissatisfaction is related to the difficulty of keeping up the old versions of the R/3 and also to the pressure from the vendor to force the company to adopt upgraded versions of the system. This is a touchy point in the management of the ERP system, since implementation of new versions may entail significant risks and costs.

FIGURE 11.20
Company Satisfaction with SAP

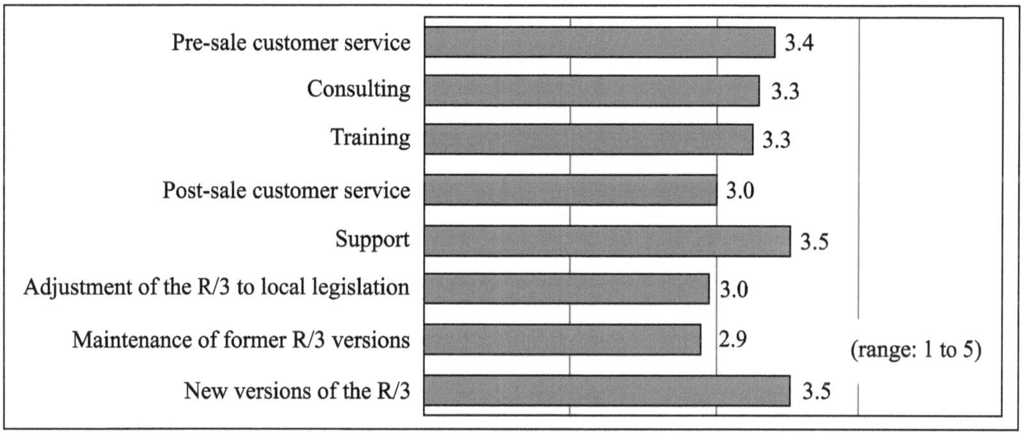

Pre-sale customer service	3.4
Consulting	3.3
Training	3.3
Post-sale customer service	3.0
Support	3.5
Adjustment of the R/3 to local legislation	3.0
Maintenance of former R/3 versions	2.9
New versions of the R/3	3.5

(range: 1 to 5)

Source: Authors.

CORE CAPABILITIES

Figures 11.21 to 11.23 disclose some results related to Feeny and Willcocks' (1998) IS core capabilities model. Companies were requested to classify seven items linked to the capabilities, attributing a classification of 1 as the least important and a classification of 7 as the most important. The mean of the classifications of each item are presented in Figure 11.21 where the brackets indicate the corresponding linked capability number. Knowledge of the company's processes was considered most important, followed by knowledge and control of the R/3 system.

FIGURE 11.21
Importance of Some Capabilities to ERP Systems Management

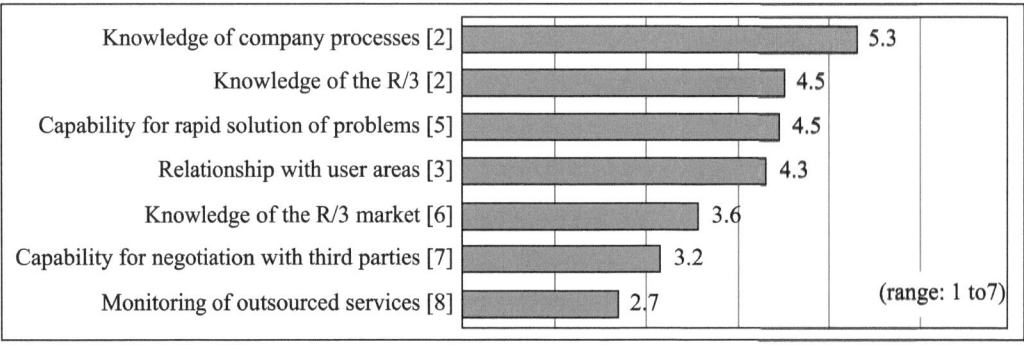

Source: Authors.

FIGURE 11.22
Knowledge of those Involved in Management of the ERP System

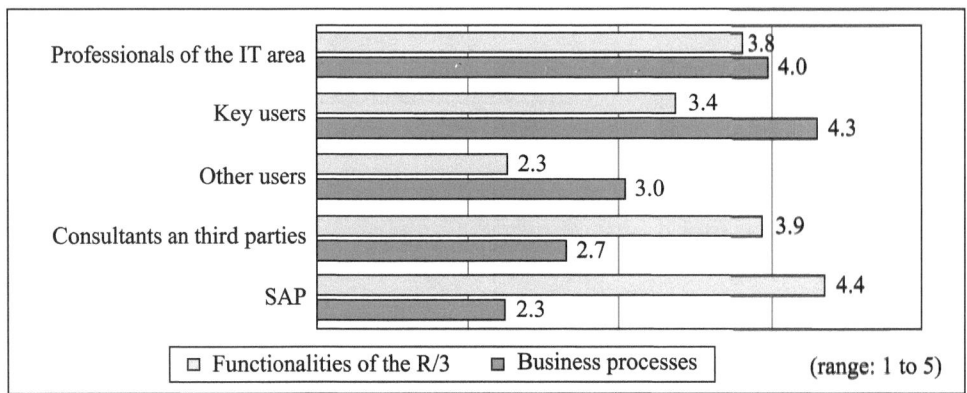

Source: Authors.

FIGURE 11.23
Handling of Contingency Situations

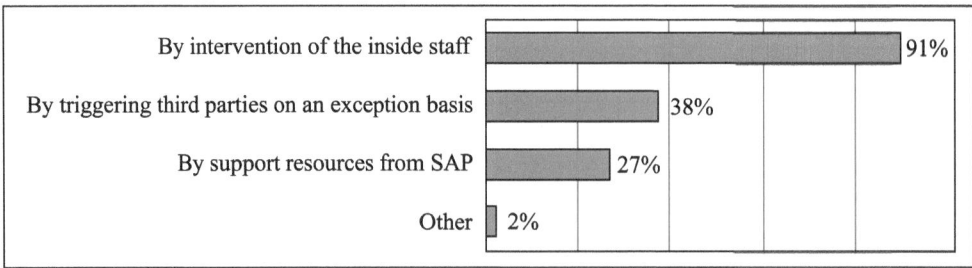

Source: Authors.

Monitoring of outsourcing was considered the least important, once again pointing to the high rating of services carried out internally. Likewise, capability of negotiating with third parties was also not considered important.

Generally speaking, knowledge of the company's processes is held inside (by key users and IT area) while knowledge of the ERP is held outside (ERP vendor and consultants). But companies also believe that they detain a high level of knowledge of the ERP. The need to adjust the system to the processes or vice versa and the fact that knowledge on this adjustment is held by different actors, as seen in Figure 11.22, often brings about tensions and difficulties during the implementation and use of the system's functionalities.

Finally, the capability to quickly solve problems was also assessed in the survey. Figure 11.21 shows that it is considered the third in importance and Figure 11.23 records where this capability resides. Most companies keep this capability inside, but some also take simultaneous avail of other resources. It is clear that third parties and the ERP vendor do not manage to successfully handle contingency situations in accordance with the company needs.

IMPLICATIONS FOR FUTURE ERP IMPLEMENTERS

As survey results have shown, the implementation of an ERP system is viewed by companies as a significant technological step forward with definitive impacts on the integration of processes and improvement of the operational controls. The ERP system then becomes a critical tool for the company requiring compliance with extreme requisites of availability and performance, with repercussions on the capabilities required from those with responsibilities regarding the system. So, it is important to firms envisioning an ERP implementation to be aware of the need to develop or maintain such capabilities.

The achievement of a constructive engagement of business areas with IT issues is the maxim of relationship building capability. Relationship-building pervades the efforts of ERP management and the approach advocated by ERP's vendor about formal user involvement during the system implementation certainly contributes to this. The figure of key users, the Users Committee, and the effort stated by the IT area in the relationship with users and in the supply of support clearly disclose that in the ERP context capability is understood by the company as being very important. This is thus an area of attention for ERP management, the maintenance of such governance arrangements.

Also architecture planning through conception of a consistent technology platform to meet current and futures needs pervades the efforts of the IT area. Likewise, making technology work or have the capability to quickly solve unexpected problems and sustain delivery of services is essential to the ERP area. Results show that these capabilities continue to be internalized and that pertinent decisions are merely supported by the vendor or by third parties.

IMPLICATIONS FOR ERP RESEARCH

Survey results also pose implications and possibilities for future ERP research, also connected with the study of the necessary capabilities for ERP management.

The leadership capability expressed in the form of integration of IT efforts with the objectives and activities of the business was only indirectly perceived through the observed influence of the IT area on the user areas, insofar the participation of these areas at ERP decisions seems still limited. Anyway, it cannot be evidenced that the leadership capability is clearly exercised by the IT areas of the companies. Future research could further investigate the role of IT leadership in ERP management, specially in the continuous alignment of the ERP with business needs. This research stream could also explore the relation of the many IT governance arrangements present in the companies and ERP management activities.

On the other hand, the business systems thinking as the capability to discern procedures made possible by technology seems to be intrinsically driven by ERP technology. Users as well as the IT area endeavour to seize all the functionality that technology makes available. Exploitation of the R/3 possibilities and the redesign of processes are ongoing matters and signal that this capability continues to be acquired. Substantiation that knowledge of the company's processes is clearly internalized and that users and the IT area are its main holders suggests that business systems thinking is part of the everyday matter of the ERP management of companies. This poses the possibility of deepening the study of the relationship between business process management (BPM) and ERP system and ERP management, which could further explore and identify possibilities and advantages of this relationship.

Contrary to what was originally expected in the survey, outsourcing issues related to the ERP were not on the list of the important concerns of companies' IT managers. Companies are essentially tied to a large-sized supplier with whom, in principle, they are satisfied, as survey results have shown. The relationship with consultants is in general longstanding, which is closely related to the knowledge they have already acquired on the technological environment and processes of the company. Eventually, it can be concluded that companies are accommodated and guaranteeing success of the service contracts ends being treated in a centralized manner by the IT area, when it takes over all the intermediation and contact of third parties with the user areas. Business analysts, supported by the key users, end up as the company's contact facilitators with consultants. Nevertheless, the level of conflict with user areas does not signal irrelevance. This fact, associated to the finding that less importance is given to contract monitoring to protect the contractual position of the business and virtual ignorance in relation to the possibilities of supplier development, suggests that the company and IT area may progress in terms of these capabilities. It can be argued that the outsourcing characteristics of ERP systems and potential value that may be added by vendors and service suppliers needs to be more intensively explored by research.

Another possibility of further research is the study of the possibilities brought forth by participation in users' groups for ERP management. Survey results showed that companies place emphasis in knowledge exchange, but the understanding of the influence these users' groups may have on the evolution of the ERP systems might offer interesting insights in terms of ERP management research.

CONCLUSIONS

In the ERP context, sharing of the decision-making responsibility between the IT area and user areas seems natural. It also seems natural that a significant part of the IT efforts are outsourced to the ERP vendor and consultants. Therefore, it is a scene for various actors with defined roles that to be well-played requires abilities and capabilities that may not yet have been acquired. This study brought forth data leading to the conclusion that one of the actors, the IT area of the companies, is maintaining or acquiring these capabilities. Eventually the model proposed in this chapter may be fine-tuned to further encompass the desired capabilities of other actors in this scenario.

ACKNOWLEDGMENTS

The authors thank the collaboration of the 2003/2004 Board of Directors and professionals responsible for the management of ASUG-Brasil.

REFERENCES

Agarwal, R. and V. Sambamurthy. 2002. 'Principles and Models for Organizing the IT Function', *MIS Quarterly Executive*, 1(1): 1–16.

Feeny, D. and L. Willcocks. 1998. 'Core IS Capabilities for Exploiting IT', *Sloan Management Review*, 39(3): 9–21.

Souza, C.A. and R. Zwicker. 2005. 'ERP Systems Management', in L. Lau (ed.), *Managing Business with SAP: Planning, Implementation and Evaluation*. Hershey: Idea Group Publishing.

Starre, D. and B. Jong. 1998. 'IT Governance and Management', Nolan Norton Institute. Available online at http://www.nolannorton.com/3intell/pages/rm/pdf/govern.pdf

Willcocks, L. and D. Feeny. 2006. 'IT Outsourcing and Core IS Capabilities: Challenges and Lessons at Dupont', *Information Systems Management*, 23(1): 49–56.

Willcocks, L. and R. Sykes. 2000. 'The Role of the CIO and IT Function in ERP', *Communications of the ACM*, 43(4): 32–38.

12

Critical Success Factors for the Acquisition of Enterprise Resource Planning (ERP): Empirical Validation

TARIQ BHATTI

College of Business Sciences, Zayed University
P.O. Box 19282, Dubai, United Arab Emirates
E-mail: tariq.bhatti@zu.ac.ae

VEERAPPAN JAYARAMAN

College of Business Sciences, Zayed University
P.O. Box 19282, Dubai, United Arab Emirates

INTRODUCTION

The business environment is changing dramatically and in order to stay competitive in the market, organizations must improve their business practices and procedures. Organizations within all departments and functions upgrade their capability to generate and communicate accurate and timely information. The organizations which have successfully implemented the Enterprise Resource Planning (ERP) systems are reaping the benefits of having integrating working environment, standardized process, and operational benefits to the organization. Not all ERP implementations have been successful. There have been horror stories of ERP implementation and improper implementation has taken the companies to bankruptcy and in several cases organizations decided to abandon the ERP implementation projects. The questions many academicians and researchers have asked are what are the reasons of success and failure of ERP implementations. Some of the reasons cited in the literature are lack of support of top management support, resistance from employees, poor selection (acquisition) of ERP systems and vendor, etc. Majority of these studies have used case studies to conclude their findings and very few have used the empirical to study the ERP. This research is an attempt to extend the ERP acquisition research by defining the conceptual domains constructs and operational measures specific to ERP acquisition critical success factors (CSFs) to advance ERP research. The objective of this chapter is to develop an instrument for measuring ERP acquisition CSFs.

Two step processes have been followed. First, 12 constructs covering CSFs for ERP acquisition have been identified. Second, because the constructs are latent variables, a rigorous procedure has been applied for ensuring the psychometric adequacy of the resulting new multi-item measurement scales.

In the next section of this chapter integrated model is presented. In Section 3, constricts and the definitions for the study are presented. In Section 4, scale development process is discussed. In Section 5 field survey and data analysis is presented. In the last section of this chapter a conclusion is made with a discussion of the implications of the results and usage of the scales, review the limitations of this study, and offer some concluding thoughts.

We conducted a cross-disciplinary literature review encompassing organizational behaviour, change management, MIS, strategic management, innovation diffusion, and operations to develop a framework, construct definitions, and item generation for this study. This process yielded the baseline model depicted and a set of initial measurement scales for 12 theoretically important CSFs.

MODEL DEVELOPMENT

Figure 12.1 illustrates the conceptual model developed for this study. Drawing from multiple literature bases, an integrative, conceptual framework of what is called 'integrated ERP implementation', was introduced which is comprised of a set of theoretically important constructs. This framework has been developed based on the organizational buying behaviour, in which the ERP acquisition goes through different processes before it is implemented. There are a number of factors that affect the ERP acquisition process which are termed in this study as acquisition CSFs. Upon the completion of ERP acquisition project the project is implemented and performance is measured by a mix of acquisition and implementation success.

CONCEPTUAL DOMAINS OF CSFs FOR ERP ACQUISITION

Since the model constructs are latent variables, which cannot be measured directly, multi-item scales, each composed of a set of individual items, were needed to obtain indirect measures of each construct. The items listed in this section represent the scales as drawn from the practitioners, and refined through an expert judge-based manual sorting process (Stratman and Roth, 2002). These scales were further refined (and some items were dropped) as a result of an empirical test of a survey instrument containing these initial scales.

CSFs are widely used in the information systems arena (Rockart, 1979). He presented CSFs as an aid to assist the management to focus its time and effort by monitoring results in those areas that are most important in helping to attain organizational goals. CSFs are those areas

FIGURE 12.1
Enterprise Resource Planning Systems Acquisition Framework

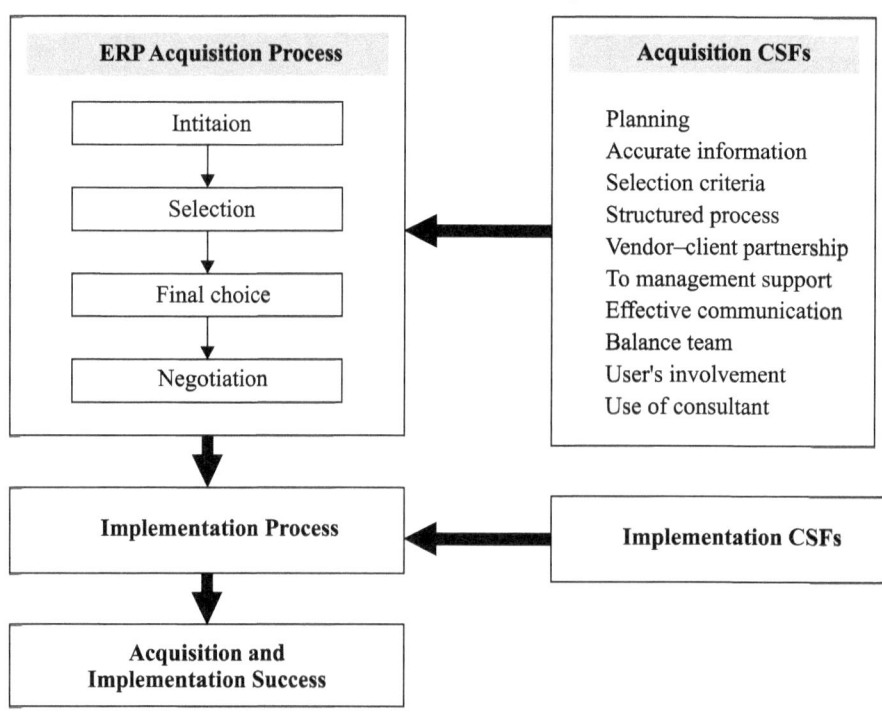

Source: Authors.

of organizational effort that must meet certain predetermined results for the entity to attain its goals. The ability of an organization to monitor performance in those areas and measure results is essential for success.

CSFs can be understood as the few key areas where things must go right for the implementation to be successful. Past studies have identified a variety of CSFs for ERP implementation, among which context-related factors consistently appear. The ERP acquisition process begins after the organization has decided to adopt an ERP system. It is a set of phases and activities that involve initiation, selecting, evaluating, and negotiating to acquire an ERP system for an organization. Following are the commonly identified CSFs identified by several researchers and are pertinent for the success of ERP implementation project. Implementation process stages and implementation are not included the current research study. CSFs are the number of factors that may affect the ERP implementation process, and the probability of conversion success has been identified in the information technology (IT) implementation, IT failures, and business process re-engineering literature. Among the more important factors are top management support and involvement, need for a project champion, user training, technological competence, project planning, change management, and project management (Somers and Nelson, 2001). From the perspective of ERP implementation, additional issues which could be incorporated are business process re-engineering, business teams, and others.

In the next section, a list of CSFs associated with implementation has been derived through a process that involved identification and synthesis of those critical requirements for implementation that have been recommended by practitioners and academicians through an extensive review of the literature (Somers and Nelson, 2001).

Nah et al. (2003) studied the Chief Information Officers' (CIO) perceptions on CSFs for ERP implementation. Hong and Kim (2002), in their study, explored the root of the high failure rate of ERP implementation from an 'organizational fit of ERP' perspective. Al-Mashari and Al-Mudimigh (2003) presented a novel taxonomy of the CSFs of the ERP implementation process. Nah et al. (2001), based on a literature review, found 11 factors critical for ERP implementation. Teamwork and composition in the ERP implementer is a key factor influencing the ERP implementation success. Bingi et al. (1999) proposed 10 factors critical for the implementation of ERP systems. Some of these factors include: top management commitment; integrating; finding and retaining competent consultants; selecting a suitable ERP package; and user training among others. Jung and Goldenson (2003), in a survey of 117 firms from 17 countries, found that companies attribute ERP success to three elements: user training and effective change management; handling the risks of project management; and continued executive commitment.

Nah et al. (2003), in a survey of 1,000 companies, found that CIOs rated top management support, project champion, ERP teamwork and composition, project management, and change management programme and culture to be the most critical for successful ERP implementation. Their findings on the CIOs' ranking of ERP CSFs are largely consistent with the literature. The Somers and Nelson (2004) research study results suggest that the early literature- and case-based research on enterprise systems does not take into account the importance of several key variables. Esteves et al. (2003) proposed a unified model of CSFs for ERP implementation. They collected an extensive number of CSFs from the literature and categorized them from four perspectives: strategic, tactical, organizational, and technological. Shanks (2000) proposed a model of ERP project implementation using two case studies. Eleven CSFs from an ERP project team and users of the system were identified as management support, best people full-time, empowered decision-makers, deliverable dates, champion, vanilla ERP, smaller scope, definition of scope and goal, balanced team, and commitment change. Somers and Nelson (2004) proposed CSFs across the stages of ERP implementations using the responses from 86 organizations that completed, or are in the process of completing, an ERP implementation. The results provide advice to management on how best to utilize their limited resources to choose those CSFs that are mostly likely to have an impact upon the implementation of the ERP system.

A brief description for each CSF for acquisition of ERP system is presented now.

Proper planning for an ERP acquisition project with adequate time frame is a key factor in successfully acquiring an ERP system. It involves outlining proposed strategic and tangible benefits, resources, costs and risks, and the timeline is critical.

It is imperative that the 'information' about ERP vendors and systems be accurate and reliable during the acquisition process. Achieving this involves verification and cross-checking of the information sources for their reputation and credibility.

Selection criteria refer to the criteria developed by the project team and management for the selection and evaluation of ERP systems.

The structured process refers to defining the structure of the acquisition phases. This includes techniques that would be used to manage the process at the very beginning of the planning phase of the acquisition process. A well-defined structure for the acquisition process presupposes the need, also, for a clear authority for the process.

Vendor–client partnership refers to partnership during the acquisition and then implementation of ERP systems between the vendors and organization intending to acquire and implement ERP systems. This relates to the mutual understanding of each other's respective needs and capabilities and creating a mutual trust for long-term relationships.

Evaluation techniques are the procedures used for evaluating the potential vendors and ERP systems. Acquisition team members decide which techniques are more suitable, given the system attributes and selection criteria.

Top management support refers to the involvement and support of top management during the ERP acquisition process. Providing the required human, technical, and budgetary resources is a critical part of this support. However, the most successful acquisition projects have benefited from full-time executive champion who participate in team meetings, monitor the acquisition efforts, and provide clear direction of the project.

Effective communication in the ERP acquisition process refers to the extent and frequency of information-sharing between management, employees, and users. This means not only sharing information in the management, but also communicating with the users and non-users of ERP system in the organization.

Having a balanced team means selecting a project team that consists of cross-functional people and the best people from various functional departments that are associated with the system.

Users' involvement refers to the involvement of users in the acquisition process, which is an important factor in the success of acquisition process. Involving users in the acquisition process with the project could minimize conflict with the project team by addressing their needs.

Consultants' involvement refers to the involvement of consultants during the acquisition of ERP systems. Organizations frequently use outside consultants for acquisition of their software, availing themselves of the consultants' experience. Consultants may have experience and knowledge in certain ERP modules and can guide the organization to choose the better fit system for the clients.

Clear goals and objectives of the ERP acquisition process refer to the management establishing and adhering to the goals and objectives of the project in advance. The project objectives should be clear, measurable and controllable, and the savings quantifiable.

SCALE DEVELOPMENT FOR CSFs OF ERP ACQUISITION

Scale development, or the design and refinement of multi-item scales employed to measure the constructs are vital to empirical research in management information systems (Stratman and Roth, 2002) Establishing the validity of the scales is dependent first upon establishing that they are reliable measures (Churchill, 1995). One of the goals of this research study is to create reliable and valid multi-item scales for measuring the 12 constructs described in Section 2. The content validity of these constructs was tentatively established by extensive literature reviews and interviews with managers and customers of technology-mediated services.

ITEM GENERATION

Constructs brief description is provided in Section 3 are necessary, but not sufficient, to advance our understanding of the CSFs of ERP acquisition. Thus, the first step in constructing new multi-item measurement scales is to generate sets of items that tap into the latent constructs and permit us to accurately and reliably assess these constructs from management' perspectives (Churchill, 1995). Some of the constructs involved in this research have been operationalized in previous studies and scales were available for these constructs. However, none of the existing scales was exactly appropriate for re-application in the context of ERP acquisition.

ITERATIVE ITEM REFINEMENT

To refine the scales, we adapted (Churchill, 1995) was widely adopted used methodology for instrument development. This method recognizes that the complexity inherent in many business processes cannot be adequately measured by a single scale. Multi-item measures can reduce measurement error by providing a more robust construct of complex variables through averaging several individual items. The challenge is to develop a set of items that capture the essence of the construct with the desired reliability and validity.

After the initial item pool was generated, the items were purified. This purification step is designed to remove the potential for measurement error from the new construct to improve their reliability. Collecting data from an initial sample of respondents helps to address these issues. Specifically, a manual factor technique (Menor, 1998) was used to establish tentative scale reliability and validity, as well as to assess potential problems with the unidimensionality of the constructs. The manual sorting procedures was conducted iteratively, using independent panels of expert judges for each round. The judges had recent industry experience with the implementation and use of ERP software in a business environment.

Each expert judge was given a questionnaire containing short descriptions of each of the proposed constructs, together with a randomized list all of the items generated from the literature. In each round, the panel of expert judges was asked to assign each item to one of the identified constructs. Items that were not consistently grouped into their target construct during this process were considered for rewording or elimination. It should be noted that this sorting procedure follows the technique described in (Moore and Benbasat, 1991), which differs from the traditional Q-sort technique (Stephenson, 1953: 78) in that there are no restrictions on the number of items which may be placed in any of the defined construct categories.

In the first round the six expert judges on ERP implementation from the academia were selected to go through the constructs and initial items generated from the literature. The experts were asked to assign each item to one of the defined constructs. The items which were not associated with any construct were reworded and revised. In the second stage of item purification, six experts from the industry with wide experience in acquisition of ERP system were invited for panel discussions. All of the six experts who were grouped in three panels with two to three members each were given these items with a short description of each construct and also a list of items which were generated from the literature and discussion with academicians. Some of the items were revised and reworded to include in the relevant construct. To assess the pre-test scale reliability of the qualitative judgments made during the sorting process, an item placement ratio (Stratman and Roth, 2002) was used.

Although the method for content validation for this study is the literature review, input from experts (using manual sorts) was used in addition to the literature review for validating the content of the construct scale. A scale is said to have content validity if the scale's items form a representative sample of the theoretical domain of the construct (Stratman and Roth, 2002).

The item placement ratios assess both the validity of the generated items and the reliability of the proposed measurement scales. If there is a high degree of inter-judge (expert) agreement, then the percentage of items placed in the target construct will also be high. In addition, scales based on constructs with a percentage of correct item placement ratio of 70 per cent or greater is generally considered acceptable. Moore and Benbasat's (1991) technique was applied to determine the item placement ratios for the constructs of this study. Most of the constructs scored above 70 per cent, which is good indicator for the acceptance of these constructs.

The manual sorting process produced refined multi-item scales for the constructs discussed in the previous section. Although our panel members of industry and academic experts are experienced in acquisition and implementation of ERP system and are qualified to assess the content validity of proposed constructs and items, empirical testing was performed to ensure the validity of the scales for the purposes of analysis for this study and to contribute in the area of ERP systems planning. This is evidenced from Churchill (1995), who proposed the development of measurement instrument norms as the final step in new scale development. This was performed using data obtained from the mail survey.

FIELD SURVEY

Satisfied by the apparent reliability and parsimony of our new measurement scales, we moved into the next phase of testing our survey instrument in a field setting. For this phase, the mail survey was targeted at decision-makers within the Australian companies that had acquired ERP system. The questionnaire used in this study attempted to measure the theoretical model illustrated and discussed in Section 2.

Initial survey instrument was pilot tested during mid-2003 and it was further refined to be ready after a pilot survey was undertaken. The final survey was sent out to the respondents in November–December 2003 and comprised of 18 questions in eight sections. Data used to test the CSF instrument were obtained from 53 respondents from Australia. Each respondent company had implemented ERP system and the respondents had experience in either been involved in ERP implementation of their organization. The questionnaire was sent through mail to the 500 organizations and 53 usable surveys were received making the response rate to be around 11 per cent. Most of the items in this study were itemized using Likert Scale, in which respondents were asked to indicate their level of importance for each of the construct items (CSFs) using their response on a seven-point scale.

The measurement analysis emphasizes explanations of the reliability and validity of the new instruments for measuring these constructs. The validity and reliability measure indicate that the instrument has the potential for use in further studies.

RELIABILITY ANALYSIS

Reliability is one of the most critical elements in assessing the quality of the construct measures (Churchill, 1995), and it is a necessary condition for scale validity. A statistically reliable scale provides consistent and stable measures of a construct. Composite reliability estimates are used to assess the inter-item reliability of the measures. Estimates greater than .70 are generally considered to meet the criterion for reliability. Some items may be removed from the construct scales if their removal results in increases in the reliability estimate, however, care must be taken to ensure that the content validity of the measures is not threatened by the removal of a key conceptual element.

As shown in Table 12.1 reliability of each factor is above .75. In it are listed the composite reliability estimates for each of the measurement scales.

CONTENT VALIDITY

The content validity of a questionnaire refers to the representativeness of item content domain. It is the manner by which the questionnaire and its items are built to ensure the reasonableness

TABLE 12.1
Constructs (CSFs) Items and Reliability Values

Constructs	Items	Alpha
Planning	8	.92
Accurate information	4	.83
Selection criteria	6	.90
Structured process	5	.87
Vendor–client partnership	5	.89
Top management support	5	.89
Effective communication	4	.85
Balanced team	5	.89
Users' involvement	5	.84
Consultants' involvement	5	.92

Source: Authors.

of the claim of content validity. The conceptualization of survey instrument constructs are based on preliminary literature review to form the initial items, the personal interviews with practitioners, and experts used for scale purification suggest that the survey instrument has strong content validity.

CONSTRUCT VALIDITY ANALYSIS

Construct validity is established by showing that the instrument measures the construct it is intended to measure. Construct validity is evaluated by performing correlation and factor analysis. High correlations considered to indicate construct validity. The Appendix shows the results of factor analysis performed on the items important for the success of ERP acquisition process. These items formed 10 factors with a high variance and reasonable eigenvalue.

Factor 1: Factor analysis results show that the first factor was associated with the Planning CSF of ERP acquisition. The items from 'planning' and 'clear goals and objectives' constructs merged under one factor. After the extraction, the items 'ERP acquisition objectives are identified' and 'Organisations define the reasons for acquisition of ERP system' were removed from this factor, due to the low loading factor. The remaining eight items with factor-loading are shown in the table in the Appendix under the 'Planning' factor. The factor-loading ranges between .72 and .83. All the items indicate the importance given to planning as a CSF.

Factor 2: Four items formed this factor. The item 'Acquisition team needs to consider and gather a lot of information before deciding on ERP vendor and system' had a very low loading value and therefore was deleted from the accurate information construct. The remaining four items with the factor loading are shown in the table in the Appendix.

Factor 3: The six items of 'selection criteria' and 'evaluation technique' constructs merged into this factor, with a high loading factor. The remaining four items of these constructs had very low factor-loading and loaded on other factors with weak factor-loading, hence were removed. The items 'attributes for evaluation of ERP systems are identified precisely', 'establish possible list of suitable ERP vendors', 'integrate the knowledge and judgment of external experts to choose an ERP project', and 'use appropriate evaluation techniques to determine ERP suitability' were removed due to their weak loading. The remaining one item was loaded into the selection criteria and was included in this factor.

Factor 4: All the five items belonging to structured process loaded into this factor, with factor-loading ranging between .71 and .89.

Factor 5: This factor is associated with the items of the vendor–client partnership CSF. All items of this construct loaded into one factor with the loading ranging from 0.78 to 0.85.

Factor 6: All the five items belonging to top management support formed one factor with high factor loading. Factor loading for this factor are shown in the Appendix table.

Factor 7: The seventh factor was associated with items of effective communication in the acquisition process, with the greatest load ranging from 0.78 to 0.86, except for 'acquisition team-members are clearly informed about the project's scope, objectives and tasks', which had a factor-loading below .40 and hence was removed from this factor. The remaining items of this factor with the loading are shown in the Appendix table, underneath the 'Effective Communication' factor.

Factor 8: Cross-sectional team members, roles and responsibilities of team members, their knowledge, and ability to make decisions and team-members' experience in the acquisition of similar system items formed this factor with the greatest factor loading. The items of this factor have a high factor-loading and relate to the balanced team CSF for ERP acquisition process.

Factor 9: This factor is associated with all items of users' involvement, with the greatest load ranging from 0.72 to 0.85. All five items indicate the importance given to users' involvement in ERP acquisition.

Factor 10: Five items with reasonably high factor-loading formed this factor. The factor-loading of these items ranges between .82 and .92.

The results of the factor analysis presented in the Appendix proved that these factors were indeed representing major constructs in addition to being significant.

Prior research in similar area suggests that validation strategies for establishing construct validity include item-to-total correlation as well. It measures the correlation of each of the items to the total scale. Items with a low correlation can be deleted. The minimum value of each corrected item-to-total correlation was above 0.40.

Table 12.2 presents the results of all the items of CSFs for ERP acquisition. All the 51 items of 10 constructs were included in this analysis. Values for all item-total correlations for the eight CSFs were greater than .60 (range .60–.82) indicating that each scale of the items had good correlation with the other items comprising the overall scale score. Whereas the values of accurate information and vendor–client partnership were moderate, internal consistencies of the item-total correlations were more than 0.42. In general, the coefficients of all the constructs were greater than 0.42, confirming validity of these constructs are highly acceptable. Based on the ratings and mean values, results indicate the top five CSFs for ERP acquisition as ranked by the respondents are effective communication, planning, top management support, user involvement, and balanced team. As narrated by Somers and Nelson (2001), effective communication is essential for the project team, between the team and the rest of the organization, and with the vendors. These findings are similar to implementation literature (Esteves and Pastor, 2002; Somers and Nelson, 2004), in which the studies have identified that top management and effective communication are the two important success factors for ERP system. Similarly, the importance of top management support in providing resources, commitment, and champion is very important for acquisition. Planning has been also identified as one of the important CSFs in the literature by Verville and Halington (2003) as well. The survey result demonstrates that most organizations believe that planning, top management support, and effective communication in the first place are critical for successfully acquiring ERP systems. User's involvement in the implementation of ERP has been cited by several studies. It is important for the acquisition because users, when they are involved in the selection and evaluation, process suitable system for the organization considering the current processes of the organization.

TABLE 12.2
Ranking and Item-to-total Correlation for Acquisition Critical Success Factors (CSFs)

Measure	Mean	Items	Item-to-total correlation
Effective communication	6.01	4	.62, .68, .76, .71
Planning	5.90	8	.79, .65, .70, .73, .71, .78, .76, .65
Top management support	5.88	5	.80, .70, .77, .74, .70
Users' involvement	5.85	5	.58, .75, .61, .70, .63
Balanced team	5.81	5	.77, .82, .73, .68, .72
Vendor–client partnership	5.66	5	.60, .42, .62, .60, .59
Structured process	5.63	5	.76, .82, .72, .65, .57
Selection criteria	5.61	6	.80, .78, .65, .79, .72, .67
Accurate information	5.60	4	.51, .72, .75, .65
Consultants' involvement	5.55	5	.75, .69, .74, .61, .70

Source: Authors.

CONCLUSION

The primary contributions of this chapter are the definition of new constructs associated with the ERP acquisition and development of new multi-item measurement scales for measuring these constructs. Unlike much prior ERP acquisition research, this study takes a grounded theory approach using ERP experts' perceptions. Future ERP implementation empirical research linking these constructs in causal models in an ERP will benefit significantly from the existence of relevant construct definitions and good measurement scales. A secondary contribution of this work is the demonstration of a rigorous empirical scale and item development process.

APPENDIX

Results of Factor Analysis of ERP Acquisition Critical Success Factors

Critical success factors for ERP acquisition	Factor loading
Factor 1: Planning	
Whole process is adequately documented	.84
Selection/evaluation priorities are identified	.72
Contingency issues are considered	.76
The request for proposal (RFP) for the system is sought from the potential vendors	.81
Acquisition process goals and expectations are defined	.78
Acquisition process goals need to be realistic and operational	.83
Acquisition process goals are consistent with overall organizational goals and objectives	.84
Acquisition process goals and objectives are set with the consent of top management	.84
Factor 2: Accurate Information	
Acquisition team knows exactly what information is needed for ERP acquisition	.70
The sources of information about ERP vendors and ERP systems are reliable and credible	.86
The sources of information for ERP vendors and systems are assessed	.88
Unbiased information about ERP vendors and ERP systems is important for the success of acquisition process	.81
Factor 3: Selection Criteria (SC)	
SC is established based on the users' information requirements	.88
SC are based on the requirements of the organization	.87
SC is based on the functional requirements	.77
Define ERP evaluation attributes precisely (such as ease of installation process, interfaces with legacy system, ease of upgrade, etc.)	.86
Establish possible list of suitable ERP vendors	.80
Integrate the knowledge and judgment of external experts to choose an ERP project	.76
Factor 4: Structured Process	
ERP acquisition process is handled to a large extent by standard procedures	.87
The acquisition structure is defined at the initial stage of ERP acquisition process	.89
ERP acquisition process should be recursive	.83
ERP acquisition process should be handled by 'the rule book'	.78
Clear authority is needed for managing the structure of the ERP acquisition process.	.71

(*Appendix Continued*)

(Appendix Continued)

Critical success factors for ERP acquisition	Factor loading
Factor 5: Vendor–client Partnership	
Commitment between the vendor of choice and the ERP acquisition team	.85
Trust between vendor of choice and the ERP acquisition team	.78
A close cooperation between vendor of choice and the ERP acquisition team	.84
Mutual satisfaction between the vendor and the ERP acquisition team	.81
Vendor supports the acquisition team during the ERP acquisition process	.80
Factor 6: Top Management Support	
Top management provides commitment and support during the ERP acquisition	.88
Top management must continuously monitor ERP acquisition process's progress	.80
Top management provides necessary resources required	.86
The process is headed by an executive-level project champion	.84
Top management identifies this process as a top priority	.80
Factor 7: Effective Communication	
Effective communication plan is developed for the acquisition process	.78
Acquisition process's progress is communicated periodically to the stakeholders	.82
Open communication policy is maintained among the acquisition team-members	.88
Changes to the organizational structure due to the acquisition process are communicated to employees	.86
Factor 8: Balanced Team	
Cross-functional team-members are selected for managing the acquisition process	.87
The roles and responsibilities of acquisition team-members are defined	.88
Acquisition team-members have sound knowledge about organization's business processes and ERP systems	.84
Team-members are empowered to make quick decisions	.80
Team comprises members with experience in acquisition of ERP systems	.83
Factor 9: Users' Involvement	
Users should be involved in defining the ERP system requirements	.72
ERP users must be involved in the acquisition effort	.85
Input from users of ERP is sought on a routine basis to help evaluate the system	.75
Users assist the project team in developing selection/evaluation criteria	.82
User involvement in the process enhances their perceived control over their work	.77
Factor 10: Consultants' Involvement	
Consultants play an essential role in the success of ERP acquisition process	.91
Consultants need to have expertise in different ERP systems	.82
Consultants need to have business and technical knowledge	.92
Consultants are able to recommend a suitable ERP system and a vendor to acquisition team	.85
Consultants need to have good interpersonal skills	.87

REFERENCES

Al-Mashari, M. and A. Al-Mudimigh. 2003. 'ERP Implementation: Lessons from a Case Study', *Information Technology & People*, 16(1): 21–34.

Bingi, P., M.K. Sharma, and J.K. Godla. 1999. 'Critical Issues Affecting an ERP Implementation', *Information Systems Management*, 16(3): 7–14.

Churchill. 1995. 'A Paradigm for Developing Better Measures of Marketing Constructs', *Journal of Marketing Research*, 16(3): 64–73.

Esteves, J. and J. Pastor. 2002. 'A Framework to Analyze Most Critical Work Packages in ERP Implementation Projects', *Proceedings of the International Conference on Enterprise Information Systems (ICEIS)*, Spain, April 2002.

Esteves J., J. Pastor, and J. Carvalho. 2003. 'Organizational and National Issues of an ERP Implementation in a Portuguese Company', IFIP (w8.2+w9.4), Athens (Greece), June 2003, 139–53.

Hong, K.K. and Y.G. Kim. 2002. 'The Critical Success Factors for ERP Implementation: an Organizational Fit Perspective', *Information & Management*, 40(1): 25–40.

Jung, Ho-Won and D.R. Goldenson. 2003. 'CMM-Based Process Improvement and Schedule Deviation in Software Maintenance', CMU/SEI-2003-TN-015. Available at www.sei.cmu.edu/reports/03tn015.pdf, (accessed on January 2009).

Menor, L.J. 1998. 'An Empirical Investigation of New Service Development Competence and Performance', working paper, Kenan–Flager Business School.

Moore, G.C. and Benbasat. 1991. 'Development of an Instrument to Measure the Perceptions of Adopting an Information Technology Innovation', *Information Systems Research*, 2(2): 192–272.

Nah, F.H., L. Lau, S. Janet, and J. Kuang. 2001. 'Critical Factors for Successful Implementation of Enterprise Systems', *Business Process Management Journal*, 7(3): 285–96.

Nah, F.H., K.M. Zuckweiler, and J.L.S. Lau. 2003. 'ERP Implementation: Chief Information Officers' Perceptions of Critical Success Factors', *International Journal of Human–Computer Interaction*, 16(1): 5–22.

Shanks, G. 2000. 'A Model for ERP Project Implementation', *Journal of Information Technology*, 15(4): 289–303.

Rockart, F. 1979. 'Chief Executives Define their Own Data Needs', *Harvard Business Review*, 57(March–April): 81–93.

Somers, T.M. and K. Nelson. 2001. 'The Impact of Critical Success Factors Across the Stages of Enterprise Resource Planning Implementation', *Proceedings of the 34th International Conference of System Sciences (HICSS)*, Big Island, HI, USA.

Somers, T.M. and K.G. Nelson. 2004. 'A Taxonomy of Players and Activities Across the ERP Project Life Cycle', *Information & Management*, 41(3): 257–78.

Stephenson, W. 1953. *The Study of Behavior: Q-technique and its Methodology*. Chicago: University of Chicago Press.

Stratman, Jeff and Roth. 2002. 'Enterprise Resource Planning (ERP) Competence Constructs: Two-stage Multi-Item Scale Development and Validation', *Decision Sciences*, 33(4): 601–26.

Verville, J. and A. Halington. 2003. 'Analysis of the Decision Process for Selecting ERP Software: Case of Keller Manufacturing, Integrated Manufacturing Systems', *International Journal of Manufacturing Technology Management*, 14(5): 423–32.

13

Integrating Enterprise Resource Planning Systems and the Balanced Scorecard in Performance Management

NOORHAYATI MANSOR
Universiti Malaysia Sabah, Kota Kinabalu, Malaysia
E-mail: nhayati@ums.edu.my

ASNIATI BAHARI
Universiti Malaysia Sabah, Kota Kinabalu, Malaysia
E-mail: asniati@ums.edu.my

INTRODUCTION

Dynamic transformation is now a common denominator among businesses worldwide. Rapid swings in consumer demands, shorter product lifecycle, and increased competition have radically changed the business landscape especially for manufacturers. In coping with these challenges, manufacturers are continuously pursuing improvements and innovations in strategic aspects of operations, including information system management. Information technology (IT) has now become one of the critical success factors to create sustainable competitive advantage (Porter and Millar, 1985). Unlike information produced under the conventional system, a widely used integrated system of information known as Enterprise Resource Planning (ERP) provides strategic decision support across organizations and locations (Bendoly and Jacobs, 2005).

ERP refers to a broad set of activities supported by multi-module applications software that help businesses to manage effectively. Organizations assemble the ERP systems by mixing and matching prefabricated software components to best meet their business requirements. The systems are multiple-modules, evolved primarily from the traditional Material Requirements Planning II (MRP II) systems. Compared to MRP II, ERP improves company's information management (Hall, 2007). According to the cybernetic control theory, organizations require continuous and timely feedback on key performance indicators in order to act, react, and survive (Vancouver, 1996; Wier et al., 2007). The ERP systems provide real time information (Rashid et al., 2002) and thus, allow for timely decisions to drive competitive advantages (Hall, 2007).

When combined with strategic key performance indicators using the Balanced Scorecard (BSC) concept, ERP further align individual, organizational, and cross-departmental initiatives towards common goals (Kaplan and Norton, 1996: 25). To date, research findings are inconclusive with respect to the advantages for ERP (e.g., Hunton et al., 2003; Rikhardson and Kraemmergaard, 2006), however their benefits can ostensibly be extended to customers (Table 13.1) through improved services and prices (Kakouris and Polychronopoulos, 2005).

Similar to ERP, the BSC is globally accepted since its introduction by Kaplan and Norton in 1992. In the BSC framework of performance measurement, three qualitative perspectives are added to the traditional financial measures. Hoque and James (2000) report a positive relationship between BSC usage and performance. Ittner et al. (2003) conclude that BSC is associated with

TABLE 13.1
Causes of ERP System Implementation Benefits

Benefit	*Cause of the benefit*
Inventory reduction	• Netting: By netting demand against inventory to determine market net requirement • Purchasing: The company buys what is needed through correct Bill of Materials (BOM), using parametrical optimum quantity algorithms • BOM: All changes in the BOM are encountered, thus preventing obsolete inventories • Planning: Production orders are processed faster, resulting in better control for the work-in-process inventories • Manufacturing: It produced what is demanded from time phased plans • Delivering: Deliveries match the actual quantities on the right dates
Labor cost reduction	• Fewer shortages, disruptions, and interruptions • Less rework, overtime, and rush jobs • Better visibility of required work, so that capacity is properly scheduled to meet demands • More free time for production personnel who are now used better and more constructively
Improved customer service	• Integration among forecasting (sales) and production planning and inventory planning can create better customer service and fewer lost sales
Improved visibility	• As the system provides a basis for linking operations, it allows for real time visibility. For example, production planners can now view what and where the orders are, thus allowing them to schedule against the forecast. This visibility has triggered co-operation and coordination between operations and allowed for a better decision-making
Others	• Flexibility and better access to information, less prone to errors • Elimination of most of the manual (paper) work • Applying the 'one set of data' principle • Integrating a holistic corporate attitude

Source: Adapted from Kakouris and Polychronopoulos (2005).

a high measurement system satisfaction. When carefully integrated and balanced, BSC provides a timely performance report card (Braam and Nijsen, 2004). Furthermore, Papalexandris et al. (2005) report that BSC improves transparency in performance management.

This chapter reviews the existing literature of ERP and BSC systems. The two major objectives of this study are: (*a*) to examine the current practice of performance management; and (*b*) to determine managers' perception of the combined effect of ERP and BSC. A framework to examine the effects of integrating the two systems on organizational performance is proposed. Existing work on these systems includes Rosemann and Wiese (1999) and Chand et al. (2005). The former uses a modified BSC approach to evaluate the implementation of ERP within an IT department. However, the research did not examine the combined benefits of ERP and BSC. The BSC systems fall within the framework of responsibility accounting which covers concepts and techniques in measuring performance consistent with achieving goal congruence (Hilton et al., 2006). The major purpose of responsibility accounting is to promote, monitor, and reinforce behaviours in organizations consistent with organizational philosophies and strategies. The remainder of the chapter is organized as follows. Section 2 describes the literature review on ERP and BSC systems in relation to performance. A review of research work on the combined effects of ERP and BSC on profitability and performance is presented in Section 3 while Section 4 briefly discusses the ERP implementation in Malaysian government-linked companies. A new research framework is proposed in Section 5. Finally, Section 6 concludes this chapter.

LITERATURE REVIEW

Even though ERP systems are now commonly used, the empirical evidence of their benefits on firms' performance is still inconclusive. Recent studies on ERP focus on strategic issues to increase performance and firms' survival. Current literature on how to sustain and improve business performance using ERP systems is still relatively limited (Chand et al., 2005). This section highlights the current findings of ERP and BSC research with respect to their impact on firm performance.

ENTERPRISE RESOURCE PLANNING (ERP) SYSTEMS

ERP is a business management system comprising of integrated business applications including financial and cost accounting, sales, distribution, materials management, human resource, production planning, and customer information. The systems also enhance supply chain network by reducing cycle times (Adam and Sammon, 2004; Cotteleer and Bendoly, 2006; Hsu and Chen, 2004; Jacobs and Bendoly 2003; Rashid et al., 2002). This integration is accomplished through a database shared by all application programs. Unlike its predecessor, MRP II, the ERP systems are flexible, allowing for multiple languages and currencies in the real time mode. The term ERP was coined by the Gartner Group and is widely used today (Hall, 2007) especially in developed countries. North America, Europe, and Asia control 66 per cent, 22 per cent, and 9 per cent of the ERP markets, respectively. However, the speed of economic growth in Asia and Latin America is now making them major targets of large ERP vendors (Huang and Palvia, 2001).

ERP Implementation Success

Studies to identify determinants of information systems (IS) success are widespread. Delone and McLean (1992) review 180 existing empirical studies and classify IS success into six major categories: *(a)* system quality, *(b)* information quality, *(c)* usage, *(d)* user satisfaction, *(e)* individual impact, and *(f)* organizational impact. Markus et al. (2000) conclude that the measures of success differ according to system lifecycle. At the implementation phase, the targets are fast implementation and cost-effective projects. Mabert et al. (2003) report that firms whose ERP implementation is under-budget tend to rate the system value (goal success and business case attainment) higher than the over-budget firms, and vice versa. Wu and Wang (2005) claim that the key user-satisfaction is closely linked to perceived system success. Further, it was found that satisfaction criteria are multidimensional including contractor service, knowledge, and involvement. ERP product satisfaction itself includes accuracy, reliability, response time, completeness, system stability, auditing and control, and system integrity.

The advantages of ERP system come with high cost, privacy issues and lack of trained personnel, challenges in implementation and time (Yen et al., 2002). Thus, implementing the ERP is risky (Davenport, 1998), particularly for organizations with multiple site implementations in dispersed locations (Markus et al., 2000). According to Tchokogué et al. (2005), strategic, tactic and operational considerations are prerequisites to effective system implementation. At the *strategic level*, the vision, scope and scale of the ERP project must be established together with resource commitment. At the *tactical level*, organizational redesigned is required to increase coherence and rigor, and clear measurement indicators are developed to assess progress. At the *operational level*, the leadership and knowledge transfer play crucial roles. In addition, Wu and Wang (2005) suggest that selection of suitable consultants and suppliers for ERP implementation also form critical elements of success.

ERP Implementation and Firms Performance

Kalakota and Robinson (1999) document major advantageous of the ERP systems. These are: *(a)* improve customer order-processing systems; *(b)* consolidate and unify business functions (such as manufacturing, finance, distribution, and human resources); *(c)* integrate a broad range of disparate technologies into a common denominator of overall functionality; and *(d)* create a foundation to develop the next-generation applications. Information integration is the key benefit of Enterprise Systems (ES) and results in savings of infrastructure support costs and improved firm performance. ERP implementation is judged successfully if it leads to faster response time, increase interaction, accelerate business processes; improve order management and order cycle, and lower inventory levels.

Hitt et al. (2002) provide one of the earlier comprehensive studies of stock price reactions to ERP implementation. They report improved financial performance immediately associated with the event, however, Hitt and his co-authors also discuss the general difficulty in identifying long term-performance gains from such systems. Unfortunately these authors fall short of formally examining the kind of relevant post-implementation information that would argue for a case either way. In stark contrast, Bendoly and Cotteleer (2008) recently studied the effect of investments in ERP systems on a firm's long-term performance. They report that the long-term performance of firms can be stymied in particular by behavioural dynamics inherent to the settings in which the applications are active.

Other case studies have also used to determine the effects of ERP investments on performance. For example, McAfee's (2002) case study looks at the implementation effect on the performance of a single firm. A survey by Mabert et al. (2003) found some improvements in managers' perceptions of performance but found that few firms had reduced direct operational costs. Hunton et al. (2002) test the relation between ERP and performance using a hypothetical case. Comparing analysts' initial earning forecasts with the revised forecasts after knowing these firms have committed to invest in ERP, their results suggest improved earnings revisions. Thus, the study supports the positive relationship between ERP implementation and performance.

Gupta and Kohli (2006) as well as Jacobs and Bendoly (2003) provide operations managers a brief overview of ERP systems and highlight its implications for operations function. Specifically, the work gives a broad-based overview of ERP systems. Using SAP R/3 as an example system, they elaborate how ERP systems assist in strengthening business strategy and operations decisions, process design, production planning and scheduling, inventory management, quality management, and human resource management. ERP provides the enterprise-wide solution to deliver many benefits such as low operating costs and improved customer service, thus enhances their business operations in many areas (Yen et al., 2002).

The Balanced Scorecard (BSC) Model

Among others, Kaplan and Norton (2001), Valiris et al. (2005), and Chenhall (2005) emphasize that choosing the right performance measurement is a strategic issue in ERP implementation decision. Managers place great importance on multiple measures to determine the association (if any) between firm performance and strategic resources (Widener, 2005). Multiple measures are widely applied in established tools such as the BSC system, Business Process Reengineering (BPR) system, and Medori and Steeple's system (Folan and Browne, 2005). The most famous of them is the BSC, and it can help make better quality decisions (Bremser and Chung, 2005; Valiris et al., 2005). The scorecard enables managers to see the breadth and totality of company operations (Kaplan and Norton, 1993). The BSC system has been widely adopted since first introduced by Kaplan and Norton in 1992 and considered the most visible performance measurement model (Bremser and Chung, 2005). The system uses a top-down approach, formulated at the top and cascaded downward. When integrated carefully and in a balanced manner, BSC provides a timely and summarized report-card of performance (Braam and Nijsen, 2004).

Kaplan and Norton (1993) argue that financial measures alone are inadequate and ineffective to capture the qualitative dimensions of performance. They introduce three additional key areas or perspectives and these are: *(a)* customers, *(b)* internal business process, and *(c)* learning and growth (infrastructure). The financial perspective summarizes the economic consequences of actions implemented under the other three perspectives. The customer perspective describes the market niche and target customers the organization is competing. The internal business process perspective defines the major internal processes required to create value for owners and customers. The final perspective describes the capabilities needed for the organization to establish long-term growth and improvement.

BSC promotes transparent performance (Papalexandris et al., 2005) and its multi-layered evaluation process is recommended for appraisal of large information and communication technology investment (Milis and Mercken, 2004). A number of studies related to companies' success in adopting the BSC have been documented. For example, a survey of 66 Australian manufacturing companies suggests that the BSC usage is associated with improved performance (Hoque and James, 2000). Another survey conducted using a sample of 140 United States financial service firms documents that the use of BSC is associated with a higher measurement system satisfaction (Ittner et al., 2003). A study in the United States banking industry indicates that bank branches implementing the BSC outperformed non-BSC-implementing branches on key financial measures (Davis and Albright, 2004). A research conducted in Finland (Malmi, 2001), and another one in Poland (Michalaska, 2005) also support the success of BSC as a strategy-focus performance tool.

ALIGNING THE BENEFITS OF ERP WITHIN THE BSC SYSTEMS

The ERP systems are now at its second wave and this phase corresponds to the stabilization period following the implementation period (Tchokogué et al., 2005). One important research question that arises at this point is whether integration of the ERP and BSC systems leads to improved performance. The idea of developing an ERP BSC has been suggested by several authors. However, only Rosemann and Weise (1999) and Chand et al. (2005) have attempted to apply the BSC approach to the specific task of managing the ERP systems. To date, no published work has empirically examined the combined effects of integrating ERP and BSC on company's performance. The following presentation summarizes the existing research findings of the ERP benefits according to the perspectives offered by the BSC framework.

THE EFFECTS OF ERP ON CUSTOMER SATISFACTION

ERP implementation integrates customer order information and results in improved coordination and information sharing for departments (Davenport, 1998) leading to better customer services. Mabert et al. (2003) use case studies of 18 manufacturing companies and a survey of 193 companies to determine areas that benefit firms the most as a result of ERP implementation. They report that: *(a)* availability of information; *(b)* inventory management; *(c)* interaction with customers; and *(d)* quality of information receive the highest benefits while the areas benefiting the least are: *(a)* costs of information technology; and *(b)* personnel management. Overall, both the case study and surveyed companies report very similar trends on the impact of ERP systems on performance.

Similarly, Hsu and Chen (2004) study the benefits of ERP implementation on customers' satisfaction. Their results provide evidence of positive relationship between the two variables. More specifically, ERP implementation improves product quality, response time to customers order and inquiries, service quality, and the overall customer satisfaction and loyalty, resulting in sales growth. This conclusion is consistent with Shang and Seddon (2000) based on their analysis of features of ERP systems.

THE EFFECTS OF ERP ON INTERNAL BUSINESS PROCESSES

According to Davenport (1998) ERP system standardizes and accelerates business processes. ERP saves time and increases productivity by reducing administrative overhead, simplifying business processes, and reducing paper work. Further, companies are able to manage multiple sites as a single entity. In addition, it reduces inventory and integrates supply chain. One of the greatest benefits of ERP system is that it unites all business processes within a single family of software modules (Gupta and Kohli, 2006). This integration simultaneously enhances operational, financial, and managerial principles.

Shang and Seddon (2000) in Adam and Sammon (2004: 11) present a comprehensive framework of business benefits achievable using the ERP systems. Prior to that, Rashid et al. (2002)

claim that ERP system is expected to improve both organizational backbone and front-end functions simultaneously. Mabert et al. (2003) report that ERP implementation benefits the most from: *(a)* business processes integration; *(b)* information availability; and *(c)* information quality. In addition, ERP implementation improves inventory management and supplier management or procurement. Other internal benefits of ERP include: *(a)* support for production capacity planning; *(b)* increase accuracy in market demand forecast; and *(c)* improve manufacturing flexibility (Hsu and Chen, 2004). Benefits are further categorized into tangible benefits and intangible benefits (Table 13.2).

TABLE 13.2
Tangible and Intangible Benefits of ERP System Implementation

Tangible benefit	*Intangible benefits*
• Support capacity planning	• Allocate enterprise resource better
• Provide more accurate market demand forecast	• Increase communications among departments
• Facilitate mass customization and improve manufacturing flexibility	• Integrate information across the enterprise
• Increase inventory turnover rate	• Increase the ability of critical operational and decision support information to provide visibility of enterprise planning activities
• Decrease inventory level and cost	• Access to real-time business intelligence
• Control and improve product quality	• Improve information flow among departments
• Speed up new product development cycle and time-to-market	• Increase response time to customer order and inquiries
• Reduce the cycle time of order fulfilment	• Improve service quality
• Achieve operational excellence	• Improve customer satisfaction and loyalty
	• Growing purchase from customers

Source: Hsu and Chen (2004).

THE EFFECTS OF ERP SYSTEM ON ORGANIZATIONAL GROWTH

Wang and Chen (2006) state that group cohesion of an ERP project team is important to attain organizational benefits. The study involves a sample of 126 senior managers in Taiwan's manufacturing companies. Cohesive groups know the members better and are motivated to complete the task successfully. In addition, willingness to participate and commitment to learn have significant effects on the outcome of group cohesion in implementing organizational innovations. Since a collective participation capability is critical to the realization of innovation benefits, it is important for management to develop appropriate participation mechanisms for organizational innovation.

Reported organizational impacts of ERP implementation include changes in IT function and increase in: *(a)* informational technology literacy; *(b)* accounting and business process integration; *(c)* financial performance; and *(d)* competitive positions (Rikhardson and Kraemmergaard, 2006). This study concludes that organizations simplify their system processes as a result of

ERP implementation. Companies also increase employees training to increase IT awareness and improve understanding of the organizational issues. ERP implementation improves personnel management (Mabert et al., 2003) and knowledge sharing (Jones et al., 2006) since knowledge requirements in the ERP environment is diverse.

Empirical evidence suggests that ERP implementation positively affects the growth ability of companies. According to Hsu and Chen (2004), among the benefits of ERP implementation includes increase in: *(a)* communication among departments; *(b)* availability of decision support information; and *(c)* access to real-time business intelligence. Spathis and Ananiadis (2005) further report that ERP improve the maintenance of common database and document circulations. Other reported benefits include increase in labor productivity due to online procurement (Falk, 2005) and improves organizational alignment (Gupta and Kohli, 2006).

THE EFFECTS OF ERP SYSTEM AND FINANCIAL PERFORMANCE

Financial outcome has and always been the most crucial determinant of a firm's success. Thus, research studies on the impact of ERP on firms' profitability are broad and extensive. However, the findings are yet inconclusive. Among them include Poston and Grabski (2001) who compare the pre- and post-ERP implementation profits. The study documents no evidence of performance improvement in each of the three years following implementation. A significant reduction in the ratio of cost of goods sold to revenues is detected three years after implementation. Further, a significant decrease in the ratio of employees to revenues is reported for each of the three years examined. In contrast, Hunton et al. (2003) examine the profitability impact of ERP by matching 63 adopters with non-adopters. Results indicate that return on assets (ROA), return on investment (ROI), and asset turnover (ATO) were significantly better over a three-year period for adopters compared to non-adopters. They also report a significant interaction between firm size and financial health for ERP adopters with respect to ROA, ROI, and return on sales (ROS).

Motivated by the mixed results, Nicolaou and Bahattacharya (2006) examine the long-term financial effects of ERP changes for firms that have previously reported ERP adoptions. They study the extent to which discrete changes to ERP systems during post-implementation affects long-run financial results. Using a sample of 247 firms, they conclude that ERP-adopting firms, which initiate early enhancements (add-ons or upgrades), report superior profits compared to other ERP-adopting firms.

Rikhardson and Kraemmergaard (2006) classify the financial impact of enterprise systems (ES) into: *(a)* income effects and *(b)* cost effects. They argue that it is not clear if ES directly increases income indirectly through enhanced customer services, achieved through ES. Other factors such as improved training of sales personnel, promotional campaigns, and the bankruptcy of a competitor may inject intervening effects. They also suggest that studying the impact of ES on costs is easier than on revenues. Specific cost effects include reduced inventory costs and cost of capital. Inventory costs reduction of up to 25 per cent is attributed to better planning and coordination with suppliers and customers, better integration between purchasing, productions, and sales, and shorter order cycle times. The cost also decline due to lower error rates in purchasing, production and sales.

Using the Lexis-Nexis system, Hunton et al. (2003) access the SEC database and annual reports of the same firms studied by Hayes in 2001. They perform additional search on foreign firms and access International Company Reports. A sample of 21 out of 63 firms that announced ERP adoption (33.33 per cent) responds to the survey. The findings show that ROA, ROI, and ATO are significantly better over a three-year period for adopters, as compared to non-adopters. According to Mabert et al. (2003), companies of different sizes approach ERP implementations differently. Also, the benefits differ by size where large companies report improvements in financial measures and small companies experience better performance in manufacturing and logistics. They also document that ERP system improves direct operating costs, inventory levels, and cash management.

According to Poston and Grabski (2001), economic and industrial organization theories provide the basis for examining how ERP systems affect firms coordination and transaction costs. ERP systems are expected to: *(a)* reduce costs by improving efficiencies through computerization; and *(b)* enhance decision-making by providing accurate and timely enterprise-wide information. These effects should be associated with improved firm performance. However, using 50 ERP system adopters, the do not find evidence of improvement associated with residual income or the ratio of selling, general, and administrative expenses in each of the three years following the implementation of the ERP system. However, a significant improvement in firm performance resulting from a decrease in the ratio of cost of goods sold to revenues was found three years after the ERP system implementation (but not in the first or second year after implementation). Further, there was a significant reduction in the ratio of employees to revenues for each of the three years examined following the ERP implementation.

ERP SYSTEMS IMPLEMENTATION IN MALAYSIA

Previous sections highlight the direct and indirect benefits of implementing ERP in today's challenging business environment. However, none of the studies look at the importance of ERP in managing developing countries. Since ERP is IT-based, its capabilities and benefits are directly linked to the availability and use of technology. Unlike the developed economies, companies in developing countries rely mostly on their governments to initiate, promote, and invest in information technology. In order to gauge the current state of ERP implementation in Malaysia, a series of interviews was conducted involving the CEOs of government-linked companies (GLCs). Malaysian GLCs represents roughly 44 per cent of the total market capitalization of Bursa Malaysia and worth more than RM200 billion. These companies are relatively large in size and mostly global in operations.

The GLCs were chosen based on their willingness to participate in this study. Initially, formal letters were sent to CEOs of Malaysian GLCs informing them of the objectives of the research and requesting for face-to-face interviews. Each CEO who agreed to be interviewed was asked to choose the most convenient date and time for the session on the reply slip attached with the introductory letter. Once the reply slip was received, the proposed session was confirmed in writing. At the same time, the general guidelines and topics to be covered during the interview were sent via facsimile to the prospective respondents. Each interview session consumed an estimated one hour and conducted in a very informal setting. The main objective of the interview is to assess the opinion of the highest level management with regard to the benefits and relationship of ERP to companies' performance. Aside from that, the interviewer also attempted to gather CEOs opinions and exposure to the BSC perspectives and its application in the design of performance evaluation system. Equally important, the CEOs were asked to describe the preferred approach if they were to integrate the ERP systems with the performance management systems of their companies. These additional insights provide the basis for developing the proposed framework for the integrated ERP and BSC system.

A total of eight publicly listed GLCs responded positively to the requests and indicated their preferred dates and time for the sessions. All but two of them are among the top 10 largest GLCs in the country. These companies are involved in various industries including financial (37.5 per cent), petroleum, shipping, plantation, timber, and energy (12.5 per cent each). All of these GLCs have undergone restructuring or in the process of so doing. This preliminary study indicates that ERP was initially implemented by one of the GLCs as early as 2003. Interestingly, two of them (22 per cent) are yet to implement integrated information systems in their organizations. The remaining 62.5 per cent currently uses some form of ERP-based information systems for operational purposes.

All interviews took place at the respective offices of the respondents. Generally, the CEOs expressed their organizational support for the research. All of them are in the opinion that integrated information systems do contribute to performance improvement. The benefits are derived basically in terms of the speed of information retrieval and the quality of decisions achieved. Further, it was noted that all of the CEOs are exposed to and familiar with the four BSC perspectives in performance management through workshop and training. CEOs representing the petroleum and electricity companies indicate the use of consultants to develop customized, in-house ERP systems that are linked with the performance measures. All of the CEOs agree that non-financial measures of performance are as important as the financial indicators for the purpose of performance evaluation. Based on the interviews, all CEOs view the use of BSC perspectives encourages them to focus on balancing their performance. Overall, the CEOs support a research proposal that combining ERP and BSC leads to improvement in companies' performance. Unfortunately, all of them indicate that such a system may not be cost-effective to all organizations due to the extent of initial investment outlay and the requirement for IT experts in the organizations. A summary of the interview is presented in the Appendix.

A RESEARCH FRAMEWORK FOR ERP-PLUS AND FIRM PERFORMANCE

The preliminary study of CEOs' opinions reveals a consensus among them for a positive performance impact of ERP and BSC systems. Given that most GLCs are in specialized industry, and at various stages of restructuring, a more detailed and industry-specific research is required to accommodate for information system uniqueness. Accordingly, a future study is proposed to examine the performance impact of a combined ERP and BSC system, termed as ERP-Plus (ERP+). This new system further integrates information and performance management systems according to the BSC's perspectives. The new system provides management with the combined advantages of the ERP and BSC systems. The former allows companies to share common databases and access information in a real-time environment (Wier et al., 2007). The BSC, on the other hand, provides a visible performance measurement model (Bremser and Chung, 2005) and a timely and summarized report-card of performance (Braam and Nijsen, 2004).

Wier et al. (2007) compare the effects of firms using: *(a)* ERP alone (n = 139); *(b)* Non-Financial Performance Incentives (NFPI) alone (n = 40); and *(c)* the combination of ERP and NFPI (n = 85). They report significantly higher return on assets for the combined effects of ERP and NFPI. Thus, the ERP+ system is expected to improve organizational strategic decisions and strengthen their long-term survival.

A case study to further integrate the ERP and BSC in an academic environment is deemed appropriate considering the growth potential and increased competition of this industry. Such a work shall provide additional insights into the full potentials of information systems in strengthening the competitive edge of institutions with unique information needs and operational characteristics. The combination of ERP and BSC is expected to further increase the efficiency and effectiveness of the university management in the global market. The study shall focus on: *(a)* the current systems of information management; *(b)* the current practice of performance management; *(c)* recommending an integrated ERP and BSC systems (ERP+) systems to improve the organizational performance consistent with research findings. Figure 13.1 present the suggested framework for the study.

The impact of ERP attributes such as the number of years of ERP adoption, specific modules adopted, implementation approach, ERP system quality, vendor service satisfaction, and knowledge are included. This is combined with the BSC perspectives (i.e., financial, customer, internal processes, and ability to learn and growth). In this study, the impact of having separate systems of ERP and BSC is compared to the direct effects of the combined model on company's performance. Thus, it is hypothesized that the ERP+ systems result in higher performance than

FIGURE 13.1
Suggested Research Framework

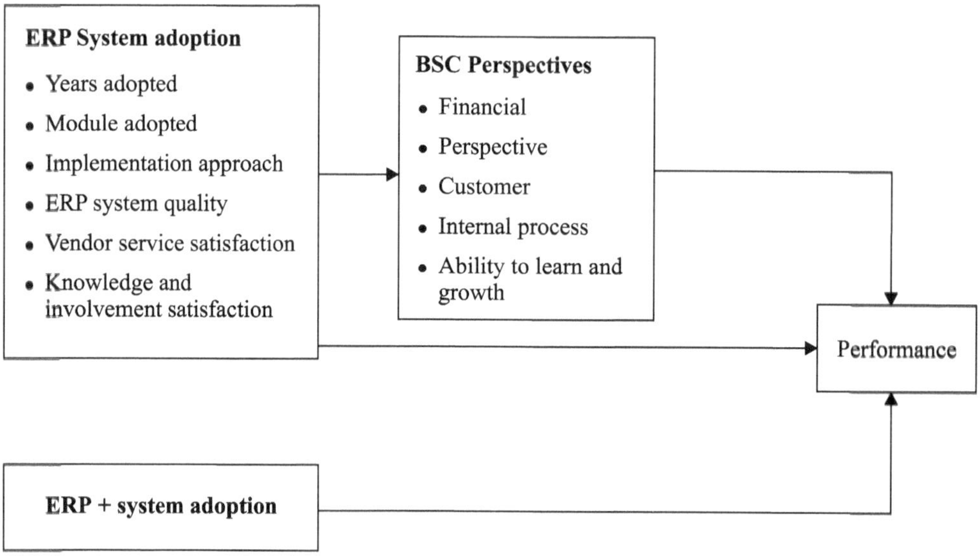

ERP System adoption

- Years adopted
- Module adopted
- Implementation approach
- ERP system quality
- Vendor service satisfaction
- Knowledge and involvement satisfaction

BSC Perspectives

- Financial
- Perspective
- Customer
- Internal process
- Ability to learn and growth

Performance

ERP + system adoption

Source: Authors.

the ordinary ERP or BSC solution. The research may add to the current body of knowledge in responsibility accounting by uncovering the optimal potentials of the ERP systems. The findings will also enhance our knowledge in the area of Accounting Information Systems as well as Management Information Systems.

CONCLUSION

ERP systems provide the means by which organizations develop competitive edge to improve performance and thus, survival. Key performance indicators developed using the BSC model help organizations to signal priorities and focus on specific targets. Even though the review of the literature generally points to the direction of positive impact of ERP on performance, inconsistent research results do exist. Thus, the findings are still inconclusive with respect to the performance effects of integrated information systems. Many factors contribute to this outcome. First, ERP is IT-based and places great reliance on the quality of the system itself. Second, the flexibility of the ERP systems accommodates a high degree of system unique-ness through customization. This in turn makes generalization of research findings across indus-tries and companies less meaningful. Third, the requirement for IT experts may not be met and thus, reduces the benefits of ERP in improving performance.

Empirical evidence supports the positive consequences of adopting the BSC perspectives in enhancing performance management. Based on our preliminary study, the framework is widely used by Malaysian GLCs following their restructuring. Overall, CEOs indicate the benefits derived from ERP implementation result in improved performance. However, the interviewed companies reveal that the ERP systems are implemented in stages and applied in selected priority areas or functions. Also, the uniqueness of each industry generally determines the scope and investment in ERP and BSC.

The findings from the preliminary study of Malaysian GLCs suggest that a case study approach is preferable to further examine the impact of ERP and BSC on firm performance. Thus, a study framework is suggested for future research. This chapter concludes with a proposal to conduct a study in an academic setting in line with the importance, growth rate, and competitiveness of this industry.

APPENDIX

No.	Code	Industry	*Question No. 1* *Do you currently implement integrated information systems in your operations?*	*Question No. 2* *Do you think combining ERP with the BSC Perspectives Management improve company's performance?*
1.	A	Shipping	Yes, only for shipment activities	Yes, the company use SAP vendor to develop information systems
2.	B	Banking	Yes, the company is developing the ERP systems	Yes, in future we need information system to support BSC
3.	C	Banking	Yes, only for customer services	Yes, but for the time being we use excel for KPIs
4.	D	Plantation	Not for the whole company, only for shop-floor. Separate units has different software	Yes, but we cannot afford that yet. In future, we plan to adopt it
5.	E	Electricity	Yes, we use ERP since 2003 by using in-house consultants to develop the systems	Yes, information system can prepare information for performance measurement
6.	F	Petroleum	Yes, the company implements customized ERP linked with performance management	KPI is a tool. Information is matter. That is the reason for adopting ERP
7.	G	Shipping	No	Yes, we still studying to adopt one of integrated software
8.	H	Timber	No	We are in the process of learning the integrated information systems

Source: Authors.

REFERENCES

Adam, F. and D. Sammon. 2004. *The Enterprise Resource Planning Decade: Lesson Learned and Issues for the Future*. Idea Group Publishing.

Bendoly, E., and F.R. Jacobs. 2005. *Strategic ERP Extension and Use*. Stanford Press.

Bendoly, E. and M. Cotteleer. 2008. 'Understanding Behavioral Sources of Process Variation following Enterprise System Deployment', *Journal of Operations Management*, 26(1): 23–44.

Braam, M. and E. Nijsen. 2004. 'Performance Effects of Using the Balanced Scorecard: A Note on Dutch Experience', *Long Range Planning*, 37: 335–49.

Bremser, W.G. and Q.B. Chung. 2005. 'A Framework for Performance Measurement in the Ee-business Environment', *Electronic Commerce Research and Applications*, 4(4): 395–412.

Chand, D., G. Hachey, J. Hunton, V., Owhoso, and S. Vasudevan. 2005. 'A Balanced Scorecard Based Framework for Assessing the Strategic Impacts of ERP Systems', *Computers in Industry*, 56(6): 558–72.

Chenhall, R. 2005. 'Integrative Strategic Performance Measurement Systems, Strategic Alignment of Manufacturing, Learning and Strategic Outcomes: An Exploratory Study', *Accounting, Organizations and Society*, 30(5): 395–422.

Cotteleer, M. and E. Bendoly. 2006. 'Order Lead-time Improvement following Enterprise-IT Implementation: An Empirical Study', *MIS Quarterly*, 30(3): 643–60.

Davenport, T.H. 1998. 'Putting the Enterprise into the Enterprise System', *Harvard Business Review*, 76(4): 121–31.

Davis, S. and T. Albright. 2004. 'An Investigation of the Effect on Balanced Scorecard Implementation on Financial Performance', *Management Accounting Research*, 15(2): 135–53.

Delone, W.H. and E.R. McLean. 1992. 'Information System Success: The Quest for Dependent Variable', *Information Systems Research*, 3(1): 60–95.

Falk, M. 2005. 'ICT-linked Firm Reorganization and Productivity Gains', *Technovation*, 25(11): 1229–50.

Folan, P. and J. Browne. 2005. 'A Review of Performance Management: Toward Performance Management', *Computers in Industry*, 56(7): 663–80.

Gupta, M. and A. Kohli. 2006. 'Enterprise Resource Planning Systems and its Implications for Operations Function', *Technovation*, 26(5–6): 687–96.

Hall, J. 2007. *Accounting Information Systems*, 5th edition. Thomson, South Western.

Hilton, R.W., M.W. Maher, and F.H. Selto. 2006. *Cost Management: Strategies for Business Decisions*, 3rd edition. McGraw-Hill.

Hitt, L.M., D.J. Wu, and X. Zhou. 2002. 'Investment in Enterprise Resources Planning', *Journal of Management Information Systems*, 19(1): 71–98.

Hoque, Z. and W. James. 2000. 'Linking Size and Market Factors to Balanced Scorecards: Impact on Organizational Performance', *Journal of Management Accounting Research*, 12(1): 1–17.

Hsu, L. and M. Chen. 2004. 'Impacts of ERP Systems on the Integrated-interaction Performance of Manufacturing and Marketing', *Industrial Management and & Data Systems*, 104(1): 42–55.

Huang, Z. and P. Palvia. 2001. 'ERP Implementation Issues in Advanced and Developing Countries', *Business Process Management*, 7(3): 276–84.

Hunton, J.E., B. Lippincott, and J.L. Reck. 2003. 'Enterprise Resource Planning Systems: Comparing Firm Performance of Adopters and Nonadopters', *International Journal of Accounting Information System*, 4: 165–84.

Hunton, J.E., R.A. McEwen, and B. Wier. 2002. 'The Reaction of Financial Analysts to Enterprise Resource Planning (ERP) Implementation Plans', *Journal of Information Systems*, 16(1): 31–40.

Ittner, C.D., D.F. Larcker, and T. Randall. 2003. 'Performance Implications of Strategic Performance Measurement in Financial Service Firms', *Accounting, Organizations and Society*, 28(7–8): 715–41.

Jacobs, F.R. and E. Bendoly. 2003. 'Enterprise Resource Planning: Developments and Directions for Operations Management Research', *European Journal of Operational Research*, 146(2): 5–12.

Jones, M.C., M. Cline, and S. Ryan. 2006. 'Exploring Knowledge Sharing in ERP Implementation: An Organizational Culture Framework', *Decision Support Systems*, 41(2): 411–34.

Kakouris, A.P. and G. Polychronopoulos. 2005. 'Enterprise Resource Planning (ERP) System: An Effective Tool for Production Management', *Management Research News*, 28(6): 66–78.

Kalakota, R. and M. Robinson. 1999. *E-bussiness: Roadmap for Success*. Masssachusetts: Addison–Wesley.

Kaplan, R.S. and D.P. Norton. 1993. 'Putting the Balanced Scorecard to Work', *Harvard Business Review*, September–October: 134–47.

———. 1996 *The Balanced Scorecard: Translating Strategy into Action*. Harvard Business School Press.

———. 2001. 'Transforming the Balanced Scorecard from Performance Measurement to Strategic Management: Part I', *Accounting Horizons*, 15(1): 87–104.

Mabert, V.A, A. Soni, and M.A. Venkataramanan. 2003. 'The Impact of Organization Size on Enterprise Resource Planning (ERP) Implementations in the US Manufacturing Sector', *Omega*, 31(3): 235–46.

Markus, M.L., C.T. Tanis, and P.C. Fenema. 2000. 'Multisite ERP Implementations', *Communications of ACM*, 43(4): 42–46.

McAfee, A. 2002. 'The Impact of Enterprise Information Technology Adoption on Operational Performance: An Empirical Investigation', *Production and Operations Management*, 11(1): 33–53.

Michalaska, J. 2005. 'The Usage of the Balanced Scorecard for the Estimation of the Enterprise's Effectiveness', *Journal of Materials Processing Technology*, 162–163(15 May): 751–58.

Milis, K. and R. Mercken. 2004. 'The Use of the BSC for the Evaluation of Information and Communication Technology Projects', *International Journal of Project Management*, 22(2): 87–97.

Nicolaou, A.I. and S. Bhattacharya. 2006. 'Organizational Performance Effects of ERP Systems Usage: The Impact of Post Implementation Changes', *International journal of Accounting Information Systems*, 7(1, Spring): 18–35. Elsevier.

Papalexandris, A., G. Ioannou, G. Prastacos, and K.E. Soderquist. 2005. 'An Integrated Methodology for Putting the Balanced Scorecard into Action', *European Management Journal*, 23(2): 214–27.

Porter, M.E. and V.E. Millar. 1985. 'How Information Gives you Competitive Advantage', *Harvard Business Review*, 64(4, July–August): 149–74.

Poston, R. and S. Grabski. 2001. 'Financial Impacts of Enterprise Resource Planning Implementations', *International Journal of Accounting*, 2: 271–94.

Rashid, M.A., L. Hossain, and J.D. Patrick. 2002. *The Evolutioin of ERP systems: A Historical Perspective*. Idea Group Publishing.

Rikhardson, Pall M. and Pernille Kraemmergaard. 2006. 'Identifying the Impacts of Enterprise System Implementation and Use: Examples from Denmark', *International journal of Accounting Information Systems*, 7(1): 36–49.

Rosemann and Weise. 1999. 'Measuring the Performance of ERP Software—a Balanced Scored Approach', *Proceedings of the 19th Australian Conference on Information Systems*. Available online at http://www2.vuw.ac.nz/acis99/Papers/PaperRosemannWiese-089.pdf

Shang, S. and B.P. Seddon. 2000, 'A Comprehensive Framework for Classifying the Benefits of ERP Systems', paper presented at the Americas Conference on Information Systems (AMCIS), Long Beach, CA, 10–13 August, 2000.

Spathis, Charalambos and John Ananiadis. 2005. 'Assessing the Benefits of Using an Enterprise System in Accounting Information and Management', *The Journal of Enterprise Information Management*, 18(2): 195–210.

Tchokogué, A., C. Bareil, and C.R. Duguay. 2005. 'Key Lessons from the Implementation of an ERP at Pratt & Whitney Canada', *International Journal Production Economics*, 95(2): 151–63.

Valiris, G., P. Chytas, and M. Glykas. 2005. 'Making Decisions Using the Balanced Scorecard and the Simple Multi-attribute Rating Technique', *Performance Measurement and Metrics*, 6(3): 159–71.

Vancouver, J.B. 1996. 'Living Systems Theory as a Paradigm for Organizational Behavior: Understanding Humans, Organizations, and Social Processes', *Behavioral Science*, 41(3): 165–204.

Wang, E.T.G. and Chen J.H.F. 2006. 'The Influence of Governable Equilibrium on ERP Project Success', *Decision Support Systems*, 41(2): 708–27.

Wier, B., J. Hunton, and H.R. HassabElnaby. 2007. 'Enterprise Resource Planning Systems and Non-financial Performance Incentives: The Joint Impact on Corporate Performance', *International Journal of Accounting Informations Systems*, doi: 10.1016/j.accinf.2007.05.001.

Wu, J.H. and Y.M. Wang. 2005. 'Measuring ERP Success: The Key Users' Viewpoint of the ERP to Produce a Viable IS in the Organization', *Computers in Human Behaviour*, 23: 1582–96. Elsevier.

Yen, D.C., D.C. Chou, and J. Chang. 2002. 'A Synergic for Web-based Enterprise Resources Planning Systems', *Computer Standards & Interface*, 24(4): 337–46.

14

Upgrade your 'Renovation Cycles' to 'Innovation Waves' Using Knowledge Management and Enterprise System Capabilities

RAKESH KUMAR MISHRA

Senior Principal Consultant, Enterprise Solutions,
Infosys (NASDAQ), Electronics City, Hosur Road, Bangalore 560100, India
E-mail: rakeshmishra@infosys.com

ABSTRACT

If organizations can empower their innovation engine by continuous fuelling it with organization's knowledge flow, they can really accomplish the state of 'optimization' and experience the 'Performance Nirvana'.

All leading industry analysts anticipate that innovation and knowledge management are going to be key differentiators in tomorrow's enterprise. Hence, enterprises must understand the complete anatomy of innovation such as what is the return an enterprise can expect from innovation, how does the innovation process work, what nurtures the innovation, what hinders the innovation, what are the human factors involved, etc. There is very strong link between innovation and knowledge management and according to the author, a strong knowledge management platform can enable the innovation to great extent if organizations are able to figure out how to leverage the knowledge management platform to integrate and resonate with the innovation life-cycle.

This chapter will discuss some of these issues in detail and also explore the role of Enterprise Systems in supporting and enabling 'innovation' in organizations.

INTRODUCTION

As the pace of information technology (IT) development is getting more and more aggressive and organizations are becoming hypersensitive towards cost performance of IT, corporate executives are pinning their hopes on enterprise Knowledge Management to address the effectiveness of the organization to deal with cost pressures and IT productivity.

Knowledge Management by nature is reflection of organization's maturity because any organization that is yet learning to bring its processes in order or struggling to streamline the discipline of operation is less likely to be ready to undertake the challenge of Knowledge Management on the risk of serious investment loss. So fundamentally, Knowledge Management as a discipline to process the structured information accumulated through raw experience and convert it into corporate intelligence can only be undertaken by organizations that have accomplished certain level of maturity in terms of their processes, attitude, commitment, and skills. Gartner report (Harris, 2006) suggests: 'From 2006 to 2010, organizations will continue to invest in KM as one of the critical competencies in high-performance workplace (HPW) initiatives.'

Similarly, organizations like Google, IBM, Kodak, or Nokia have proven the worth of 'innovation-led' business growth strategies. Consumers today have lot of options to choose from and their choices change every month. With that kind of business environment, just 'doing more' is not sufficient. Enterprises are forced to adopt the innovation as their instrument to differentiate and compete in the environment that is becoming more and more unpredictable day by day. Gartner report (Broadbent et al., 2003) says: 'Innovation through electronically enabled services, processes and products has only just begun, and CIOs still need to lead the enterprise forward with risk-managed innovation.' Further to that, Harris (2002) says:

> Innovation is an emerging core competency. Leading enterprises will have a dual focus: embrace the innovations of others and drive the marketplace with their own innovations. Active management of innovation will become a required competency for all enterprises during the 2002 to 2007 planning horizon.

Now, if organizations can empower their innovation engine by continuous fueling it with organization's knowledge flow, they can really accomplish the state of 'optimization' and experience the 'Performance Nirvana'.

This chapter will deliberate upon the dynamics of innovation and ways to use the Knowledge Management practices for supporting the innovation demands in subsequent sections.

ANATOMY OF INNOVATION

In this section, the facets of innovation, especially those that are critical for administering the outcomes of innovation will be examined.

EFFECTIVENESS OF INNOVATION

The way outcomes of innovations within enterprise benefits really will depend on the area enterprise is focusing for innovation and the way specific results of innovations impact the concerned enterprise areas. Senior management can only commit to innovation investments at enterprise scale if they have clear visibility and understanding of returns that are expected from innovation. If the enterprise believes that its business landscape demands innovation for business growth, it must create a strong foundation of innovation vision including clear articulation of areas where enterprise will focus on for innovation, results that are expected from the innovation, and quantitative goals of returns that will drive the scale and focus of innovations.

NURTURING THE INNOVATION

To make the innovations work for the enterprises in a sustainable manner, it is very essential for enterprises to discover the ways and elements that nurture the process and outcomes of innovation. Though such ways and elements could vary from enterprise to enterprise both in terms of degree of their effectiveness and applicability, there are some more generally applicable themes that promote innovation process. Few of such themes are highlighted further:

- *Interest to ask 'why'*: In general, people who have natural trait to question the 'Status Quo' of the matters and who always seek novelty in what ever they do, they are more likely to use their curiosity and knowledge to deliver innovations. Enterprises not only should identify such staff members and give them support but as well mentor the rest of the staff to encourage the 'inquisitive' traits.
- *Well-defined process and methods of harvesting innovation*: Harvesting the innovation is all about using the methodical ways to create the opportunities of innovation and maximize the returns for the enterprise from the outcomes of innovations. Many enterprises simply leave the process of innovation to become matter of 'accidental' discovery and thus let it happen by chance. According to CBI and 3M Innovation Survey (Amidon, 2003) as quoted by Entovation International News of March 2003, 'few companies have the processes and infrastructure in place to manage innovation. A survey of 350 organizations found that less than 15% of companies have any IT systems in place to manage innovation, and only 40 per cent have established any formal procedures'. Innovation-oriented enterprises are expected to adopt mature processes for complete lifecycle of innovation in order to 'manage' the innovation.
- *Cross-functional integration of innovation champions*: As indicated earlier, enterprises with mature processes and discipline are more likely to succeed at differentiation through innovation. One of the great enablers for innovation available in such organization is strong integration between cross-functional departments or teams. When enterprises integrate small innovations happening at department level and create resonating focus, it is more likely to deliver large scale business benefits.
- *Focus and perseverance*: As Dr Clayton Christensen, a Harvard Business School professor says, 'there isn't anything about the process of innovation per se that makes it

unpredictable,' (www.hbs.edu) innovations by nature are dependent on creative forces and are subjected to unpredictable timelines for 'idea-to-cash' lifecycle. As enterprise mature and perfect the process of innovation, this predictability of outcomes from innovation gets better but until then, enterprise must persevere the focus for innovation.

- *Simplicity of innovation initiative execution*: One of the most common hurdles in the area of innovation is the complexity of implementation where an idea might sound simple but taking the idea to reality could be highly complex in the existing ecosystem of the enterprise. Simpler the execution, higher the chances that innovation endeavour will succeed in the enterprise and hence during evaluation of innovative ideas, implementation simplicity focus must be included.

- *Increasing the relevance of innovation*: While innovation can be done for a variety of purposes including business growth, social transformation, academic excellence, or political interests, for the purpose of this chapter, the driver of innovation will be considered to be the business value. It also implies that relevance of innovation for the interest of business value delivery will be an important criterion while making investment into innovation process. Some of the elements that are helpful in accomplishing the relevance of innovation with business stakeholders are highlighted ahead:

  - *Focusing on end-user objectives and usability*: One of the most important aspects of the innovation is the perspective of usability (Kalbach, 2001) and value addition for end-users. End-user here could be internal to organization (e.g., users of any system or process) or external users. Typically, prototyping is a good practice that involves major stakeholders early in the lifecycle of innovation and validates the relevance of the innovation from stakeholder or user perspective.

  - *Iterative model for deploying the innovation*: Real value of innovation is in its implementation. To increase the relevance of innovation, the enterprise should use the power of learning in iterative manner (Boothby, 2005) while deploying the outcomes of innovation. The use of Knowledge Management for improving innovation will be further deliberated in this paper subsequently.

  - *Quick wins*: For continuous sponsorship of innovation initiatives within organization, it is highly recommended to implement some quick wins or low hanging fruits to keep the stakeholder interest and confidence high in the innovation initiatives.

  - *Linking innovation initiatives with business planning cycles*: Best way to bring direct business relevance into innovation is to link the innovation initiatives with business planning cycles. A mature organization will induct the innovation teams with understanding of business planning cycles, create specific vision of business context for innovations, and align the lifecycle of innovation in such a manner that outcome of innovation ideation can be fed into business planning. This way, innovations can be tagged with specific business planning objectives which is more likely to boost the relevance of innovation initiatives.

DEALING WITH THE COMPLEXITY OF THE HUMAN TOUCH

The process of innovation is really in the human mind. All external processes merely streamline and formalize the delivery of innovation from human mind to tangible outcomes. This is one of the prime reasons why process of innovation can not be completely bound and tamed (of course until human mind is entirely understood). There are a lot of human factors involved in the instrumentation of innovation process. Some of the example scenarios of such human factors are provided here:

- *Individual vs. team innovation*: Organizations should promote both individually contributed innovations as well as team-collaboration based innovations depending on type, complexity, and scale of the innovation. Organizations can get better returns from investments into innovations if they are able to understand if specific types of innovations are best suited for individually-managed initiatives or team-collaborated initiatives (Anklam, 2003).
- *Integration of disparate individual strengths*: Well-managed knowledge can enhance the innovation process outcomes but individual capacities and organization culture still play such an important role as discussed earlier. One individual typically cannot do it all in most cases and hence as a collective process of innovation, different individuals need to play their strengths where it is most applicable in the lifecycle of innovation development. Some are good at ideation, some at finding problems with new ideas, and others in creating good operational plan for any idea. Organizations must integrate all of these to make a cohesive continuum of strengths that can act as an engine to thrive on innovation and take ideas from concepts to implementation (Wiig, 1999).
- *Opportunity to move up the value chain*: Unfortunately, one can find a lot of cases where individuals withhold the knowledge and information with them in order to create their demand and differentiation (Wiig, 1999). Such people are absolute hindrance and threat to maturity of the organization. As enterprises mature in Knowledge Management, improve the general availability of information to everyone in the organization, and visibly reward those who contribute to growth of the enterprise knowledge pool (Boothby, 2005), it naturally forces people to release information, share knowledge, and evolve to differentiation by innovation.
- *Difference between creativity and innovativeness*: Very often people do not differentiate between creativity and innovativeness. They are tightly linked but are not same. A creative thinking is about a variety of ideas that reflect non-obvious or non-stereotyped options while innovation is about taming the creativity to produce relevant and tangible outcomes. This implies that innovation has lot more to it than just being creative. Some of the other elements of innovation that may not be necessarily part of 'creativity' are:

- *Context of business vision*: Innovation as described earlier is not matter of accidental inventions. Innovation must be based on the context of a vision that will drive the valuation, design specifics, and expected outcomes of the innovation (Hammer, 2006).
- *Strategic Intent:* Innovation has to be approached with a strategic intent based on context of the vision that aligns the end-to-end lifecycle of the innovation to other business activities of the organization. This strategic intent defines the distinct interests of the stakeholders and creates a long-term view of how specific innovations can change the organizations from 'as-is' to 'to-be' state.
- *Domain foresight*: It is important that innovators have foresight in the domain with in which innovations is being ideated. This foresight enables the innovators to deliver innovations that are highly relevant for the enterprise in the context of global business environment. Otherwise, innovators could produce extremely creative ideas that may not necessarily result into any strategic benefits for the organization or alternatively could only produce results that are short-lived owing to changes occurring in the domain.
- *Tangible outcomes:* This is fundamental quality of the innovation. A creative thought may not result into any think tangible, instead could be just an experience while innovation must have tangible outcomes that are directly linked to the context of vision within which it has been delivered.

PRE-REQUISITES OF INNOVATIONS

Having understood the other facets of innovation, the pre-requisites for making innovation as business growth strategy should now be examined. These are again only illustrative list and by no means an exhaustive or complete list:

- *Well-organized and structured information*: Access to right information can be highly instrumental in making innovations faster and meaningful. Before organizations embark on serious innovation initiatives, they must first strengthen the organization of the information and make it available to innovator community in structured form. Innovators should be able to search the global knowledge database of the enterprise in real-time and be able to perform relevant analysis without having to resort to manual hardship of information provisioning as far as possible.
- *Tolerance for risk*: As discussed, innovations do have unpredictable side of their returns and timelines for outcomes. This is definitely a risk for the organization and, hence, before organizations accept innovation as a strategy, they must commit to great degree of tolerance of risk for the investment being made in innovation. Lack of such tolerance could inculcate unnecessarily aggressive and rigid behaviour among sponsors or stakeholders which can be extremely detrimental for the environment of innovation.

Once enterprise accepts the risks, they must manage the risk by deploying methods that increase the chances of success and reduce the roadblocks.

- *Acceptance of failure*: Since innovation has inherent elements of risks, it is fairly possible that some of the risks will eventuate and certain innovation initiative could be failure. Along with tolerance to risk, enterprises must agree on acceptance of failure for certain percentages of innovation initiatives. An enterprise should define success expectancy ratio (ratio of failed innovation to total number of innovations) that is pragmatic and as enterprise matures the process of innovation, this target ratio must be aimed for reduction.
- *Low resistance for change*: Innovation implies organizational change since innovation is for something that does not exist. For an enterprise to be good at using innovation as a strategy, they must create an environment that has low resistance for change. Enterprises that have great degree of resistance are likely to be content with current state of affairs and less likely to be successful with innovation as a strategic instrument.
- *IP management strategy*: Typically innovations result into specific intellectual properties that bring differentiation to enterprises against their competitors. In today's world, enterprises need to have a very strong intellectual property management strategy (Siemens PLM Software Division, 2007) that allows them to protect their intellectual properties (both internally as well as externally) and at the same time ensure that innovators are not in violation of any intellectual property right while attempting certain ideas. Today a lot of organizations have specialized Internet Protocol (IP) management groups that completely focus on management or intellectual property management including formalized creation of IPs, IP protection, IP filing and approvals and IP awareness within the organization.

INNOVATION ON BACKBONE OF KNOWLEDGE MANAGEMENT

A mature and effective Knowledge Management framework in the enterprise can make innovation delivery significantly accelerated and promising. A number of facets of innovation lifecycle can be examined to understand opportunities that a good Knowledge Management framework provides as highlighted further:

- *Faster access to required information*: Access to well-managed knowledge repository and resources assures greater relevance of innovation idea from perspective of competition, market and industry and definitely helps moving past the trivia in the area of innovation so that the innovation team can use valuable time for true innovation (Bellinger, 2004).
- *Higher productivity*: Focus more on innovation process than on information gathering and dealing with low-value information. This also reduces the total cost of innovation. Studies show that today organizations spend enormous amount of time in searching for the right information that impacts the pace at which innovation is carried out and

ultimately impacts the time-to-market for the final product of the innovation (Siemens PLM Software Division, 2007).

- *Gets contribution from larger network of staff*: As discussed, core of innovation is in people's mind that defines organizational intelligence. Greater the network of innovative people within enterprise, higher the quality and speed of innovation. To make it happen, it is essential that organizations integrate the resources of knowledge, both people and assets and provide them platform to interact, collaborate, and integrate their efforts in win-win manner. When it comes to Knowledge Management, many organizations focus just on 'asset' part which is direct knowledge source. It is very essential that organizations equally manage the knowledge that resides in people's mind and may not be readily available in any form. Such Knowledge Management primary entails creation of networks of subject matter experts and integrating their efforts on common objectives in collaborative manner (Anklam, 2003; Bellinger, 2004).

- *Avoiding re-invention of the wheel*: In the area of research and innovation, failures are as important as successes are. For one, failures give great insight into limitations or constraints that need to be taken into account for converting the ideas into reality and second, translating the failure into knowledge helps save time and money by avoiding the future innovation attempts reaching the state of failure because of reasons that have been already discovered.

ROLE OF ENTERPRISE SYSTEMS IN ENABLING THE BUSINESS INNOVATION AND KNOWLEDGE MANAGEMENT

Most of the large enterprises today use technology infrastructure as the backbone for their business operation. Clearly technology itself has evolved in last decade from being just an office automation and data-recording tool to business process automation and now emerging as a great platform for innovating business solutions. So far the dynamics of Knowledge Management and innovation processes have been understood. This section will focus on establishing the relevance and significance of the enterprise systems in enabling the both.

- *Business Intelligence Capabilities*: One of the most prominent segments of the enterprise systems that have direct influence on the enterprise capability to delivery business innovation. Business intelligence systems as well as predictive complex event processing systems today offer wide variety of information synthesis options. Through these capabilities, today, businesses have a lot more visibility to meaningful information and have great opportunity to creative innovative business alternatives based on the insights provided by these analytical and predictive modelling tools. Organizations are investing more and more today to gain competitive advantages by leveraging the business intelligence knowledge and integrating it into their core business innovation processes (Pohl, 2003).

- *Real-time cross-functional integration of the enterprise information*: While a lot of business intelligence related capability could be just aggregated offline processing of enterprise information, it is getting better today with real-time information processing capability. Enterprises are already enabling their key roles of business innovation by providing them real-time access to the enterprise knowledge (Siemens PLM Software Division, 2007). This information is not just real-time but is cross-functional as well so that the roles doing business innovation have full visibility to what is happening in their enterprise across all functional areas. This is especially very important because in today's scenario, enterprises are in dire need of dynamic innovation based on changing market conditions (Pohl, 2003; Anklam, 2003).

- *Advance application development platforms*: Enterprise systems like SAP, Oracle, etc., provide highly evolved development environments. Such development platforms allow quick composition of the business solution without needing to hand code the solution. Many such application development platforms are configuration-driven where a business solution can be quickly composed. This way, non-technical community (business analysts typically) can easily participate in the solution development process and directly material the business innovation into reality without getting stuck in solution development complications. So in essence, it has made the business innovation realization faster and easier.

- *Adoption of wider consumer technology into enterprise systems*: One of the key changes in business computing that has taken place in recent times is adoption of wider end-consumer technologies like Facebook, Google Search, web 2.0 applications, web-conference and audio features, etc., into enterprise systems. SAPs and Oracles or the world are integrating with end-consumer focused platforms like Microsoft to innovate better user experience for enterprise users. That allows enterprises users to easily share the knowledge and use these technologies to further innovate the methods of alternative business solutions for their customers.

- *Formal innovation and collaboration platforms*: As part of enterprise systems, enterprises have started launching formal innovation platform with the help of popular collaboration platforms like blogs, wiki, etc. So basically innovation is being recognized as one of the formal enterprises processes and is further supported by technology platforms to manage the workflow and collaborations needs of the innovation processes. Blogs and Wiki platforms have made it easy to bring individual level knowledge to a larger enterprises ecosystem of innovators. Such platform also unleash the freedom of lateral thinking to bring elements from outside of the enterprises and let the innovation be developed in a continuous process instead of a discrete and restricted process. It means that now innovation is not restricted to only a few in the enterprises but allows people in the enterprise at all levels to participate in the innovation process.

MY EXPERIMENTS WITH INNOVATION AND KNOWLEDGE MANAGEMENT

Portfolio Think Tank: This is the Innovation and Knowledge Management initiative that I myself had undertaken in the capacity of both sponsor and chair person. I would like to describe my experience with this initiative.

Background and drivers: I had been managing a large portfolio of a client for delivery of enterprise integration services that includes complete lifecycle starting from idea development till product support and maintenance. After I had taken over the portfolio management responsibility, as part of delivery improvement programme planning, I observed that despite having a large size team, total amount of innovation coming out from the portfolio is not satisfactory. When we carried out the root cause analysis, the top three reasons that were contributing to lack of innovation were:

- Teams were busy in delivery engagements and not spending time in capitalizing the significant experience to deliver any innovation largely due to mind set. Large part of teams thought innovation is not their responsibility.
- There were no active platforms and frameworks to use the knowledge gained into innovation for future.
- There was no direct linkage between performance of individuals or the organization for innovation and the incentives either the individuals or organizations can receive.

The experiment: Based on the root cause analysis, I, together with my leadership team, launched an initiative to establish a Think Tank entity in the portfolio that can actively look after the need of innovation using strong Knowledge Management frameworks. To do this, here are the key elements of the initiative that were successfully implemented:

- As a foundation, entire knowledge base for the portfolio irrespective of its size and location was discovered by individual team members, consolidated and made available on a web-based portal in a structured taxonomy, well-categorized by area of knowledge and service. This to large extent facilitated the easy access to right and correct information to portfolio members.
- Next step was to actively create and share the knowledge at large scale. We created a central repository where all body of knowledge can be stored in controlled manner and it was made accessible to portfolio members to the portal that was already established. Additionally, an e-mail–based communication mechanism was established to introduce any new body of knowledge that had been created within portfolio. Team members that delivered body of knowledge in their specialized areas were given credit and entire status of knowledge creation progress was available on the portal for people to see what body of knowledge is being created, who is contributing and how as a portfolio we are performing on knowledge creation.

- Now that portfolio has established foundation of creating, sharing, and managing the knowledge, we approached the issue of innovation through means of Knowledge Management framework we had already established including the team that has much more motivation and active participation now. We establish a 'Think Tank' team for the portfolio where people who were interested in contribution towards innovation were brought together on voluntary basis. A charter of Think Tank team was created so that everyone follows same values and principles and focuses on right objectives. Core principle of this team was an entrepreneurship model in which portfolio team members were given opportunity of sponsorship of their ideas. As operational process, Think Tank team members submitted their proposal with some basic information which was scrutinized and evaluated for its merit and when approved was taken forward as full blown initiative with a dedicated team. Entire ownership of planning, networking with subject matter experts, relevant industry research, and executing the initiative was with this virtual Think Tank team in which team took genuine pride. Typically team had been always faced with the bandwidth availability but owing to self-driven motivation and adequate support from senior portfolio execute team, initiatives were delivered with great value to client and to portfolio, even if it took slightly longer than what we might have desired. Now this Think Team is working in steady state mode where initiatives are conceptualized as ongoing practice, they are evaluated and then approved ideas are converted into initiatives that are put into innovation delivery cycle every quarter. This way, innovation delivery has become the life-line of the portfolio and with that, there is great deal of satisfaction within client as well pride in the staff from the outcome that we are able to accomplish together as a highly motivated innovation team.

CONCLUSION

Innovation as a strategic process for business is relatively a new paradigm and hence it is still evolving, both in terms of process maturity as well as acceptance and adoption in the industry. However, as the chapter suggested, business competition dynamics is going to force enterprises to adopt innovation as key strategy to sustain the business differentiation. In order to deliver effective innovation results, enterprises will require very strong and functioning Knowledge Management framework as a backbone for innovation. If the essence of the chapter has to be summarized, it can be concluded with the following three key hypotheses:

1. Enterprises need to adopt innovation as a mainstream philosophy for business in order to sustain competitiveness over industry change cycles.
2. Innovation as enterprise level strategic platform for business differentiation needs strong Knowledge Management platform.

3. Knowledge Management to become the backbone of innovation, must expand its scope, transform value delivery maturity, and become core operational domain in the enterprise.

REFERENCES

Amidon, Debra M. 2003. 'The Praxis of Knowledge Innovation: The Case for SME's', Entovation International News. Available online at http://www.entovation.com/whatsnew/praxis.htm

Anklam, Patti. 2003. 'KM and Social Networks', *InsideKnowledge*, 6(8). Available online at http://www.kmmagazine.com/xq/asp/sid.45D056BE-8625-11D7-9D4D-00508B44AB3A/articleid.F79B4E31-7854-4B6A-9202-164FB18672D3/qx/display.htm

Bellinger, Gene. 2004. 'Knowledge Management—Emerging Perspectives'. Available online at http://www.systems-thinking.org/kmgmt/kmgmt.htm

Boothby, Rod. 2005. 'Turning Knowledge Workers into Innovation Creators'. Available online at http://www.innovationcreators.com

Broadbent, Marianne, Ken McGee, and Mark P. McDonald. 2003. Gartner Research Paper ID: FT-20-0693. Available online at http://rte.gartner.com/resources/114800/114867/it_success_requires_discipli_114867.pdf

CBI and 3M Innovation Survey. 2000. Entovation International News, March 2003, www.entovation.com/info/archives.htm

Gartner Insight. 2003. Volume 4, Issue 3 (March 2002) www.gartnerinsight.com accessed January 2009.

Harris, Kathy. 2002. Gartner Research Paper ID: AV-15-0808. Available online at http://www.gartner.com/resources/104000/104061/104061.pdf

———. 2006. Gartner Research Paper ID: G00136928. Available online at http://www.gartner.com/resources/136900/136928/knowledge_management_enables_136928.pdf

Hammer, Roger L. 2006 'Strategic Innovation: The Engine that Propels Business', Strategic Business Innovation. Available online at www.SBInnovation.com

Kalbach, James. 2001. 'Understanding Innovation', Razorfish reportReport # 045, 8 January. Available online at http://comminfo.rutgers.edu/~kalbach/understanding_innovation.pdf

Pohl, Jens. 2003. 'The Emerging Knowledge Management Paradigm: Some Organizational and Technical Issues', InterSymp Paper, CADRC. Available online at http://www.cadrc.calpoly.edu/pdf/baden2003.pdf

Siemens PLM (Software Division). 2007. 'Enabling Innovation through Knowledge and Intellectual Property Management', White paper, Available online at http://www.plm.automation.siemens.com/en_in/Images/knowledge_intellectual_property_mgmt_wpW6_tcm641-4182.pdf

Wiig, Karl M. 1999. 'Knowledge Management: An Emerging Discipline Rooted in a Long History'. Available online at http://www.krii.com/downloads/km_emerg_discipl.pdf

Section 3

Enterprise Systems—Case Studies and Field Applications

15

Balanced Scorecard and Its Role in Strategic Management of Information: A Review of Practice

D.P. SINHA

Professor, XLRI Jamshedpur and Ex-Vice President, Birla Group of Companies
E-mail: sinhadp@xlri.ac.in

ABSTRACT

The chapter discusses the evolution of the use of balanced scorecard (BSC) in managing organizations. The authors have traced the use of the BSC by a number of industries and present the zones of effectiveness in this usage. The use of enterprise systems in this process for strategic management of the enterprise is then discussed.

THE CONCEPT AND DEVOLUTION

Nearly 2,500 years ago the Greek playwright Euripides noted the importance of balance in life. He said:

The best and safest thing is to keep a balance in your life: Acknowledge the greatest power around us and in us: If you can do that, and live that way you are really a wise man.

In the modern economy, businesses find themselves involved in a constant act of balancing— balancing between normal management activities like budgeting, planning, coordinating and keeping track of financials on one hand and the processes, innovations and strategies on the other. These processes and strategies drive the results, and also prepare an organization for future success. Organizations have been searching for a management tool that is not only appropriate to give a more meaningful and holistic picture of the business and its day to day activities, but also provide a business logic by inter-relating the critical components in a logical framework.

It is true that no manager can ignore the bottomline—a key indicator of what happened (lagging indicator). But at the same time it is equally important to know 'how well we are doing' (current indicators) and more importantly 'what can we expect to do in future' (the leading indicators). Then only we will get a clear picture of the business in totality. If the focus is only on financial health of the organization, several unfortunate consequences arise—the need to identify the causal factors or events that influence these numbers (that is, the lagging indicators).

To solve the problem of an excessive focus on lagging financial indicators, Kaplan and Norton (1992) created a unique high level business performance model that synthesizes and links each of the key components—a new mechanism to take a holistic view of organizational performance. They argued that accounting or financial numbers are not the real drivers of performance and are not capable of assessing and managing business performance. Many organizations in United States, Europe, and Asia have adopted this model popularly known as the Balanced Scorecard (BSC). This concept has also been embedded into business software known as ERP systems, and this fusion forms the basis of the current article.

Creelman et al. (2005) interviewed a number of thought leaders from the Asian region and conducted an extensive survey of balanced scorecard implementation in South-East Asian companies for their book titled *Succeeding with the Balanced Scorecard*. A Study of organizations implementing Scorecard after the concept was first introduced by Kaplan and Norton reveals that BSC was seen generally as yet another performance measurement and management system combining both financial and non-financial components. Too little emphasis was put on its use as a strategic management system. After some experimentation with the concept, organizations discovered its potential and found that the Balanced Scorecard has much more to offer than what meets the eyes.

This chapter briefly reviews the state of practice of the Balanced Scorecard 15 years after the introduction of the concept and its adoption. About 50 cases of Balanced Scorecard implementation were analyzed by the author, and the key points are illustrated through six representative case studies. These case studies are also used to illustrate how the Balanced Scorecard is embedded into ERP systems for use in strategic management of information.

A MULTI-DIMENSIONAL TOOL—ONE SCORECARD, MULTIPLE INTERPRETATIONS

As the concept matured over a period of time, new implementation methodologies and BSC designs emerged, and this led to a broadening of the aims, definition and scope of the BSC. Kaplan and Norton (2003) subsequently described BSC as a framework comprising three strategic parts:

- Strategic Themes
- Strategic Targets and Measurement
- Strategic Action Plan

Lawson et al. (2008) have reported the results of a survey to study the best BSC practices in organizations across the world. As there are more than one way of defining a scorecard system, the survey respondents were asked to document their own definition. Based on the documentation provided by the organizations, scorecard is defined as a style of user interface, designed to deliver user-specific metrics related to an explicitly stated strategy that typically focuses on:

- Forward looking strategic information, rather than historic information.
- Collaboration and Communication about strategic goals and progress towards achieving them.
- Primarily on outcome measures rather than output (or throughput) measures.

Thus, the unique features of scorecard management system are its 'flexibility' and 'adaptability'. These features facilitate businesses to re-interpret the perspectives in relation to the importance of the context in their organization. They may be related to customers, stakeholders, employees, safety, efficiency, waste, learning, innovation, growth, processes, or operations. Organizations determine which perspectives best define their aspirations to re-present their business model and provide the best view for their current and future performance.

This implies that organizations need to clearly define and communicate the reason why they feel the need to deploy the scorecard system. The reasons influence both the design of the system and the resulting benefits. The survey helped the researchers in developing best practice criteria for implementing and using the scorecard system. According to the study, 16 out of 382 organizations in the international survey met these criteria. The group of these 16 organizations were referred to as 'Best Practice (BP) organizations'.

The adopters of BSC those who responded to the survey reported the following benefits from the BSC system:

- Ability to measure performance
- Increased communication
- Organizational alignment
- Ability to align employee behaviour with strategy
- Understand measure and strategy and cause and effect relationship
- Ability to link performance to compensation
- Decreased cost
- Ability to make strategic decision faster with better data
- Increased Revenue

STRATEGIC INFORMATION MANAGEMENT

Apart from the challenges discussed above, organizations often find it difficult to decide on measurement metrics. Managing information strategically so that the key parameters are measured and monitored at the correct level of aggregation, is also a challenge with which most organizations struggle. We now intend to focus more in-depth on the importance of strategic management of information, data, and knowledge essential for successful implementation of scorecard system. It is very important because information, data, and knowledge are the critical raw materials for creating value for the organization. Their value can, however, be realized only in the context of a strategy. No matter how good the design of the balanced scorecard and how well structured the implementation process, it might fail to meet the strategic objectives unless the basic raw material (information, knowledge, and data) is suitably aligned to the companies strategies. For example, if a company decides to pursue low cost strategy, its information and data access and management systems need to focus on quality, process improvement, resource optimization, and productivity. Similarly, if the strategy is to enhance customer-retention, the information system needs to provide knowledge that will reveal customer preferences and behavior (Customer Relationship Management?). Likewise, if a product leadership strategy requires knowledge and information related to product features, design and development process (Product Lifecycle Management).

A critical requirement for getting intended benefit for the BSC system, therefore, is to ensure that relevant information about organization's vision, strategies, and goals are stored, retrieved, analyzed, and used by the employees collectively across the organization. In other words, continuous management of 'in-put' (storage of data/information) and 'out-put' (its retrieval and use) is a critical pre-requisite for success of BSC.

In order to meet this requirement most BSC-implementing organizations design their own solutions which could provide information automatically or retrieve the same from some other transaction system such as ERP. The software companies from different segments in IT Industry discovered the potential and developed specialized applications designed to suit the BSC system. As the BSC concept gained acknowledgement as an effective system, the demand for appropriate software-based technical system also grew, and simultaneously a variety of software and advance solutions. Over a period of time technology companies have focused so much on technical aspects of BSC solutions that balanced scorecard implementation system is being seen were as an IT project. Fact is that 'scorecard software solution' which can be plugged and played is not possible. A technical system cannot replicate the critical process of senior executive team debating and agreeing on critical few objectives and measures that will deliver strategic success. What is necessary is the BSC software design which in addition to number crunching functionality, could validate strategy maps, connect to organizations vision, strategic goal measures and action plans and also provide business logic to senior executives to debate and share their knowledge and insights.

A FRAMEWORK FOR STRATEGIC INFORMATION MANAGEMENT

Thus a system devised suitably to facilitate communication of organization's strategic priorities to the employees to enable them to apply appropriate information, knowledge, and data to realize the intended strategies is a key requirement for the success of the BSC process. As we saw, there are two basic requirements constituting such a system: first, a package of information, knowledge, and data for strategic application, and, second, a technology infrastructure to capture, update, store, and retrieve them as and when needed. Explaining technological aspects its features, technicalities, advantages, and disadvantages of the system are beyond the scope of this paper. The focus instead is on identification and description of information, knowledge, and data that is required for application to support the strategic priorities flowing from each of the four perspectives (financial performance, customer management, internal processes, and learning and growth) and their strategic management.

Thus, defining strategic priorities, describing corresponding information, knowledge, and data and their applications for the intended purpose are the key components strategic information management system. The structure evolved by Kaplan and Norton (1992, 2003) begins with the definition of strategic priorities and translating them into strategic objectives in the strategy map. For example, strategic priorities as given in their structure has two critical objectives: first, to focus on value creating processes (such as innovation, customer management and operations management), and, second, to add knowledge, information, and learning for better asset utilization (see Table 15.1).

Kaplan and Norton identified the following three categories of applications of information, knowledge, and data (information capital) as key components to structure the framework for strategic information management system.

As observed by Kaplan and Norton, investment in information technology has been increasing steadily for more than three decades. Yet 90 per cent of sizeable annual expenditure in a typical IT budget are locked into operating and maintaining existing applications. Only 10 per cent is typically available for discretionary investment, though it is discretionary IT investment that creates strategic alignments as they support application of new information, knowledge, and data for strategic purposes.

The conclusion of the analysis therefore is that strategic management of information, knowledge, and data and their alignment with the strategic priority is critical for the success of BSC project. A good BSC design and well structured implementation are not enough to guarantee intended benefit from the BSC system.

Information, knowledge, and data constitute basic raw material for creating value for the organization. They will however create value only if linked appropriately to the strategy. Thus, linking information, knowledge, and data and aligning them to strategy and to the internal processes is critical pre-requisite for the success of the scorecard system. To meet this requirement, it is necessary to evolve a suitable technical system to support the BSC system. The technical system could also be either Excel-based solution or Web-based internal BSC portal or an 'add-on module' to the ERP system (see Table 15.2).

CASE STUDIES

What works, what does not and 'why', in scorecards? Where is it most effective? Based on experiences across a broad range of businesses, a variety of challenges emerge while putting

TABLE 15.1
Strategy Maps for Defining the Strategic Vision and the Associated Activities Contributing to the Plan

STRATGEY MAPS (Defining strategic priorities)

	Value creating processes			Information capital portfolio	Asset readiness	
	Internal perspective				Learning and growth perspective	
	Innovation perspective	Customer management	Operations management	Financial perspective	Human resources	Strategic management
Transformational Applications	Interactive Customer Design	Call Center Sales Protocol	Package Tracking JIT Supply	Shareholder Value	Human Capital Management	Balanced Scorecard
Analytical Applications	Product Analysis Product Development Knowledge Management	– Customer Analytics – Customer Management System – Customer Profitability	– Cycle Time Analytics – Quality Analysis – Activity and Process Costing	Financial Analytics Financial Consolidation Activity based costing	e-recruiting e-learning Compliance Reports	Activity Based Management Budgeting Forecast Dynamic Simulation
Transaction Processing Applications	Pipeline Management CAD/CAM	Customer Relationship Management	Supply Chain Management Manufacturing	Financial Management	Employee Records (ERP/HR) Employee self service	
Technological Infrastructure	Physical Infrastructure				Management Infrastructure	

Source: **Adapted from Kaplan and Norton (2003).**

TABLE 15.2
Three Levels of I.T. Applications for Information, Knowledge, and Data

Application	Description
• Transanction Processing Applications	– To automate the basic repetitive transactions (Such as ERP System)
• Transformational Applications	– To change the prevailing business model—distinguished by their Significant potential impact on strategic objective such as share holder value
• Analytical Applications	– To analyze, interpret and share information/knowledge (Relevant to organizations adopting operational approach to BSC)

Source: Laudon and Laudon (2005).

scorecards into operations. Success or failure of scorecards depends largely on how correctly these are managed.

Since the focus of the article is on the adoption and practice of the BSC system by organizations, the process of development and use of the scorecard will be demonstrated through some representative case studies. These case studies have been chosen from a larger pool of about 50 case studies which were examined in-depth to study the actual implementation of the BSC in detail.

CASE STUDY 1: SKANDIA

A Swedish insurance and long-term savings company, often considered a pioneer in intellectual capital, found specialist knowledge as an organization's most important asset. Skandia in their scorecard model called 'Navigator' put emphasis on human resources as the most important resources. 'Human Resources' was therefore placed at the heart of the model as shown in Figure 15.1. The argument of Skandia was that if planned and managed well, human focus plays a multiplier role in value creation in the organization. The Swedish Insurance Company used

FIGURE 15.1
Skandia's Navigator

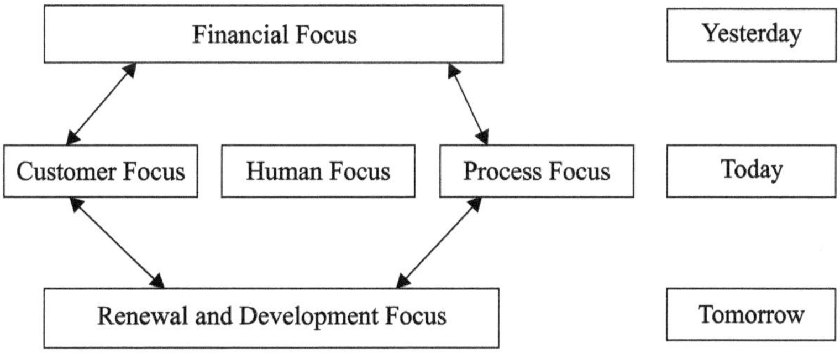

Source: www.oldmutal.com/skandia

the scorecard framework to emphasize on human recourses as the most important resources in the organization.

Skandia was built in a unique way. Jan Carendi, the CEO of Skandia, regarded that the specialist knowledge of distributors in selling long-term savings products to the established customer base, was the most important asset of the company for continuously improving the customer service. This thought triggered a search for new tool to visualize and manage organizations intangible asset (specialist knowledge of distributors). The company came out with a major multi-dimensional management tool based on Kaplan and Norton's scorecard principles. This tool was named as 'Navigator' (see Figure 15.1). Skandia's ambition was to spread the organization-wide use of this tool and every body was encouraged to develop their own 'Skandia Navigator'—a management system.

In order to make organization-wide use of Navigator a success, Skandia took several initiatives to get employees accept and use this as a tool. The success of Navigator, however, depended largely on the extent to which it is supported by an appropriate technical system to ensure storing, recording, updating right knowledge, and information for use by the employees for the intended purpose. Skandia developed a system to meet this requirement. It was named 'Dolphin System'. 'Dolphin' linked Skandia's vision, strategies, and success factors and the requisite information, knowledge, and data, creating cause-and-effect linkages.

Skandia's BSC implementation process, thus, ensured that relevant information knowledge, data is recorded as critical 'input' and used to realize the key objective (output). The gap between intended and actual benefit from BSC is caused mainly by the failure to manage effectively the 'input–output' challenges.

CASE STUDY 2: TATA MOTORS

The Commercial Vehicle Business Unit (CVBU) of Tata Motors initiated BSC implementation in 2000. The company had adopted Business Excellence Model based on the Malcolm Baldrige Criteria. In an assessment of CVBU against the Malcolm Baldrige Criteria, lack of strategy was found as a significant weakness in the unit. The CEO (Mr Ravi Kant) evolved a strategy for the unit's turnaround and sustained growth and profitability. The core issue around which strategy was structured was 'being the lowest cost producer '. After an intensive internal deliberation it was concluded that deployment of scorecard could offer solution to strategy implementation and create involvement of all its employees.

Being the lowest cost producer was the central feature of the strategy. It was felt that delivering to its strategy would require involvement of all its employees. This was something of a challenge because so far the unit has been highly operational and short-term result oriented. The unit agreed, after intensive internal deliberation, to launch the BSC programme.

The BSC proved a success in Tata Motors—the revenue and profit improved. The success of BSC is described using three words: ' Focus ', 'Accountability', and 'Ownership'—organization-wide focus on strategic goals, improving critical processes and customer satisfaction. The ownership of performance and accountability for targets were clearly defined, integrated, and aligned across the organization. The unit created over 300 scorecards and evolved a strategy map which clearly defined strategic objectives comprising four conventional perspectives: financial, customer, business process, and learning and growth. The top objective was 'to be among the top five commercial vehicle manufactures globally'. The measures, targets, ownership, and initiatives to support the strategy were described for businesses processes.

The key challenges that the unit encountered in effective implementation of the system were:

1. Integrating and creating interface between 300 scorecards covering different functions, linking each other to its higher level scorecard through strategic objectives.
2. Sharing the company's vision, mission, future direction, and strategies with employees across the organization and creating their meaningful involvement.
3. Aligning individual compensation with performance of the organization. This alignment is relatively simpler in case of a sales and marketing organization.
4. Data and information management (input and output) for the effective management of BSC system and online review. Tata Motors has adopted a non-exclusive software such as Excel and Power Point to support the BSC.

CASE STUDY 3: MAGMA CHEMICALS AND FERTILIZER

Back Ground

Magma (name changed) is a large fertilizer company in India, catering to markets in western and southern parts of the country. The company has been reporting a turnover in excess of ₹ 1,500 crores. The company was established in mid 1970s jointly by a leading Indian industrial house and an American company.

TABLE 15.3
Company's (Magma's) Profit in the Last Six Years

Year		Profit After Tax (PAT) (in rupees crore)
02–03	...	20.84
03–04	...	19.57
04–05	...	26.82
05–06	...	26.17
06–07	...	40.00
07–08	...	75.00
08–09	...	115 Cr

Source: www.magma.co.in

Scorecard Initiative—The Beginning

- In 2004 the company started preparing for the implementation of scorecard management system. The company's profit which used to be more than ₹65 crore till 1998–99 was plummeting every year. Financial projections made indicated that by 2005–06 the profit will go down as low as ₹5 crore unless major transformational initiatives were taken.
- Early processes involved a number of off-site deliberations to evolve a consensus on industry and company situation. The direction the company should take and the business model were discussed in detail. A series of such deliberations involving the entire work force were held spread over one-and-a-half years. The emerging scenario was carefully analyzed.
- At the end a consensus emerged that the organization was in crisis. Every possible improvement was important and urgent. Three key areas were identified:

    - Revenue Enhancement
    - Efficiency Improvement
    - Re-think Business Model

- Since there were constraints in increasing the volume of the company's own product, revenue enhancement was possible only by procuring products from other sources and diversifying into trading. Efficiency improvement particularly in logistics, operational cost, and manpower rationalization was considered as a priority task.
- Though awareness was created at the organizational level, for deploying scorecard management system, marketing and sales functions were chosen for making a beginning. These functions were chosen because they were externally focused, more customer centric, and in constant contact with the market. The managers in these functions were encouraged to define their own set of performance indicators independently. The only thing these managers were told was to use the scorecard to describe marketing operations beginning with the mission, the strategy, and the action plan, and define the metric to measure the progress.
- Functional level scorecard was cascaded into individual scorecard. The approach was different from the text book formula that is 'strategy to operations'. This approach was from operations to strategy—a bottom-up approach.
- The initiative had the support of the top management team because it was steered by Head of Marketing and Head of HR. Both were the members of top management committee and also aware of the changes at industry and the company level. They were deeply involved in key strategic business decisions.
- The efforts have paid handsomely. It has successfully surmounted the constraints in raising revenue only through its own products and achieved all round efficiency in all functional areas without changing the technology. The profit after tax has gone up to ₹75 crore from as low as ₹19 crore.

- Another crucial necessity for the success of the scorecard is to secure buy-in of employees throughout the organization. This requires the management to promote the scorecard as a set of simple functional structures linked to managements multi-dimensional performance evaluation network. This may be done at the functional level, even if the company level strategy maps and scorecards have not been evolved. Magma Chemicals was involved in initiating the BSC process and its successful implementation.

- Magma was passing through a stage of deeper industry level changes such as technology obsolence, change in the feed stock, and regulatory changes altering the fundamentals of policy which formed the very basis for growth and success of the industry.

  The customer loyalty, company's market position, and demand growth trend however remained unaltered. Because of the changing industry environment, it became imperative for the company to stipulate the new dimensions of performance relevant to the changing context and to communicate to people the linkage between 'how doing the right thing will create a new source of competitive advantage and produce long-term rewards'.

- Magma believed that BSC was the right tool to be deployed in the given situation before the company. The question was 'how' to use it? There were multiple choices before the company to pursue BSC as a control tool or a change management tool or a measurement tool or a communication tool. Knowing fully well the internal organizational dynamics, culture, resistance to change, and peoples awareness about the changing business conditions and their concerns and apprehensions, the company introduced BSC as a simple tool to enable people to take a holistic view of the business and appreciate its different perspectives, strategies, and objectives flowing from each of the perspectives and their inter-relationship or cause and effect assumption basis.

  This helped people to clearly distinguish between what they are doing and how they are doing and what is right thing and right way to do these in the changing context. They could also establish a linkage between their own performance on the dimensions stipulated in the company's mission and the strategies and objectives flowing from different perspectives. People in Magma started viewing BSC as a 'Support Tool'—a tool which supports and provides business logic to the performers. This was first key preparatory step in convincing people 'why' the organization needed a scorecard.

- The second step was 'how'—'how' did Magma go about deploying the scorecard. The first thing was to decide where from to start BSC process in Magma. There was a fair amount of apprehension about the process reaching down if started for the top echelon. Deploying BSC system at the company level was also difficult considering diversity of functions, involvement of multiple divisions, and inter-functional coordination and control. The proposal to deploy BSC management system was considered by the top policy making body, The Management Committee, and the approval to go ahead was accorded. The Management Committee also agreed to extend full support to the implementation of the system and provide necessary resources.

- The next step was to choose an unit/division or business activities which is right for making a beginning. After careful consideration, Magma chose Marketing and Sales function for scorecard deployment. Marketing and Sales was chosen because it is self contained, revenue generating, more customer centric, remaining in constant contact with the market, and operates on 'outside-in' basis. Also, managers in this function are aware about the changing business conditions and environment.
- Adequate knowledge about business, changes in the industry, market conditions and their short-term and long-term impact on Magma was provided to the managers. Neither any formal corporate level scorecard nor strategy maps were drawn—'instead functional managers were told to evaluate the situation themselves, define the destination (mission) they want to reach, chart the route (strategy), set milestones (goals), and define the metric to measure the progress. Formulating and evolving consensus on 'mission', 'strategy', 'goals', and the criteria for 'measurements' was thrown as an 'intellectual challenge to the managers' in a group.

A key difference in case of Magma was that there was no corporate level scorecard; the Marketing and HR Heads who initiated and steered the process fully understood the industry changes at macro level and their impact in the short-term and long-term, on the company and its strategic requirements. Both were permanent members of the Management Committee—a top policy formulation and review body. This approach helped Magma in reiforcing the BSC concept and its need in the organization and overcoming the initial challenge of involving people.

IN SUMMARY

Magma Chemicals and Fertilizers implemented a scorecard at marketing and sales function level across the company. This case highlights how a scorecard can be implemented without any formal corporate level scorecard or a strategy map. The functional managers were apprised of the deeper industry level changes and their impact on Magma. They were told to evaluate the situation themselves, come to a consensus and set their own destination and road map. Subsequently, the initiative was translated into the marketing division's mission, strategy, goal, and metric for measurement. This case illustrates that depending on the situation, it is not always necessary to start the BSC project at the top level of management. It may begin with a pilot project somewhere down the line and follow a bottom-up approach.

CASE STUDY 4: ZUARI (MARKET DIVISION EXECUTIVE)

Scorecarding organizations across the world adopt different systems and practices to diminish the gap between intended and actual BSC benefits. Some prefer in-house developed Excel Based

Solutions which they find to be flexible and easy to adjust to local and specific situations, some go for Web Based internal BSC portal, while others develop 'Add-ons' to the ERP system.

'Add-on' is a module designed to serve as a source of information, data, and knowledge for the BSC that can be integrated with the company's existing ERP system. The benefit of using 'Add-on' to ERP is that it is tightly integrated to all other components in ERP solution and it will enable easy retrieval of necessary information. 'Add-on' could be to any function in the organization such as HR management, production planning, inventory management, purchase, sales or any process regarding which the organization believes that any or all its value is created through process and wants to adopt 'process transformation' as strategy and develop add-on to process transformation. For example, let us consider the case of IBM between 1996 and 2002. The then CEO, Lou Gerstner, led IBM through an enterprise process transformational model which evolved into a 'Value chain transformation model'. Gerstner contended that process transformation model aligns business strategies and value chain transformation objectives. IBM identified seven value chains.

Similarly Nordea, a leading financial service group in Nordic and Baltic Sea region, implemented an 'add-on solution' to their ERP package. Nordea introduced a 'new planning and performance management' (PPMM) model. PPMM is the key central management tool of Nordea. Balanced scorecard is one of three constituent parts of PPMM—two other being Rolling Financial Forecasts (RFF) and Service level agreements (SLA). Nordea added PPMM as an 'add-on' to the existing ERP package.

CASE STUDY 5: BRITISH AIRWAYS (HEATHROW)

- British Airways (BA) service network is one of the largest in the world. It invested substantially to improve the quality of service and passenger comfort during the last decade. The airline has its head office outside London near Heathrow. It serves both Heathrow and Gatwick airports in London. It employed approximately 60,000 people in 1999.

- Heathrow is the world's biggest international airport. It is also one of the biggest Cargo ports. In 1997, the operations at Heathrow needed immediate improvement through an appropriate change programme. The performance of British Airways was poor. A new manager from British Airways cargo was brought in to steer the change programme. To begin with, the scope of his responsibility was baggage handling at Heathrow. The new manager was earlier involved in re-structuring the initiatives deploying BSC system. He considered using scorecard as a tool to steer the change process.

- He immediately decided to hold a brainstorming conference to discuss what needed to be done to turn around the operations. The focus of the conference was to pay attention to details rather than to challenge the business division's vision and strategic goals. He decided to do that because the organization was in crisis and every possible immediate improvement was important. Each department, was, therefore, encouraged to describe how they thought customers judged their performance, and adopt this as the reference point to derive appropriate measures.

- The new manager encouraged each unit head to define their own set of indicators independently as long as they could explain why each metric was an important indicator from the customer's point of view and could tailor it to the specific situation. The results of the management conference made scorecard very tangible as each unit head understood the metrics. The new manager at the end mandated that each unit head should use the scorecard to describe the unit's operations. Looking at the success of the change programme through BSC, new operations were added to the scope of the manger.

- One challenge that the manager faced was to get every unit head accept the outcome according to the scorecard. In the beginning some managers argued that the figures were incorrect and that the performance in their unit was much better than what the scorecard suggested. Some managers claimed that poor results depended on quality of metrics, not the actual performance.

- The idea of deploying the scorecard is often initiated by some enthusiast, for example, the new manager in this case. He intended to deploy BSC in his division as a pilot project, allow positive experience to generate interest in other parts of BA, and spread BSC as a management practice in BA. This means that recommendations in the text to use corporate strategy as a strategy point cascading down is not the right approach always.

CASE STUDY 6: MIGUEL FINANCIAL SERVICES

- Miguel (name changed) is a leading financial services company in the European region. It describes itself as world leader in internet banking. The spread of its business covers Retail Banking, Corporate and Institutional Banking, etc.

- The company was formed after the merger of four major financial institutions. A new management structure was created after the merger. Some of the divisions of the erstwhile companies before merger were using scorecard management system. The CEO of the company was not only familiar with the BSC concept but also had previous experience regarding this.

- Soon after the new company came into being a review of the planning process was carried out and it was decided to evolve a model which will be the central management tool of Miguel. The tool was termed as the New Planning and Performance Management Model (PPMM). Through PPMM was deployed as new tool in the organization, the traditional budget was also used.

- The new PPMM consists of three parts, namely Balanced Scorecard, a system for making quarterly Rolling Financial Forecast (RFF) which together with BSC will replace budget gradually, and a Service Level Agreement (SLA) used for the internal service provider. To put in other words, BSC in Miguel drives strategy into action, rolling financial forecasts gives an updated view on future financial performance, and service level agreement fosters cooperation between internal service providers and receivers.

- The New Planning and Performance Management Model services three key purposes: focus on shareholder value creation, strategy implementation, create alignment, and support company wide common cultural. The Miguel case is a classic example of how BSC can be integrated with other planning and operational tools and techniques and control system in the organization.

SCORECARD SUCCESS—LESSONS AND INSIGHTS

As a key resource person in initiating BSC process in his corporate career, subsequently in his consulting assignments, and now as a teacher in a leading B-school, the author has come across a variety of situations where the scorecard has been a success and also where it did not yield expected result. The author identified issues that organizations commonly encounter in putting scorecards into operations at various stages—initial stage, during the continuous process, and in measuring the outcome, and these have been classified as under:

- Defining purpose/usage of scorecard (Why?)
- Implementation process/Methodology (How?)
- Where to start? Top-Down/Bottom-up
- Which activity of the business?
- Securing 'employee buy-in' (people involvement)
- Strategic Information Management—Input/Output Challenge (Information/Knowledge/Data)

A key challenge, to begin with, at the initial stage is to present the reasons as to 'why does an organization need BSC'? Developing reasons for deploying the scorecard system depends on the organization's belief and approach to managing business performance—some adopt an operational approach while others, strategic. Those adopting operational approach predominantly view scorecard as a way to perform the assigned task-as an organizational process—a measurement tool with multi-dimensional measurement methodology. In such a situation, application of knowledge, information, and data is limited to transactional purposes. Contrary to this, those adopting strategic approach look at the business and performance on a different horizon—understanding fundamental logic of 'what we do and why we do'?, creating a business language visualizing strategy, and identifying the 'path' to strategic 'destination'. They apply information, knowledge, and data for transformational purposes. The BSC process helps in addressing the challenge of meaningful integration and alignment of different aspects of business.

BSC, in earlier cases, was used mainly for exercising management control (micromanage and enforce compliance in operational process) while later, after 2000, it was used as a tool for strategic control (communicating and delivering strategic goals). Defining belief and approach is subject to the industry and business situation, organizational dynamics, and the management of change. Belief dictates the purpose and intended use of BSC system, which in turn determines the design structure and implementation process.

As experience shows, the reasons why scorecard does not yield expected results include failure to define its usage, design appropriate system for its implementation, and evolve the right implementation methodology.

A multi-division oil company in middle-east, in late 1990s needed a strategic and performance management tool for monitoring its progress towards its strategic goal. To meet this requirement, the company implemented a series of scorecards at corporate and operational unit levels. The BSC development process began with a strategic review and identifying new strategic priorities. Subsequently, a total of seven balance scorecards were developed: corporate and those for sub-units such as Lubricants, Retail, Commercial, Distribution, Terminal Operations, and Group Business Services.

Although the expected benefit from the scorecard centered around communication of strategy and monitoring the delivery of strategic goals, the company adopted 'bottom-up' approach to scorecard development. The corporate design was completed last which was based on the results of the sub-units. As a result, scorecard was found to be relating more to operational issues than strategic implementation. The scorecard initiative ultimately did little in terms of improving the clarity of what the organization was trying to control.

We discussed some of the challenges we believe exist in the initial stage of BSC implementation process. We talked about defining and presenting the reasons 'why' (purpose/usage) organizations need scorecard, where to start (top-down/bottom-up), which activity of the business to begin with, how to initiate the process and how to secure buy-in of employees across the organization and the implications if BSC design and implementation methodologies are not aligned with the intended purpose.

A few examples of the aims and usage for which organizations deploy scorecard are:

- To create a culture of accountability.
- As a communication tool.
- A system design for performance management with select set of measures.
- To facilitate intellectual capital management.
- As a format to discuss strategy.

In order to make the scorecard adaptable to one's own situation and put it in practice, organizations re-configure BSC design to suit their situations.

So the balanced scorecard is:

- A total system.
- It has high synergistic potential.
- Key purpose—Its use can be broadened from a narrowly defined management system to a strategy formulation, implementation, and control system.
- The term BSC may go but the fact remains that complexities in business, and the multiplicity of factors and changing stakeholder needs will continue to increase the act of balancing.

CONCLUSION

Whether the term Balanced Scorecard remains or not, but the fact that new dimensions in complexities and perspectives in the business in modern economy will continue to emerge and so will be the web of stakeholders and their wants and needs. As a result, businesses will remain in the constant act of 'balancing' in the modern economy.

Success will be redefined in terms of how well the organization is able to balance between the short- and the longer-term, the tangible and the intangible, the leading and lagging performance parameters, and the internal and external conditions.

The scorecard management system will face new challenges such as linking strategy to budget, aligning employee behaviour to strategy, and establishing appropriate performance measures to key strategic drivers like intellectual capital, value from R&D, innovation, and customer lifetime value.

'Best practice organizations achieve greater number of benefits from their scorecard systems and with higher frequency' (Creelman et al., 2005). All the best practice organizations claimed better organizational alignment and better ability to measure performance. All the Best Practice organizations agreed to some extent that the use of the scorecard system had driven performance improvement in their organization.

Whether your organization is using scorecard or considering to use it or looking for getting more out of the system, you will definitely benefit from the experiences of the organizations summarized in this chapter.

REFERENCES

Creelman, J., N. Makhijani, and D. Norton. 2005. Succeeding with the Balanced Scorecard: Mastering Business in Asia Series. New York: Wiley (1st Edition).

Kaplan, R.S and D.P. Norton. 1992 (January–February). 'The Balanced Scorecard—Measures that Drive Performance', Harvard Business Review, 70(1): 71–79.

Kaplan, R.S and D.P. Norton. 2000. *The Strategy-Focused Organization: How Balanced Scorecard Companies Thrive in the New Business Environment.* Harvard Business Press (1st Edition).

———. 2003. *Strategy Maps: Converting Intangible Assets into Tangible Outcomes,* Boston: Harvard Business School Press (1st Edition).

Laudon, K. and J. Laudon. 2005. *Management Information Systems* (9th ed.). New York: Prentice Hall.

Lawson, R., D. Desroches, and T. Hatch., 2008. *Scorecard Best Practices: Design, Implementation, and Evaluation.* New Jersey: John Wiley and Sons.

16

A Case of MRO Process Transformation through ERP: Enabling Growth through Improved Intra- and Inter-company Collaboration

ALEXANDRA BIZEROVA
Goizueta Business School, Emory University, Atlanta, GA
E-mail: alexandra_bizerova@bus.emory.edu

INTRODUCTION

ERP implementation is often associated with the need of a company to change. The transformation is often viewed as one complete process rather than giving different weight of the contribution of each of the activities. There are studies which are focused on evaluating the performance effect of the complementarities between information systems, marketing, manufacturing, and supply chain. Within that context the task for evaluating the effectiveness of the ERP component as part of the entire company transformation is limited and not-representative. The usefulness of the systems solution and its effect toward achieving the company goals can be assessed by comparing user satisfaction and actual usage data.

In the evaluation of the success of the Inventory Component Exchange program in Delta Air Lines, the criteria have been user satisfaction, time savings achieved, and improvement of service (increase in the number of transactions, fewer days for service, decrease in overdue exchanges).

DELTA AIR LINES OVERVIEW

Delta Air Lines (NYSE: DAL) is a Delaware corporation headquartered in Atlanta, Georgia. It offers regular flights to 311 destinations in 52 countries which are more destinations covered than any other global airline. Adding more than 60 new international routes in 2007, Delta has grown its international flights at a faster rate than any other major US airline. It has become the leader across the Atlantic with flights to 32 trans-Atlantic destinations. Delta is a founding member of SkyTeam, a global airline alliance that provides customers with extensive worldwide destinations, flights, and services. Including its SkyTeam and worldwide codeshare partners, Delta can offer flights to 462 worldwide destinations in 98 countries.

Delta is subject to government regulation under the Federal Aviation Act of 1958, as amended, as well as many other federal, state, and foreign laws.

DELTA AIR LINES MRO SERVICES

With 75 years of experience in maintenance service and industry innovation, in addition to offering the standard services of an airline company, Delta Technical Operations division has extended its service portfolio to offer aircraft maintenance, repair, and overhaul (MRO) to other airlines. The Technical Operations Center facility in Atlanta has been providing a comprehensive range of maintenance support since 1983. Among the key services offered are airframe maintenance, aircraft overhaul, repair, overhaul, and test facilities for electromechanical components and avionics, engine maintenance, and more.

Customer airlines benefit from Delta Technical Operations infrastructure, experience, and commitment. More than 6,500 Technical Operations employees systemwide provide the same services within Delta and have become industry experts. With a flexible workforce, Delta's technicians are among the most productive in the industry. The technical dispatch reliability is greater than 97 per cent fleetwide. Safety is Delta's operations brand. Delta's employees are provided with aggressive continuing education, training, and advanced computer knowledge to keep the expertise on the cutting edge.

The TechOps logistics centre in Atlanta manages the inventory necessary to support the day-to-day operations of Delta's 440 plus aircraft and also many customers' aircraft. It uses the latest technologies to ensure inventory accuracy and component traceability. Customers can depend on the qualified logistics specialists to provide fast and accurate service. Delta provides storage, distribution, transportation, worldwide procurement, initial provisioning, and customized support, access to Delta's own inventory parts system.

The MRO services are not separated in an independent division but are a line of business within each of the functions in Delta's Technical Operations. In this way the MRO services provided to the external and internal customers share the same benefits and learning curves. The organizational structures which provide the MRO services within the Delta Technical Operations are: Technical Sales and Marketing; Maintenance Operations; Materials and Planning; Quality; Engineering; and Training. Within Materials and Planning division employees who provide day-to-day MRO services are in the Logistics and Resources planning functions. Within the Technical Sales and Marketing departments these are account managers in the Sales and Customer Service function.

In 2007 Delta's Technical Operations division is the largest airline MRO in North America. Delta TechOps earns more than $ 310 million in revenue in 2006. The growth of Delta as an MRO leader has three major aspects: expanding customer base; expanding supplier agreements; and providing the platform for growth. Delta has been successful in the implementation of each of these three aspects.

Delta's Inventory Exchange program is the technological platform which allowed the MRO business unit to grow. Having the workforce and experience already in place for the standard Delta Air Lines operations, the information system is the factor which allowed collaboration in order to improve customer service. The expansion of Delta's MRO business has been attributed to multiple factors, such as industry recovery, optimization of internal processes, improved resource allocation, and others. However, the fact is that in 2005, Delta's Technical Operations Executive Vice President Tony Charaf set the goal for the business unit to be the 'The Feared Player in the MRO industry'. In 2007 Delta was the largest airline company in North America for MRO and served over 100 clients all over the world. The transformation for Delta's MRO unit did not occur overnight but it took the efforts of all internal business units such as Technical Sales, Operations, and Materials and Planning.

The ERP system implementation described as a case study in this chapter is the technological solution which facilitates the communication between the clients and Delta Air Lines users in the core process for the MRO industry—the exchange of components. The simple and scalable SAP solution and its web-portal interface give the opportunity to end users to view and make changes to their orders and easily acquire the basic reports needed for operations. Internal users have benefited most from improved workflow and time savings.

The implementation of the Enterprise Resource Planning (ERP) solution for the inventory component exchange processes has brought Delta Air Lines closer to the fulfilment of two major objectives. First, giving access to customers to data previously available only on the Delta Air Lines network has improved the quality and speed of service provided and facilitated the collaboration between clients and service-provider. Building strong relationships with customers is one of the key goals for the sustainable growth of the MRO unit. Second, adding a new process to the SAP technology map smoothes the progress of the company technological integration. ERP implementation is a gradual process in companies of the size of Delta Air Lines. Therefore, there is a higher return on the investment by adding new processes to the company-wide platform.

THEORETICAL FOUNDATIONS FOR CONSIDERATION

Some of the frameworks frequently used to assess software systems include a holistic perspective on the project implementation, the system performance, and the environmental impact on the users and stakeholders (Boloix, 1995). The approach toward the evaluation of ERP's success has an objective component (including the system fit in the task and user context) and subjective assessment (based on user and supervisor perception).

Extensive research has been conducted to understand the impact of different user beliefs with respect to the judgment of ERP systems. The results of these studies prove that supervisors value the ERP system higher within environments with operational interdependence (Bendoly et al., 2008). The task specificity and need for collaboration between teams to deliver a product or service make people perceive resource planning systems more highly effective than employees in a different setting. This perception has a direct effect on the actual use of the system and its adoption.

In addition to the resource planning systems different communication tools exist which have been used to facilitate collaboration. The goal of ERP implementations is to decrease the dependence on these various means of communication, standardize data definitions, and structures and channel the workflow within the systems. However, the non-transactional capabilities of the resource planning software when left at the discretion of each user are not utilized completely. Non-transactional capabilities include report development for performance evaluation or ad-hoc data access for problem definition. Therefore, users tend to underestimate the usefulness of these benefits.

Managerial support is another factor critical for the 'success' of the ERP. On the one hand system capabilities and fit within the context of tasks is important. On the other hand the perception of usefulness is the result of previous experience to which managers are exposed. In general the more supervisory experience a manager has had, the more likely he is to view the intra-organizational communication capabilities of the system. (Bendoly et al., 2008). The research has shown that throughout the supervisory experience, managers learn through trial and error. Experienced supervisors tend to pursue combination of media for communication among subordinates in order to improve collaborative efforts. The asynchronous use of shared database as an alternate media has the tendency to be more highly valued by supervisors with more experience and especially in interdependent settings.

An important distinction is the individualistic versus collectivistic culture which research shows to give bias toward the perceptions of resource planning capabilities. In collectivistic cultures, such as Delta's technicians, the driving force is to attain group goals. There is decreased tendency for social loafing (or contribute less to the group efforts and rely on others more) than in individualistic cultures (Bendoly et al., 2008). As a result supervisors are more likely to view the intra-organizational capabilities of resource planning systems as 'useful' than managers from individualistic cultures.

METHODOLOGY

In order to measure the usefulness of the Inventory Component Exchange Program for the Delta Air Lines MRO business both user perceptions and actual data needed to be acquired. Surveys were conducted to reflect the opinion of the internal users and Delta customers' users.

The interpretation of the survey results is based on interviews conducted in advance with key users from each group. In addition to the results of the survey, system reports have also indicated some trends after the implementation of the Inventory Component Exchange Program.

INVENTORY COMPONENT EXCHANGE PROGRAM

The exchange of components is part of the complete service solution provided by Delta Technical Operations to its MRO customers. Flexibility and accuracy in the process is crucial because the sooner the aircraft is repaired, the customer can put it back into operation. Therefore, Delta's processes need to be streamlined and effective to provide the best possible service to its customers.

The inventory component exchange between Delta Air Lines and its customers has two main business processes called Standard and Advanced. In the standard process each order is completed before the unserviceable component is received from the customer. The steps for the standard exchange are the following:

1. The customer orders the component to Delta using any of the contact methods provided.
2. Delta's team sends the serviceable part to the customer from a location where the component is available.
3. Customer starts repairing the aircraft using the serviceable part.
4. Customer sends back the unserviceable part to be serviced at Delta's component shops.
5. If the customer does not send back the unserviceable unit within the contracted period of time, it is charged a late fee.

The advanced process is different from the standard in that the order is fulfilled after the customer sends back the component for replacement. It has the following steps:

1. The customer sends back the unserviceable part to Delta's warehouse.
2. Delta's team inspects the part and if possible repairs it.
3. Delta's warehouse sends back the needed serviceable component to the customer.
4. Customer either starts aircraft repair or usually hold the serviceable component as a spare unit, when the component arrives.

These processes have customer specific days of return and components and types of aircraft included which are negotiated by Delta's Technical Sales as part of the contract signed with the customer. Customer specific information needs to be tracked and fees to be accrued and charged toward customer invoices.

Some of the critical information to be monitored in the processes described earlier is:

- Tracking the number of days needed to send back the components.
- Tracking the number of days needed by Delta to send (or send back) the component.
- Tracking customer specific components within the process.
- Tracking order status and component position by customers.

In 2005 while Delta Air Lines was recovering from bankruptcy, the company audit identified that Delta TechOps controlled manually the exchange of parts with its MRO customers. The existing inventory component exchange database was a stand-alone access-based system used for parts tracking and invoicing. Customer specific part information was not possible to be included in the database. Coordinators made exchanges based on limited knowledge. The auditors estimated that the existing inventory component exchange process results in $ 1.5 million loss per year in late fees and marked it to lead to incorrect asset transfer processes.

After the crisis of 11 September the MRO industry and the airlines market were in the process of growing back to and beyond the 2001 levels of activity. Component exchanges related to integrated inventory programmes have increased from 50 per month to an average of 350–400 per month in 2005.

The Inventory Component Exchange Program was initiated in 2006 following the audit recommendations and the need to develop the MRO business unit. It had the following specific goals:

- To satisfy corporate audit concerns regarding late fees calculation and asset transfer process.
- To improve the monitoring and standardization of contract terms.
- To enhance customer experience through giving more visibility to the exchange orders.
- To provide customer specific parts list.
- To eliminate access database.
- To create sustainable process to facilitate the growth of component exchange business.

EXPECTED BENEFITS

The primary goal for the Inventory Component Exchange Program was the ability to grow the MRO business by 10 per cent per year. The exchange programme was expected to give the technological basis to facilitate the expected scope growth of the MRO business unit within Delta Air Lines. The expected benefits at 10 per cent growth rate and a 35 per cent margin were calculated to reach $ 8.5 million over five years.

The 10 per cent growth in the business would be the result of a team effort of Technical Sales and Customer Contract Desk (CCD), both departments within TechOps. It was expected to be achieved by signing new contracts and making it possible for each of these teams to serve more customers. Especially important for achieving that goal is the time savings in the CCD department, which currently was servicing manually all customer requests coming over the phone, e-mail, or teletype.

PROGRAM IMPLEMENTATION

The Inventory Component Exchange Program was initiated with representatives from Delta's Technology, Technical Operations, and Customer Competency Center (CCC) departments. It was developed following Delta's long-term Information Technology strategy of implementing SAP as a platform for streamlining the business processes. After evaluation of the business requirements Delta Technology considered SAP Sales and Distribution module to be the most applicable to serve the goals of the project. In addition to that automatic upload and storage of scanned documents for proof of delivery was to be integrated in order to facilitate the exchange of documents and reduce paper use. Another feature to be implemented is a web portal which would give access to customers to information stored in SAP and previously available only within Delta's network. As part of the project Delta Technology considered integration with AeroExchange, an industry-wide platform used by airline carriers for component exchange.

The project implementation was split in two phases. The first phase integrated the component exchange process into SAP, providing the ability to manage exchange orders more effectively. The planned start was in June 2006, design completion in July 2006, and the planned beginning of implementation in October 2006. The second phase provided for basic interactive web-based functionality for all customers and internal users, including parts list visibility. The planned start was in June 2006, design completion in December 2006, and the implementation during February 2007. The project was expected to require altogether 10 full time employees for a period of five and six months. The risks which were identified were partially technological such as SAP updates and third party vendor dependencies, while others included the lack of experience of the team because the team was developing a new technological solution.

During the system implementation the requirements of the inventory component exchange process were successfully built into the SAP system as part of the Sales and Distribution module. In addition to the functionality in the ERP system, during the second phase of the project implementation a web portal was added to give customers access to data otherwise available only internally to Delta's system users.

The first phase of the Inventory Component Exchange Program developed the internal processes within Delta Air Lines. There are three types of system users within Delta, who have different roles. Delta's Technical Sales are responsible for negotiating the contract with the customer and entering the contract data in the system. Invoicing customers and entering customer financial details are also part of the sales person role in the ERP system. All these responsibilities are fulfilled by using transactions in the SAP system.

CCD is the largest unit benefiting from the implementation of the Inventory Component Exchange Program. Part of the SAP functionality implemented in the first phase of the project is the CCD workbench. The workbench is a central place for the most commonly executed transactions by the CCD. It gives quick access to component availability in plant and storage locations, inventory data, and interchangeability reports. From the workbench it is easy to track status of orders, pending proof of deliveries, open inquiries, and returns.

The administration and configuration of the system within Delta's team is done by CCC. They are the third role in the processes of the inventory component exchange. For various reasons the planned cooperation with AeroExchange could not be fulfilled. However, Delta Technology and CCC came up with simple workaround of the obstacle. The development of a web portal interface to SAP functionality opened the system to external customers allowing better collaboration between the parties.

Delta Air Lines' customers extracted the biggest benefit of the web portal. The web portal gave each user access to the information and actions which previously were not available. Some of those are request part, view order details, search for the exchange number, view shipping details, exchange messages, generate reports for return time, fill rate, open exchanges, closed exchanges, parts list, and view or upload proof of delivery.

The second phase made possible transactions to which customers also have access to be executed by Technical Sales in non-SAP environment. Thus, Delta's Technical Sales had an easy and user-friendly access to the SAP system from any computer outside the Delta's network. Information regarding new customers and contract details continue to be executed in the SAP environment.

The web-portal provides the opportunity for real-time subscription events available for the different order status changes. Some of the status changes or the standard exchange include: Pending part; Accepted or Rejected; In-transit; Delivered; Closed or Closed under review; and Overdue. The advance exchange process includes the following status changes: Pending part; Received; In- transit; and Closed. Access to the web portal was given to customers through the Delta Passport credential assignment. It makes possible tracking of the SAP licence usage and is integrated with Delta Passport Self-serve account management portal.

OVERALL RESULTS

OPERATIONAL PROCESSING CHANGES REALIZED

Before discussing general benefits derived from the implementation, it is worth reiterating the changes that took place during this natural experiment. The implementation of the ERP module together with the web portal solution leads to optimization and streamlining of the processes. Table 16.1 gives a brief overview of the major changes in the component exchange process.

TABLE 16.1
Process Changes before and after MRO Implementation

	Before	*After*
Take order	E-mail	Website
	Phone	E-mail
	Teletype	Phone
Create order	Access db	Website
		SAP transaction
Check availability	Access db	CCD workbench
		SAP inquiry
Component interchangeability	No specific database	SAP inquiry
Check if unserviceable part included	No specified process	SAP inquiry
Messaging	Phone	Website
Proof of delivery	Paper based	In documentum
Tracking	Phone	Website
Reports	Phone	Website
	Access	SAP inquiry
Customer specific parts	Not possible	SAP inquiry

Source: Author.

Taking orders by the CCD team has been changed from the manual taking by e-mail, phone or teletype to the automatic one on the website. Currently all ways of taking orders are available to Delta's customers, but even when customers use phone or e-mail, the CCD team records the order through the website functionality. Customers can also create orders by themselves using the website functionality.

Checking component availability has been facilitated through the SAP inquiries available and the consolidated workbench for the CCD team. Checking component interchangeability and unserviceable parts has been difficult process for the CCD team, since they did not have the needed information readily available. Only experienced people usually in the warehouse were well acquainted about the interchangeability of the parts. The sales team negotiating the terms of the contract was aware of which parts were to be serviced by Delta Air Lines.

Before the web interface to SAP messaging was not available. Any information exchanged about the process was via phone or e-mail and it was up to the carefulness of the employee whether it will be recorded in the access database order. Proof of delivery was paper-based and information whether components have been exchanged between warehouses or between Delta and its customers was transmitted via fax. The ERP system allowed the storage of a scanned version of each proof of delivery to be stored in Documentum, an environment which allowed information from the scanned copy to be automatically filled in data fields in the orders created. The scanned proof of delivery can be attached to the respective order and changes its status when needed.

Tracking of the order status and the component location was a time-consuming and tense process. The website allows for real-time tracking of the component, integration with Delta's flight information system, and integration with third-party forwarder's systems used to track shipments online.

Reports availability is one of the biggest advantages of the web portal. Customers benefit from the information available regarding return time, open exchanges, or available parts list. The reports are based on SAP inquiries and give real time information. Identifying unique customer specific parts has not been possible in the access database. SAP allowed for the unique tail numbers to be used to assign components to customers and track parts within the system.

HIGHER LEVEL RESULTS

Overall Satisfaction: Delta's employees are more satisfied with the functionality of the Inventory Component Exchange Program. The overall score for employees is 7.55, while for customers it is 5.63 out of maximum 10. The interesting part of the results is that 27.3 per cent of Delta's internal users have answered with a maximum of 10 as its score. This indicates the improvement in the work process for the employees as compared with the previous manual process. The CCD group have greatly benefited by the introduction of the Inventory Component Exchange Program.

Most used features: The three most used features of the implemented solution for the internal users are Execution of SAP transactions, Messaging, and Proof of Delivery. For customers the three most used features are Real time order status information, Tracking of shipments through Delta sites, and Reports regarding overdue exchanges, late fees, and open or closed exchanges. The results of the surveys are consistent with the expectations of Delta Air Lines. However, the survey has a bias toward the customers who are more Internet and technologically inclined. These customers would be also more willing to use the Inventory Component Exchange web portal as well.

Most useful features: Delta's employees find most useful the following three functionalities: Execution of SAP transaction; Reports; and Update unserviceable return part information. For customers the most useful features are: Reports, Real time order status information; and Tracking of shipments. The results reflect the general opinion of employees that their work in SAP has been made easier and more accurate by implementing the web portal. The system reports also show that the average time for a 'proficient user' to create the inquiry directly in SAP is about two minutes. The same user can create the inquiry from the web in about 30 seconds assuming that they are already logged on. Logging on will add about 45 seconds. Therefore, for employees, web interface has proved really useful, saving them time to complete the basic transactions.

Time savings: For both groups, employees, and customers, the solution saves on average between one and two hours per week. Assuming Delta's heavy users to be 25 and external customer users about 20, this translates into overall savings of 67 hours per week or around eight FTE for both parties. Only for Delta Air Lines these are savings of approximately 18 FTE per month. Another interesting point in Delta's employee survey results is that 22 per cent answered that the Inventory Component Exchange solution saves them more than five hours per week. These findings are consistent with the expectations that the technological solution would have beneficial effect on the work previously done manually in the warehouse.

More transactions completed: Delta's employees agree that they are able to conduct more transactions after the SAP solution for the Inventory Component Exchange. For the customers using the web portal there has been no significant change in the number of transactions and the answers are split in half. A comparison of the number of transactions for a randomly selected customer based on the report from the access database and from the SAP module shows that for a three-month period cumulative transactions have increased from 76 to 107. The average days for execution of exchange have decreased from 4.7 to 4.3. In addition to that the number of active records has shown improvement from 300 to 130 open records.

Overdue exchange decrease: Overdue exchanges survey results show difference in the answers as well. From Delta's employees perspective there has been a decrease in the number of overdue exchanges. Customers' perception is that the web portal has had no effect on the overdue exchanges. System reports show that the number of exchanges which are overdue more than 30 days has fallen from 40 to 37.

DISCUSSION

The results of both user perception and report data show that there is a discrepancy on the solution adoption by internal and external users. Although the web solution has been launched six to eight months later than the SAP solution, the rate of acceptance among the customers is much lower than Delta's employees using it. In addition to that, although customer calls to initiate orders were expected to drop by 70 per cent, after the second phase of the project, this has not happened. Comparing this fact with the results indicates that there are a certain number of customers who do not use the complete benefits of the online service provided by Delta Air Lines. Several reasons for the low rate of adoption may exist, such as insufficient information on the website availability, insufficient training or training conducted not on actual users of the system, and lack of additional stimuli to use the web service.

The SAP solution implementation has greatly optimized and improved the work of internal users which is confirmed both by the project implementation and the user perceptions. Not only CCD survey responses indicated the benefits of the platform, but also the feedback from Technical Sales department validated their excitement. The CCC which is responsible for the system support after the implementation has substantiated the claims about the usefulness of the solution. Some of the feedback it has provided as part of the interview process included the low number of change requests as compared to other solutions and stable usage statistics.

A positive perception bias regarding the ERP within Delta's team can exist because of the many years of supervisor experience and the overall collectivistic culture within the company.

Delta's teams are in general characterized by very close and collaborative atmosphere built during years of working together. Delta's customers do not necessarily enjoy similar internal culture which can be a reason for the lower evaluation of the system benefits.

One of the reasons for better system adoption is Delta's management support. Having gone through several ERP modules implementations and already reaping the benefits of using the system, management and users are convinced of the software capabilities. Therefore the learning curve and adoption rate is expected to be higher than that in environment in which new ways of working have not been recently developed.

In order to extract more benefit from the improved inventory component exchange processes, based on the interviews conducted and the survey findings, there are two recommendations for future system success. First, more customer education on the benefits of using the web portal is needed. Current customer users should be trained again if needed and managers should be informed on the benefits of using the website solution. The number of companies which are using the website should be increased to include all types of customers.

Second, the Technical Sales should provide incentives for self-service. The web solution portal is intended to give customers access to the SAP system during any time of the day. The more customers are using the website the more time CCD has for actual execution of the orders. The effects of lock-in should also be considered when creating the stimuli for customer website self-service.

Albeit suggesting, the results of the web survey are likely biased towards technologically oriented individuals who would also use the web solution. The fact that limited number of customers responded to the web-survey is indicative of the lack of motivation to improve the use of a technological platform for collaboration. This corresponds to the lack of incentives to use the sales portal. The time period in which the website and the SAP solution has been used is together is limited in order to assess the effects on the financial performance of the MRO unit.

CONCLUSION

Besides the beneficial business effects the implementation of the Inventory Component Exchange Program has brought Delta Air Lines one step closer to better integration of its processes. The Program involved the development of process and procedures to track and monitor the component exchanges. The Technical Sales department acquired access to reports detailing the customers' activity and facilitates the communication regarding invoices and late fees. CCD managed to distribute the responsibility for the component exchange to other parties within Delta Air Lines.

The overall goal for the program implementation has been achieved when the Corporate Audit Review has stated that: '[There have been] considerable improvements in the process related to the tracking of the part issued to the customer and the subsequent receipt of the unserviceable unit sent from the customer. The risk of lost revenue (fees) or assets due to (remaining) concerns is low.'

REFERENCES

Bendoly, E., D.G. Bachrach, and B. Powel. 2008. 'The Role of Operational Interdependence and Supervisory Experience on Management Assessments of Resource Planning Systems', *Production and Operations Management*, 17(1).

Bachrach, D.G., H. Wang, E. Bendoly, and S. Zhang. 2007. 'Task Interdependence and Culture: Moderating Effects on the Importance Attributed to Organizational Citizenship Behavior', *Management and Organization Review*, 3(2): 255–76.

Boloix, R. 1995. 'A Software System Evaluation Framework', *Computer*, 28(12): 17–26.

17

The Role of Mobile Computing and Communication Technologies in Mobile Governance

SHASHANK GARG
*Vice President, Advanced Projects at Encore Software Limited, Bangalore,
and Founder-trustee of Sarvatva Foundation*
E-mail: garg.shashank@gmail.com

KRISHNA SUNDAR DIATHA
*Associate Professor, Indian Institute of Management Bangalore,
and Founder-trustee of Sarvatva Foundation*
E-mail: diatha@iimb.ernet.in

INTRODUCTION

In this chapter the following issues are discussed:[1] how mobile computing and communication technologies, when applied to address specific problems in governance, can potentially improve the lives of the people and reduce the economic and social divide that exists in society. The focus on mobile computing and communication technologies is deliberate. While mobile communication technology, as manifested in the mobile phone, is already a large part of our daily lives, one needs to move beyond communication to actual computing. This next generation of mobile devices will have the ability to deliver many applications in the hands of the citizen on the move, beyond telephony. Hence, it is necessary to move beyond the concept of e-governance to mobile or m-governance, thereby enabling the provision of government services to the 'door-step' of the citizen or, essentially, wherever she may happen to be at any instant in time. Of course, this would require a complete end-to-end enterprise level solution comprising front-end data collection and back-end services to facilitate seamless transactions

---

[1] The views expressed in this chapter are those of the authors in their individual capacities, and do not represent the views of their respective organizations.

between the various stakeholders such as the rural population, field-based retail service providers, back-end governmental entities, and policy planners.

Amongst the hundreds of important services expected to be delivered by an elected government to its citizens, the services dealing with the Public Distribution and Public Health are amongst the most critical to a nation's well being. The Public Distribution System (PDS) deals with the nation's food security and the Public Health System, including Disease Surveillance which performs a sentinel role against epidemic and other threats, caters to the primary health needs of a vast majority of the medically under-served rural population. Mobile technology can enable a disruptive transformation in these services by improving systemic efficiency, reducing response times, reducing transaction costs, increasing coverage, and introducing transparency, with the potential to create maximum positive social impact. Of course, reducing the socio-economic divide will also help reduce the digital divide because rural citizens will begin to use information and communication technology (ICT) in their daily lives to access meaningful government services.

Therefore, two specific areas will be addressed in this chapter: the PDS and Public Health.

THE PUBLIC DISTRIBUTION SYSTEM

Let us first examine the PDS, the oldest and one of the most comprehensive anti-poverty programmes in terms of budgetary expenditures provided by the central and state governments. Since independence the PDS has evolved into a price support-cum-quantity-rationing-cum-subsidy programme. While we have moved from the food scarcity of the first two decades after independence to the relatively happier situation of food availability and surpluses, the PDS remains corrupt and inefficient because of serious systemic defects. There is evident disconnect among the needs of the various stakeholders, ranging from citizens (primarily poor people) to supplier's (poor farmers) to the government, all amidst a complex web of information dependencies like the monsoon, the annual budget, and political constituencies. Lack of timely and relevant information from the field has led to the formulation of inefficient food security policies and non-remunerative pricing for producers and consumers. As a result, the poor consumer as well as the poor farmer suffers and large parts of the population suffer from food insecurity despite tremendous progress in agricultural production. A quick and dynamic feedback system could potentially even out the imbalances in the system to improve efficiency, but the PDS remains divorced from any technological interventions.

It is an imperative of governance that it should be seen as transparent, minimally invasive, effective, and implementable at minimal cost so that the scarce resources can be deployed for real societal development, the infrastructure, and for enhancement of quality of life of citizens. Mobile and communications technologies will play an enabling role in delivering governance to the door-step of the citizens if we treat this PDS similar to an enterprise supply chain with seamless transactions between the front-end user and back-end service providers.

A NEW E-GOVERNANCE FRAMEWORK FOR PUBLIC DISTRIBUTION SYSTEM

In a paper titled 'Creating e-Chains to enable E-Governance through Embedded Technologies' (Sundar and Garg, 2003), a conceptual framework for e-governance has been formulated that typically consists of Knowledge Aggregation, Process Constructs, Content Constructs, and Delivery Methods with appropriate connectivity as depicted in Figure 17.1.

FIGURE 17.1
A Conceptual Framework for E-Governance

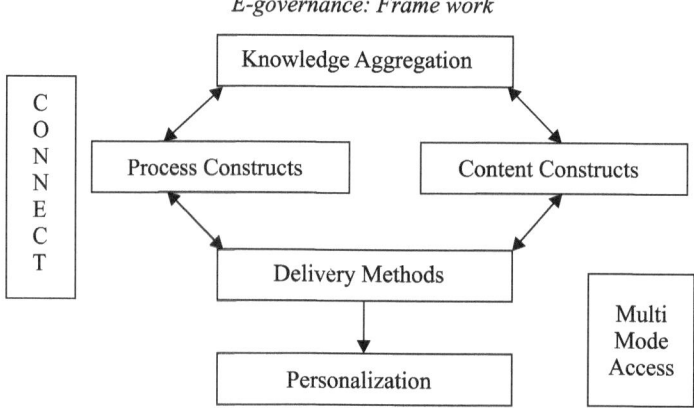

In the same paper, this framework has been extended to depict the specific example of a PDS, as shown in Figure 17.2.

FIGURE 17.2
The Public Distribution System

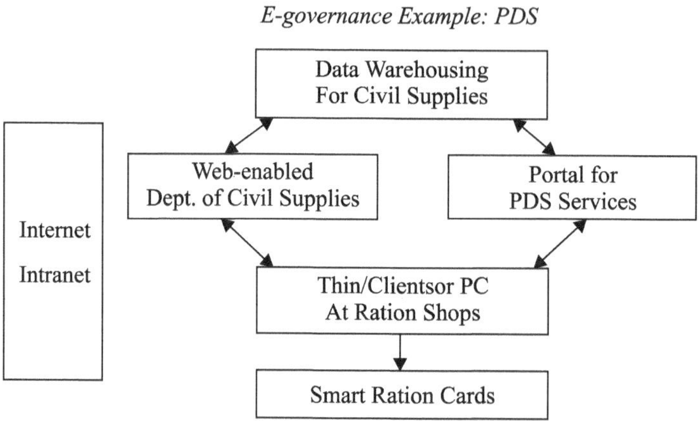

This shows how information technology may be used effectively in the PDS. There is no doubt that the 'Information Technology Revolution' that the world, including India, is currently witnessing seems to be an urban-centric phenomenon which increases the friction already prevalent in the rural–urban divide and the socio-economic divide through the addition of a deep 'digital divide'. As our economy transforms into a knowledge economy, the digital or information divide will certainly widen. This imbalance occurs primarily when one section of society has relatively easy access to information over other sections of society, resulting in loss of competitiveness for those affected sections. However, a well-planned and implemented e-governance infrastructure can not only help reduce the basic socio-economic divide between rural and urban sections of society, but also reduce the digital divide as citizens become comfortable in using information technology (IT) services in the normal course of interacting with government services provided to them through the mobile governance infrastructure.

The PDS was designed as a deliberate tool of social policy by the Government of India, with the following objectives:

- To provide food-grains and other essential items to vulnerable sections of society at reasonable prices which are normally subsidized.
- To provide a moderating influence on the open-market prices of cereals, the distribution of which constitutes a fairly big share of the total marketable surplus.
- To ensure equitable distribution of essential commodities so that vulnerable sections of society are not left out to fend for themselves in the market.

However, the PDS has not been particularly efficient in meeting the stated objectives for reasons such as:

- Inefficient procurement, storage, and delivery mechanisms:
    - Often resulting in the government godowns overflowing with food-grains (wheat and rice), of which a significant proportion of stocks are believed to be rotten and generally unfit for human consumption.
    - The cost of holding a huge inventory of food-grain is massive.

- Procurement and handling costs in the PDS are generally twice as high compared to private traders whereas the quality of food-grains procured and supplied is generally sub-standard and of lower quality.
- Food-grains are often lost in transit between warehouses in the supply-chain through systemic leakage, thefts, and corruption.
- The salaries and perks of the PDS workers consume a significant portion of the PDS budget.
- The productivity and performance level of PDS workers is amongst the lowest in the country.

ESSENTIAL COMPONENTS FOR AN IMPROVED PUBLIC DISTRIBUTION SYSTEM (PDS)

It can clearly be identified that to provide an efficient PDS, at the very least, a few critical components of the system need to be improved through the use of ICT. These critical areas are:

- Logistics Management
- Consumer Identity Management
- The Government–Citizen Interface

Logistics management involves a two-level staging, with the first stage being the transfer of food shipments from the central warehouse to a state's warehouse and the second stage being the transfer of goods from a state warehouse to the thousands of geographically dispersed fair-price shops run by the state government. A typical logistics management supply-chain consists of:

- Shipment tracking.
- Notification service.
- Billing and payments between state and central governments.
- Warehouse integration and management for both central government and state government.
- Logistics management: Responsibility of entire logistics requirement of the process.

LOGISTICS MANAGEMENT

A logistics hub needs to be developed in order to track a shipment in its journey from a central warehouse till it reaches the state warehouse, and subsequently from the state warehouse to the fair-price shop at the final destination. A combination of relatively low cost radio-frequency identification (RFID) technology and global positioning system (GPS) technology can be deployed in the shipment chains. RFID tags should be used for tracking individual palletized shipments electronically and GPS-enabled trucks and railway wagons would enable the tracking of bulk shipments in real-time. Each truck should be fitted with a mobile tracking platform consisting of a GPS receiver that periodically records location information, and a GSM communications module that reports information in real-time to a central server that can track the travel trajectory of each track on a map. RFID technology is cost-effective and the tags are reusable if designed properly. This will help minimize losses and thefts in transit, one of the main problems in the traditional PDS delivery chain. This will bring about tremendous transparency into the entire process and will help to pinpoint problem areas.

Similarly, inter-government payments can be speeded up through electronic fund transfer between state and central government. Each participating entity could generate reports on the system in order to track a particular shipment.

The architecture of a typical logistics hub that can be maintained for centre-to-state warehousing within the PDS has been shown in Figure 17.3.

FIGURE 17.3
The Logistics Hub for Public Distribution Systems

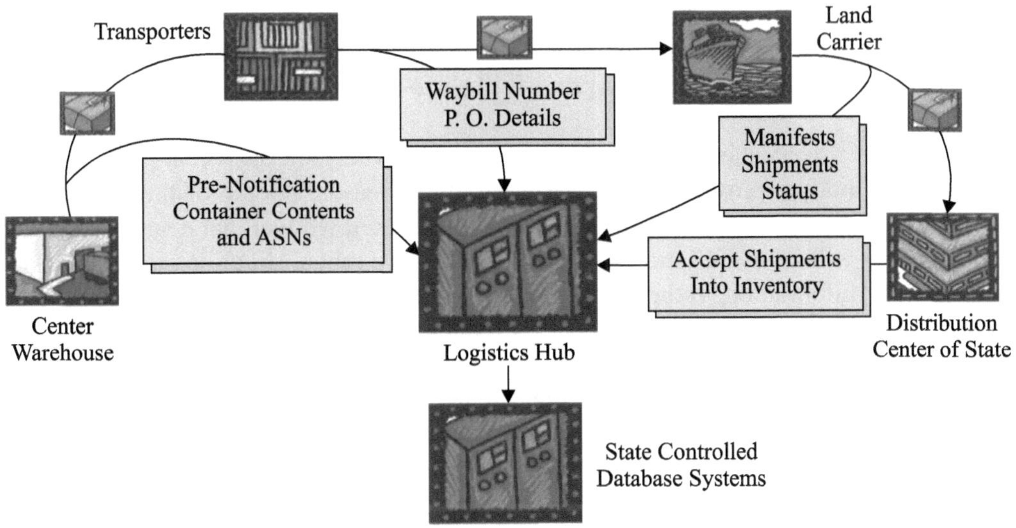

Source: Authors.

CONSUMER IDENTITY MANAGEMENT AND THE RETAIL CONSUMER

Consumer identity is at the core of the business process of food distribution at the end of the chain in any successful PDS since it is important to properly identify the target beneficiaries to provide them the services and entitlements in a transparent manner. Duplication of identities and masquerading often occur at this stage, leaving the real poor uninformed of their rights, and robbed of essential goods and services.

State governments have traditionally used various forms of paper-based 'ration cards' to help in this identification process. Ration cards are assigned on a per-household basis and define whether the card holder is 'above poverty line' (APL) or 'below poverty line' (BPL) since each categorization has its own set of entitlements. Obviously, BPL card holders deserve special handling as they form the poorest of the poor in our society. Unfortunately, paper-based ration cards have not proven to be very effective as various socio-economic studies have pointed out that the benefits of the PDS fail to reach the targeted beneficiaries. Hence it is absolutely critical that the process of Consumer Identity Management be as efficient, transparent, and auditable as possible.

This is an area that can be well addressed by low-cost technology like smart-cards for maintaining consumer identity in a digital form as it allows the implementation of secured and authenticated access to private identity and consumer data (Windley, 2005).

A unique digital identity can be assigned to each individual member of a household and a single family-owned smart card can hold the digital identities of all members of a typical household. In addition to textual identity information, the smart card should also include a digitized picture of each member, as well as bio-metric data such as finger-prints for multi-level identification. A system that combines several identification techniques such as physical verification through pictures and finger-prints is likely to be more successful than a paper-based ration card.

While smart cards have been tried out in various pilot studies in the recent past, smart card technology has not yet proved popular for a variety of reasons. Some of these reasons are cost and lack of availability of applications. For this reason, we feel that a smart card based identity system will be useful and cost-effective only if a range of applications can use the digital identity information, rather than having single application-specific smart cards. Of course, the cost of smart cards is progressively reducing and will come down much further as volumes increase.

So a smart card based digital identity management system has been suggested that spans across a diverse range of government services that are available:

- Electronic Digital Identity Management:
  - For ration card in the PDS application
  - For voter identification
  - For driving licence
  - For income-tax (electronic PAN card)

- Other Applications such as:
  - Electronic land records
  - Electronic cooperative bank passbook
  - Electronic health records (public health applications)

It must be mentioned here that individual privacy and confidentiality of information are important for the success of any government scheme. It is the ethical and moral responsibility of any governance system that collects individual data to maintain and protect the confidentiality of each individual's personal identifying information. It is also important to prevent willful and accidental misuse of such data for profiling and linkage of sensitive data to any specific individuals. Access to such information must be provided through a set of authentication procedures based on a strict need-to-know basis.

A smart card based consumer identity management system is proposed for the implementation of security and authentication procedures. Different levels of access to information can be assigned, with the retail personnel operating the mobile devices for the specified applications only. A robust identity management system with multiple levels of security and authentication is essential for ensuring organizational efficiency, security of transactions, prevention of fraud, privacy of data, and rapidness of response (NECCC, 2002).

THE GOVERNMENT–CITIZEN INTERFACE

Traditionally, the government–citizen interface has been based on the classic client–server model wherein government departments provide a few sets of services to their citizen clients through a form-filling mechanism. A client requiring a specific service visits the concerned government office and fills out a request for that service. The government office provides that service in a non-real time way by asking the client to come back when the office is ready with its answer.

The next step in the growth of e-governance has been to make these forms and services available on a web-based portal. The proliferation of low-cost broadband Internet access makes such services more commonly available. However, even that is not entirely appropriate or adequate for larger rural populations which do not have access to broadband Internet access. It is important to recognize the ground reality that rural citizens would be better served through mobile connectivity since a large portion of the day is spent out in the fields away from an Internet kiosk or a physical government office. Cellular telephony should be leveraged for this purpose. The cell-phone and other low-cost mobile devices will play a significant role in enabling this transformation towards universal availability of government services at the door-step.

Cellular telephony has already touched the lives of over 250 million people in India, making it the second largest market after China, and it maintains a healthy growth rate. The e-governance infrastructure must now leverage this cellular infrastructure by offering services that the citizens need. The PDS is one such service that awaits this transformation through a 'disruptive' evolution into a transparent, efficient and cost-effective service to those living at the margins.

THE 'SMART PDS OUTLET'

To facilitate the deployment of PDS services, it will be essential for each retail PDS outlet to be plugged into the technology infrastructure of smart cards and logistics tracking. We define a 'Smart PDS Outlet' as a retail outlet that is able to read smart cards presented by the clients for identification in real-time. A device incorporating a smart card reader and cellular communication for instant connectivity to a back-end server would be a minimal requirement at each retail outlet. The smart PDS outlet, therefore, requires the following minimum functionality:

- A built-in smart card reader.
- A retail outlet identifier (an electronic tag can be used).
- A cellular connection to the back-end server.
- An optional biometric sensor (finger-print scanner) for authentication.
- An RFID reader for reading RFID tags from pelletized shipments delivered to the retail outlet.

It should be noted that government services being supplied at the door-step of the citizen are also being envisaged, a critical step in reaching the goal of 'mobile governance'. Many rural communities comprise nomadic tribes who are always on the move. Such tribes have significantly higher poverty levels as they are forced to live on the fringes of the already impoverished rural communities. It is important that government services and facilities be provided to these communities too. Ideally, a mobile PDS van could be used for delivery of such services. So a smart PDS outlet should also have the capability to deliver goods to the door-step of rural communities. This introduces an element of mobility within the delivery system itself and calls for a mobile retail PDS outlet. Therefore, the minimal requirement can be redefined with the following minimal functionality:

- A built-in smart card reader.
- A retail outlet identifier (an electronic tag can be used).
- A GPS receiver for recording and reporting of location coordinates.
- A cellular connection to the back-end server.
- An optional biometric sensor (finger-print scanner) for authentication.
- An RFID reader for reading RFID tags from pelletized shipments delivered to the retail outlet.

Only a GPS receiver has been added because it can record location information in real-time and therefore allow the system to track the mobility of a mobile PDS outlet when desired. Since the location of the mobile retail outlet can be tracked in real-time, it creates a certain amount of accountability for the last-mile service provider.

A low-cost mobile device with a small liquid crystal display (LCD) display, a built-in smart card reader, an RFID reader, GSM cellular connectivity, and some non-volatile storage for handling and storage of data would be essential. Non-volatile storage would be primarily for situations when connectivity to back-end servers may not be available. Thus the mobile PDS system should be fully capable of disconnected operation for limited periods in which cellular connectivity might not be available.

Mobile devices like the Simputer, developed by one of the authors, already incorporate the above functionality and are fully capable of being deployed in the PDS as well as for many other e-governance applications.

THE BUSINESS PROCESS FLOW IN A SMART PDS OUTLET

A business process diagram shown in Figure 17.4 gives a simplified overview of the business processes involved when a retail consumer drives visits a retail PDS outlet for purchasing food on her smart ration card.

FIGURE 17.4
The Smart Retail PDS Outlet

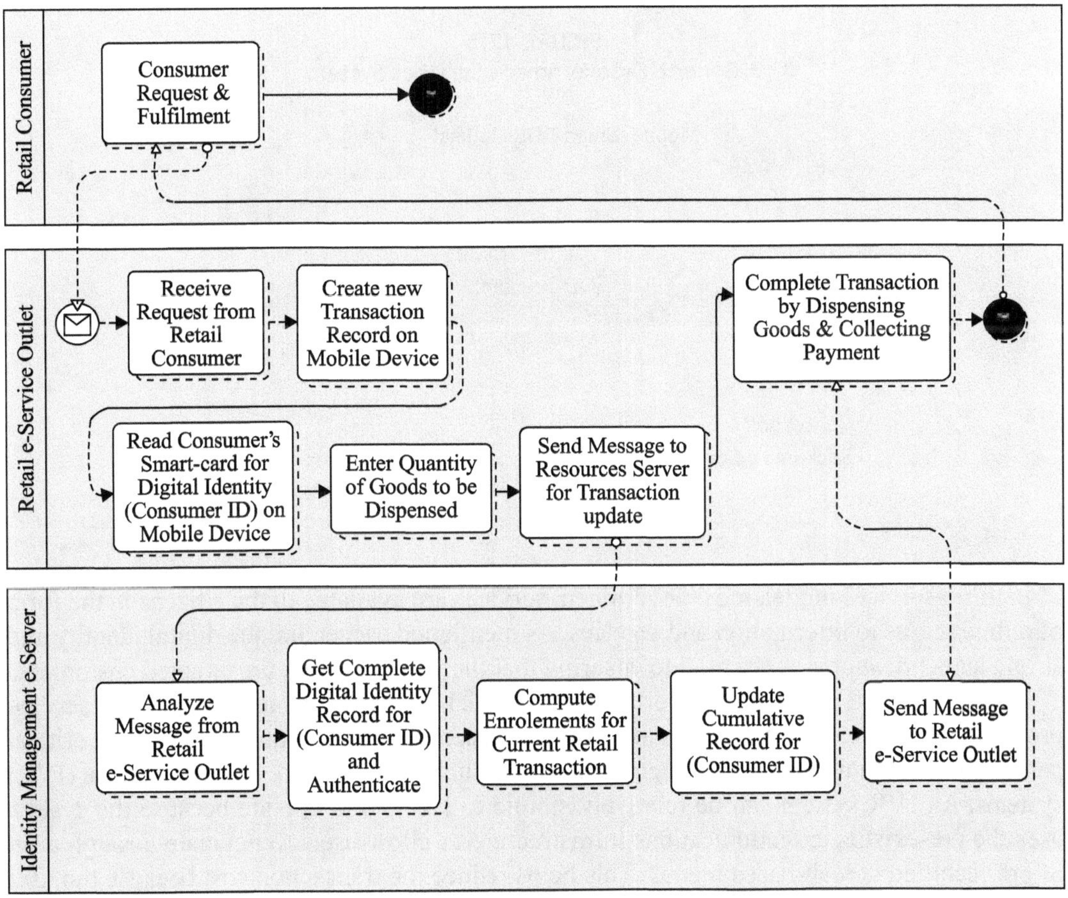

Source: Authors.

A simplified notation from the Business Processing Modeling Notation (BPMN) Specification has been used to describe the functional tasks and interactions in the parallel processes at the retail PDS outlet and the back-end e-Server (OMG, 2006).

THE E-SERVICES SYSTEM

Some of the modules are back-end processes that run on the server. The mobile device is used for data capture at the retail outlet, validation, security and authentication, communications, and messaging. The back-end services consist of Consumer Identity Management and the management of e-services to which a retail consumer has specific entitlements.

This same process model can be extended to other government services, besides food products distributed through the PDS, is depicted in the Figure 17.5.

FIGURE 17.5
A Generic E-Government Services System

Mobile 'Smart PDS Outlets'

The Internet

Back-end e-Server

An e-Government Services System

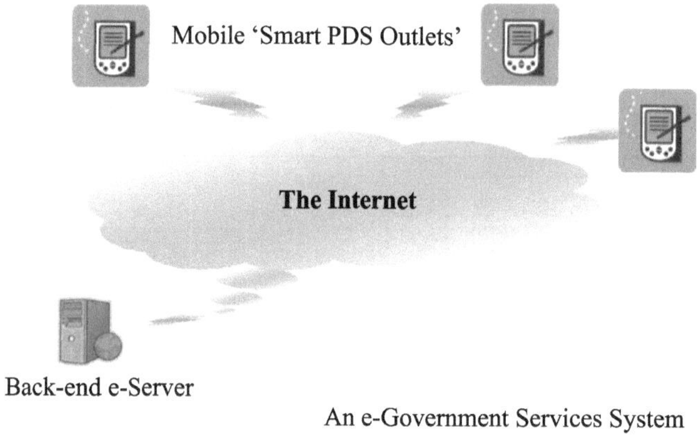

Source: Authors.

In this e-services model, most government services are available to the citizens in the form of online access to information and services. As mentioned earlier, unique digital identity and strong authentication are essential to ensuring that the services reach the targeted customers.

Consumers will always have certain needs which require interaction with the service provider and cannot be met through mere on-line access to information. IT will play a critical part in providing interactivity through other media such as Interactive Voice Response (IVR) systems. An IVR system can be relatively simple to set up and operate because the system uses the pre-existing communications infrastructure to allow users to navigate through a set of pre-recorded speech-based menus. This helps reduce the transaction cost because the user no longer has to visit the government office to acquire the service. A generalized model of this approach is successfully followed by call centers where trained operators respond to customer queries and satisfy the client's needs. The broad parameters under which call centres operate are as follows:

- Provide domain-specific services to clients:
  - Improve operational efficiencies through automation of information.
  - Automation of repetitive tasks.

- Reduce Transaction Cost to Service Provider:
  - Geographical location in low-cost service areas.

- Provision of 24-hour, seven-day access to services.

However, the IT-enabled services model does not go far enough in being able to reduce transaction cost and increasing operational efficiency. Various reasons can be attributed to this failure of the traditional IT-enabled services model:

- Lack of service provisioning in local languages.
- Lack of appropriate applications that service community needs:
  - Information on cropping patterns, irrigation techniques, soil conditions, weather reports, markets, etc., for the benefit of farmers.

- Distributed access to services:
  - Farmers spend most of the time in remote fields where services should be available.

- High transaction costs.

Embedded technology can play an effective role in creating e-Chains in the proposed e-Governance Framework to reduce transaction cost and improve operational efficiencies. In order for the benefits of e-Governance to percolate to the target audience, it is essential to analyze the Delivery (transportation) Methods in this Framework and also analyze the specific aspect of personalization. These aspects are discussed with specific reference to PDS in India.

THE CURRENT SCENARIO OF PUBLIC HEALTH IN INDIA

India has made tremendous economic progress in the last 15 years since economic liberalization was kicked off in the early 1990s. Though the trajectory of economic reforms has been quite tentative, with frequent political roadblocks along the way, the country is steadily poised to become an economic powerhouse over the next few decades. However, it is increasingly accepted that social sector development has not kept pace with economic development. It is known that economic development has not been equitable, geographically widespread and socially inclusive. Since economic and social development is inextricably interlinked, it is imperative that social indicators are given equal primacy when we talk about the development of appropriate metrics to measure socio-economic performance.

On most social development indicators India is still a laggard and civil society must not accept this inequitable situation as fait accompli. Just as we accepted the low 'Hindu rate of growth' for several decades before economic opportunity helped change our collective mindset, we have to apply the same disruptive stimulus to our collective national conscience. For example, while we have made advances in the practice of modern medicine in the metros, the public health system remains sadly untouched by such advances in medical research. While medical tourism is often highlighted to showcase the success of our advances in medicine primarily through our corporate hospitals, this showcase hides the pathetic state of the public health system (Garg and Sundar, 2008).

The poor state of the public health infrastructure and pathetic delivery mechanisms have left a huge rural population of over 700 million people that are medically under-served and ignored at our own peril. Even basic medical facilities are not available to people living on the edges of urban pockets or at the fringes of society. Poor sanitation, lack of awareness about personal hygiene, poor quality of the sources of water, rural poverty, low levels of education amongst the target population, and various socio-economic factors contribute to a vicious cycle of neglect and apathy in public health system. This is further compounded by the non-availability of quality data in real-time.

Most social development indicators such as primary education, literacy, development of human resources, consumption of fuel and power, availability of public transport, lack of access to timely, and cost-effective government services, all point to poor all-round governance.

A vicious export-oriented economic engine that primarily serves external markets and generally ignores the enormous economic potential that exists at the bottom of our pyramid is a poor indicator of the success of our socio-economic reforms. Our economic activity is essentially geared towards an export economy in which labour arbitrage is our unique value. This labour arbitrage as a competitive advantage could vanish as other developing economies coming into the marketplace at a lower cost of labour and services. The Indian Information Technology industry's penchant for chasing the 'low-hanging fruit' is already well known. Undoubtedly, it is much harder to service the local market and provide economic value at reasonable cost but it is nevertheless essential. So a complete change of mindset is needed to provide encouragement to social entrepreneurship, or entrepreneurship with clear social goals as a primary focus. There is also a need to develop appropriate products and services that will meet local market needs at a cost that the local markets can afford.

Many such socially relevant initiatives are needed across industry segments as we now have the basic tools and infrastructure for social entrepreneurship. There is also a need to co-opt all sections of civil society and government in active partnership for economic and social development. Instead of waiting for economic benefits to trickle-down to the outer fringes to cover those who have been left behind, we need to move at an accelerated pace with the technological tools we now possess.

ICTs, including mobile computing technologies, should play the enabling role of a force-multiplier in social and economic development. Mobile computing must play a vibrant and increasingly important role in improving delivery mechanisms for social sector services. Hopefully, this article will trigger some introspection within Indian civil society and more specifically within the Indian IT industry.

THE IMPORTANCE OF DISEASE SURVEILLANCE IN PUBLIC HEALTH

In this section of the chapter a few examples of the use of mobile technology in public health will be concentrated upon to demonstrate the potential for great social impact.

The economic burden of disease is a well-accepted concept for determining the economic costs that are directly or indirectly attributable to a disease. Direct costs are normally attributable to expenditure on hospitalization, expenditure on drugs, physician consultation, capital infrastructure for health-care, etc. Indirect costs attempt to measure loss of economic opportunity due to illness, disability, and mortality costs. This economic burden of disease needs to be lowered through better public health infrastructure.

As a result, the Government of India has recently launched the hugely ambitious National Rural Health Mission (NRHM) and the Integrated Disease Surveillance Programme (IDSP) with a clear recognition that a healthy public–private partnership is absolutely essential and critical to the success of any large public health-care initiative of such scope. In addition, these programmes also emphasize the importance of decentralized decision making through the involvement of local communities as stakeholders within a broader framework that will enable innovation and enterprise through a sense of ownership of such public health programmes at a local level.

Disease surveillance is an important aspect of any public health-care programme that serves two essential purposes, one of which is monitoring the progress of ongoing medical interventions for disease reduction, and the other is for the early detection of outbreaks to initiate investigative and control measures. Disease Surveillance is also a basic tool for the field epidemiologist as surveillance data provide a scientific basis for implementation of an appropriate health-care policy, disease control decisions, the evaluation of the efficacy of surveillance initiatives, and for the allocation of resources in the primary health-care system.

The NRHM and IDSP initiatives will use trained health-care workers from local communities to collect field-level data for dissemination of information and delivery of basic health-care services to local communities. Unfortunately, in the current scheme, health-care workers will maintain pen-and-paper-based records for their target populace and periodically transfer this information up the hierarchical tree till it reaches the district headquarters for evaluation, analysis, and response.

The availability of quality health-related information in near real-time is a pre-requisite for a disease surveillance system to be an effective sentinel to a successful public health programme. Paper-based data collection and reporting systems are generally inflexible, and not easily replicable or scalable across different regions. Mobile technology can play a role in creating a flexible, reliable, scalable, and replicable framework for collection and analysis of field data in near real-time which would be at the core of a successful public health programme.

THE CHRONIC KIDNEY DISEASE (CKD) SURVEILLANCE PROJECT

One example of an independent initiative in public health improvement is a longitudinal study being initiated for the causes of chronic kidney disease, in which the authors of this article are active participants. This collaborative project between various non-governmental entities and several medical departments of St. John's Medical College, Bangalore, is working on a disease surveillance system for the study of chronic kidney disease (CKD) which is a growing public health problem in developing countries such as India.

The aim of our project is to prove that early detection of CKD through a process of screening the target population for CKD, hypertension, and diabetes mellitus and the management of high risk groups for CKD with simple cost effective interventions at the primary health centre level, can result in reducing the economic burden of CKD. For this purpose, there is a plan to use indigenously developed mobile devices for baseline demographic surveillance, periodic follow-up, and monitoring of the population over a five-year period.

Early detection of abnormal renal function, prompt initiation of therapy, and close monitoring are essential to delaying the progression of CKD towards end-stage renal disease (ESRD). Interventions for treatment of ESRD require considerable medical infrastructure, skill, and resources. The large financial burden alone of renal replacement therapy precludes dialysis as a treatment option for most people who reach ESRD. Thus, for the large majority of patients who reach ESRD, it is a uniformly fatal diagnosis.

Although infectious diseases clearly remain a public health priority, chronic diseases are now prevalent in pandemic proportions and represent major causes of morbidity and mortality worldwide. CKD, in particular, warrants increased attention given the rapid increase in prevalence, the rising cost of treatment, its role in increasing the risk of cardiovascular disease, and the discovery of effective measures to prevent progression. In addition, CKD must be viewed in light of its complex interrelationship with cardiovascular disease, diabetes, and hypertension.

Early detection and effective initiation of therapies to delay progression of CKD must be tailored to local requirements.

Early detection and prevention programmes for CKD have been limited by lack of awareness amongst policy makers, the medical community, and patients, competing health care priorities, and lack of funding. However, several controlled studies have shown that it is feasible to reduce the burden of CKD in the developing world through targeted programmes in communities with vulnerable populations.

THE PROBLEM OF THE PEN-AND-PAPER-BASED APPROACH

The typical elements of any effective disease surveillance solution are:

- Widespread screening, accessible and effective interventions when needed, and ensure close follow-up.
- Data collection tools to collect basic epidemiological data and assess efficacy.
- Capacity to include co-morbid cardiovascular disease, diabetes, and hypertension data.
- Capacity to tailor programme to the individual community's conditions and requirements.
- Adequate financing for scaling and replication to increase population coverage.

Traditional pen-and-paper-based systems have often experienced several problems that limit their utility in disease surveillance including:

- Duplication of efforts as the same data are required to be filled into several forms and registers.
- Inaccuracies in data collection due to transcribing of data from paper to electronic form through an array of paper forms and surveys.
- Non-detection of many cases due to lack of timeliness and accuracy of health surveillance data.
- Lack of scalability in manual systems for increasing coverage to larger populations at risk.

These issues are especially problematic for chronic disease care because they result in delayed detection of disease, delayed response times for medical interventions, and inadequate follow-up. This gap in timely collection of data can be addressed with the use of mobile technologies quite effectively.

An active surveillance system must be designed to prevent and localize outbreaks, and provide timely and appropriate response where most needed. A mobile data collection solution will provide the following benefits:

- Improvements in the quality and accuracy of field data:

  - Using XFORMS, an XML-based technology, for data entry and surveys.

- Reduction in time required to detect outbreaks through timely transmission of data:

  - Using cellular communication for exchange of between the mobile device and back-end services.
  - Messages for providing feedback to field workers.

- Reduction in response time.
- Reduction in transaction cost.
- Provide feedback mechanism through short messaging services.
- Ease of data collection and management for longitudinal cohort studies for non-communicable diseases.

THE ROLE OF MOBILE TECHNOLOGIES IN DISEASE SURVEILLANCE

Mobile computing and wireless communication technologies provide an essential element of a comprehensive solution by expanding the size of the population that can be reached, by improving the quality of the information transfer and data accuracy, and by creating a mode for timely communication for medical interventions and enhanced patient monitoring.

Our objective is to use hand-held mobile devices in the detection and prevention of chronic kidney disease. We believe that the use of mobile and wireless technologies will result in several benefits. First, this will help create a flexible data collection solution with the potential to scale to include other co-morbid diseases. Second, it will reduce the transaction costs and time required for field data to be communicated to specialists at tertiary referral centres. Third, it will allow health-care workers to cover larger populations than would otherwise be possible. Finally, it will allow timely communication between specialist nephrologists and health-care workers in the field to allow intensive management of CKD and related conditions.

The Mobilis is a low-cost mobile device indigenously developed at Encore Software Limited, Bangalore. This recent invention continues a strong tradition of innovative product development at Encore, starting with the development of the Simputer, a personal digital assistant (PDA) specifically developed as an enabling tool to help bridge the Digital Divide. The development of the Mobilis was partially funded through CSIR's New Millennium Indian Technology Leadership Initiative (NMITLI) funding programme.

The Mobilis family of products caters to a broad range of mobile computing applications that require the high mobility of a PDA with a larger form-factor display, wireless connectivity and long battery life. The embedded appliance is built around modular hardware architecture and an open-source software environment that provides easy extensibility and customizability for target applications.

The device incorporates a range of hardware features such as smart card interface, GPS receiver, general packet radio service (GPRS) modem, Ethernet, WiFi, and high capacity non-volatile storage. Built-in software such as a Java Virtual Machine, web browser, and productivity tools enable the mobile appliance to be used for a wide range of applications.

Since this section focuses on the application of mobile technologies to Public Health, with a specific example of Chronic Kidney Disease Surveillance, it is important to point out a few other applications areas in Public Health that could benefit from technology interventions through the Mobilis mobile appliance and other mobile devices:

- Disease surveillance systems
- Reproductive and child health
- Long-term cohort studies
- Mobile health-care and telemedicine
- Patient bed-side information delivery
- Health education and dissemination in the community
- Anthropology and population studies

PATIENT IDENTITY MANAGEMENT

Patient Identity is once again at the core of the business process of a successful Public Health and Disease Surveillance programme since it is essential to properly identify the target population and maintain long-term records for effective delivery of health-care services. Longitudinal studies can often extend over five years, with periodic follow-up. Smart card based management of identities will be most appropriate and highly scalable. Since we have already discussed smart card based identity management, it is enough to mention that same smart card will work for applications in Public Health. In fact, an Electronic Health Record will use the Patient Identity information as the starting point for gathering and maintaining information about individual patients.

Once again, patient privacy is absolutely critical to the success of a public health programme. Hence personal identity is expected to be hidden through the appropriate transformations as data travels between different applications on a stringent need-to-know basis.

THE POTENTIAL SOCIAL IMPACT OF THE CKD PROJECT

In our CKD Pilot Study we plan to use 20 Mobile Devices configured with GPS and GPRS capability. The built-in GPS receiver will be used to record location information to enable us to develop a Geographical Information System- (GIS) based health-map of the target community. The mobile devices will also have a built-in GPRS modem which will allow health-workers to send data from the field and thereby reduce transaction time for data availability to the medical experts.

With each GPS and GPRS enabled mobile device costing approximately ₹25,000 and being used for surveillance coverage of a target population of 2,000 people, this works out to an incremental cost of just ₹12.5 per person. The potential gains in productivity, accuracy, and timeliness of data collection due to mobile technology induction are likely to be well beyond this initial cost of the technology. The cost of implementing a mobile solution using indigenous mobile technology and cellular communication is relatively low and is capable of being scaled up because a single mobile device can handle data collection and manage the study for almost 2,000 people.

Figure 17.6 highlights the potential social impact of such a project on the target community:

FIGURE 17.6
Potential Impact of Mobile Technology on CKD Pilot

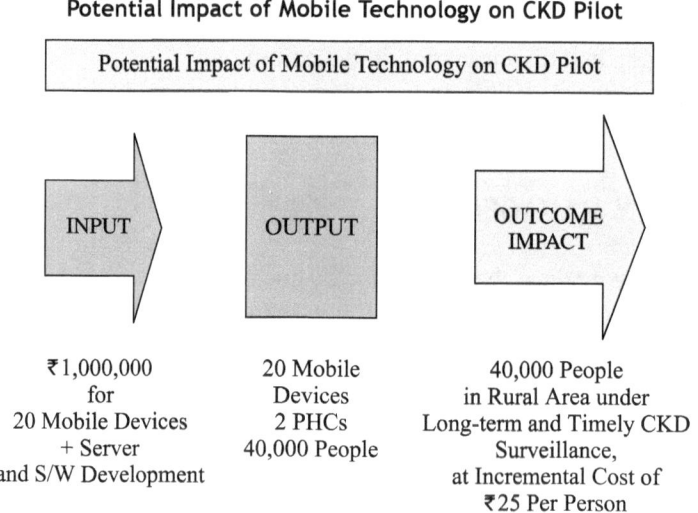

Source: Authors.

Of course, the CKD Project is a five-year study whose real social impact will be determined at the end of the study. But it is essential to develop the metrics that will be used to measure social impact.

OPEN-SOURCE IMPLEMENTATION OPTIONS

The implementation of a complete PDS or a Public Health System would pose tremendous challenges if we were to start developing these systems from scratch. Fortunately, the open-source world provides a vast range of implementation options to choose from and we would like to highlight for the benefit of the interested reader a few of the open-source projects that are relevant to the Public Health System.

First of all, let us start with the specification of the business processes. The BPMN is a well-established industry standard of the Object Management Group (OMG), and Business Process Modelling Initiative (BPMI). BPMN provides businesses a graphical notation that helps in the understanding of internal business procedures in a graphical manner and to give planners the ability to communicate these procedures in a standard manner. The graphical notation helps facilitate the understanding of interactions between different entities involved in the business transactions between the organizations. For example, a BPMN diagram has been used to depict the basic transactions between three critical entities in the PDS chain: the retail consumer; the retail service provider; and the back-end services. These diagrams could be used for a variety of purposes such as documentation of procedures, as well as for generation of code, depending on the capabilities of the software tools available to the designer (OMG, 2006).

We have used Intalio BPMS Designer to implement our business processes diagrams for PDS. The processes in the Public Health System can also be defined using BPMN methodology.

There are several choices for the electronic health-care record:

- OpenMRS
- OpenEHR
- WorldVistA

These major health-care projects focus on the electronic health record, medical ontologies, software tools, and a flexible health computing framework that can be easily customized for individual requirements.

OpenMRS has been specifically chosen because of its flexible and customizable framework that enables us to integrate mobile technology for field data collection. OpenMRS provides a flexible web-based server environment for using electronic health records in a variety of medical applications. In the Public Health domain it is essential to conduct baseline demographic surveillance surveys and subsequently periodic follow-up surveys over the lifetime of a longitudinal study. Electronic forms are a desirable replacement of the traditional pen-and-paper based forms because of the advantages outlined earlier.

The EpiHandy Study Designer software is used for development of questionnaires and surveys. EpiHandy is a generic data collection and management tool with extensive data collection capabilities including support for various data-types, branching and skip logic, and synchronization with the back-end server. In addition, EpiHandy has now been upgraded to generate forms compatible with the XFORMS specification. This enables us to use a light-weight open-source XFORMS engine on a mobile device to render those forms for data collection.

The javaROSA project is an interesting embedded Java (J2ME) application promoted by the OpenROSA community, a consortium formed to create open source, standards-based tools for mobile data collection, aggregation, analysis, and reporting. JavaROSA is designed to run on mobile phones and PDAs with a J2ME run-time environment. Hence a vast range of mobile devices could potentially be used for field data collection without a vendor lock-in.

A GIS is a very useful software tool for studying spatial clustering in the context of epidemiological surveillance. Open Source Geospatial Foundation is a community that encourages the development of community based geospatial software for diverse needs. One of its initiatives is Geographic Resources Analysis Support System (GRASS), an open-source GIS package used for geospatial data management and analysis, image processing, graphics or maps production, spatial modeling, and visualization. GRASS is now also available for PDAs.

Of course, a comprehensive Public Health System requires several other software modules beyond the scope of this article. A few important modules have been merely highlighted for the interested reader.

CONCLUSION

Two important government services, PDS and Public Health, as representative of the improvements that are possible in general governance through the enabling role of mobile and computing technologies in delivering government services at the door-step of the rural user haveb been highlighted. A unique digital consumer identity management system through modern smart card technology will play a critical role in ensuring a safe and secure delivery of services to the target population.

The intent of this chapter was to point out that economic development cannot be effective or equitable unless it moves in sync with social development. An inclusive approach demands that the economic engine serves the needs of the local marketplace through appropriate products and services, better governance, and equitable distribution. Mobile computing and communication technologies will play an increasing role in enabling the design of better products, applications, and services with better delivery mechanisms for these services. Governments must leverage these technologies as enabling tools for better service delivery and transparency.

The government and private sector enterprises have to step up and create vibrant ecosystems that will nurture social entrepreneurship as well as entrepreneurship in general.

REFERENCES

Garg, Shashank and Krishna Sundar. 2008. 'Euro mGOV 2008', Conference on Mobile Government: A Mobile Technology Framework for Consumption-based Dynamic Pricing of Gasoline for Developing Countries (to be published). The Third International Conference and Exhibitions on Mobile Government, 15–16 September, 2008, Antalya, Turkey.

National Electronic Commerce Coordinating Council (NECCC). 2002. 'Identity Management', A White Paper, NECCC, December. Available at www.ec3.org

Object Management Group (OMG). 2006. 'Business Process Modeling Notation (BPMN) Specification DTC/06-01-01', January. Available at http://www.omg.org/bpmn/Documents/OMG_Final_Adopted_BPMN_1-0_Spec_06-02-01.pdf

Sundar, D. Krishna and Shashank Garg. 2003. 'Creating E-Chains to Enable E-Governance through Embedded Technologies', Proceedings of First International Conference on E-Governance, 2003, New Delhi, India.

Windley, P.J. 2005. *Digital Identity*. Sebastopol, California: O'Reilly Media Inc.

About the Editors and Contributors

EDITORS

Sanjay Kumar is Associate Professor, Operations Management and Information Systems, School of Management, XLRI Jamshedpur. He has taught ERP internationally at AIT-XLRI Alliance, Dubai.

Jose Esteves is Chair and Professor of Information Systems, IE Business School, Spain.

Elliot Bendoly is Associate Professor, Information Systems and Operations Management at the Goizueta Business School, Emory University, Atlanta, USA.

CONTRIBUTORS

Jan Aalmink is a Senior Software Architect. He was responsible for Enterprise Systems Engineering in the areas of Logistics Controlling, Cost Containment, Financial Services, Foundation, Manufacturing, and Supply Chain Management.

Minwir Al-Shammari is Professor of Management and Director of Graduate Studies at the University of Bahrain, College of Business Administration, Bahrain.

Maria Argyropoulou is currently working on her PhD thesis at Brunel Business School/UK. She is a Research Associate in the Management Science Laboratory of the Athens University of Economics and Business, Athens, Greece.

Asniati Bahari is currently pursuing a doctoral degree in Accounting Information System at Universiti Malaysia Sabah.

Silke Balzert joined the Institute for Information Systems (IWi) at the German Research Center for Artificial Intelligence (DFKI) as a researcher in 2008. Her research activities comprise Business Process Management, Process-oriented Knowledge Management, Corporate Performance Management and Business Intelligence.

Tariq Bhatti teaches at the College of Business Sciences, Zayed University, Dubai, UAE.

Alexandra Bizerova is a Professor at the College of Business, Emory University, Atlanta, USA.

Thomas Burkhart is a researcher at Institute for Information Systems (IWi) at the German Research Center for Artificial Intelligence (DFKI).

Cesar Alexandre de Souza is an industrial engineer and Professor of Management at the School of Economics, Administration and Accounting of the University of São Paulo, Brazil (FEA-USP).

Shashank Garg is Vice President, Advanced Projects, Encore Software Ltd, Bangalore, and Founder-trustee of Sarvatva Foundation.

Jorge Marx Gómez is a member in the following institutions: German Association of Computer Science (Gesellschaft für Informatik e.V., in short GI), OFFIS e.V. (Oldenburg Institute of Informatics), SAP Roundtable for Business Intelligence, German Association of University Professors and Lecturers (Deutscher Hochschulverband, in short DHV), German Forum of Interoperability (in short DFI), German Oracle Users Group e.V. (in short DOAG) and reviewer and expert in DAAD selection committee for Latin-American research proposals.

George Ioannou is Professor of Production & Operations Management at the Department of Management Science and Technology of the Athens University of Economics and Business, Athens, Greece. He serves as the Acting Director of the International MBA Program, and directs the Operations & ERP Systems Center (Management Science Laboratory).

Veerappan Jayaraman is Professor, College of Business Sciences, Zayed University, Dubai, UAE.

Manoj Jha is Senior Consultant, HRMS, Aricent Technologies.

Sebastian Kämper works at the Institute of Information Systems (IWi) at the German Research Centre for Artificial Intelligence (DKFI), Saarbrücken, Germany.

Dimitrios N. Koufopoulos is Senior Lecturer at the Brunel Business School, Brunel University. He is the Director of the Hellenic Observatory of Corporate Governance, and Managing Partner of the Gnosis Management Consultants.

Gita A. Kumta is Professor in Information Systems at the School of Business Management, NMIMS (Deemed-to-be-University), Mumbai, India.

Peter Loos is the Chair for Information Systems and Business Administration at the Institute of Information Systems (IWi) at the German Research Center for Artificial Intelligence (DKFI).

Vincent A. Mabert is currently Editor-in-Chief of the *Production and Inventory Management Journal* and Professor Emeritus of Operations Management in the Operations and Decision Technologies Department at the Kelley School of Business, Indiana University, Indiana, USA.

Sudeep Mallick is a Principal Research Scientist with the Distributed Computing Lab at SETLabs, Infosys.

Noorhayati Mansor currently serves as a Trustee of the Malaysian Accountancy Research and Education Foundation (MAREF), KL, Malaysia.

Rakesh Kumar Mishra is currently the Industry Principal in Enterprise Solutions at Infosys. He currently heads Technology Innovation Center for one of the largest business units in Infosys.

Sachin B. Modi is an Assistant Professor of Supply Chain Management in the Department of Information Operations and Technology Management at the University of Toledo.

Jaideep Motwani, PhD, is a Professor and the Chair of the Management Department at Grand Valley State University.

Jayanthi Ranjan, PhD, is a Professor of Information Technology at the Institute of Management Technology, Ghaziabad, Uttar Pradesh.

B.S. Sahay is the Director of Management Development Institute (MDI) Gurgaon, India.

Judy E. Scott is an Associate Professor of Information Systems at the University of Colorado Denver, Denver, USA.

D.P. Sinha is a visiting professor at XLRI, Jamshedpur, and Ex-Vice President of the Birla Group of Companies.

Krishna Sundar Diatha, PhD, is a Professor at Indian Institute of Management, Bangalore, and Founder-trustee of Sarvatva Foundation.

Dirk Werth is Head of Project Group Business Integration Technologies at the German Research Center for Artificial Intelligence (DFKI), Germany.

Ronaldo Zwicker is a Chemical Engineer and has a PhD in Business Administration. He is Full Professor of Information Technology at the Business and Economics School of the University of São Paulo (USP), Brazil.